SELECT WORKS OF EDMUND BURKE

VOLUME 3

Select Works of Edmund Burke

A NEW IMPRINT OF THE PAYNE EDITION

VOLUME 1

Thoughts on the Cause of the Present Discontents

The Two Speeches on America

VOLUME 2

Reflections on the Revolution in France

VOLUME 3

Letters on a Regicide Peace

Miscellaneous Writings

EDMUND BURKE

SELECT WORKS OF EDMUND BURKE

A NEW IMPRINT OF THE PAYNE EDITION

Foreword by Francis Canavan

VOLUME 3

LETTERS ON A REGICIDE PEACE

LIBERTY FUND

INDIANAPOLIS

Frontispiece is Thomas Hickey's *Edmund Burke in Conversation with His Friend Charles James Fox.* By permission of the National Gallery of Ireland.

99 00 01 02 03 C 5 4 3 2 1
99 00 01 02 03 P 5 4 3 2 1

Library of Congress Cataloging-in-Publication Data
Burke, Edmund, 1729–1797.
[Selections. 1999]
Select works of Edmund Burke : a new imprint of the Payne edition / foreword and biographical note by Francis Canavan.
p. cm.
Vols. 1–3 originally published: Oxford : Clarendon Press, 1874–1878.
Includes bibliographical references.
Contents: v. 1. Thoughts on the cause of the present discontents. The two speeches on America—v. 2. Reflections on the revolution in France—v. 3. Letters on a regicide peace—[4] Miscellaneous writings.
ISBN 0-86597-162-5 (v. 1 : hc : alk. paper).—ISBN 0-86597-163-3 (v. 1 : pb : alk. paper)
1. Great Britain—Politics and government—18th century. 2. Great Britain—Colonies—America. 3. France—History—Revolution, 1789–1799. 4. Great Britain—Relations—France. I. Canavan, Francis, 1917– . II. Payne, Edward John, 1844–1904. III. Title.
JC176.B826 1999
320.9'033—dc21   97-34325

ISBN 0-86597-166-8 (v. 3 : hc : alk. paper)
ISBN 0-86597-167-6 (v. 3 : pb : alk. paper)
ISBN 0-86597-253-2 (set : hc : alk. paper)
ISBN 0-86597-254-0 (set : pb : alk. paper)

LIBERTY FUND, INC.
8335 Allison Pointe Trail, Suite 300
Indianapolis, IN 46250-1687

CONTENTS

EDITOR'S FOREWORD

This volume includes Burke's four *Letters on a Regicide Peace,* his last published writings on the French Revolution and the policy toward it that he would have Great Britain follow. There is no need to explain here the historical circumstances in which Burke wrote these works or the details of their composition and publication, since E. J. Payne has so thoroughly done that in his Introduction. A few comments will be enough—possibly more than enough.

As Payne says, there were contemporaries of Burke, "chiefly among the Foxite Whigs, who saw in the 'Reflections' the beginnings of a distorted view of things which in the 'Regicide Peace' letters culminated and amounted to lunacy." It is a criticism that has often been repeated since then: Burke's attack on the Revolution became simply hysterical. But Payne thinks otherwise and holds that in the letters Burke expressed "a far bolder, wider, more accurate view" than that expressed in the *Reflections* and wrote "as a statesman, a scholar, and a historical critic." The *Letters on a Regicide Peace,* he concludes, are entitled "to rank even before the 'Reflections,' and to be called the writer's masterpiece."[1]

Nonetheless, Payne maintains that, although Burke was substantially right in his judgment of the French Republic under the Directory, he was wrong in his defense of the ancien régime as it existed not only in France but also throughout Europe. "That political system of Europe," he says, "which Burke loved so much, was rotten to the heart; and it was the destiny of French republicanism to begin the

1. Pp. 56–57.

long task of breaking it up, crumbling it to dust, and scattering it to the winds. This is clear as the day to us."[2] Without nostalgia for that political system, however, we may once again note a touch of nineteenth-century optimism in Payne's remark. For one could also point to the difficulty France has had in establishing a stable democratic regime. One might also agree that the Russian Revolution of 1917 and the following years destroyed a system that was rotten to the heart and deserved to perish. But are we willing to assign a historical destiny to Leninism and Stalinism? Our experience with revolutions in the nineteenth and twentieth centuries suggests that we should maintain a certain caution about historical destiny and the ideologies that foster belief in it.

John Gray, a Fellow of Jesus College, Oxford, has warned us not to neglect "the oldest lesson of history, which is that no form of government is ever secure or final." The liberal democratic regime, he believes, suffers from a weakness that derives from "the cultural sources of liberal self-deception that emerged from the French Revolution," which in turn was a product of the Enlightenment. But he wonders whether "the Enlightenment cultures of the West can shed these disabling utopias without undergoing a traumatic loss of self-confidence." It would be highly optimistic, he believes, to hope for "Enlightenment without illusions."[3]

It was the illusion of a secular utopia, proclaimed by such of his contemporaries as the Marquis de Condorcet and Joseph Priestley, that Burke feared in the Revolution. As the French political scientist Bertrand de Jouvenel was to say in the twentieth century, "there is a tyranny in the womb of every Utopia."[4] Burke was right in pointing out the dan-

---

2. P. 55.

3. *National Review* 48 (April 8, 1996): 53–54.

4. *Sovereignty: An Inquiry into the Political Good* (Indianapolis: Liberty Fund, Inc., 1997), p. 12.

ger of political utopianism. His mistake was to tie the causes of civilization and Christendom too closely to the political regime of monarchy and aristocracy that existed in his time. The flaw in the democratic revolution that began at that time was that it justified itself with a political theory rooted in the philosophy of the Enlightenment. Today it would seem that the future of democracy depends on developing and adopting a sounder political philosophy than one based on what is, to an increasing degree, an intellectually and morally bankrupt liberalism. To that project Burke, for all his devotion to a social and political order that was dying as he wrote, can make a valuable contribution.

FRANCIS CANAVAN
Fordham University

Editor's Note

In this volume, the pagination of E. J. Payne's edition is indicated by bracketed page numbers embedded in the text. Cross references have been changed to reflect the pagination of the current edition. Burke's and Payne's spellings, capitalizations, and use of italics have been retained, strange as they may seem to modern eyes. The use of double punctuation (e.g., ,—) has been eliminated except in quoted material. In the present volume, footnotes in Letters 1, 2, and 4 are Burke's. Footnotes in Letter 3 are explained in the two advertisements preceding Letter 3.

All references to Burke's *Correspondence* are to the 1844 edition.

SELECT WORKS OF EDMUND BURKE

VOLUME 3

LETTERS ON A REGICIDE PEACE

INTRODUCTION

BY E. J. PAYNE

THE AUTUMN OF 1795 OPENED A NEW SCENE in the great drama of French affairs. It witnessed the establishment of the Directory. Five years had now passed since Burke had published his famous denunciation of the French Revolution. Those five years had witnessed portents and convulsions transcending all living experience. The Revolution still existed: but it had passed through strange transformations. The monarchy had perished in attempting to compromise with the Revolution. The dethroned King had been tried and executed as a traitor. The Queen and the Princess Elizabeth had met the same fate. The Dauphin, a mere boy, had been slowly murdered in a prison. The King's brothers, with the remnant of the anti-Revolutionary party, had fled from French soil to spread terror and indignation through Europe. Meanwhile, the destinies of France had been shaped by successive groups of eager and unscrupulous politicians. Those whom Burke had early denounced had long disappeared. Necker was in exile: Mirabeau was dead: Lafayette was in an Austrian dungeon: Barnave and Bailly had perished on the scaffold. To their idle schemes of constitutional monarchy had succeeded the unmixed democracy of the Convention: and to themselves that fierce and desperate race in whom the spirit of the Revolution dwelt in all its fulness, and in whom posterity will ever regard it as personified—the Dantons, the Héberts, the Marats, the Talliens, the Saint-Justs, the Santerres, and the Robespierres. The terrible story of the Convention is summed up in a few words. The Gironde and the

Mountain had wrestled fiercely for power: and the victory had fallen to the least moderate of the two. The ascendancy [vi] of the Mountain in the Convention had produced the domination of Robespierre. The fall of Robespierre had been followed by the Thermidorian reaction, and the White Terror: and the Convention, rapidly becoming more and more odious to the people, had at length dissolved, bequeathing to France as the result of its labours the constitution of the Directory. In the midst of all these changes France had been assailed by all Europe in arms. Yet she had shown no signal of distress. Neither the ferocious contests of her leaders, nor their deadly revenges, nor their gross follies, nor their reckless policy, had wasted her elastic powers. On the contrary, France was animated with a new life. That liberty which she had purchased with so many crimes and sacrifices she had proved herself able to defend. Nor was this all. In vindicating that liberty, she had wrested from her assailants trophies which threw into the shade the conquests of the Grand Monarque himself. In less than three years she had become actual mistress of nearly all that lay between the Rhine, the Alps, the Pyrenees, and the ocean, and potentially mistress of all the rest. She had attained a position, which, if maintained, would prove the destruction of the old balance of power in Europe.

In the eyes of outsiders, the establishment of the Directory was the most important incident since the abolition of the monarchy. It confirmed the republican form of government: and its filiation with the Convention justified the transfer to it of the epithet Regicide. The execution of Louis XVI, though of small importance in the internal politics of France, had been the turning point in the relations of the Republic to the European world. But European intervention, in a feeble and undecided form, had commenced long before the tragedy of January 1793. The King's treason had been the breach of his sworn fidelity to the new order of things, followed by an attempted flight to the camp of a general who was plotting the destruction of the Revolution by arms. Two months after that attempt, the Emperor and the King of Prussia had held the meeting of Pilnitz: in the following year the forces of the Armed Coalition were on the soil of France. The capture of Longwy struck terror into none save those who were profoundly ignorant of the state of the opposing elements. The invasion of Champagne, if such it can be called, acted on France like an electric stroke. [vii] Longwy was taken on the 23rd of August, 1792. Before the end of the year, the generals of France had not only hurled the Germans back on the Rhine, but had sprung in all its parts that deep mine which was destined to shatter the ancient fabric of Europe. They had seized Spires, Worms, and Mentz. They had levied contributions on the rich city of Frankfort: they had incorporated Savoy with France, by the name of the Department of Mont Blanc: they had annexed the county of Nice. On the northern frontier they had been even more successful. A few years before, the Austrian throne had been occupied by a sovereign whose head was full of modern ideas. Joseph the Second was a man of progress and enlightenment. Relying on the alliance with France which had been cemented by the marriage of the French king with an Austrian princess, he had ordered the demolition of all the Austrian fortresses on the Flemish frontier, and transferred his military strength to the frontiers of Bavaria and Turkey. The consequences, as soon as France became an enemy, were obvious. The single fight of Gemappe laid Austrian Flanders prostrate. Mons, Tournay, Nieuport, Ostend, Bruges, and finally Brussels itself, threw open their gates to Dumouriez and Miranda: and the Convention, in defiance of the feeble Dutch, had decreed the invasion of Holland and the opening of the Scheldt. The forces of the Armed Coalition, consisting of Austria and Prussia alone, were scattered by the Republican armies like chaff before the wind.

The year 1793 opened a new phase of the struggle. France

was no longer the helpless object of intervention and plunder. France had braced herself for resistance: she had proved her strength. Europe began to dread as well as to hate her. Meanwhile a fiercer element was added to the ferment. The dark days of December had witnessed the trial of Louis at the bar of the Convention: the 21st of January witnessed his execution. The attitude of England had for above two years been one of utter carelessness. Burke's voice had been raised almost alone in tones of alarm: and Burke had been unanimously laughed down. The English nation were not unlike the Spanish Admiral Don Alonzo del Campo, with his fleet peaceably riding at anchor in the lake of Maracaibo. Two days before the redoubtable Morgan destroyed that fleet, a negro, says the chronicler, came on board, telling him, "Sir, be pleased to have great [viii] care of yourself: for the English have prepared a fire-ship, with design to burn your fleet." But Don Alonzo, not believing this, answered: "How can that be? Have they peradventure wit enough to build a fire-ship? Or what instruments have they to do it withal?" The English parliament gave as little attention to the alarms of Burke. But as the year 1792 wore on, more and more came to light of the intrigues between French revolutionists and English sympathizers. English representatives now presented themselves in the Convention. The deepest anxiety filled those who feared the effect in England of the Revolutionary example: and some thought a civil war, in which France would be the ally of a revolutionary element, to be at hand. Without going beyond the actual, the system of plunder which the French pursued in Belgium excited English indignation: and when Holland was invaded and the Scheldt declared to be open, the unprincipled and reckless aims of the Convention became clear. They were boldly avowed by Danton: France intended to grasp all that lay within her natural boundaries, the Ocean, the Rhine, the Alps, and the Pyrenees. Since the abolition of the Monarchy, England had held no regu-

lar communication with the French government. The French
Minister, however, remained in London: and through him,
though unofficially, the English ministry endeavoured to recall the politicians of France to peace and moderation. But
there was in truth no common ground of negotiation. Cred-
iting the reports of English sympathizers, the Parisian politicians believed the English Monarchy to be on the verge of a
dissolution as complete as that which had befallen their own.
They showed no respect to Grenville's remonstrances: and by
the middle of January war was known by diplomatists to be
a certainty. The execution of the French King precipitated
it. George III then broke off all negotiation with the French
Minister, and ordered him to quit England in eight days. England was at war with France, and the Armed Coalition was
thus reinforced by all the wealth, power and authority of
the leading nation in Europe. The rest of Europe soon followed. Before the summer of 1793 Austria, Prussia, England,
Holland, Russia, Spain, and all Italy except the Republics of
Venice and Genoa, were at war with the French Republic.

Pitted against such a Coalition France might well expect
[ix] reverses. She could hardly expect to keep her bold and
reckless conquests: she might well have been content to purchase the right to choose her own government with the loss
of a considerable part of her own territory. Austria and Prussia were bent on dismembering her: England coveted her
rich possessions beyond seas. Disaster after disaster befell
the armies of the Revolution. The Austrian generals, better
skilled in tactics and in command of veteran soldiers, quickly
rescued Flanders from the undisciplined levies of the French.
At Neerwinden the French were totally defeated: and before
the end of March they were driven to their own soil. The
Armed Coalition now seemed to have its way made plain before its face. The second invasion of France was a different
matter to the desultory irruption of the preceding summer.
The task, if achieved, was certain to accomplish its end: but it

was no easy one. The famous Iron Frontier had to be forced. Condé and Valenciennes were invested: and the capture of Condé was the first-fruits of the invasion. On the 28th of July, 1793, Valenciennes was taken by the Duke of York. In every quarter the prospects of the Republic darkened. Mentz was retaken. From the lower Loire came the news of the formidable and famous insurrection of La Vendée. Toulon was occupied by Lord Hood, in the name of Louis XVII. British ships seized the French islands in the West Indies, and did not even spare the petty fishing stations of St. Pierre and Miquelon, which were all that remained to the French of their vast and rich titular empire in North America. British troops seized the poor remains of the once brilliant French empire in India. Greater ills than the loss of Tobago and Pondicherry were menacing at home. Famine stalked through the people. Bankruptcy threatened the treasury. In that dark hour France drew strength from her perils. Throughout the departments the people cheerfully gave up their all to the imperious necessities of the public cause. France became one vast camp. The cathedrals were turned into barracks: the church bells were cast into cannon. The decree went forth that all Frenchmen should be in permanent readiness for military service. Custine, the general who had surrendered Mentz, was executed. Meanwhile, the Duke of York was besieging Dunkirk; and the existence of the Republic depended on the defence of the Iron Frontier. On all sides, indeed, the defence of France aroused [x] all the energy and ingenuity of the French character. The French were now no longer in the hands of generals who hesitated between the Dauphin, the Duke of Orleans, and the Assembly: who had not decided whether to play the part of a Cromwell or of a Monk. They were led by stout and earnest republicans: by Carnot, Moreau, and Jourdan; Pichegru and Hoche defended the Rhine: Davoust and Labourdonnaye the Pyrenees: Kellermann and Massena the Alps. Before the end of the year, La Vendée was pacified: Toulon was recovered: while Moreau and Jourdan had not only stayed the progress of the Allies on the Iron Frontier, but had a second time effected a lodgment on the soil of Flanders. The end of the year 1793 found France, though surrounded by the whole world as an enemy, in a far stronger position than the beginning.

The fortunes of France steadily rose from the hour when the Duke of York was forced to raise the siege of Dunkirk. During the winter, the army in Flanders was reinforced to the utmost: and early in 1794 the command of it was transferred from Jourdan to Pichegru. Meanwhile, the spirit of the Allies began to flag. There was little union or sympathy among them: and as for Austria and Prussia, they hated each other with their old hatred. Prussia, jealous of the aggrandisement of Austria, left her unsupported: there was no combined plan: and the spring was wasted in desultory fighting on the Sambre and the Meuse. The French gained daily: but it was not until the 26th of June that the decisive action was fought on the plains of Fleurus. The French now entered Brussels. Before the summer of 1794 was ended, the Allies were swept from the Austrian Netherlands and driven back on Holland. Here the reality of their success was at once tested by its effect on the Dutch. The party of the Stadtholder had long maintained with great difficulty a doubtful ascendancy. The French sympathizers now took fresh heart: and throughout Holland the approach of the French produced a powerful revival of the republican party. Everywhere the Revolution reproduced itself. Province after province of the United Netherlands gladly capitulated as the French advanced. While the Stadtholder fled to England, the British contingent was falling back on Gröningen and Friesland: and it at length retired to German soil, and sailed homeward. The French had conquered the key of Europe.

[xi] The policy of the Coalition throughout the war was so bad that no French patriot could have wished it worse.

Union among them there was none: they had not even united plans for the Flemish campaign. Of the French royalists they made no account whatever. They did indeed consult, as advisers, the worthless emigrants: but they never sought by any practical means to gain as allies the strong anti-Revolutionary elements which existed within France. Early in the history of the Coalition, Burke had taken up his pen to expose these fundamental errors. He had predicted that the Coalition as it stood could be no match for French energy. "Instead of being at the head of a great confederacy," he wrote, "and the arbiters of Europe, we shall, by our mistakes, break up a great design into a thousand little selfish quarrels. The enemy will triumph, and we shall sit down under the terms of unsafe and dependent peace, weakened, mortified, and disgraced, whilst all Europe, England included, is left open and defenceless on every part, to Jacobin principles, intrigues, and arms."[1] A provisional government, he insisted, ought to be formed out of the French emigrants, and this government should be formally recognized. The powers that were in France ought to be considered as outlaws. "France," he wrote, "is out of herself. The moral France is separated from the geographical. The master of the house is expelled: and the robbers are in possession." The Parliament of Paris should be organized, and it should recognize the Regent according to the ancient laws of the kingdom. Burke emphatically denounced that change which was fast transmuting a holy war into a war of mere plunder. France was, and always ought to be, a great nation. The liberties of Europe could only be preserved by her remaining a great and even a preponderating power. Yet England was foolishly bent on depriving her of her commerce and her marine, while Austria was bent on despoiling her of her whole frontier, from Dunkirk to Switzerland. This was enough to unite everything that was French within the

1. Remarks on the Policy of the Allies, 1793.

boundaries of France; and to make an enemy to the Coalition out of every Frenchman who had a spark of patriotic feeling.

In little more than a year the predictions of Burke had been [xii] accomplished. The fortunes of the Armed Coalition now rapidly declined. In the eyes of the whole world it stood defeated: and its dissolution followed as a matter of course upon its defeat. A third-rate Italian State led the way. Tuscany is by nature indefensible; and the fact that its only commercial centre of any importance, the port of Leghorn, was at the mercy of the Toulon fleet, had hitherto kept the Grand Duke of Tuscany in subordination to France. Dreading the vengeance of the conqueror, he hastened to make his peace the moment victory declared for the French, apologizing abjectly for his desertion, on the ground that he had been compelled to it by threats. The defection of Prussia was more serious. The King of Prussia had only engaged in the war in the hope of adding to his Rhenish territories at the expense of France. Liberally subsidized by the English, he sent a few troops for show to the army of the Coalition, and employed the bulk of the loan in an expedition for the dismemberment of Poland. At Basle, on the 5th of April, 1795, the treaty of peace between Prussia and the Republic was signed by Von Hardenberg and Barthélemy. Prussia was to leave in the hands of the French, pending a general pacification, all her possessions on the left bank of the Rhine: for these she was to be indemnified out of the rich fund of the Ecclesiastical Sovereignties. Holland was revolutionized. The Stadtholderate was extinguished, and an alliance effected which practically annexed the United Netherlands to France as completely as the Austrian Netherlands, which had been formally incorporated with France by a law of the Convention. Spain was the next to make peace. Basle was the scene of Spanish humiliation, as it had been of Prussian humiliation. The rich island of St. Domingo, and the fertile tracts of Florida were ceded to France: and the favourite Manuel Godoy, already created

Duke of Alcudia, was rewarded with the title of Prince of the Peace. Thus did Spain sow the seeds of which she reaped the fruit in the expulsion of her dynasty, in the loss of her American possessions, in her financial ruin, and in her exclusion from the number of the great nations of Europe. Thus did Prussia sow the seed of which she reaped the fruit in the bloody fields of Jena and Friedland, in her bitter servitude, and in a hazard, as near as nation ever escaped, of total extinction.

These desertions left nothing remaining of the Coalition, save [xiii] England and Austria. Austria had a substantial reason for standing out. Austria had great things at stake: she hoped for the subjection of Suabia and Bavaria, and she had set her heart on the annexation of Alsace. Even if she banished her dreams of conquest, she could not withdraw from the contest worsted and reduced in territory. The French had conquered the Netherlands, her richest possession, and indeed for their size the most populous and flourishing provinces of Europe. They did not merely hold the Austrian Netherlands as conquerors: a law incorporating these with the French Republic had been among the last acts of the Convention. The Convention had a passion for abolishing old names and substituting new ones in their place. They called their conquest by the name of Belgium, a name long appropriated to the Netherlands by Latin-writing diplomatists and historians, but henceforth exclusively applied to the Austrian Netherlands. It was worth the while of Austria to go on with the war if there were any prospect of recovering the Netherlands. But there was small prospect of this after the spring of 1794: and month by month that prospect had been diminishing. Austria, staggering under her reverses, was fast drifting into a peacemaking mood; and in April 1797, even while Burke was writing his famous Third Letter, England's only ally was arranging at Leoben the preliminaries of that "Regicide Peace" which was consummated in the autumn at

Campo Formio: a peace which yielded to the French everything for which Burke was urging England to fight, and diverted the whole force of the enraged French nation to her
sole antagonist across the Channel. England had been slow
to join the Coalition: she was now the only member of it who
was in earnest. "British interests," as the phrase now goes,
would have lost nothing by a peace. On the contrary, they
would have gained: for what England had won beyond seas,
she might, if she were so minded, have retained.

On the question of the war with France, English public
opinion had been passionately divided. Fox had opposed it
from the beginning with the utmost force of his eloquence
and his authority. It was when this war was looming in the
distance that Burke had formally confirmed his alienation
from Fox, and finally broken with that great party to which
he had formerly been bound by his convictions, his personal associations, and his public [xiv] acts during a career
of nearly thirty years. Fox had denounced the war even before it began. On the 15th December, 1792, he had made his
motion for sending a minister to Paris, to treat with the Convention. That motion, which was seconded by Grey, involved
the entire question now at stake. Speaking on that motion in
his most eloquent mood, and animating the majority by his
usual arguments for an inexpiable war with France, Burke
had quoted some lines of Virgil which might serve for the
key-note of his subsequent utterances:

Tum vos, O Tyrii, stirpem et genus omne futurum
Exercete odiis; cinerique haec mittite nostro
Munera: nullus amor populis, nec foedera sunto.
Litora litoribus contraria, fluctibus undas
Imprecor, arma armis: pugnent ipsique nepotes.

Lansdowne had raised a similar discussion in the Lords; but
in both houses the disposition to war predominated. When
the war actually broke out, the question was debated with re-

doubled ardour. But the advocates of peace were nowhere. In vain did the calm, penetrating, practical statesmanship of Lansdowne, based upon his unrivalled knowledge of continental affairs, protest to the Lords against England being made the "cat's-paw of Europe." Nor had the heated sympathies of Fox any more effect in the Commons. The nation was pledged to the war; and for a while it prosecuted the war with vigour.

In these early debates on the war Burke had brought the Ministry an important accession of strength. When he seceded from the Whig ranks, he carried with him a large and respectable section of the party: the Portlands, the Fitzwilliams, and the Windhams. Like Burke, these men served the cause of general liberty and good government with a firm and genuine devotion: like him, they believed that cause to be disgraced and profaned by the crimes committed by the French government in its name. Like Burke, they believed in an England flourishing at home, but so using her wealth and her power as to make herself potent abroad: in an England which would not tamely suffer by her side aggressors who defied the public law of Europe, insulted its diplomatists, and rearranged the relations of its peoples by the standard of their own rapacity, or convenience, or caprice. These were the most strenuous supporters of the war. The [xv] original following of Mr. Pitt was less in earnest. Pitt never loved the war. He never bent to it the whole force of his powerful mind. Conceiving the war to be mainly the business of those great military powers who had been robbed of their territories by France, he thought his part done, so far as concerned Europe, when he had persuaded Parliament to vote them their subsidies, and equipped a small contingent to help them. He was for extending the power of England, on the old Whig principle, through its commerce and its colonies. Tidings of the capture of islands in the West Indies, and comptoirs in the East, were more welcome to his ear than tidings of the occupation of Toulon and the beleaguering of Dunkirk. Beyond seas, the war-ships of England were as irresistible as the legions of Pichegru and Buonaparte. As years went on, England gained one by one those rich and productive settlements whose growth had for a century and a half been her envy and her temptation. She left the French not a single colony. She stripped the Dutch, rejoicing in their new servitude, one by one of those famous possessions whence they had drawn the fatal wealth which had demoralized and blotted them out from the powers of Europe. Pitt lived to become master, according to a sarcasm then current, of every island in the world, the British Islands only excepted.

So long as the Allies were successful, the war was popular enough. When the Coalition was defeated, and that process of defection began which ultimately left England standing alone against the victorious Republic, the tide of opinion naturally turned. Burke's idea of a war for the old régime, steadfastly and sternly waged until the old régime should be restored, had gradually fallen into disrepute: and in the end it may be doubted whether any one believed in it except himself and Lord Fitzwilliam. Europe had made a cat's-paw of England: but it wanted that convenient instrument no longer. And Pitt's real impulse to the war was counterbalanced by the damage it wrought on commerce and manufactures at home. For in Pitt's view, the war against France was almost as much a war of plunder as in the view of the Emperor or the King of Prussia. The French cared little for their colonies. "Perish the colonies, rather than a single principle," had rung through the Assembly, in a famous debate on the consequence of granting political rights to the [xvi] Haytian mulattoes: and the sentiment gained thunders of applause. Pitt was for conceding to the French their beloved principles, so far as these tended to put England in possession of the French sugar islands. He remembered the days, thirty years ago, when his father had annexed Dominica, and

Grenada, and Tobago, amidst the applause of English merchants and politicians. But England in the present war had
been less successful: so little successful, hitherto, that it was
beginning to be thought that she had already gone quite far
enough. She felt the loss of her trade with France, Holland,
and Spain more than she felt the small advantages she had
gained in the East and West Indies. In this third year of the
war the mercantile interest of England, an interest on which
Pitt greatly relied, began to protest against its continuance.
The commerce of England with her nearest neighbours was
paralysed. No sooner was the question of England's continuing the war, deserted by all her Allies, raised in Parliament
early in 1795, than petitions in favour of peace poured in
from all her seats of commerce, from Southampton, from
Manchester, from Hull, and from Liverpool. It was now two
years since Grey had first challenged Ministers to justify to the
house their action in plunging the nation into an unnecessary
war with the Convention. Now that the Armed Coalition had
failed and dissolved, he returned to the charge. On the 26th
of January, 1795, he moved "To declare it to be the opinion
of the House of Commons, that the existence of the present
government in France ought not to be considered as pre-
cluding at that time a negotiation for peace." In other words,
England was invited to make a "Regicide Peace"—a peace
with that government which not only had murdered a mild
and lawful monarch, but had declared war against monarchs
and monarchies throughout the world.

Grey had stated his motion too categorically. Pitt was
determined neither to accept nor to reject it. He honestly
wished to end the war: but he did not wish to be driven to it
by Mr. Grey. He did not wish to tie himself to negotiate immediately, or to negotiate at any definite distance of time. He
wished to persuade the nation, at the same time, of his own
willingness to end the war, and of his own fitness to decide
on the time when, and the persons with whom, and the cir-

cumstances in which, any negotiations for ending it should be undertaken. He therefore [xvii] carried an amendment, resolving to prosecute the war "until a pacification could be effected, on just and honourable terms, with any government in France capable of maintaining the accustomed relations of peace and amity with other countries." This device neither helped nor retarded the disposition for peace in England. It only embittered the politicians of the Convention. It fixed in them a belief in the duplicity and the Punic faith of England. They had long believed extravagant falsehoods contrived to poison them against England. Here at least there was no room for doubt. England was still full of her old animosity: she was still resolved on an inexpiable war with the Republic. The real meaning of this, in the eyes of France, was simply that England was determined to take every advantage afforded by her naval position for the reduction and impoverishment of France, on pretence of restoring that tyrannous and detestable government from which she had escaped. At the same time, England had not the honesty to confess this in the face of Europe. That England should be so nice and delicate, so anxious to avoid the contagion of Regicide, must have seemed ridiculous indeed. The sovereigns of Prussia, of Spain, and of Naples, not to mention lesser ones, were known to be willing to treat with the Convention, stained though it was with the blood of a king. The Emperor was on the point of negotiating: the Pope himself could not be regarded as irreconcilable. England, a republic in all but name, ruled by men whose halls were hung with the portraits of Cromwell, of Hampden, and of Sidney, whose great grandfathers had seen their monarch perish on a scaffold, whose ministers had always feared the people more than they feared Crown or Assembly—England was making the Regicide Government a mere stalking-horse to cover her greed and her ambition, to gratify a jealousy pent up during twenty years, and to avenge on France the loss of that fairest empire an European nation ever grasped, now grown into the independent United States of North America.

These considerations were not without an impression on thoughtful people in England. On the 6th of February, 1795, Grey again returned to the charge. The previous question was moved, and he was again defeated. It was not a full house: but the majority against him was numerically less. And it was less in [xviii] moral weight by one vote, that of Wilberforce, who on this occasion divided with the minority.

When Parliament met for the Session of 1794–1795, though the failure of the Coalition was plain, its dissolution was only foreseen. It took place during the spring and the summer. When Parliament next met in October 1795, all Europe, save England and Austria, had made peace with France: and Austria was only waiting to see if she could perchance make better terms through the help of England. The defection of Prussia had produced one curious result. It forced that peace which Prussia had accepted on the smaller states of Western Germany. Those states hastened to make their peace, to save themselves from annexation: and among the rest, the King of England was forced to make peace as Elector of Hanover. Another ill-judged blow at the Republic had been fruitlessly attempted. The Quiberon expedition had failed, having served no other purpose than to deepen French hatred and distrust of England. And a change had taken place which tended to discredit the argument of Mr. Pitt, that no peace could be made with the blood-stained Republic. The Convention, with all its follies, all its crimes, and all its glories, was gone. It had not passed away in the throes of revolution. It had quietly expired in a time of comparative domestic tranquillity, bequeathing its power and its prestige, purged of the horror which attached to its name, to a new constitution of its own devising. This new constitution was the Directory.

The new scheme of government differed essentially from

the mass of those paper-constitutions which Burke described Sieyes as keeping assorted in the pigeon-holes of his desk. Ostensibly, it was a step in the direction of constitutional government on the English model: practically, it was the first stepping-stone to a military despotism. It was really an anarchy of the worst type. It was a despotism not strong enough to despise opposition, not bold enough to scorn vacillation, not quick and sagacious enough to efface the results of its inherent defects before they had wrought its destruction. It indulged freely in the safe and easy cant of republicanism. The republic was "one and indivisible": the sovereignty resided in the universality of French citizens. There was universal suffrage, to be exercised in primary assemblies: these elected the secondary or elective assemblies; these elected [xix] the legislative body. This legislative body consisted of a Council of Ancients, and a Council of Five Hundred, one third of each going out every year. So far all was in accordance with the first ideas of the Revolution. But added to, and overriding all this, was a power which discharged functions necessary to the well-being of France—functions which had been discharged by the Committee of Public Safety, and which in a very short time were concentrated in the person of a single man. France had need of a strong and legitimate executive power. Where was such a power to be found? Where but in her own best-approved citizens? Of these France had many: and that struggle for power which had hitherto led to so much rancour and bloodshed could easily be avoided by the method of divided authority, based on a system of secret voting. The executive power was therefore vested in a council of Five Directors. They were chosen as follows. The Council of Five Hundred balloted for fifty candidates: and out of these, the Council of Ancients balloted the Directory. One Director was to retire every year, the retiring member during the first year being determined by lot. Each Director in his turn was to be President of the Republic for a term of three months. The Directors had official costumes, guards, military honours, messengers of state, a large annual salary, and a residence in the Palace of the Luxembourg. Given these preliminaries, it was easy to guess what would be the composition of the highest body in the State. If the chicaners and wire-pullers did their best, they could at least return a majority, let public worth and tried statesmanship, if such things existed, meet with what recognition they would. The ballot resulted in the election of five men not only unconnected with, but radically opposed to each other. The first lot for President fell upon Rewbell, a country lawyer, or rather land-bailiff, of Alsace, who had been returned to the Convention by that peasantry of whom he had been the hired oppressor. He was a Convention politician of the most reckless and sanguinary type. The same may be said of another of the Directors. Lareveillère-Lepaux, an ugly and deformed creature, the malignity of whose face, according to his opponents, did but reflect the depravity of his soul, had been bred to the law, like Rewbell. He and Rewbell stood and fell together. The third Director was the famous soldier Carnot. In the Convention, [xx] Carnot had been a man of blood: in the Directory he proved himself a statesman and a man of peace. Letourneur, the fourth Director, a nonentity whose only known exploit was that of having made some bad verses, was the first to retire in twelve month's time. The lot was an unlucky one: for Letourneur, under the influence of Carnot, was in favour of peace on reasonable terms. Barras, the fifth Director, was a profligate and extravagant nobleman, one of whose mistresses, Josephine Beauharnais, had been married to an ambitious young officer of artillery, for whom he interested himself to procure promotion and active employment. This young man was Napoleon Bonaparte.

Those essential vices of the Directorial constitution, which soon wrought its disruption, remained for the present unnoticed. Except Carnot, the men who were at its head were little known beyond the circle of Parisian politicians. For Burke, the Directory was a mere Committee of the Regicide Convention, inheriting in all fulness its reckless policy, and its infamous principles. One fact amply justified him in extending to the Directory that hateful epithet "Regicide," which he had bestowed upon the Convention. The new law provided that no man should be a Director who had not given his vote in the Convention for the death of the King. All the Directors were thus in the strictest sense of the word Regicides. While Carnot was planning the restoration of peace, at the imminent risk of his own head, Burke was not altogether without justification when he described him as a sanguinary tyrant, sunk on the down of usurped pomp, not satiated with the blood of his own sovereign, but indulging his ravening maw in the expectation of more. Such a picture may indeed not misrepresent the party who had dominated in the Convention, and succeeded in dominating in the Directory. But it misrepresents Carnot, who resisted while resistance was possible, and at length fell from his elevation, and fled for his life.

Apart from the merits or demerits of its constitution, the establishment of the Directory was an opportunity not likely to be lost by those politicians, on both sides of the house, who whether openly or secretly wished to put an end to the war. It coincided with the end of the Parliamentary vacation of 1795. We have seen how fast the necessity for peace had meanwhile grown upon the allies. The Ministry now boldly reversed their policy. Their attitude hitherto had drawn no signs of a peaceable disposition [xxi] from the French Government. With the view of doing so, a pamphlet was prepared by Lord Auckland, a noted and able adherent of the Ministry. Auckland, a man of liberal views, an accomplished diplomatist and a shrewd politician, had hitherto been one of the most strenuous supporters of the war. It was he who had penned the pregnant manifesto to the Dutch, dated from the Hague in January, 1793. In the early debates of this very year, he had opposed the weight of his authority to the arguments of Lansdowne and Stanhope in favour of peace. He now bent himself to the facts of the situation. The old dream of re-establishing the Monarchy, the Church, and the emigrant nobility, he pronounced to be at an end. France had undergone a radical and lasting change, of which the events of the past year were a guarantee. Robespierre and the Convention had passed away: the politicians of France were mending their ways, and had formed at last a constitution based on the time-honoured English principle of a separation of the legislative and the executive powers. France had sown her wild oats, and was seriously beginning a quiet and progressive national career. He had been of opinion, with Pitt, that peace could not be made with the Convention: with Pitt, he caught at every straw which pointed at the chance of a peace with the Directory. He quieted the alarms of those who dreaded the ambition of the French politicians, and the already portentous growth of France, by a venerable historical paradox. If the French were fools enough to build up too big an empire, it must before long fall to pieces by its own weight. France was fostering the smaller republics which she had created on her frontier: she was very likely to crumble into separate republics herself. Auckland had an argument or two to soothe the Whig adherents of Burke and Portland. The continuance of the war could not but favour that coming despotism of which Pitt's Gagging Acts were a sign. The longer it went on, the more powerful must the Crown become, and the more unpopular the Whig anti-Jacobins with the people. So far, the Revolution had been a wholesome lesson to headstrong kings. But it had been a wholesome lesson also to the upper classes of all political societies. Let the English landed interest take warning by the example of the landed interest of France. Let England wisely make the best of the past, secure what compensation she could get, save what remained of the independence of Western Europe, and think herself well [xxii] rid of

her selfish and useless allies. Such were the views set forth in
Auckland's pamphlet of the last week of October, 1795.

The attitude of Burke in this changed situation could not
be to the Ministry a matter of indifference. He had swayed
public opinion towards the war: he had strenuously supported it: and though now broken by sorrow and disease, no
longer in Parliament, and living in strict retirement at Beaconsfield, he had given striking proof that the power of his
pen had not abated. The failure of the Hastings prosecution had bitterly disappointed him: and after the acquittal,
he ceased for a time to busy himself with public affairs, not
even, as he declared to a correspondent, reading a newspaper
for months together. A personal attack roused him: and his
famous "Letter to a Noble Lord," which had surprised the
world by its fiery and bitter eloquence, indicated that he was
still a prominent man in the country. Lord Auckland, though
never an intimate friend, and never until lately even a political ally, addressed to him a respectful letter, accompanying it
with a copy of the October pamphlet. He preserved Burke's
reply: and on the publication of Burke's posthumous works
many years afterwards he supplied a copy of it for insertion
among them. Burke's letter breathed no gust of passion at
finding that the Ministry had at length deliberately abandoned that policy which had tempted him from his life-long
allegiance. He employed to express what he felt no stronger
terms than grief, dismay, and dejection. But he declared that
the policy of Fox and Lansdowne, now advisedly embraced by
the Ministry, could lead to nothing but ruin, utter and irretrievable. He declared that in that ruin would be involved not
only the Ministry, but the Crown, the succession, the importance, the independence, the very existence, of the country.
These expressions, however, were private. Burke still hoped
that the Ministry had not come to their final decision. He still
hoped that the English people would hesitate before casting
in their lot with Jacobinism and thus taking, as he believed,

the first step to the dissolution of their own established government.

The King's Speech at the opening of Parliament contained a passage which more guardedly foreshadowed the same conclusion. Should the crisis in France, it declared, terminate in any order of things compatible with the tranquillity of other countries, and affording a reasonable expectation of security and [xxiii] permanence in any treaty which might be concluded, the appearance of a disposition to negotiate for a general peace on just and suitable terms would not fail to be met, on the part of the Government, with an earnest desire to give it the fullest and speediest effect. Briefly, if the Directory stood its ground, and wished for peace, Mr. Pitt would make peace with the Directory. Mr. Pitt spoke to the same effect in the Debate on the Address. Five months before, Mr. Pitt had declared his resolution not to acknowledge the then Government. The Convention, he said, was a government reeking with the blood of their sovereign. With the Convention, had it lasted, he would have waged an inexpiable war. But France had now seen the error of her ways. The Convention, after bringing France to the verge of ruin, had vanished. A new constitution, embracing, as far as the French politicians were able, the political principles of England, had been adopted. It had been ushered in with a solemn recantation of all the pernicious maxims hitherto in repute. Boissy D'Anglas, adopting the now trite philosophy with which Burke himself had familiarised the European world, had shown how that melancholy succession of crimes and blunders, which formed the recent history of France, had come about. Constitutions could not be built up anew from the ground. Men could not live by blotted paper alone: society was an organism, not a machine which could be altered and regulated at will. These invaluable truths had convinced the French of the folly of their *à priori* politics. They now resorted to the practical lessons of experience. All this time, however, no one in England knew what was the nature of the constitution, which had now been in existence a day and a half. No one knew who were the persons in power. And Mr. Pitt could not therefore speak in positive terms as to the particular measures the Government would be able to adopt. He took the opportunity, however, of solemnly affirming one of Burke's main arguments. He declared himself still in favour of a crusade against Jacobinism. If the principles of the Convention still swayed the French Government; if the Directory persisted in the policy of spreading their republicanism and irreligion throughout Europe by fire and sword; if France became the Rome of an atheistic Inquisition; then the war should be maintained, so far as the Ministry were able to maintain it.

Six weeks passed. The Directory began with every possible [xxiv] assumption of moderation, and every possible manifestation of a desire of conciliation both at home and abroad. They professed to maintain the war only as a war of self-defence. What more could be desired? The Ministry hastened to pronounce that the new government of France really was all that had been anticipated in the Royal Speech, and that they meant to make peace with it—if they could. A Royal Message, followed by an address from Parliament, embodied this solemn approval of the Directory: and Pitt vindicated his policy in one of his greatest speeches. The French, he declared, had adopted that grand panacea of all social difficulties, a mixed form of government. The pure democracy of the Revolution was at an end. In time, the course of events would suggest gradual improvements in the new constitution, and it would probably grow like the English constitution, every year more useful, more capable of being applied to the wants of the people, more intrinsically excellent. Such a constitution ought to be stable, and capable of supporting a stable peace with other nations. He could not presume to say this prospect was certain. It was enough, for those who had peace and the common welfare of Europe at heart, that

it was reasonably probable. The Ministry would now negotiate. What the issue of their negotiations might be, depended
on the views and the temper of France. If France wished for
peace on reasonable terms, she could not now allege a contrary disposition on the part of England.

Lord Auckland's pamphlet had now reached a second
edition. It had been translated into French. It began with a
French motto: *Que faire dans une telle nuit? Attendre le jour.* The
night of Revolution was now far spent: the daystar of peace
and moderation was arisen. Such was the gay vision with
which the Ministry dazzled the English people. But it created
the deepest alarm in those who looked below the surface. England was now on the verge of the precipice: and the ghastly
depth of that precipice was easily measured by a glance at
Holland. Holland had made her peace: England was now on
the verge of making hers. Negotiations for peace might at any
moment be commenced and ended: and before England had
realized what she was doing, she might find herself fast bound
in a treaty with the Regicide Republic. Such a treaty would
lead to an alliance: such an alliance to the fatal assimilation
of the two [xxv] governments which had already taken place
in Holland. The Stadtholder of Holland and his family were
safely lodged in Hampton Court: where would be the asylum
of George the Third, and the Royal Family of England?

Feeble and broken as Burke was, he did not shrink from
taking up his pen for what could not but be a sustained controversy. He began with the pamphlet of October, which he
examined, from beginning to end, in a letter addressed to
the Earl Fitzwilliam. This letter he never published: he never
even finished it. It was found by his executors among his
papers, and published with other posthumous works in 1812
as the "Fourth Letter on a Regicide Peace." It is so published
in the present volume: but it is really the First. The task animated Burke to an extraordinary degree. Nothing more gay
and vivacious than the first part of this letter ever came from

his pen. It breathes at first that spirit of pure and good-humoured raillery which had so often won the author the ear of the Commons when it had been deaf to his deeper and more studied irony, to his prophetic warnings, and to his lavished stores of knowledge and wisdom. But these elements were not wanting. As the writer warms to his subject, he opens the vial of that fierce and blasting contempt which none knew better how to pour forth upon occasion. Burke's representatives, in preserving this relic to the world, preserved to it a literary treasure of high value. Its interest, however, is little more than literary. Its scope does not extend beyond the four corners of the October pamphlet, except towards the end, where the first Editor has tacked on to it one of Burke's old philippics against Jacobinism. It proves that Burke was not deceived by the Directorial imposture. He, for one, saw clearly that the mantle of the Committee of Public Safety had descended on the Directory. He saw that France was still at heart Jacobin, and still bent on a war with the ancient political system of Europe; a war whose principle was fanaticism, whose object was conquest, and which was everywhere attended with insult, with plunder, and with destruction. This war could not be judged by any modern standard, or indeed by any single standard in the records of history. It resembled in some degree the wars of Attila and the wars of Mahomet. But adequately to shadow forth those who planned and conducted it, Mahomet and Attila must be rolled into one. [xxvi] A peace with France would lay Europe prostrate at the feet of a horde of greedy, cruel, fanatical savages.

The grant of his well-earned pension had done something to restore the balance of Burke's powers. It assured him ease in his affairs during what he knew must be the short remainder of his career: and during the spring he now busied himself with his farm, with his pamphlet, and with the establishment of a school for the children of French emigrants at the village of Penn, a mile or two from his door. In this school he took a keen delight: he visited it almost daily; and he declared it to be the only pleasure which remained to him. Many a Frenchman who twenty years afterwards served the restored Bourbon dynasty, had worn the blue uniform and white cockade of the Penn school, and had eagerly turned his eyes to greet the worn face and emaciated figure of the famous Englishman who had stirred up Europe in their cause. At present, it was not Burke's policy to thrust the peace controversy into prominence. Time, unveiling slowly and surely the character of the new government, would do more. But the opposition still continued the agitation. Peace was no nearer than when the government, towards the end of the previous year, had signified their gracious approval of the constitution of the Directory. The opposition, pushing their success, demanded that the peace negotiations should be accelerated. Why did the Ministry delude the nation with the prospect of a peace, while nothing was done, and every day brought news of some fresh success to the arms of the French? Mr. Pitt could only reply that steps towards a negotiation were being taken. His situation was not without difficulty. Though his own imperious mind was set upon a peace some of his best supporters were swayed by Burke's disapproval of it. Windham was against peace: Loughborough, the Chancellor, was against it: Fitzwilliam and Portland were against it. All these united in urging Burke to publish the pamphlet he was known to be writing: and the Ministry, yielding to the pressure of the opposition, now took a more decided step. Burke now hastened to finish his pamphlet. He laboured at it from time to time: sometimes he carried what he had written to the sick chamber of his wife, and read it aloud to the sole companion of his declining years. But before he had completed it, he was himself stricken down by a violent attack of his fatal malady, which compelled him to retreat at once to Bath.

[xxvii] When his labours were thus interrupted, the long-promised steps towards pacification had been taken: the vista

of those negotiations which his pen was to make famous, and which were to be its last employment, was opened. At Basle, the scene of the humiliating peace made by Prussia, and of the more humiliating one made by Spain, in the previous year, an English diplomatist had been deputed to open negotiations with Barthélemy, who, on the part of the Directory, had conducted both negotiations on the part of France. Mr. Wickham was deputed to propose a Congress, and to enquire upon what terms France was willing to make peace with England. The proposal for a Congress was at once viewed with suspicion: and the Directory in the clearest and promptest manner declared that if England made the restoration of the Austrian Netherlands a necessary condition of peace, negotiation must be at an end. The Netherlands were now part of France. They had been incorporated with the Republic by a law which the Directory had not the power, even if they had the will, to alter. The French government thus took a stand which they unswervingly maintained throughout the whole business. Nor can there be any question that they were right. Every argument of policy, almost of moral right, justified the French in maintaining this trophy of the famous campaign of '94.

In adding the Belgian Netherlands to France, French statesmen were not guilty of the gross folly of annexing the ancient territory of a neighbouring nation, inhabited by a patriotic and high-spirited population. Flanders and Brabant had no more to do with Ducal Austria than Hanover had to do with England. They had descended to its reigning family by an accident: they were the remains of a once-flourishing kingdom, itself nearly allied to France. The people were unanimous for the French incorporation. It was here that the aggression of the Allies had commenced. Belgium was the gate of France: its surrender would be the surrender of her hard-won guarantee for the security of her territory against future invasion. The surrender of Belgium involved the loss of another inestimable advantage. The possession of it was the sole guarantee for the independence of Holland. Cut off Holland, to France or to England an equally desirable ally, by surrendering Belgium, and a counter-revolution would have brought the Stadtholder back to the Hague in a month.

[xxviii] The Basle negotiations thus put an end to all hope of restoring peace, unless by surrendering the principle of a balance of the European power in which France should not disproportionately predominate. For above a century the maintenance of this principle had been a primary maxim of English politics. England had never even sanctioned a negotiation into which entered any contemplation of its surrender. For that principle William had organised the Grand Alliance: for that principle the war begun by him had been steadily maintained and brought to a glorious end by the great ministers and generals of Queen Anne. At the peace of Aix-la-Chapelle, at the first treaty of Paris in 1763, it had been triumphantly affirmed. Even at the peace of 1783, when England retired in defeat from an inglorious and disastrous contest, it had not been assailed. Advocates of peace in England were thus confronted by a serious dilemma. Peace on the French terms meant, in Burke's words, nothing less than the surrender of Europe, bound hand and foot, to France. But out of this dilemma the advocates of peace contrived to make new capital. What had produced the failure of the negotiations? Simply the absence of full authority on the part of the ministerial delegate. The whole transaction was informal: and besides, on many other grounds, the French had reason to distrust the sincerity of the English Ministry. Nor were the English Ministry in truth really desirous of peace. The negotiation was a mere trick to take the wind out of the sails of the Opposition: a trick to persuade the country to go on granting useless supplies and squandered subsidies. If a peace were to be made, France must see a complete change of men and measures in England. She would make no peace

with Mr. Pitt: but it did not therefore follow that she would not cheerfully confide in the sincerity of Mr. Fox, Mr. Sheridan, and Mr. Grey. But Mr. Pitt dexterously converted this identical version of the affair to his own use. The proposals of Basle could indeed hardly be said to amount to a negotiation. They indicated only a perverse and suspicious temper on the part of France, which had prevented the negotiations from being matured. Some power among the former Allies, which had already made its peace, might yet by interposing its assurances of the honesty, good faith, and ultimate reasonableness of the English Ministry, if only a serious and formal negotiation could be arranged, bring about the desired end, without throwing [xxix] England into the hands of Mr. Fox. With this view, Mr. Pitt sought the mediation of Prussia. But this attempt came to nothing also.

But fortune suddenly put a new resource into Mr. Pitt's hands. A war of aggression carried on on every frontier could not be long carried on without reverses: and the French arms in the summer of 1796 sustained a serious check. Secure on the side of the Netherlands, France was pushing to the utmost the advantages she had gained on the Rhine and in Italy. The plan of the war was bold and simple. On the Rhine were Jourdan and Moreau: in Italy Bonaparte had established a base of operations by the submission of Sardinia. Jourdan and Moreau were to unite and push on by the valley of the Danube, while Bonaparte, after sweeping Northern Italy of the Austrians, was to force the passes of the Tyrol, unite with Moreau and Jourdan, and pour the whole forces of the French Republic on Vienna. Fortune steadily attended the French arms in Italy: and nothing in the world seemed more unlikely than reverses in Germany. Once more Frankfort was occupied and pillaged: the important princes of Baden and Wirtemberg, and the nest of petty sovereigns who were included in the Circle of Swabia, hastened to buy peace by submission and contributions. The defence of the Empire had been entrusted to the Archduke Charles, a young general not wholly unworthy of the praise which Burke bestows upon him. Placed between the two armies of Moreau and Jourdan, he was compelled to retreat before them step by step, until a blow well-directed on the former general at Donauwerth separated him from his artillery and stores and compelled him to a temporary pause. Turning his success to instant advantage, Charles left a small force to keep Moreau in check, and drew off the bulk of his army to fall with crushing force upon Jourdan. After a few days' skilful manoeuvring, he completely defeated him in the battle of Amberg. This victory completely frustrated the plans for the German campaign. Jourdan was obliged to flee in disorder to the Lower Rhine, losing in his retreat, if it could be dignified with the name, nearly half his army. Moreau pushed on into Bavaria: but the disaster sustained by Jourdan, and the daily reinforcements poured into the Imperial ranks, made it necessary to commence a retreat, which he effected in so masterly a manner as to entitle it to high celebrity among military exploits.

[xxx] Jourdan's failure naturally kindled fresh hopes in those who believed the French might yet listen to reasonable proposals of peace. So severe a blow could not but tend to bring the Directory to reason. The English Ministry at once seized the opportunity. As soon as the news reached the Cabinet, a note was despatched to the Danish Minister in London, enclosing a request to be delivered to the Directory through the Danish Minister at Paris. The enclosure was brief, and intended to bear in every line marks of plainness and sincerity. It requested a passport for an English envoy, who was to proceed at once to Paris, and ascertain, by direct consultation with the French Government, if any base of pacification could be laid down. Such an application, at such a moment, could not but prepossess the French in favour of English sincerity. It would show that in spite of the favourable turn taken by the war, England was anxious to put an end to it.

INTRODUCTION

Unfortunately for the salutary effect which might have been wrought in the French mind by Jourdan's disaster, it had been more than counteracted by the extraordinary advance of the French in their second line of attack on Austria. In Italy a campaign more rapid and more brilliant than anything on record had been made by the youthful protégé of Barras. A force of forty thousand picked French troops, well inured to a hot climate by service against Spain in the Pyrenees, was set free for further operations by the peace which had been made by Godoy. Early in the year these troops were sent to reinforce the French army in the maritime Alps: and the command of the whole was given to Bonaparte. Hardly had the first blow been struck, when the King of Sardinia sued for peace, and opened to French garrisons those famous fortresses which made Piedmont the key of Italy. The Duke of Parma followed his example. Bonaparte was in a week or two in possession of Milan, and overrunning the whole of Lombardy. Before the end of May, he had passed the Mincio, forcing the Austrians partly into Mantua and partly into the uplands. Not a single disaster stayed his progress. News of the great victories of Castiglione and Arcola, of the siege of Mantua, of the submission of Naples, and of the formation of the Cispadane Republic, came like a succession of thunderclaps to Paris and to London. The young Corsican adventurer had brought to pass the favourite dream of French ambition. He [xxxi] had conquered Italy. He had done far more: he had almost revived the Empire of Charlemagne.

After some formal parley, the French Directory at length granted a passport for an English envoy to be sent to Paris. But this double issue of the year's events complicated the negotiation at the outset. The English based their hopes of the abandonment of French military ambition on the successes of the Archduke Charles, on the failure and mismanagement of the internal resources of France, prominently insisted on by the moderate party in the debates of the two

Assemblies, and not least on the pacific disposition of one or two of the Directors themselves. They believed it to be worth the while of the Directory to sacrifice the Austrian Netherlands to secure a peace which should ensure the stability of the new constitution. But had the Directory no reason to suppose that the renewal of the negotiations by England indicated a disposition to concede this very point? Barthélemy's answer to Wickham had been explicit enough. The conquest of Italy far outweighed the disasters in Germany: and the Directory might very well imagine that the latter rather than the former had suggested the initiative now taken by England. Had Lord Grenville hinted through the Danish Minister the grounds which induced him to offer peace, and made it known that his terms would be substantially the same which had been rejected at Basle, there can be no doubt that the Directory would have indignantly refused to treat. The new negotiation was thus based from the very outset on mutual misunderstandings.

A few months had so changed the situation that scarcely a line of all that Burke had written before his compulsory retreat to Bath was now applicable to it. Peace with France was no longer obscurely hinted at. It was openly avowed as a foremost object of policy: it was sought by every possible means, at the sacrifice of ministerial consistency, almost of national dignity and honour. Twice, at Basle and Berlin, had the British Ministry held out the hand of conciliation, and each time they had been met with a haughty rebuff. Yet the experiment was about to be repeated at Paris. All this was so much gain to those who opposed on principle all dealings with the Regicide Republic. Every repetition of the experiment weakened the cause of the peacemakers. If the present negotiation could be made to end in failure, all peril [xxxii] of a French alliance would be nearly over. Should the French Government only maintain its insolent attitude and arrogant demands, and the British plenipotentiary therefore return unsuccessful, a great step would have been gained. The old war-cry might then be effectually raised. The British public might then be roused to an indignant enthusiasm: the fortune of war might turn: a new Armed Coalition might be formed: and the troubles of France might be ended at some distant period by a Restoration.

Such were the hopes with which Burke began, before the name of the British envoy was known, to write his First published Letter on a Regicide Peace. The contemplation of the past vicissitudes of France suggested that brilliant historical phantasmagoria with which the volume opens. In the mutable scheme of human events, all things were possible. That terrible and unnatural spectre which now stalked over paralysed Europe was liable to the same fate which had befallen the murdered French Monarchy. The ends of Providence were often accomplished by slight means. Nearly four centuries ago the power that was then devastating France had been broken by a poor girl at the door of an inn. Who should say that Providence had no second Joan of Arc, to save France from an enemy a thousandfold more cruel and hateful?

In an exordium of greater length than he commonly allowed himself, before reaching the main question of argument, but turning with such life and swiftness to almost every element contained in the question, that it seems unusually brief, Burke went on to sketch out the true position of England and the Allies, and the true relation of France with the rest of Europe. He then turned to the history of the overtures for peace. Omitting the Auckland pamphlet, and dating the negotiations from the King's Speech which accompanied it, he pictured with bitter irony the crowned heads of Europe patiently waiting as suitors in the antechamber of the Luxembourg, and among the rest, the proud monarchy of Britain bidding for the mercy of the regicide tyrants. He next states the result of the Basle negotiations, which was briefly this. All that the Republic had incorporated with itself, by a "law" which it arrogantly assumed to be irreversible, it meant to keep. The Austrian Netherlands in the North, Savoy in the East, Nice in the South, had been thus incorporated. [xxxiii] The possession of the Austrian Netherlands, provinces in themselves of the highest value and importance, had a secondary operation. It fettered at the feet of triumphant France, with links of steel, the captive republic of Holland. The possession of Savoy threatened a similar degradation for Switzerland. The possession of Nice threatened a similar degradation for Italy. When Burke was writing, Italy had actually been trampled under the iron heel of Bonaparte: and only two years passed before the prediction was fulfilled to the letter in Switzerland.

The conquest of Italy, together with the over-running of half Germany, came in opportunely for Burke's argument. Here was the best commentary on the pacific professions of the Directory. In the counsels which projected this crusade against the liberties of Europe there was no halt or hesitation. Europe might sue for peace: the Directory could afford to refuse it, and ultimately to impose on Europe its own terms. From the previous conduct of the Directory, from its ascertained character, and from the present situation of affairs, Burke drew the conclusion that no terms which England could accept would be offered. He then passed on to consider how far the minority, in proposing peace, could be considered as expressing the public mind of England. None but regicide sympathizers could really desire a regicide peace: the rest of the nation, if once roused to a full consideration of the question, and to a sense of its enormous moment, must be in favour of maintaining the war. What proportion did the Jacobins, with Lansdowne, Fox, and Grey at their head, bear to the English nation? Burke was ready with an answer: and his answer, based as it was on data which he thought sufficient, is a curious and valuable piece of statistics. He estimated the number of Englishmen and Scotsmen capable of forming political opinions at four hundred thousand. One-fifth, or eighty thousand, of these he reckoned as Jacobins. The remainder he assumed to be supporters of the ancient and natural policy of England.

How, then, was the present unpopularity of the war to be accounted for? How was it that the English people, a people of sympathies easily kindled into a warlike flame, and in general only too ready to support a policy of action, were petitioning on all sides against a war in which England and her Allies had everywhere [xxxiv] been worsted, a war which, in an age of prolonged wars, had not lasted four years, and in which the strength of England had not yet been half put forth? How was it that the English people were willing to surrender everything for which the war had been declared — the independence of Holland, the right of their Austrian allies to the Netherlands, the cause of monarchy, religion, and property, in France, and on all the borders of France? To see a republican propaganda securely established in the heart of Europe, destined to work what changes none could foresee, not only throughout Europe, but throughout the civilized world? The answer was obvious. In order that a war may be popular, it must affect British interests. In other words, it must be a mercenary war: a war either to gain plunder, or to protect from spoliation, or both.

In contrasting the mercenary war of 1739 with the War of the Grand Alliance a generation before, and tracing the analogy between that famous struggle and the present one, Burke employed a method which the reader of his works has already seen well exemplified in the Speech on Conciliation with America. It was the method of applying reason to historical example: and Burke's natural examples were the wars which Britain had waged during the preceding century. Wars, he maintained, must not be judged by the impulse which leads to them, or by the spirit with which they are first prosecuted. A popular war is generally a mercenary war, and

therefore, as likely as not, an unjust war. That famous war of
1739, in which the English nation had been roused to an enthusiasm so memorable, Burke pronounced, after a careful
examination of the original documents of the times, to have
been an extremely unjust war. In that other great war for
the balance of power, which had been waged in the preceding generation by William III at the head of the Grand Alliance, the conditions were reversed. That war was a righteous
and necessary one, if any ever were such. But was that war a
popular one? Was it even carried on with spirit and vigour
when the break-up of the hollow peace of Ryswick called the
British people to redoubled exertions? On the contrary, all
classes of the people, sodden with ignorance and toryism,
detested it. The great Whig ministers themselves despaired
of it. "The sober firmness of Somers, the undaunted resolution of Shrewsbury, the adventurous spirit of Montagu and
Orford, were [xxxv] staggered. They were not yet mounted
to the elevation of the King." The ministers begged the King
to reconsider his policy. Strong in his wise determination,
the King refused: and as time rolled on, his policy was amply
justified. The march of events gradually animated the Lords,
the Commons, and the people at large.

This fine historical argument is stated by Burke in his happiest manner—a manner which irresistibly recalls his arguments on Conciliation with America. He naturally changed
his style in passing on to his next task, that of animating
the English people by exhibiting to them a picture, painted
in the most glowing colours, of their abominated enemy.
Macaulay, in a clever jeu d'esprit, has described Burke as a
merry, good-natured Irishman, who liked to go out at nights
to a children's party carrying a magic lantern, with which
he alternately amused and terrified them. Such a picture of
the effect upon England of a Jacobin Peace concludes the
Fourth Letter. In such a spirit he had astonished the House
by flinging the Birmingham dagger on the floor. Very dif-

ferent is that calm analysis of the French Republic which concludes the First Letter, and is continued in the Second. Keen of eye, and firm of hand, like some skilled anatomist, he gradually lays bare the structure of this political monster. Less, however, is now made of the natural and inborn atrociousness of the French republic, less of the crimes and follies of the Assembly and Convention. The main point insisted on is that France, once a scene of chaos, a proverb for anarchy, has become a vast, united, sagacious, and terrible power: a power which Europe must boldly face, but to face which Europe has hitherto been totally lacking in resolution. The exposure of the true aims and the actual character of the new French ambition is the main point of the present letters: and in this great and central point it may safely be said that Burke was perfectly and invariably right. How the spirit which animated France was aroused, of what elements it was compounded, whether its prevalence might have been prevented, what might and ought to have been the policy of the leading men in France, were questions that had really passed into the limbo of chroniclers. On these subordinate questions we think that Burke was often wrong: on the main question we are sure that he was right. He was as right as he had been [xxxvi] in arguing upon the Double Cabinet, upon the Taxation of America, upon the Irish Penal Laws, upon Economical Reform, upon the wrongs of India, and upon almost every real question, that is, upon every practical question, staring the world in the face and demanding solution, with which he was brought in contact. Here was a new power repudiating not only law and diplomacy, but moral right, aggressive in its nature, powerful in its resources, served by sagacious minds and iron sinews, avowedly warring against the rest of the world to make it like unto itself, or in other words, to conquer it. Such a pest ought to be resisted, and such resistance ought to be continued, through failure and through discouragement, until the tyranny should be overpast. In this general conclusion the events of the next fourteen years proved Burke to have been right, as fully and as clearly as events are capable of proving anything.

We have said that the French were in the right to keep fast hold on the Austrian Netherlands. Had it been clear that the French merely wished to retain them for purposes of defence, as a compensation for the outrage attempted upon the French nation by what was really a war of plunder, and as a recognition on the part of Europe of the great alteration which the Revolution had wrought in both the outward and the inward aspect of the French nationality, we think that England ought to have made peace. But it was not so: the Belgian annexation, as the sequel soon proved, was but the beginning of a policy of Conquest. And in any case, England could make no peace yielding up the Netherlands to France, unless her Austrian ally assented to it. To have made such a peace would have been to drink of that cup of humiliation which had been eagerly drained by Spain and Prussia, and to have yielded that position the firm maintenance of which in succeeding years sufficed to save the whole of Europe from the all-levelling despotism of Bonaparte. In any case, no equitable peace could be made in haste. The changes we have related, few and simple in themselves, had penetrated to the very base of all European relations: and the reparation of the strains and fractures they had wrought was a task demanding in the highest degree patience, moderation, firmness, and good sense. These were not wanting on the side of England. They were totally wanting on the side of France.

The messenger of peace whom Pitt despatched to Paris in [xxxvii] October 1796 was James, first Earl of Malmesbury: a diplomatist who had well earned his honourable rank by public services. None of the politicians at Pitt's disposal knew Europe better: none could have dealt with the Directory more wisely. Malmesbury was a thorough Englishman. His frank manners and commanding presence, added to a fine face, piercing eyes, and abundant white hair, had gained him among his friends the byename of "the Lion." No man was better calculated to restore French confidence in England, and to satisfy the Directory of the sincerity of England's desire for peace. As soon as it was known who was to be the envoy, it was felt that in his person the cause of the peacemakers must stand or fall. In due time Lord Malmesbury set out on his mission. The anxiety which prevailed as to its result suggested the remark that his journey to Paris was a slow one. Burke contemptuously replied that this was not wonderful, seeing that he went all the way on his knees. His journey thither may have been tardy: but his return to England was precipitate. Among articles of less importance, Lord Malmesbury was to offer to France equivalents from among the English conquests, in exchange for the restoration, on the part of France, of Belgium to Austria. This restoration England still insisted on. The Directory, through their negotiator, Delacroix, declared that this was impossible. No publicist could possibly construe the Act of Constitution so as to admit of it. Belgium was annexed to France by a law which was of the very essence of the constitution. The Emperor, if he pleased, might take his equivalent elsewhere in Europe. France proposed to secularise the three Ecclesiastical Electorates, and to seize the rich bishoprics which filled up the nooks and corners in the geographical mosaic of Germany and Italy. If there must still be the same number of Electors, the Stadtholder, the Duke of Brunswick, and the Duke of Wirtemberg would be convenient substitutes for the Prince-Bishops. The objections to all this were obvious. It still left France in a dominant military position, which there was no reason to suppose her indisposed to abuse: and it would have been accomplished, not at the expense of France, but at the expense of all that remained of Austrian influence in the Empire.

The history of the failure of the negotiations is amply detailed in the Second Part of the Third Letter. Malmesbury's last [xxxviii] interview with Delacroix, during which the whole proposal of England was amply exposed and discussed, took place on the 17th of December. Next day, the two memorials containing the English proposals, the one relating to France, the other to Holland, were returned by the Directory to him on the ground that they were not properly signed, and that they contained no ultimatum. The Directory wished for an ultimatum: they did, in fact, with indecent haste and utterly undiplomatic manners, demand of Lord Malmesbury an ultimatum within twenty-four hours. Malmesbury must then have seen that the negotiations were all moonshine, and that the Directory were determined on war. He complied, however, as far as he was able, with this peremptory demand. He affixed his signature to the memorials. He pointed out that they contained no ultimatum: that they represented nothing more than a basis of discussion: and that to ask for an ultimatum, at the present stage of affairs, was to snuff out the negotiation. He therefore invited the Directory to produce, if they were so disposed, a counter-project. Immediately on receiving this temperate reply, and without an hour's delay, the Directory gave him notice to quit Paris within eight and forty hours. The pacific intentions of the Directory may be estimated by the fact that on the evening of the 16th, the day preceding the final conference between Malmesbury and Delacroix, a fleet set out from Brest for the Irish coast, carrying a force of eighteen thousand men, the command of which was entrusted to Hoche.

The British Ministry lost no time in publishing their comment on the failure of the negotiation. In a long and laboured Declaration, dated December the 27th, they evinced the strongest disappointment, and cast the whole blame on the French. They "lamented" its abrupt termination, and solemnly engaged, "in the face of all Europe," to renew negotiations as soon as the French should be disposed to recommence them. This undignified attitude had at least the merit of consistency. It sealed and confirmed that abject apostrophe to the French in the name of Pitt and his colleagues, which Burke in his contemptuous mood had already penned —"Citizen Regicides! . . . . Nothing shall hinder us from renewing our supplications. You may turn us out at the door: but we will jump in at the window" (p. 83).

Burke had foreseen the failure of the negotiations: and it was [xxxix] natural for him to hail its announcement with a satisfaction bordering on triumph. The ground was cut from under the feet of the peacemakers: and nothing remained but to prosecute the war. He now took up the pen for the last of its many labours—to write a Third and final Letter, characterising the recent negotiations, pointing out how inevitable was their failure, and animating the nation to the continuance of the war, by proving at large, in answer to those who held that the war was ruining the country, the sufficiency of British resources for its maintenance. Pitt's purpose in the Declaration was to soothe the national resentment, and to stifle the warlike spirit, if such there were, of the English people. It was impossible to foresee what force or form that spirit might assume. If the people were bent on peace, they would see that the French Republic would make none with a Ministry which had done its best to destroy it. If the people were bent on war, they would see that Mr. Pitt was lacking in spirit, as he had gone far to prove himself lacking in ability, to conduct it. In either case, Mr. Pitt and his colleagues must lose their places. Burke was anxious to avoid the dilemma. He knew that Windham and Fitzwilliam were not strong enough to form a Ministry: he knew that a revulsion of feeling would throw the nation into the hands of the Regicide Peace party, of Shelburne and Fox, who had quenched their old mutual hostility, and agreed on a coalition. Erskine had published a pamphlet early in the year in furtherance of this object: and the disposition of the nation may be estimated by the unparalleled fact that thirty-three editions of it were called for during the year. In this pamphlet Erskine appealed, in answer to Burke's First and Second Letters, to the principles which the great statesman had laid down in his famous speech on "Conciliation with America." Boldly denying, as he did, all Burke's recent conclusions, and contrasting them with those contained in his collected works, then recently republished, Erskine tempered his criticism with the confession that when he looked into his own mind, he found "all its best lights and principles fed from that immense magazine of moral and political wisdom." A sense, he said, of mingled awe and grati-tude checked him, even in that respectful liberty which he allowed himself in the controversy. Erskine went on, in words as truthful as they were appropriate, to mark out the posi-tion which Burke had taken up, and in which he was now left. [xl] "When I look," he wrote, "at his inveterate consistency, even to this hour, when all support of men and things has been withdrawn from him: when I compare him with those who took up his errors only for their own convenience, and for the same convenience laid them down, he rises to such a deceptive height in my imagination, that, with my eyes fixed upon ministers, I view him as upon an eminence too high to be approached."[1] This estimate was not Erskine's alone. Those who wish to see to what intellectual eminence it is possible for a man to attain in his life-time, should read the Parliamentary debates of this time. Burke's opinions, on all subjects, are there quoted, like Scripture, by all parties, and in the most opposite senses.

The composition of the great fragment of a Third Let-ter on a Regicide Peace was spread over the last six months of Burke's life. It was begun in January, and the rest was probably written during the short intervals of ease which he enjoyed, while his incurable malady was slowly hasten-

1. View of the Causes and Consequences of the Present War with France, p. 119.

ing his end. Burke spent the early part of the year partly at Beaconsfield and partly at Bath. To the latter place he went much against his inclination: for his sincere wish was to die as quietly as might be at home. His political allies drove him to the crowded pump-room of Bath in hopes of prolonging a life so necessary, as they thought, to the welfare of the country. "Your life," Windham had written on the 22nd of January, "is at this moment of more consequence than that of any other man now living." The cause of the Regicide war had now become indeed precarious. The hopes of those who wished to reanimate the nation rested, as Windham put it, on Burke's pen and Hoche's sword. The events of April added new force to the latter argument. Bonaparte, at the gates of Vienna, had driven Austria herself to sue for peace: and England now stood alone. In full expectation of speedy invasion, Windham turned anxiously to Burke. Unwilling as he was to tax Burke's declining powers, he begged him to write only a short letter indicating the measures necessary to be taken for the immediate safety of the country. "The danger," he wrote, "is coming thundering upon us. We are miserably unprepared, in means, and in spirit, for the crisis." But while the need was [xli] growing more urgent, Burke was growing less and less able to respond to it. The end was fast approaching. Towards the end of May, having spent four months at Bath to no purpose, he returned to his house at Beaconsfield. It was, as he expressed it, so much on his way to the tomb. "There," he wrote, "I shall be nearer to a habitation more permanent, humbly and fearfully hoping that my better part may find a better mansion." Six weeks after this he died. Events had by that time far outrun the labours of his pen. Malmesbury was fruitlessly repeating the peace negotiations at Lille; while the French war-party were thwarting all attempts at compromise, and hastening on the Revolution of Fructidor, which extinguished all moderate counsels, and paved the way for the ambitious and unscrupulous despotism of Bonaparte. The

---

Lille negotiations were yet going on, when Canning wrote to a member of the embassy: "There is but one event, but that is an event for the world — Burke is dead! . . . . He is the man that will mark this age, marked as it is in itself by events, to all time."[1]

Dr. French Laurence, an eminent civilian, whose association with Burke during the Hastings Impeachment had led to the closest political and social relations with him, and Dr. Walker King, Bishop of Rochester, were Burke's literary executors. The Third Letter on a Regicide Peace was prepared for the press by the former; the Fourth, by the latter. The exact condition in which the Third Letter came to the hands of Laurence is described in the Advertisements, prefixed to it on publication, and reprinted in the present volume. Laurence added to it what was necessary to fill up the design: and the added portions are easy to be distinguished from the original. In the part written by Burke's own hand it is impossible to trace any marks of declining intellectual power. But it is easy to trace in it a declining disposition or ability to employ the old weapons of authorship. The rare exuberance, the inextinguishable force and vivacity which mark the "Letter to a Noble Lord," and are not wanting in the "Fourth Letter," are gone. In part, no doubt, they were extinguished by pain and debility. Nothing remains but the clear vision, the unimpaired judgment, the stern penetration which fact and reason alone survive, and the large conception [xlii] which appears, to any other mind becoming for the first time familiar with it, almost a revelation.

The "Regicide Peace" Letters form a natural complement to the two volumes of Burke's Select Works already issued in the present series. The main topic of the Tract and Speeches contained in the first volume is the relation of Government to the people in the mass, whether at home or in the colo-

---

1. Malmesbury's Correspondence, Vol. III. p. 398.

nies. The main topic of the famous work contained in the second volume is the relation of the present generation of men, viewed as a political body, to those which have passed away, and to those which are to come. The question in the present volume is the almost equally inexhaustible one of the relation of separate nations to that great family of nations which is called the civilized world. Of this question the interest is inexhaustible because it is perpetual, and because the conditions which surround it are perpetually changing. It is one which is passed on from one generation of Englishmen to another, with the continuous life of the great community itself which they compose. The duty and interest of England as a member of the European family of nations is indeed a large subject. We have it in the present volume discussed by a large and forethoughtful mind. In times when the duties of nations to their neighbours are as little settled, so far at least as belongs to practice, as were the duties of man in the Hobbesian state of nature, and when political conditions all over the world are rapidly becoming such that the attitude of nations to each other is practically determined, and determined in a very short space of time, by the capricious impulses of a majority told by the head, the mature conclusions of one so wise and so well-informed as Burke on this subject should possess some interest. Let us see, as briefly as possible, to what those conclusions amount.

In the preface to a previous volume of Burke's works[1] we have sketched out Burke's doctrine of the position of the individual man in relation to mankind at large. Man is so formed as to be entirely controlled by instincts arising from intercourse with his neighbours. Severance from his fellow-men means the extinction of those controlling instincts, and the extinction, in and through them, of all the power that gives to man's natural eminence in the [xliii] animal world its natural

1. Select Works of Burke, Vol. II. p. 45.

extent and significance. Now the common intercourse, the mutual relations and interests, the jealousies, the gains, the losses, of men in society, as well as the sentiments and the reasonings which practically guide them, each and all have their parallel in the relations of the nations. No nation can isolate itself from the rest of the world, without committing moral suicide. No nation can cast off its responsibility, whether to its neighbours, or to its own children, or even to its yet unborn descendants. The nation that shows any signs of this betrayal of its inherited trusts is on the high road to dissolution.

But how far does this analogy between the human individual and the body politic hold good? Limits it unquestionably has. The human individual, for instance, presuming him to escape casual causes of death, is absolutely certain of dissolution in the ordinary course of nature within a space of time not exceeding, except in the rarest cases, a well-ascertained limit. But it is false to argue from this to similar conditions in the body politic. The body politic, well says Mr. Mill, may indeed die: but it dies of disease or violence, not of old age. Again, that grand and beautiful relation which subsists between an old country and the offshoots from its own flesh and blood which it has settled beyond seas, has been the subject of misconception more pernicious, because more influencing practice. What business, Burke had heard it gravely argued in Parliament, has a child to rebel against its parent, and therefore, what business have the Colonies to resist taxation from home? It is clear, therefore, that the analogy has its limits; perhaps very narrow ones.

The general question to which Burke's arguments belong is, When is a nation bound to go to war with its neighbour, and having once gone to war, when is it justified in making peace? Wars, said Burke, using the words of Bacon, are suits to the tribunal of God's justice. That fearful tribunal is not to be lightly invoked. *Justa bella quibus necessaria.* A war is only just when it is also necessary: and it only becomes necessary when all other means of accomplishing its object have been tried, and have failed. Seeing that war is to the community of nations what the ordinary means of justice are to single societies, it is clear that whatever conditions may attend it we may be sure of this—that nothing can banish it from the world which does not also banish international justice. Those who say otherwise can [xliv] scarcely impose even upon themselves. When diplomacy has failed, war is the sole means of obtaining redress among nations: and nations, in their own suits, fulfil the functions both of advocate and judge. In civil society, a man has ceased to be judge in his own cause as soon as he has emerged from the Hobbesian state of nature. Here, then, the analogy of the state and the individual terminates. A state makes war, after it has itself decided upon the justice of its cause. On the question of that justice itself, the analogy is still valid. Justice is either civil or criminal. To obtain his civil rights, a man has recourse to the law; he has recourse to the same law to protect himself from wrong by punishing the malefactor in such a way as shall deter generally from the commission of the offence. Criminal justice, in its true aspect, is strictly preventive: the murderer is sent to the gallows, not because he has murdered a man, but that men may not be murdered. Of vindictive or avenging justice, fully civilized society knows nothing. That form of justice, in its strict sense, has long been left by legislators to other and not less potent instruments; to social penalties, to the guilty conscience, and to the awful Power which says "Vengeance is mine, I will repay." Both these forms of justice have their analogies in that transcendent justice which a nation demands by making war. But England stands with regard to the appeal to war in a different relation from the rest of Europe: in a relation, indeed, so far as relates to offensive war, which may be described as intermediate between that of the rest of Europe and that of America. So far as relates to defensive war, the case is otherwise. Here England must fully realize and amply guard against the strategic dangers which are peculiar to her position. The relations of England with the rest of Europe differ widely from the relations among themselves of the nations which compose the rest of Europe. The physical cause, in Burke's phrase, is "a slender dyke of five and twenty miles." This insular position has been the occasion, while other powerful elements have been the efficient causes, of England's vast commerce, and of England's naval superiority. England's interests lie less on the continent than on the sea-shore: her neighbours inhabit the coasts of the whole world. New York and Bombay are nearer to her than Paris and Vienna; disturbances in the highlands of India and China, war in the Drakenberg or the Rocky Mountains, touch [xlv] her more nearly than such events at her own door as the annexation of Holstein, or the separation of Belgium and Holland. But her navy and her purse are tempting objects to the designing politicians of Europe: and happy is the European schemer who can make a cat's-paw of Great Britain. And there are a mean sort of Englishmen who are anxious that England should be ever huffing and swaggering in the councils of Europe, as if this great kingdom, with her six hundred years of national glory, with her splendid offshoots and dependencies on every habitable shore of the globe, were in peril of being cast into the shade by some brand-new Republic or Empire of yesterday. The difference between England and the rest of Europe is a difference in kind. The deduction which in Burke's time was unhesitatingly drawn from this, and which in a modified form has survived all subsequent changes in the European system, was well expressed by Waller, in his famous comparison of the situation of England to that of the mysterious powers of the air:

Angels and we have this prerogative,
That none can at our happy seats arrive:
While *we* descend at pleasure to invade
The bad with vengeance, and the good to aid.

England was the natural arbitress of Europe. This position had been aspired to by Henry the Eighth: it had been seized by Elizabeth: it had been gloriously held by Cromwell: it had been extended and confirmed by William of Orange: within living memory it had been pushed to the utmost, amidst the plaudits of the world, by Chatham. To most Englishmen in those days the doctrine of Waller's lines was a matter not only of belief, but of sentiment. England believed herself, and not without reason, the supreme court of appeal in the transcendent lawsuits of Europe. Moral causes alone could put her mighty forces in motion: and these moral causes might lie not only in wrongs attempted on herself, but in those attempted on others. As to what England should construe as a wrong to herself, it was unnecessary to examine; it was sufficient that England was always able to make up her mind on the question when the contingency occurred. The question of the wrongs of others was more difficult. Now, both these questions were united in the case of the war with France. England had at her door a political nuisance which [xlvi] was fast spreading over Europe, and even propagating itself within England's own limits. Was England justified in going to war? In the circumstances, according to the standard maxims of eighty years ago, unquestionably she was.

By which of the different forms of justice enumerated by the philosophers was England's war with France justified? Burke answered, in the first place, by the civil law itself. Suppose your neighbour's house to have been seized by a gang of thieves and assassins, who after murdering the owner, and driving out his family, settled into an organized gang of marauders, infesting the whole neighbourhood. From an obvious point of view, this is what France might be said to have done. Even if such a gang of thieves and assassins abstained from molesting yourself, and confined themselves for a time to attacking those who occupied a less defensible position, was it a wise policy to let them go on confirming their position and adding to their strength, instead of doing your utmost to crush them at the outset? And intervention in France was, he thought, justifiable on much more limited grounds. Put the case in a much more modest way. Suppose your neighbour to have set up at your door a new erection in the nature of a nuisance. Were you not justified in taking immediate steps to abate it? Clear as might be his right to do what he would with his own, the rights of ownership are regulated and restrained by the rights of vicinage. The court-leet of Christendom, the grand vicinage of Europe, were therefore bound to ascertain and to prevent any capital innovation which might amount to a dangerous nuisance. This was the ground that had been taken up in the famous Whitehall Declaration. All the surrounding powers, it was there said, had a right, and felt it a duty, to stop the progress of an evil which attacked the fundamental principles by which mankind was united in civil society.

Burke readily admitted great limitations to this right of making war upon a neighbouring nation for misgovernment. The evil to be attacked must have declared itself by something more than casual or temporary manifestations. It must be shown to be radicated in the nature of the thing itself: to be permanent in its action and constant in its effects: to be progressive, and not stationary; and to be curable by no other means than the knife. Burke had remarked that such communities existed in Europe long anterior to the French Republic. In one memorable [xlvii] passage in his book on the Revolution, he had denounced to the whole of the Christian world the "barbarous and anarchic despotism of Turkey." Here was a power more barbarous and anarchic, more destructive, in its policy and in the tendency of its whole being, to the human race, than even the monstrous despotism of Turkey. It enjoyed a less advantageous position. It was a new wrong, and could plead no prescription. It had destroyed a great nation: that nation ought to be reinstated. It had discomposed Europe: Europe ought to be rearranged in its old relations. Of its doings, if left to itself, none could foresee the end: let another end then be put to them, and that right speedily.

Such had in a great measure been the grounds on which war with France had been resolved upon by the English cabinet in '92. But that resolution had beyond question been leavened by a less controllable element. Still more did that same element leaven the resolution with which England maintained her warlike attitude after the execution of Louis in '93. That element was the impulse to vindictive justice: the demand for the actual punishment of the regicides, the atheists, and the levellers. This fact Burke took small pains to conceal. When in '93 the fortunes of the Allies had given delusive hopes of success, he had even sketched out the limits to which retribution should proceed. He was totally opposed to an amnesty. He was for executing a stern vengeance on the regicides who had sat in the Convention: on those who had composed the Revolutionary Tribunal: on those who should be proved to have taken a leading part in acts of sacrilege: on all the leaders of the Jacobin Clubs. Not one of these, he said, should escape his due punishment. He was not, indeed, for taking the lives of all. Justice ought to be tempered with mercy. "There would be deaths—but for the number of criminals, and the size of France, not many." The rest was to be done by transportation, by the galleys, in some cases by mere exile. And in fortifying this opinion by the example of the English restoration, Burke half apologized for the treachery of the monarch who after granting a general amnesty had sent more than one true English patriot to a cruel death. Here, then, we see what Burke regarded as one object of the war. The restoration of the monarchy and the church was to be followed by a Bloody Assize.

[xlviii] Was the war with France really justifiable on these grounds? British public opinion soon cooled down to the

conviction that it was not: and these "second thoughts" are confirmed by the verdict of history. When these Letters were written, the war, in whatever spirit commenced, was not being waged as a Regicide War: the objection to peace was not Burke's repugnance to a Regicide Peace. It would have been as easy to reanimate the King's corpse, as to expel the Republic from France, and to reinstate the monarchy. The war was maintained on other grounds. It was maintained because the robbers in possession had carried on and improved upon the policy of the old master of the house; because the Republic and the demon of French national ambition had so readily coalesced; because under the Republic that demon had started to new life and formed more audacious plans; and because these plans were actually being executed, and that with extraordinary vigour and persistency. The character of the war had completely changed. The change had begun with the victory of Fleurus; it was clearly perceived in the last six months of Burke's life: and in the year which followed it was made plain to the dullest of politicians by the unprovoked seizure of Switzerland and the merciless sack of Rome. Had Burke lived to see '98, he would have seen the fullest confirmation of the main principles he had laid down. He would then have seen his character of the rapacious, conscienceless Republic amply verified: he would have seen England once more animated by a determination to crush its dreadful force, and placing herself resolutely at the head of a second coalition armed in defence of the public rights of Europe. But he would also have seen that the English people were no longer filled with that burning hatred of "Jacobinism" and "Regicide" which animated him, and with which he had done his best to animate them. And in such a case the people are generally in the right.

Burke has provided us, in one short sentence, with a gauge of the varying soundness and hollowness of his argument. "France," he wrote in '93, "is not formidable as a great republic, but as the most dreadful gang of robbers and murderers that ever was embodied." Burke was wrong. Whether the particular citizens who moulded its destinies were robbers and murderers, or patriots and philosophers, it was as a great republic, if at all, that France was formidable. She had forced the whole of Europe to acknowledge [xlix] her as a great republic. Even England, though she had not made peace with her, had virtually acknowledged her as a great republic ever since the negotiation at Basle. But although the old Regicide argument, so far as European public opinion was concerned, had thus been cast into the shade, it did not follow that Burke was bound to cease from employing it. For him, at least, it was as valid and cogent as while the guillotine was still wet with the blood of the Son of St. Louis. It was equally valid and cogent for thousands of English men and women, who read in the recent events in France the doom of the old political system of Europe. That doom had been pronounced by a decree which no war could reverse, though waged in the name of Chivalry and Christianity, supported by all the religious philosophy of both Churches, and by the wealth of both Indies. That political system of Europe, which Burke loved so much, was rotten to the heart; and it was the destiny of French republicanism to begin the long task of breaking it up, crumbling it to dust, and scattering it to the winds. This is clear as the day to us. But the spectator of eighty years ago might well be excused for averting his eyes from that which indicated it.

Not only was the scheme of which the author speaks at the end of the First Letter never completed, but not one of the four Letters of which the present volume consists, can be considered a finished work, complete in all its parts and members. The First most nearly approaches completion: and the Second was hastily written as a supplement to it. The First and Second Letters may really be considered as a first and second part of the same work. The Third and Fourth are merely grand fragments, running in each case into a continuation patched up by another hand out of the author's remains. The book on the Revolution (Select Works, Vol. ii.) similarly consists of one or two colossal fragments of a whole that only existed in Burke's vast imagination. The reader unavoidably compares the Reflections on the Revolution with the Letters on a Regicide Peace. Difficult as the comparison would in any case be, this condition of incompleteness and mutilation renders it more difficult than ever. But one thing will be abundantly clear to any one who reads the present volume through. Utterly wrong were those contemporary critics, chiefly among the Foxite Whigs, who saw in the "Reflections" the beginnings of a distorted view of things which in the "Regicide Peace" letters [1] culminated and amounted to lunacy. The intemperate heat, the factious preoccupation, and the precipitate judgment which vitiate so much of the "Reflections" are indeed to be traced more or less in the "Regicide Peace." But the question is altered: and a far bolder, wider, more accurate view of its elements predominates. It is a view which reminds us strongly of the writer's arguments on the American question. In the "Reflections" Burke was avowedly writing in a partial and prejudiced sense. He took upon himself to expound on the spur of the moment the unreasoned creed and the traditional sentiment of the ordinary Englishman of his day. In the present volume Burke relinquishes this "John Bull" masquerade, and writes as a statesman, a scholar, and a historical critic. The reader will find more than one of his early arguments repudiated. This was the natural result of wider and more prolonged experience. In the "Reflections," for instance, he had declared it to be the tendency of the new French state to crumble into separate republics. That argument was blindly adopted by Lord Auckland: and in the present volume it is treated with the greatest scorn, and directly confuted by a reference to facts. In the present volume, though Burke writes with opinions in the main unchanged, he also writes with knowledge vastly enlarged. He writes, moreover, with a deeper and more sustained sense of the importance of the question at issue, both to England and to Europe: and with a solemn sense of personal responsibility natural in a veteran statesman consciously taking his leave of the world. These qualities, combined with a degree of eloquence and logical ability which is to say the least equal to that displayed in the earlier work, have been thought by some to entitle the Letters on a Regicide Peace, fragmentary as they are, to rank even before the "Reflections," and to be called the writer's masterpiece.

London,

February 21, 1878.

Two Letters Addressed to a Member of the Present Parliament, on the Proposals for Peace with the Regicide Directory of France by the Right Honourable Edmund Burke

[Second Edition. Rivingtons, 1796.]

LETTER I

On the Overtures of Peace

[Argument

Introduction, pp. 62–78. Difficulties of the "philosophy of history,"
p. 62. Rise and successes of the Regicide Republic, p. 64. England
often at her strongest when she believes herself to be weakest, as in
1757, p. 67. The nation to be awakened, p. 68. Double aspect of the

LETTERS ON A REGICIDE PEACE

Wealth of England, p. 69. England cannot act apart [2] from Europe, p. 70. Discreditable issue of the war hitherto, p. 72. Disaster abroad reflected in distemper at home, p. 73, which is explained by the want of high-principled leaders, p. 75. The peculiar character of a war with a Regicide State, p. 76. This leads the author (Part I) to review the history of the Overtures for Peace already made by the English Government, and to show from them that no Peace is seriously contemplated by France. Thence (Part II) to show that these Overtures cannot accord with the sentiments of the English nation, and lastly (Part III) to show that the nature of the Regicide Republic is such that no Peace could be made with it.

PART I, pp. 78–101

History of the Overtures for Peace

Indications of French temper. Bird's mission, p. 79; Hamburg declaration, p. 81.

1st OVERTURES. Speech from the Throne, Oct. 29, 1795, and reply of 5th Pluviose (Jan. 25, 1796), p. 82.

2nd OVERTURES. Note of March 8, 1796, from Mr. Wickham to M. Barthélémy, and answer of the latter, March 26, p. 86. Downing Street Note of April 10, p. 91. Disasters of the Summer, and failure of rumoured Prussian mediation, p. 92.

PRESENT OVERTURES. Lord Grenville's request, through the Danish Minister, for a passport for an English plenipotentiary, Sept. 6, 1796, p. 93. Refusal of the French Government, Sept. 19, p. 94. Lord Grenville applies directly, by the note of Sept. 19, and the passport is despatched on the 11th of Vendémiaire. The first manifesto, issued at the same time as the passport, proves the futility of going on with the negotiations, p. 96. These views confirmed by the second manifesto of Oct. 5, p. 98. Burke mournfully contrasts the present with the former attitude of the Government, and quotes the famous WHITEHALL DECLARATION of Oct. 29, 1793, p. 99.

REGICIDE PEACE I

PART II, pp. 101–22

*The Overtures do not represent the feeling
of the British Nation*

They are contrary to the policy of England, p. 101, and to the disposition of the nation, p. 102. The Jacobins a minority, p. 105. Dulness
and inaction of the sound part of the nation, p. 106. A popular war,
such as the Spanish War of 1739, is produced by superficial causes:
the deep causes of the present war require to be explained and [3] en-
forced, p. 108. Power of the British nation under a great leader fully
illustrated by the history of the great war with France, 1689–1713,
pp. 110–22. Weakness of England then as a military power, p. 112,
an isolated nation, with little commerce, p. 113. In spite of all this,
Unanimous Address of a factious House of Commons in 1697 against
the Enemy's Overtures for Peace, p. 114. Continuation of William's
Great War, p. 115. He carries it on against the Ministry and People,
and converts the Lords to his views, p. 117, and ultimately the Commons, p. 118. Conclusion drawn from this, p. 119. If the war against
Louis XIV was thus heroically carried on, how much more should the
present war be fought out, p. 122.

PART III, pp. 122–52

Why no Peace possible with France

A state based on the principles of Regicide, Jacobinism, and Atheism
(p. 124), and fortified by the propagation of a corresponding system
of manners and morals (pp. 126–32), is a standing menace to Europe.
Europe is a moral and social unity (p. 132) in which France has violently isolated herself, and taken up a position of hostility, p. 134. Position of Europe and France illustrated from the Civil Law, p. 135, and
the war upon France justified by the principles of the *Law of Vicinage*,
p. 138. The condition of France transferred for the sake of argument
to England, p. 139. The case of Algiers distinguished, p. 143.

CONCLUSION, pp. 147–52. Popular opinion no safe guide: the decision
must rest with Ministers, p. 147. Scheme of future letters, arranged in
six heads, p. 148. Personal explanation, p. 149.]

My Dear Sir,

OUR LAST CONVERSATION, though not in the tone of absolute despondency, was far from chearful. We could not easily account for some unpleasant appearances. They were represented to us as indicating the state of the popular mind; and they were not at all what we should have expected from our old ideas even of the faults and vices of the English character. The disastrous events, which [4] have followed one upon another in a long unbroken funereal train, moving in a procession that seemed to have no end—these were not the principal causes of our dejection. We feared more from what threatened to fail within, than what menaced to oppress us from abroad. To a people who have once been proud and great, and great because they were proud, a change in the national spirit is the most terrible of all revolutions.

I shall not live to behold the unravelling of the intricate plot, which saddens and perplexes the awful drama of Providence, now acting on the moral theatre of the world. Whether for thought or for action, I am at the end of my career. You are in the middle of yours. In what part of it's orbit the nation, with which we are carried along, moves at this instant, it is not easy to conjecture. It may, perhaps, be far advanced in its aphelion. But when to return?

Not to lose ourselves in the infinite void of the conjectural world, our business is with what is likely to be affected for the better or the worse by the wisdom or weakness of our plans. In all speculations upon men and human affairs, it is of no small moment to distinguish things of accident from permanent causes, and from effects that cannot be altered. It is not every irregularity in our movement that is a total deviation from our course. I am not quite of the mind of those speculators, who seem assured, that necessarily, and by the constitution of things, all States have the same periods of infancy, manhood, and decrepitude, that are found in the individuals who compose them. Parallels of this sort rather furnish similitudes to illustrate or to adorn, than supply analogies from whence to reason. The objects which are attempted to be forced into an analogy are not found in the same classes of existence. Individuals are physical beings, subject to laws [5] universal and invariable. The immediate cause acting in these laws may be obscure: the general results are subjects of certain calculation. But commonwealths are not physical but moral essences. They are artificial combinations; and, in their proximate efficient cause, the arbitrary productions of the human mind. We are not yet acquainted with the laws which necessarily influence the stability of that kind of work made by that kind of agent. There is not in the physical order (with which they do not appear to hold any assignable connexion) a distinct cause by which any of those fabrics must necessarily grow, flourish, or decay; nor, in my opinion, does the moral world produce any thing more determinate on that subject, than what may serve as an amusement (liberal indeed, and ingenious, but still only an amusement) for speculative men. I doubt whether the history of mankind is yet complete enough, if ever it can be so, to furnish grounds for a sure theory on the internal causes which necessarily affect the fortune of a State. I am far from denying the operation of such causes: but they are infinitely uncertain, and much more obscure, and much more difficult to trace, than the foreign causes that tend to raise, to depress, and sometimes to overwhelm a community.

It is often impossible, in these political enquiries, to find any proportion between the apparent force of any moral causes we may assign, and their known operation. We are therefore obliged to deliver up that operation to mere chance; or, more piously (perhaps more rationally), to the occasional interposition and the irresistible hand of the Great Disposer. We have seen States of considerable duration, which for ages have remained nearly as they have begun, and could hardly be said to ebb or flow. Some appear to have spent their vigour at their commencement. Some have blazed out in their glory a little before [6] their extinction. The meridian of some has been the most splendid. Others, and they the greatest number, have fluctuated, and experienced at different periods of their existence a great variety of fortune. At the very moment when some of them seemed plunged in unfathomable abysses of disgrace and disaster, they have suddenly emerged. They have begun a new course, and opened a new reckoning; and even in the depths of their calamity, and on the very ruins of their country, have laid the foundations of a towering and durable greatness. All this has happened without any apparent previous change in the general circumstances which had brought on their distress. The death of a man at a critical juncture, his disgust, his retreat, his disgrace, have brought innumerable calamities on a whole nation. A common soldier, a child, a girl at the door of an inn, have changed the face of fortune, and almost of Nature.

SUCH, AND OFTEN INFLUENCED BY SUCH CAUSES, has commonly been the fate of Monarchies of long duration. They have their ebbs and their flows. This has been eminently the fate of the Monarchy of France. There have been times in which no Power has ever been brought so low. Few have ever flourished in greater glory. By turns elevated and depressed, that Power had been, on the whole, rather on the encrease; and it continued not only powerful but formidable to the hour of the total ruin of the Monarchy. This fall of the Monarchy was far from being preceded by any exterior symptoms of decline. The interior were not visible to every eye; and a thousand accidents might have prevented the operation of what the most clear-sighted were not able to discern, nor the most provident to divine. A very little time before its dreadful catastrophe, there was a kind of exterior splendour in the situation of the Crown, [7] which usually adds to Government strength and authority at home. The Crown seemed then to have obtained some of the most splendid objects of state ambition. None of the Continental Powers of Europe were the enemies of France. They were all either tacitly disposed to her or publickly connected with her; and in those who kept the most aloof, there was little appearance of jealousy; of animosity there was no appearance at all. The British Nation, her great preponderating rival, she had humbled; to all appearance she had weakened; certainly had endangered, by cutting off a very large, and by far the most growing part of her empire. In that it's acmé of human prosperity and greatness, in the high and palmy state of the Monarchy of France, it fell to the ground without a struggle. It fell without any of those vices in the Monarch, which have sometimes been the causes of the fall of kingdoms, but which existed, without any visible effect on the state, in the highest degree in many other Princes; and, far from destroying their power, had only left some slight stains on their character. The financial difficulties were only pretexts and instruments of those who accomplished the ruin of that Monarchy. They were not the causes of it.

Deprived of the old Government, deprived in a manner of all Government, France, fallen as a Monarchy, to common speculators might have appeared more likely to be an object of pity or insult, according to the disposition of the circumjacent powers, than to be the scourge and terror of them all. But out of the tomb of the murdered Monarchy in France, has arisen a vast, tremendous, unformed spectre, in a far more terrific guise than any which ever yet have overpowered the imagination and subdued the fortitude of man. Going straight forward to its end, unappalled by peril, unchecked by remorse, despising all [8] common maxims and all common means, that hideous phantom overpowered those who could not believe it was possible she could at all exist, except on the principles, which habit rather than nature had persuaded them were necessary to their own particular welfare and to their own ordinary modes of action. But the constitution of any political being, as well as that of any physical being, ought to be known, before one can venture to say what is fit for its conservation, or what is the proper means for its power. The poison of other States is the food of the new Republick. That bankruptcy, the very apprehension of which is one of the causes assigned for the fall of the Monarchy, was the capital on which she opened her traffick with the world.

The Republick of Regicide, with an annihilated revenue, with defaced manufactures, with a ruined commerce, with an uncultivated and half depopulated country, with a discontented, distressed, enslaved, and famished people, passing with a rapid, eccentrick, incalculable course from the wildest anarchy to the sternest despotism, has actually conquered the finest parts of Europe, has distressed, disunited, deranged, and broke to pieces all the rest; and so subdued the minds of the rulers in every nation, that hardly any resource presents itself to them, except that of entitling themselves to a contemptuous mercy by a display of their imbecility and meanness. Even in their greatest military efforts and the greatest display of their fortitude, they seem not to hope, they do not even appear to wish, the extinction of what subsists to their certain ruin. Their ambition is only to be admitted to a more favoured class in the order of servitude under that domineering power.

This seems the temper of the day. At first the French force was too much despised. Now it is too much [9] dreaded. As inconsiderate courage has given way to irrational fear, so it may be hoped, that through the medium of deliberate sober apprehension, we may arrive at steady fortitude. Who knows whether indignation may not succeed to terror, and the revival of high sentiment, spurning away the delusion of a safety purchased at the expence of glory, may not yet drive us to

that generous despair, which has often subdued distempers
in the State for which no remedy could be found in the wisest
counsels?

OTHER GREAT STATES having been without any regular
certain course of elevation or decline, we may hope that the
British fortune may fluctuate also; because the public mind,
which greatly influences that fortune, may have it's changes.
We are therefore never authorized to abandon our country
to it's fate, or to act or advise as if it had no resource. There is
no reason to apprehend, because ordinary means threaten to
fail, that no others can spring up. Whilst our heart is whole,
it will find means, or make them. The heart of the citizen is
a perennial spring of energy to the State. Because the pulse
seems to intermit, we must not presume that it will cease
instantly to beat. The publick must never be regarded as incurable. I remember in the beginning of what has lately been
called the Seven Years' War, that an eloquent writer and ingenious speculator, Dr. Brown, upon some reverses which
happened in the beginning of that war, published an elaborate philosophical discourse to prove that the distinguishing
features of the people of England had been totally changed,
and that a frivolous effeminacy was become the national
character. Nothing could be more popular than that work.
It was thought a great consolation to us, the light people
of this country, (who were and are light, but who were not
and are not effeminate,) that we had found the causes of our
[10] misfortunes in our vices. Pythagoras could not be more
pleased with his leading discovery. But whilst, in that splen-
etick mood, we amused ourselves in a sour critical speculation, of which we were ourselves the objects, and in which
every man lost his particular sense of the publick disgrace in
the epidemic nature of the distemper; whilst, as in the Alps,
goitre kept *goitre* in countenance; whilst we were thus abandoning ourselves to a direct confession of our inferiority to

France, and whilst many, very many, were ready to act upon a sense of that inferiority, a few months effected a total change in our variable minds. We emerged from the gulph of that speculative despondency, and were buoyed up to the highest point of practical vigour. Never did the masculine spirit of England display itself with more energy, nor ever did it's genius soar with a prouder pre-eminence over France, than at the time when frivolity and effeminacy had been at least tacitly acknowledged as their national character, by the good people of this kingdom.

FOR ONE (IF THEY BE PROPERLY TREATED) I despair neither of the publick fortune nor of the publick mind. There is much to be done undoubtedly, and much to be retrieved. We must walk in new ways, or we can never encounter our enemy in his devious march. We are not at an end of our struggle, nor near it. Let us not deceive ourselves: we are at the beginning of great troubles. I readily acknowledge that the state of publick affairs is infinitely more unpromising than at the period I have just now alluded to; and the position of all the Powers of Europe, in relation to us, and in relation to each other, is more intricate and critical beyond all comparison. Difficult indeed is our situation. In all situations of difficulty men will be influenced in the part they take, not only by the reason of the case, but by the [11] peculiar turn of their own character. The same ways to safety do not present themselves to all men, nor to the same men in different tempers. There is a courageous wisdom: there is also a false reptile prudence, the result not of caution but of fear. Under misfortunes it often happens that the nerves of the understanding are so relaxed, the pressing peril of the hour so completely confounds all the faculties, that no future danger can be properly provided for, can be justly estimated, can be so much as fully seen. The eye of the mind is dazzled and vanquished. An abject distrust of ourselves, an extravagant admiration of the enemy, present us with no hope but in a compromise with his pride, by a submission to his will. This short plan of policy is the only counsel which will obtain a hearing. We plunge into a dark gulph with all the rash precipitation of fear. The nature of courage is, without a question, to be conversant with danger; but in the palpable night of their terrors, men under consternation suppose, not that it is the danger, which, by a sure instinct, calls out the courage to resist it, but that it is the courage which produces the danger. They therefore seek for a refuge from their fears in the fears themselves, and consider a temporizing meanness as the only source of safety.

The rules and definitions of prudence can rarely be exact; never universal. I do not deny that in small truckling states a timely compromise with power has often been the means, and the only means, of drawling out their puny existence. But a great state is too much envied, too much dreaded, to find safety in humiliation. To be secure, it must be respected. Power, and eminence, and consideration, are things not to be begged. They must be commanded: and they who supplicate for mercy from others can never hope for justice thro' themselves. What justice they are to obtain, as the alms of an enemy, depends upon his character; [12] and that they ought well to know before they implicitly confide.

MUCH CONTROVERSY THERE HAS BEEN in Parliament, and not a little amongst us out of doors, about the instrumental means of this nation towards the maintenance of her dignity, and the assertion of her rights. On the most elaborate and correct detail of facts, the result seems to be that at no time has the wealth and power of Great Britain been so considerable as it is at this very perilous moment. We have a vast interest to preserve, and we possess great means of preserving it. But it is to be remembered that the artificer may be incumbered by his tools, and that resources may be among impediments. If wealth is the obedient and laborious slave of virtue and of publick honour, then wealth is in it's place, and has it's use. But if this order is changed, and honor is to be sacrificed to the conservation of riches, riches, which have neither eyes nor hands, nor any thing truly vital in them, cannot long survive the being of their vivifying powers, their legitimate masters, and their potent protectors. If we command our wealth, we shall be rich and free. If our wealth commands us, we are poor indeed. We are bought by the enemy with the treasure from our own coffers. Too great a sense of the value of a subordinate interest may be the very source of it's danger, as well as the certain ruin of interests of a superiour order. Often has a man lost his all because he would not submit to hazard all in defending it. A display of our wealth before robbers is not the way to restrain their boldness, or to lessen their rapacity. This display is made, I know, to persuade the people of England that thereby we shall awe the enemy, and improve the terms of our capitulation: it is made, not that we should fight with more animation, but that we should supplicate with better hopes. We are mistaken. We have an enemy to deal with [13] who never regarded our contest as a measuring and weighing of purses. He is the Gaul that puts his *sword* into the scale. He is more tempted with our wealth as booty, than terrified with it as power. But let us be rich or poor, let us be either in what proportion we may, nature is false or this is true, that where the essential publick force (of which money is but a part) is in any degree upon a par in a conflict between nations, that state which is resolved to hazard it's existence rather than to abandon it's objects, must have an infinite advantage over that which is resolved to yield rather than to carry it's resistance beyond a certain point. Humanly speaking, that people which bounds it's efforts only with it's being, must give the law to that nation which will not push its opposition beyond its convenience.

IF WE LOOK TO NOTHING but our domestick condition, the state of the nation is full even to plethory; but if we imagine that this country can long maintain it's blood and it's food, as disjoined from the community of mankind, such an opinion does not deserve refutation as absurd, but pity as insane.

I do not know that such an improvident and stupid selfishness deserves the discussion, which, perhaps, I may bestow upon it hereafter. We cannot arrange with our enemy in the present conjuncture, without abandoning the interest of mankind. If we look only to our own petty peculium in the war, we have had some advantages; advantages ambiguous in their nature, and dearly bought. We have not in the slightest degree impaired the strength of the common enemy in any one of those points in which his particular force consists: at the same time that new enemies to ourselves, new allies to the Regicide Republick, have been made out of the wrecks and fragments of the general confederacy. So far as to the selfish part. As composing a [14] part of the community of Europe, and interested in it's fate, it is not easy to conceive a state of things more doubtful and perplexing. When Louis the Fourteenth had made himself master of one of the largest and most important provinces of Spain; when he had in a manner over-run Lombardy, and was thundering at the gates of Turin; when he had mastered almost all Germany on this side the Rhine; when he was on the point of ruining the august fabrick of the Empire; when, with the Elector of Bavaria in his alliance, hardly any thing interposed between him and Vienna; when the Turk hung with a mighty force over the Empire on the other side; I do not know, that in the beginning of 1704 (that is in the third year of the renovated war with Louis the Fourteenth) the state of Europe was so truly alarming. To England it certainly was not. Holland (and Holland is a matter to England of value inestimable) was then powerful, was then independent, and though greatly endangered, was then full of energy and spirit. But the great resource of Europe was in England. Not in a sort of England detached from the rest of the world, and amusing herself with the puppet shew of a naval power (it can be no better, whilst all the sources of that power, and of every sort of power, are precarious), but in that sort of England, who considered herself as embodied with Europe; in that sort of England, who, sympathetick with the adversity or the happiness of mankind, felt that nothing in human affairs was foreign to her. We may consider it as a sure axiom that, as on the one hand, no confederacy of the least effect or duration can exist against France, of which England is not only a part, but the head, so neither can England pretend to cope with France but as connected with the body of Christendom.

OUR ACCOUNT OF THE WAR, *as a war of communion*, to the very point in which we began to throw out lures, oglings, [15] and glances for peace, was a war of disaster and of little else. The independant advantages obtained by us at the beginning of the war, and which were made at the expence of that common cause, if they deceive us about our largest and our surest interest, are to be reckoned amongst our heaviest losses.

The allies, and Great Britain amongst the rest (perhaps amongst the foremost), have been miserably deluded by this great fundamental error; that it was in our power to make peace with this monster of a State, whenever we chose to forget the crimes that made it great, and the designs that made it formidable. People imagined that their ceasing to resist was the sure way to be secure. This "pale cast of thought sicklied over all their enterprizes and turned all their politicks awry." They could not, or rather they would not read, in the most unequivocal declarations of the enemy, and in his uniform conduct, that more safety was to be found in the most arduous war, than in the friendship of that kind of being. It's hostile amity can be obtained on no terms that do not imply an inability hereafter to resist it's designs. This great prolific error (I mean that peace was always in our power) has been the cause that rendered the allies indifferent about the *direc-*

tion of the war; and persuaded them that they might always risque a choice, and even a change in it's objects. They seldom improved any advantage; hoping that the enemy, affected by it, would make a proffer of peace. Hence it was that all their early victories have been followed almost immediately with the usual effects of a defeat; whilst all the advantages obtained by the Regicides, have been followed by the consequences that were natural. The discomfitures, which the Republick of Assassins has suffered, have uniformly called forth new exertions, which not only repaired old losses, but prepared new conquests. The losses of the allies, on the contrary, (no provision having been made on the speculation of such an event) have been followed by [16] desertion, by dismay, by disunion, by a dereliction of their policy, by a flight from their principles, by an admiration of the enemy, by mutual accusations, by a distrust in every member of the alliance of it's fellow, of it's cause, it's power, and it's courage.

Great difficulties in consequence of our erroneous policy, as I have said, press upon every side of us. Far from desiring to conceal or even to palliate the evil in the representation, I wish to lay it down as my foundation, that never greater existed. In a moment when sudden panick is apprehended, it may be wise, for a while to conceal some great publick disaster, or to reveal it by degrees, until the minds of the people have time to be re-collected, that their understanding may have leisure to rally, and that more steady counsels may prevent their doing something desperate under the first impressions of rage or terror. But with regard to a *general* state of things, growing out of events and causes already known in the gross, there is no piety in the fraud that covers it's true nature; because nothing but erroneous resolutions can be the result of false representations. Those measures which in common distress might be available, in greater, are no better than playing with the evil. That the effort may bear a proportion to the exigence, it is fit it should be known; known in it's quality, in it's extent, and in all the circumstances which attend it. Great reverses of fortune there have been, and great embarrassments in counsel: a principled Regicide enemy possessed of the most important part of Europe, and struggling for the rest: within ourselves, a total relaxation of all authority, whilst a cry is raised against it, as if it were the most ferocious of all despotism. A worse phaenomenon — our government disowned by the most efficient member of it's tribunals; ill supported by any of their constituent parts; and the highest tribunal of all (from causes not for our present [17] purpose to examine) deprived of all that dignity and all that efficiency which might enforce, or regulate, or if the case required it, might supply the want of every other court. Public prosecutions are become little better than schools for treason; of no use but to improve the dexterity of criminals in the mystery of evasion; or to shew with what compleat impunity men may conspire against the Commonwealth; with what safety assassins may attempt it's awful head. Every thing is secure, except what the laws have made sacred; every thing is tameness and languor that is not fury and faction. Whilst the distempers of a relaxed fibre prognosticate and prepare all the morbid force of convulsion in the body of the State, the steadiness of the physician is overpowered by the very aspect of the disease.[1] The doctor of the Constitution, pretending to under-rate what he is not able to contend with, shrinks from his own operation. He doubts and questions the salutary but critical terrors of the cautery and the knife. He takes a poor credit even from his defeat; and covers impotence under the mask of lenity. He praises the moderation of the laws, as, in his hands, he sees them baffled and despised. Is all this, because in our day the statutes of the kingdom are not engrossed in as firm a character, and imprinted in as

1. "Mussabat tacito medicina timore."

black and legible a type as ever? No! the law is a clear, but
it is a dead letter. Dead and putrid, it is insufficient to save
the State, but potent to infect and to kill. Living law, full of
reason, and of equity and justice, (as it is, or it should not
exist) ought to be severe and awful too; or the words of menace, whether written on the parchment roll of England, or
cut into the brazen tablet of Rome, will excite nothing but
contempt. How comes it, that in all the State prosecutions of
magnitude, from the Revolution to within these two or three
years, the Crown has scarcely ever retired disgraced and defeated from it's Courts? Whence [18] this alarming change?
By a connexion easily felt, and not impossible to be traced to
it's cause, all the parts of the State have their correspondence
and consent. They who bow to the enemy abroad will not be
of power to subdue the conspirator at home. It is impossible
not to observe, that in proportion as we approximate to the
poisonous jaws of anarchy, the fascination grows irresistible.
In proportion as we are attracted towards the focus of ille-
gality, irreligion, and desperate enterprize, all the venomous
and blighting insects of the State are awakened into life. The
promise of the year is blasted, and shrivelled, and burned
up before them. Our most salutary and most beautiful institutions yield nothing but dust and smut: the harvest of our
law is no more than stubble. It is in the nature of these erup-
tive diseases in the State to sink in by fits, and re-appear.
But the fuel of the malady remains; and in my opinion is not
in the smallest degree mitigated in it's malignity, though it
waits the favourable moment of a freer communication with
the source of Regicide to exert and to encrease it's force.

IS IT THAT THE PEOPLE ARE CHANGED, that the Commonwealth cannot be protected by its laws? I hardly think
it. On the contrary, I conceive, that these things happen because men are not changed, but remain always what they
always were; they remain what the bulk of us must ever be,

when abandoned to our vulgar propensities, without guide, leader or controul. That is, made to be full of a blind elevation in prosperity; to despise untried dangers; to be overpowered with unexpected reverses; to find no clue in a labyrinth of difficulties; to get out of a present inconvenience, with any risque of future ruin; to follow and to bow to fortune; to admire successful though wicked enterprize, and to imitate what we admire; to contemn the government which announces [19] danger from sacrilege and regicide, whilst they are only in their infancy and their struggle, but which finds nothing that can alarm in their adult state, and in the power and triumph of those destructive principles. In a mass we cannot be left to ourselves. We must have leaders. If none will undertake to lead us right, we shall find guides who will contrive to conduct us to shame and ruin.

We are in a war of a peculiar nature. It is not with an ordinary community, which is hostile or friendly as passion or as interest may veer about; not with a State which makes war through wantonness, and abandons it through lassitude. We are at war with a system, which, by it's essence, is inimical to all other Governments, and which makes peace or war, as peace and war may best contribute to their subversion. It is with an *armed doctrine* that we are at war. It has, by it's essence, a faction of opinion, and of interest, and of enthusiasm, in every country. To us it is a Colossus which bestrides our channel. It has one foot on a foreign shore, the other upon the British soil. Thus advantaged, if it can at all exist, it must finally prevail. Nothing can so compleatly ruin any of the old Governments, ours in particular, as the acknowledgment, directly or by implication, of any kind of superiority in this new power. This acknowledgment we make, if in a bad or doubtful situation of our affairs, we solicit peace; or if we yield to the modes of new humiliation, in which alone she is content to give us an hearing. By that means the terms cannot be of our choosing; no, not in any part.

REGICIDE PEACE I

It is laid in the unalterable constitution of things—none can aspire to act greatly, but those who are of force greatly to suffer. They who make their arrangements in the first run of misadventure, and in a temper of mind the common fruit of disappointment and dismay, put a seal on their calamities. To their power they take a security against any [20] favours which they might hope from the usual inconstancy of fortune. I am therefore, my dear friend, invariably of your opinion (though full of respect for those who think differently) that neither the time chosen for it, nor the manner of soliciting a negotiation, were properly considered; even though I had allowed (I hardly shall allow) that with the horde of Regicides we could by any selection of time, or use of means, obtain any thing at all deserving the name of peace.

In one point we are lucky. The Regicide has received our advances with scorn. We have an enemy, to whose virtues we can owe nothing; but on this occasion we are infinitely obliged to one of his vices. We owe more to his insolence than to our own precaution. The haughtiness by which the proud repel us, has this of good in it; that in making us keep our distance, they must keep their distance too. In the present case, the pride of the Regicide may be our safety. He has given time for our reason to operate; and for British dignity to recover from it's surprise. From first to last he has rejected all our advances. Far as we have gone, he has still left a way open to our retreat.

There is always an augury to be taken of what a peace is likely to be, from the preliminary steps that are made to bring it about. We may gather something from the time in which the first overtures are made; from the quarter whence they come; from the manner in which they are received. These discover the temper of the parties. If your enemy offers peace in the moment of success, it indicates that he is satisfied with something. It shews that there are limits to his ambition or his resentment. If he offers nothing under misfortune, it is probable, that it is more painful to him to abandon the prospect of advantage than to endure calamity. If he rejects solicitation, and will not give even a nod to the suppliants for peace, until a change in the fortune of the war threatens him with ruin, then I think it evident, [21] that he wishes nothing more than to disarm his adversary to gain time. Afterwards a question arises, which of the parties is likely to obtain the greater advantages, by continuing disarmed and by the use of time.

With these few plain indications in our minds, it will not be improper to re-consider the conduct of the enemy together with our own, from the day that a question of peace has been in agitation. In considering this part of the question, I do not proceed on my own hypothesis. I suppose, for a moment, that this body of Regicide, calling itself a Republick, is a politick person, with whom something deserving the name of peace may be made. On that supposition, let us examine our own proceeding. Let us compute the profit it has brought, and the advantage that it is likely to bring hereafter. A peace too eagerly sought, is not always the sooner obtained. The discovery of vehement wishes generally frustrates their attainment; and your adversary has gained a great advantage over you when he finds you impatient to conclude a treaty. There is in reserve, not only something of dignity, but a great deal of prudence too. A sort of courage belongs to negotiation, as well as to operations of the field. A negotiator must often seem willing to hazard the whole issue of his treaty, if he wishes to secure any one material point.

THE REGICIDES were the first to declare war. We are the first to sue for peace. In proportion to the humility and perseverance we have shewn in our addresses, has been the obstinacy of their arrogance in rejecting our suit. The patience of their pride seems to have been worn out with the importunity of our courtship. Disgusted as they are with a conduct so different from all the sentiments by which they are them-

REGICIDE PEACE I

selves filled, they think to put an end to our vexatious solicitation by redoubling their insults.

[22] It happens frequently, that pride may reject a public
advance, while interest listens to a secret suggestion of advantage. The opportunity has been afforded. At a very early
period in the diplomacy of humiliation, a gentleman was sent
on an errand,[1] of which, from the motive of it, whatever the
event might be, we can never be ashamed. Humanity cannot
be degraded by humiliation. It is it's very character to submit
to such things. There is a consanguinity between benevolence
and humility. They are virtues of the same stock. Dignity is
of as good a race; but it belongs to the family of Fortitude.
In the spirit of that benevolence, we sent a gentleman to be-
seech the Directory of Regicide, not to be quite so prodigal
as their Republick had been of judicial murder. We solicited
them to spare the lives of some unhappy persons of the first
distinction, whose safety at other times could not have been
an object of solicitation. They had quitted France on the faith
of the declaration of the rights of citizens. They never had
been in the service of the Regicides, nor at their hands had
received any stipend. The very system and constitution of
government that now prevails was settled subsequent to their
emigration. They were under the protection of Great Britain,
and in his Majesty's pay and service. Not an hostile invasion,
but the disasters of the sea, had thrown them upon a shore
more barbarous and inhospitable than the inclement ocean
under the most pitiless of it's storms. Here was an opportunity to express a feeling for the miseries of war; and to open
some sort of conversation, which (after our publick overtures
had glutted their pride), at a cautious and jealous distance,
might lead to something like an accommodation. What was
the event? A strange uncouth thing, a theatrical figure of the
opera, his head shaded with [23] three-coloured plumes, his

---

1. Mr. Bird sent to state the real situation of the Duc de Choiseul.

body fantastically habited, strutted from the back scenes, and after a short speech, in the mock-heroic falsetto of stupid tragedy, delivered the gentleman who came to make the representation into the custody of a guard, with directions not to lose sight of him for a moment; and then ordered him to be sent from Paris in two hours.

Here it is impossible that a sentiment of tenderness should not strike athwart the sternness of politicks, and make us recal to painful memory the difference between this insolent and bloody theatre, and the temperate, natural majesty of a civilized court, where the afflicted family of Asgill did not in vain solicit the mercy of the highest in rank, and the most compassionate of the compassionate sex.

In this intercourse, at least, there was nothing to promise a great deal of success in our future advances. Whilst the fortune of the field was wholly with the Regicides, nothing was thought of but to follow where it led; and it led to every thing. Not so much as a talk of treaty. Laws were laid down with arrogance. The most moderate politician in their clan[1] was chosen as the organ, not so much for prescribing limits to their claims, as to mark what, for the present, they are content to leave to others. They made, not laws, not conventions, not late possession, but physical nature and political convenience, the sole foundation of their claims. The Rhine, the Mediterranean, and the ocean were the bounds which for the time they assigned to the Empire of Regicide. What was the Chamber of Union of Louis the Fourteenth, which astonished and provoked all Europe, compared to this declaration? In truth, with these limits, and their principle, they would not have left even the shadow of liberty or safety to any nation. This plan of empire was not taken up in the first intoxication of unexpected success. You must recollect, that it was projected, just as the report has stated [24] it, from

1. Boissy d'Anglas.

REGICIDE PEACE I

the very first revolt of the faction against their Monarchy; and it has been uniformly pursued, as a standing maxim of national policy, from that time to this. It is, generally, in the season of prosperity that men discover their real temper, principles, and designs. But this principle, suggested in their first struggles, fully avowed in their prosperity, has in the most adverse state of their affairs been tenaciously adhered to. The report, combined with their conduct, forms an infallible criterion of the views of this Republick.

In their fortune there has been some fluctuation. We are to see how their minds have been affected with a change. Some impression it made on them undoubtedly. It produced some oblique notice of the submissions that were made by suppliant nations. The utmost they did was to make some of those cold, formal, general professions of a love of peace which no Power has ever refused to make; because they mean little, and cost nothing. The first paper I have seen (the publication at Hamburgh) making a shew of that pacific disposition, discovered a rooted animosity against this nation, and an incurable rancour, even more than any one of their hostile acts. In this Hamburgh declaration, they choose to suppose, that the war, on the part of England, *is a war of Government, begun and carried on against the sense and interests of the people;* thus sowing in their very overtures towards peace the seeds of tumult and sedition: for they never have abandoned, and never will they abandon, in peace, in war, in treaty, in any situation, or for one instant, their old steady maxim of separating the people from their Government. Let me add—and it is with unfeigned anxiety for the character and credit of Ministers that I do add—if our Government perseveres, in it's as uniform course, of acting under instruments with such preambles, it pleads guilty to the charges made by our [25] enemies against it, both on its own part, and on the part of Parliament itself. The enemy must succeed in his plan for loosening and disconnecting all the internal holdings of the kingdom.

It was not enough that the Speech from the Throne, in the opening of the session in 1795, threw out oglings and glances of tenderness. Lest this coquetting should seem too cold and ambiguous, without waiting for it's effect, the violent passion for a relation to the Regicides produced a direct Message from the Crown, and it's consequences from the two Houses of Parliament. On the part of the Regicides these declarations could not be entirely passed by without notice: but in that notice they discovered still more clearly the bottom of their character. The offer made to them by the message to Parliament was hinted at in their answer; but in an obscure and oblique manner as before. They accompanied their notice of the indications manifested on our side, with every kind of insolent and taunting reflection. The Regicide Directory, on the day which, in their gipsey jargon, they call the 5th of Pluviose, in return for our advances, charge us with eluding our declarations under "evasive formalities and frivolous pretexts." What these pretexts and evasions were, they do not say, and I have never heard. But they do not rest there. They proceed to charge us, and, as it should seem, our allies in the mass, with direct *perfidy;* they are so conciliatory in their language as to hint that this perfidious character is not new in our proceedings. However, notwithstanding this our habitual perfidy, they will offer peace "on conditions *as* moderate"—as what? As reason and as equity require? No! as moderate "as are suitable to their *national dignity.*" National dignity in all treaties I do admit is an important consideration. They have given us an useful hint on that subject: but dignity, [26] hitherto, has belonged to the mode of proceeding, not to the matter of a treaty. Never before has it been mentioned as the standard for rating the conditions of peace; no, never by the most violent of conquerors. Indemnification is capable of some estimate; dignity has no standard. It is impossible to guess what acquisitions pride and ambition may think fit for their *dignity.* But lest any doubt should remain on what they think for their dignity, the Regicides in the next paragraph tell us "that they will have no peace with their enemies, until they have reduced them to a state, which will put them under an *impossibility* of pursuing their wretched projects"; that is, in plain French or English, until they have accomplished our utter and irretrievable ruin. This is their *pacific* language. It flows from their unalterable principle in whatever language they speak, or whatever steps they take, whether of real war, or of pretended pacification. They have never, to do them justice, been at much trouble in concealing their intentions. We were as obstinately resolved to think them not in earnest; but I confess jests of this sort, whatever their urbanity may be, are not much to my taste.

To this conciliatory and amicable publick communication, our sole answer, in effect, is this. "Citizen Regicides! whenever *you* find yourselves in the humour, you may have a peace with *us*. That is a point you may always command. We are constantly in attendance, and nothing you can do shall hinder us from the renewal of our supplications. You may turn us out at the door; but we will jump in at the window."

To those, who do not love to contemplate the fall of human greatness, I do not know a more mortifying spectacle, than to see the assembled majesty of the crowned heads of Europe waiting as patient suitors in the antechamber of Regicide. They wait, it seems, until the [27] sanguinary tyrant *Carnot* shall have snorted away the fumes of the indigested blood of his Sovereign. Then, when, sunk on the down of usurped pomp, he shall have sufficiently indulged his meditations with what Monarch he shall next glut his ravening maw, he may condescend to signify that it is his pleasure to be awake; and that he is at leisure to receive the proposals of his high and mighty clients for the terms on which he may respite the execution of the sentence he has passed upon them. At the opening of those doors, what a sight it must be to behold the plenipotentiaries of royal impotence, in the precedency which they will intrigue to obtain, and which will be granted to them according to the seniority of their degradation, sneaking into the Regicide presence, and with the reliques of the smile which they had dressed up for the levée of their masters still flickering on their curled lips, presenting the faded remains of their courtly graces, to meet the scornful, ferocious, sardonic grin of a bloody ruffian, who, whilst he is receiving their homage, is measuring them with his eye, and fitting to their size the slider of his Guillotine! These ambassadors may easily return as good courtiers as they went; but can they ever return from that degrading residence, loyal and faithful subjects; or with any true affection to their master, or true attachment to the constitution, religion, or laws of their country? There is great danger that they who enter smiling into this Trophonian Cave, will come out of it sad and serious conspirators; and such will continue as long as they live. They will become true conductors of contagion to every country which has had the misfortune to send them to the source of that electricity. At best they will become totally indifferent to good and evil, to one institution or another. This species of indifference is but too generally distinguishable in those who have been much employed in foreign [28] Courts; but in the present case the evil must be aggravated without measure; for they go from their country, not with the pride of the old character, but in a state of the lowest degradation; and what must happen in their place of residence can have no effect in raising them to the level of true dignity, or of chaste self-estimation, either as men, or as representatives of crowned heads.

Our early proceeding, which has produced these returns of affront, appeared to me totally new, without being adapted to the new circumstances of affairs. I have called to my mind the speeches and messages in former times. I find nothing like these. You will look in the journals to find whether my memory fails me. Before this time, never was a ground of

REGICIDE PEACE I

peace laid, (as it were, in a parliamentary record,) until it had been as good as concluded. This was a wise homage paid to the discretion of the Crown. It was known how much a negotiation must suffer by having any thing in the train towards it prematurely disclosed. But when those parliamentary declarations were made, not so much as a step had been taken towards a negotiation in any mode whatever. The measure was an unpleasant and unseasonable discovery.

I conceive that another circumstance in that transaction has been as little authorised by any example; and that it is as little prudent in itself; I mean the formal recognition of the French Republic. Without entering, for the present, into a question on the good faith manifested in that measure, or on it's general policy, I doubt, upon mere temporary considerations of prudence, whether it was perfectly adviseable. It is not within the rules of dexterous conduct to make an acknowledgment of a contested title in your enemy, before you are morally certain that your recognition will secure his friendship. Otherwise it is a measure worse than thrown away. It adds infinitely to the strength, and [29] consequently to the demands of the adverse party. He has gained a fundamental point without an equivalent. It has happened as might have been foreseen. No notice whatever was taken of this recognition. In fact, the Directory never gave themselves any concern about it; and they received our acknowledgment with perfect scorn. With them, it is not for the States of Europe to judge of their title. But in their eye the title of every other power depends wholly on their pleasure.

Preliminary declarations of this sort, thrown out at random, and sown, as it were, broad-cast, were never to be found in the mode of our proceeding with France and Spain, whilst the great Monarchies of France and Spain existed. I do not say, that a diplomatick measure ought to be, like a parliamentary or a judicial proceeding, according to strict precedent. I hope I am far from that pedantry. But this I know, that a great state ought to have some regard to it's antient maxims; especially where they indicate it's dignity; where they concur with the rules of prudence; and above all, where the circumstances of the time require that a spirit of innovation should be resisted, which leads to the humiliation of sovereign powers. It would be ridiculous to assert, that those powers have suffered nothing in their estimation. I admit that the greater interests of state will for a moment supersede all other considerations: but if there was a rule that a sovereign never should let down his dignity without a sure payment to his interest, the dignity of Kings would be held high enough. At present, however, fashion governs in more serious things than furniture and dress. It looks as if sovereigns abroad were emulous in bidding against their estimation. It seems as if the pre-eminence of Regicide was acknowledged; and that Kings tacitly ranked themselves below their sacrilegious murderers, as natural magistrates and judges over them. It [30] appears as if dignity were the prerogative of crime; and a temporising humiliation the proper part for venerable authority. If the vilest of mankind are resolved to be the most wicked, they lose all the baseness of their origin, and take their place above Kings. This example in sovereign Princes, I trust, will not spread. It is the concern of mankind, that the destruction of order should not be a claim to rank: that crimes should not be the only title to preeminence and honour.

AT THIS SECOND STAGE of humiliation, (I mean the insulting declaration in consequence of the message to both Houses of Parliament) it might not have been amiss to pause; and not to squander away the fund of our submissions, until we know what final purposes of public interest they might answer. The policy of subjecting ourselves to further insults is not to me quite apparent. It was resolved however, to hazard a third trial. Citizen Barthelemi had been established on the part of the new Republick, at Basle; where, with his proconsulate of Switzerland and the adjacent parts of Germany, he was appointed as a sort of factor to deal in the degradation of the crowned heads of Europe. At Basle it was thought proper, in order to keep others, I suppose, in countenance, that Great Britain should appear at this market, and bid with the rest, for the mercy of the People-King.

On the 6th of March, 1796, Mr. Wickham, in consequence of authority, was desired to sound France on her disposition towards a general pacification; to know whether she would consent to send Ministers to a Congress at such a place as might be hereafter agreed upon; to know whether they would communicate the general grounds of a pacification such as France (the diplomatick name of the Regicide power) would be willing to propose, as a foundation for a [31] negociation for peace with his Majesty *and his allies:* but he had no authority to enter into any negociation or discussion with citizen Barthelemi upon these subjects.

On the part of Great Britain this measure was a voluntary act, wholly uncalled for on the part of Regicide. Suits of this sort are at least strong indications of a desire for accommodation. Any other body of men but the Directory would be somewhat soothed with such advances. They could not however begin their answer, which was given without much delay, and communicated on the 28th of the same month, without a preamble of insult and reproach. "They doubt the sincerity of the pacific intentions of this Court." She did not begin, say they, yet to "know her real interests"—"she did not seek peace *with good faith.*" This, or something to this effect, has been the constant preliminary observation, (now grown into a sort of office-form) on all our overtures to this power: a perpetual charge on the British Government of fraud, evasion, and habitual perfidy.

It might be asked, from whence did these opinions of our insincerity and ill faith arise? It was because the British Ministry (leaving to the Directory, however, to propose a better mode) proposed a *Congress* for the purpose of a general pacification; and this they said "would render negociation endless." From hence they immediately inferred a fraudulent intention in the offer. Unquestionably their mode of giving the law would bring matters to a more speedy conclusion. As to any other method more agreeable to them than a Congress, an alternative expressly proposed to them, they did not condescend to signify their pleasure.

This refusal of treating conjointly with the powers allied against this Republick, furnishes matter for a great deal of serious reflexion. They have hitherto constantly declined any other than a treaty with a single power. By thus [32] dissociating every State from every other, like deer separated from the herd, each power is treated with on the merit of his being a deserter from the common cause. In that light the Regicide power finding each of them insulated and unprotected, with great facility gives the law to them all. By this system, for the present, an incurable distrust is sown amongst confederates; and in future, all alliance is rendered impracticable. It is thus they have treated with Prussia, with Spain, with Sardinia, with Bavaria, with the Ecclesiastical State, with Saxony; and here we see them refuse to treat with Great Britain in any other mode. They must be worse than blind who do not see with what undeviating regularity of system, in this case and in all cases, they pursue their scheme for the utter destruction of every independent power; especially the smaller, who cannot find any refuge whatever but in some common cause.

Renewing their taunts and reflections, they tell Mr. Wickham, "that their policy has no guides but openness and good faith, and that their conduct shall be conformable to these principles." They say concerning their Government, that "yielding to the ardent desire by which it is animated to procure peace for the French Republick, and for all nations, it will not *fear to declare itself openly*. Charged by the Constitution with the execution of the *laws*, it cannot *make* or *listen to* any proposal that would be contrary to them. The constitutional act does not permit it to consent to any alienation of that which, according to the existing laws, constitutes the territory of the Republick."

"With respect to the countries *occupied by the French armies and which have not been united to France,* they, as well as other interests political and commercial, may become the subject of a negociation, which will present to the Directory the means of proving how much it desires to [33] attain speedily to a happy pacification. That the Directory is ready to receive in this respect any overtures that shall be just, reasonable, and compatible *with the dignity of the Republick.*" On the head of what is *not* to be the subject of negotiation, the Directory is clear and open. As to what may be a matter of treaty, all this open dealing is gone. She retires into her shell. There she expects overtures from *you;* and that you are to guess what she shall judge just, reasonable, and above all, *compatible with her dignity.*

In the records of pride there does not exist so insulting a declaration. It is insolent in words, in manner, but in substance it is not only insulting but alarming. It is a specimen of what may be expected from the masters we are preparing for our humbled country. Their openness and candour consist in a direct avowal of their despotism and ambition. We know that their declared resolution had been to surrender no object belonging to France previous to the war. They had resolved, that the Republick was entire, and must remain so. As to what she has conquered from the allies and united to the same indivisible body, it is of the same nature. That is, the allies are to give up whatever conquests they have made or may make upon France, but all which she has violently ravished from her neighbours and thought fit to appropriate, are not to become so much as objects of negociation.

In this unity and indivisibility of possession are sunk ten immense and wealthy provinces, full of strong, flourishing

and opulent cities, the Austrian Netherlands, the part of
Europe the most necessary to preserve any communication
between this kingdom and its natural allies, next to Holland
the most interesting to this country, and without which Holland must virtually belong to France. Savoy and Nice, the
keys of Italy, and the citadel in her hands to bridle Switzerland, are in that consolidation. The important [34] territory
of Liège is torn out of the heart of the Empire. All these are
integrant parts of the Republick, not to be subject to any discussion, or to be purchased by any equivalent. Why? Because
there is a law which prevents it. What law? The law of nations?
The acknowledged public law of Europe? Treaties and conventions of parties? No! not a pretence of the kind. It is a
declaration not made in consequence of any prescription on
her side, not on any cession or dereliction, actual or tacit, of
other powers. It is a declaration *pendente lite* in the middle of a
war, one principal object of which was originally the defence,
and has since been the recovery, of these very countries.

This strange law is not made for a trivial object, not for
a single port, or for a single fortress; but for a great kingdom; for the religion, the morals, the laws, the liberties, the
lives and fortunes of millions of human creatures, who without their consent, or that of their lawful government, are, by
an arbitrary act of this regicide and homicide Government,
which they call a law, incorporated into their tyranny.

In other words, their will is the law, not only at home,
but as to the concerns of every nation. Who has made that
law but the Regicide Republick itself, whose laws, like those
of the Medes and Persians, they cannot alter or abrogate, or
even so much as take into consideration? Without the least
ceremony or compliment, they have sent out of the world
whole sets of laws and lawgivers. They have swept away the
very constitutions under which the Legislatures acted, and
the Laws were made. Even the fundamental sacred *Rights of
Man* they have not scrupled to profane. They have set this
holy code at naught with ignominy and scorn. Thus they treat

all their domestic laws and constitutions, and even what they had considered as a Law of Nature; but whatever they have put their seal on for the purposes of their ambition, and the ruin of their neighbours, [35] this alone is invulnerable, impassible, immortal. Assuming to be masters of every thing human and divine, here, and here alone, it seems they are limited, "cooped and cabined in"; and this omnipotent legislature finds itself wholly without the power of exercising it's favourite attribute, the love of peace. In other words, they are powerful to usurp, impotent to restore; and equally by their power and their impotence they aggrandize themselves, and weaken and impoverish you and all other nations. ∨

NOTHING CAN BE MORE PROPER or more manly than the state publication called a *note* on this proceeding, dated Downing-street, the 10th of April, 1796. Only that it is better expressed, it perfectly agrees with the opinion I have taken the liberty of submitting to your consideration.[1] I place it

1. "This Court has seen, with regret, how far the tone and spirit of that answer, the nature and extent of the demands which it contains, and the manner of announcing them, are remote from any dispositions for peace.

"The inadmissible pretension is there avowed of appropriating to France all that the laws existing there may have comprised under the denomination of French territory. To a demand such as this, is added an express declaration that no proposal contrary to it will be made, or even listened to. And even this, under the pretence of an internal regulation, the provisions of which are wholly foreign to all other nations.

"While these dispositions shall be persisted in, nothing is left for the King, but to prosecute a war equally just and necessary.

"Whenever his enemies shall manifest more pacific sentiments, his Majesty will, at all times, be eager to concur in them, by lending himself, in concert with his allies, to all such measures as shall be calculated to re-establish general tranquillity on conditions just, honourable and permanent, either by the establishment of a general Congress, which has been so happily the means of restoring peace to Europe, or by a preliminary discussion of the principles which may be proposed, on either side, as a foundation of a general pacification; or, lastly, by an impartial examination of any other way which may be pointed out to him for arriving at the same salutary end."

Downing-Street, April 10, 1796.

below at full length as my justification in thinking that this astonishing paper is not only a direct negative to all treaty, but is a rejection of every principle upon which [36] treaties could be made. To admit it for a moment were to erect this power, usurped at home, into a Legislature to govern mankind. It is an authority that on a thousand occasions they have asserted in claim, and whenever they are able, exerted in practice. The dereliction of this whole scheme of policy became, therefore, an indispensable previous condition to all renewal of treaty. The remark of the British Cabinet on this arrogant and tyrannical claim is natural and unavoidable. Our Ministry state, *"That while these dispositions shall be persisted in, nothing is left for the King but to prosecute a war that is just and necessary."*

It was of course, that we should wait until the enemy shewed some sort of disposition on their part to fulfil this condition. It was hoped indeed that our suppliant strains might be suffered to steal into the august ear in a more propitious season. That season, however, invoked by so many vows, conjurations, and prayers, did not come. Every declaration of hostility renovated, and every act pursued with double animosity—the over-running of Lombardy—the subjugation of Piedmont—the possession of its impregnable fortresses— the seizing on all the neutral states of Italy—our expulsion from Leghorn—instances for ever renewed for our expulsion from Genoa—Spain rendered subject to them and hostile to us—Portugal bent under the yoke—half the Empire overrun and ravaged, were the only signs which this mild Republick thought proper to manifest of their pacific sentiments. Every demonstration of an implacable rancour and an untameable pride were the only encouragements we received to the renewal of our supplications. Here, therefore, they and we were fixed. Nothing was left to the British Ministry but "to prosecute a war just and necessary"—a war equally just as at the time of our engaging in it—a war become ten times more necessary by every thing which [37] happened after-wards. This resolution was soon, however, forgot. It felt the heat of the season and melted away. New hopes were enter-tained from supplication. No expectations, indeed, were then formed from renewing a direct application to the French Regicides through the Agent General for the humiliation of Sovereigns. At length a step was taken in degradation which even went lower than all the rest. Deficient in merits of our own, a Mediator was to be sought—and we looked for that Mediator at Berlin! The King of Prussia's merits in abandon-ing the general cause might have obtained for him some sort of influence in favour of those whom he had deserted—but I have never heard that his Prussian Majesty had lately discov-ered so marked an affection for the Court of St. James's, or for the Court of Vienna, as to excite much hope of his inter-posing a very powerful mediation to deliver them from the distresses into which he had brought them.

If humiliation is the element in which we live, if it is be-come, not only our occasional policy, but our habit, no great objection can be made to the modes in which it may be di-versified; though, I confess, I cannot be charmed with the idea of our exposing our lazar sores at the door of every proud servitor of the French Republick, where the court-dogs will not deign to lick them. We had, if I am not mistaken, a minister at that court, who might try it's temper, and recede and advance as he found backwardness or encouragement. But to send a gentleman there on no other errand than this, and with no assurance whatever that he should not find, what he did find, a repulse, seems to me to go far beyond all the demands of a humiliation merely politick. I hope it did not arise from a predilection for that mode of conduct.

THE CUP OF BITTERNESS was not, however, drained to the [38] dregs. Basle and Berlin were not sufficient. After so many and so diversified repulses, we were resolved to make another trial, and to try another Mediator, among the unhappy gentlemen in whose persons Royalty is insulted and degraded at the seat of plebeian pride and upstart insolence. There is a minister from Denmark at Paris. Without any previous encouragement to that, any more than the other steps, we sent through this turnpike to demand a passport for a person who on our part was to solicit peace in the metropolis, at the footstool of Regicide itself. It was not to be expected that any one of those degraded beings could have influence enough to settle any part of the terms in favour of the candidates for further degradation; besides, such intervention would be a direct breach in their system, which did not permit one sovereign power to utter a word in the concerns of his equal.—Another repulse. We were desired to apply directly in our persons.—We submitted and made the application.

IT MIGHT BE THOUGHT that here, at length, we had touched the bottom of humiliation; our lead was brought up covered with mud. But "in the lowest deep, a lower deep" was to open for us still more profound abysses of disgrace and shame. However, in we leaped. We came forward in our own name. The passport, such a passport and safe-conduct as would be granted to thieves who might come in to betray their accomplices, and no better, was granted to British supplication. To leave no doubt of it's spirit, as soon as the rumour of this act of condescension could get abroad, it was formally announced, with an explanation from authority, containing an invective against the Ministry of Great Britain, their habitual frauds, their proverbial *Punick* perfidy. No such State Paper, as a preliminary to a negociation for peace, has ever yet appeared. Very [39] few declarations of war have ever shewn so much and so unqualified animosity. I place it below[1] as a diplomatick [40] curiosity: and in order to be

1. *Official Note, extracted from the Journal of the Defenders of the Country.*
"*EXECUTIVE DIRECTORY.*
"Different Journals have advanced that an English Plenipotentiary had

Regicide Peace I

better understood, in the few remarks I have to make upon a piece which indeed defies all description; "None but itself can be it's parallel."

---

reached Paris, and had presented himself to the Executive Directory, but that his propositions not having appeared satisfactory, he had received orders instantly to quit France.

"All these assertions are equally false.

"The notices given, in the English Papers, of a Minister having been sent to Paris, there to treat of peace, bring to recollection the overtures of Mr. Wickham to the Ambassador of the Republick at Basle, and the rumours circulated relative to the mission of Mr. Hammond to the Court of Prussia. The *insignificance,* or rather the *subtle duplicity,* the *PUNICK stile of* Mr. Wickham's note, is not forgotten. According to the partizans of the English Ministry, it was to Paris that Mr. Hammond was to come to speak for peace: when his destination became publick, and it was known that he went to Prussia, the same writer repeated that it was to accelerate a peace, and notwithstanding the object, now well known, of this negociation, was to engage Prussia to break her treaties with the Republick, and to return into the coalition. The Court of Berlin, faithful to its engagements, repulsed these *perfidious* propositions. But in converting this intrigue into a mission for peace, the English Ministry joined to the hope of giving a new enemy to France, *that of justifying the continuance of the war in the eyes of the English nation, and of throwing all the odium of it on the French Government.* Such was also the aim of Mr. Wickham's note. *Such is still that of the notices given at this time in the English papers.*

"This aim will appear evident, if we reflect how difficult it is, that the ambitious Government of England should sincerely wish for a peace that would *snatch from it it's maritime preponderancy, would re-establish the freedom of the seas, would give a new impulse to the Spanish, Dutch, and French marines,* and would carry to the highest degree of prosperity the industry and commerce of those nations in which it has always found *rivals,* and which it has considered as *enemies* of it's commerce, when they were tired of being it's *dupes.*

"But there will *no longer be any credit given to the pacific intentions of the English Ministry, when it is known, that it's gold and it's intrigues, it's open practices, and it's insinuations, besiege more than ever the Cabinet of Vienna, and are one of the principal obstacles to the negotiation which* that Cabinet *would of itself be induced to enter on for peace.*

"They will no longer *be credited,* finally, when the moment of the rumour of these overtures being circulated is considered. *The English nation supports impatiently the continuance of the war, a reply must be made to it's complaints, it's reproaches:* the Parliament is about to re-open it's sittings, the mouths of the orators who will declaim against the war must be shut, the demand of new taxes must be justified; and to obtain these results, it is necessary to be enabled to advance, that the French Government refuses every reasonable proposition of peace."

I pass by all the insolence and contumely of the performance as it comes from them. The question is not now how we are to be affected with it in regard to our dignity. That is gone. I shall say no more about it. Light lie the earth on the ashes of English pride. I shall only observe upon it *politically,* and as furnishing a direction for our own conduct in this low business.

THE VERY IDEA of a negociation for peace, whatever the inward sentiments of the parties may be, implies some confidence in their faith, some degree of belief in the professions which are made concerning it. A temporary and occasional credit, at least, is granted. Otherwise men stumble on the very threshold. I therefore wish to ask what hope we can have of their good faith, who, as the very basis of the negociation, assume the ill faith and treachery of those they have to deal with? The terms, as against us, must be such as imply a full security against a treacherous conduct — that is, what this Directory stated in it's first declaration, to place us "in an utter impossibility of executing our wretched projects." This is the omen, and the sole omen, under which we have consented to open our treaty.

THE SECOND OBSERVATION I have to make upon it, (much connected undoubtedly with the first,) is, that they have informed you of the result they propose from the kind of peace they mean to grant you; that is to say, the union they propose among nations with the view of rivalling our trade and destroying our naval power: and this they suppose (and with good reason too) must be the inevitable effect of their peace. It forms one of their principal grounds for suspecting [41] our Ministers could not be in good earnest in their proposition. They make no scruple beforehand to tell you the whole of what they intend; and this is what we call, in the modern style, the acceptance of a proposition for peace!

In old language it would be called a most haughty, offensive, and insolent rejection of all treaty.

THIRDLY, THEY TELL YOU what they conceive to be the perfidious policy which dictates your delusive offer; that is, the design of cheating not only them, but the people of England, against whose interest and inclination this war is supposed to be carried on.

If we proceed in this business, under this preliminary declaration, it seems to me that we admit, (now for the third time) by something a great deal stronger than words, the truth of the charges of every kind which they make upon the British Ministry, and the grounds of those foul imputations. The language used by us, which in other circumstances would not be exceptionable, in this case tends very strongly to confirm and realize the suspicion of our enemy. I mean the declaration, that if we do not obtain such terms of peace as suits our opinion of what our interests require, *then,* and in *that* case, we shall continue the war with vigour. This offer, so reasoned, plainly implies, that without it, our leaders themselves entertain great doubts of the opinion and good affections of the British people; otherwise there does not appear any cause, why we should proceed under the scandalous construction of our enemy, upon the former offer made by Mr. Wickham, and on the new offer made directly at Paris. It is not, therefore, from a sense of dignity, but from the danger of radicating that false sentiment in the breasts of the enemy, that I think, under the auspices of this declaration, we cannot, with the least hope of a good event, or, indeed, with any regard to the common safety, proceed [42] in the train of this negociation. I wish Ministry would seriously consider the importance of their seeming to confirm the enemy in an opinion, that his frequent appeals to the people against their Government have not been without their effect. If it puts an end to this war, it will render another impracticable.

Whoever goes to the directorial presence under this pass-port, with this offensive comment, and foul explanation, goes in the avowed sense of the Court to which he is sent; as the in-strument of a Government dissociated from the interests and wishes of the Nation, for the purpose of cheating both the people of France and the people of England. He goes out the declared emissary of a faithless Ministry. He has perfidy for his credentials. He has national weakness for his full powers. I yet doubt whether any one can be found to invest himself with that character. If there should, it would be pleasant to read his instructions on the answer which he is to give to the Directory, in case they should repeat to him the substance of the Manifesto which he carries with him in his portfolio.

So MUCH FOR THE *first* Manifesto of the Regicide Court which went along with the passport. Lest this declaration should seem the effect of haste, or a mere sudden effusion of pride and insolence, on full deliberation about a week after comes out a second. In this manifesto, which is dated the fifth of October, one day before the speech from the Throne, on the vigil of the festive day of cordial unanimity so happily celebrated by all parties in the British Parliament, the Regicides, our worthy friends, (I call them by advance and by courtesy what by law I shall be obliged to call them hereafter) our worthy friends, I say, renew and enforce the former declaration concerning our faith and sincerity, which they pinned to our passport. On three other points which [43] run through all their declarations, they are more ex-plicit than ever.

First, they more directly undertake to be the real repre-sentatives of the people of this kingdom: and on a supposi-tion in which they agree with our parliamentary reformers, that the House of Commons is not that Representative, the function being vacant, they, as our true constitutional organ, inform his Majesty and the world of the sense of the nation.

REGICIDE PEACE I

They tell us that "the English people see with regret his Majesty's Government squandering away the funds which had been granted to him." This astonishing assumption of the publick voice of England is but a slight foretaste of the usurpation which, on a peace, we may be assured they will make of all the powers in all the parts of our vassal constitution. "If it be thus in the green leaf, what will it be in the dry?"

Next they tell us, as a condition to our treaty, that "this Government must abjure the unjust hatred it bears to them, and at last open it's ears to the voice of humanity." Truly this is even from them an extraordinary demand. Hitherto, it seems, we have put wax into our ears, to shut them up against the tender, soothing strains, in the *affettuoso* of humanity, warbled from the throats of Reubel, Carnot, Tallien, and the whole chorus of Confiscators, Domiciliary Visitors, Committee-men of Research, Jurors and Presidents of Revolutionary Tribunals, Regicides, Assassins, Massacrers, and Septembrizers. It is not difficult to discern what sort of humanity our Government is to learn from these syren singers. Our Government also, (I admit, with some reason,) as a step towards the proposed fraternity, is required to abjure the unjust hatred which it bears to this body of honour and virtue. I thank God I am neither a Minister nor a leader of Opposition. I protest I cannot do what they desire, if I were under the guillotine, or as they ingeniously and pleasantly express it, "looking out of the [44] little national window." Even at that opening I could receive none of their light. I am fortified against all such affections by the declaration of the Government, which I must yet consider as lawful, made on the 29th of October 1793,[1] and [45] still ringing in my ears.

1. "In their place has succeeded a system destructive of all publick order, maintained by proscriptions, exiles, and confiscations, without number: by arbitrary imprisonment; by massacres which cannot be remembered without horror; and at length by the execrable murder of a just and beneficent Sovereign, and of the illustrious Princess, who, with an unshaken firmness, has

This declaration was transmitted not only to all our commanders by sea and land, but to our Ministers in every Court of Europe. It is the most eloquent and highly finished in the style, the most judicious in the choice of topicks, the most orderly in the arrangement, and the most rich in the colouring, without employing the smallest degree of exaggeration,

---

shared all the misfortunes of her Royal Consort, his protracted sufferings, his cruel captivity and his ignominious death."—"They (the allies) have had to encounter acts of aggression without pretext, open violations of all treaties, unprovoked declarations of war; in a word, whatever corruption, intrigue or violence could effect for the purpose so openly avowed, of subverting all the institutions of society, and of extending over all the nations of Europe that confusion, which has produced the misery of France."—"This state of things cannot exist in France without involving all the surrounding powers in one common danger, without giving them the right, without imposing it upon them as a duty, to stop the progress of an evil, which exists only by the successive violation of all law and all property, and which attacks the fundamental principles by which mankind is united in the bonds of civil society."—"The King would impose none other than equitable and moderate conditions, not such as the expence, the risques and the sacrifices of the war might justify; but such as his Majesty thinks himself under the indispensable necessity of requiring, with a view to these considerations, and still more to that of his own security and of the future tranquillity of Europe. His Majesty desires nothing more sincerely than thus to terminate a war, which he in vain endeavoured to avoid, and all the calamities of which, as now experienced by France, are to be attributed only to the ambition, the perfidy and the violence of those, whose crimes have involved their own country in misery, and disgraced all civilized nations."—"The King promises on his part the suspension of hostilities, friendship, and (as far as the course of events will allow, of which the will of man cannot dispose) security and protection to all those who, by declaring for a monarchical form of Government, shall shake off the yoke of sanguinary anarchy; of that anarchy which has broken all the most sacred bonds of society, dissolved all the relations of civil life, violated every right, confounded every duty; which uses the name of liberty to exercise the most cruel tyranny, to annihilate all property, to seize on all possessions; which founds it's power on the pretended consent of the people, and itself carries fire and sword through extensive provinces for having demanded their laws, their religion and their *lawful Sovereign*."

Declaration sent by his Majesty's command to the Commanders of his Majesty's fleets and armies employed against France, and to his Majesty's Ministers employed at foreign Courts.—Whitehall, *Oct.* 29, 1793.

of any state paper that has ever yet appeared. An ancient writer, Plutarch, I think it is, quotes some verses on the eloquence of Pericles, who is called "the only orator that left stings in the minds of his hearers." Like his, the eloquence of the declaration, not contradicting, but enforcing sentiments of the truest humanity, has left stings that have penetrated more than skin-deep into my mind; and never can they be extracted by all the surgery of murder; never can the throbbings they have created, be assuaged by all the emollient cataplasms of robbery and confiscation.

The third point which they have more clearly expressed than ever, is of equal importance with the rest; and with them furnishes a complete view of the Regicide system. For they demand as a condition without which our ambassador of obedience cannot be received with any hope of success, that he shall be "provided with full powers to negociate a peace between the French Republick and Great Britain, and to conclude it *definitively* BETWEEN THE TWO POWERS." With their spear they draw a circle about us. They will hear nothing of a joint treaty. We must make a peace separately from our allies. We must, as the very first and preliminary step, be guilty of that perfidy towards our friends and associates, with which they reproach us in our transactions with them our enemies. We are called upon scandalously to betray the fundamental securities to ourselves and to all nations. In my opinion, (it is perhaps but a poor one) if we are meanly bold enough to send an ambassador, such as this official note of the enemy requires, we cannot [46] even dispatch our emissary without danger of being charged with a breach of our alliance. Government now understand the full meaning of the passport.

Strange revolutions have happened in the ways of thinking and in the feelings of men. But it requires a very extraordinary coalition of parties indeed, and a kind of unheard-of unanimity in public Councils, which can impose this new-discovered system of negociation, as sound national policy, on the understanding of a spectator of this wonderful scene, who judges on the principles of any thing he ever before saw, read, or heard of, and above all, on the understanding of a person who has had in his eye the transactions of the last seven years.

I know it is supposed, that if good terms of capitulation are not granted, after we have thus so repeatedly hung out the white flag, the national spirit will revive with tenfold ardour. This is an experiment cautiously to be made. *Reculer pour mieux sauter*, according to the French by-word, cannot be trusted to as a general rule of conduct. To diet a man into weakness and languor, afterwards to give him the greater strength, has more of the empirick than the rational physician. It is true that some persons have been kicked into courage; and this is no bad hint to give to those who are too forward and liberal in bestowing insults and outrages on their passive companions. But such a course does not at first view appear a well-chosen discipline to form men to a nice sense of honour, or a quick resentment of injuries. A long habit of humiliation does not seem a very good preparative to manly and vigorous sentiment. It may not leave, perhaps, enough of energy in the mind fairly to discern what are good terms or what are not. Men low and dispirited may regard those terms as not at all amiss, which in another state of mind they would think intolerable: if they [47] grew peevish in this state of mind, they may be roused, not against the enemy whom they have been taught to fear, but against the Ministry,[1] who are more within their reach, and who have refused conditions that are not unseasonable, from power that they have been taught to consider as irresistible.

IF ALL THAT FOR SOME MONTHS I have heard have the least foundation, (I hope it has not,) the Ministers are, per-

---

1. Ut lethargicus hic, cum fit pugil, et medicum urget. —HOR.

haps, not quite so much to be blamed, as their condition is to be lamented. I have been given to understand, that these proceedings are not in their origin properly theirs. It is said that there is a secret in the House of Commons. It is said that Ministers act not according to the votes, but according to the dispositions, of the majority. I hear that the minority has long since spoken the general sense of the nation; and that to prevent those who compose it from having the open and avowed lead in that house, or perhaps in both Houses, it was necessary to pre-occupy their ground, and to take their propositions out of their mouths, even with the hazard of being afterwards reproached with a compliance which it was foreseen would be fruitless.

If the general disposition of the people be, as I hear it is, for an immediate peace with Regicide, without so much as considering our publick and solemn engagements to the party in France whose cause we had espoused, or the engagements expressed in our general alliances, not only without an enquiry into the terms, but with a certain knowledge that none but the worst terms will be offered, it is all over with us. It is strange, but it may be true, that as the danger from Jacobinism is increased in my eyes and in yours, the fear of it is lessened in the eyes of many people who formerly regarded it with horror. [48] It seems, they act under the impression of terrors of another sort, which have frightened them out of their first apprehensions. But let their fears, or their hopes, or their desires, be what they will, they should recollect, that they who would make peace without a previous knowledge of the terms, make a surrender. They are conquered. They do not treat; they receive the law. Is this the disposition of the people of England? Then the people of England are contented to seek in the kindness of a foreign systematick enemy combined with a dangerous faction at home, a security which they cannot find in their own patriotism and their own courage. They are willing to trust to the sympathy of Regicides the guarantee of the British Monarchy. They are content to rest their religion on the piety of atheists by establishment. They are satisfied to seek in the clemency of practised murderers the security of their lives. They are pleased to confide their property to the safeguard of those who are robbers by inclination, interest, habit, and system. If this be our deliberate mind, truly we deserve to lose, what it is impossible we should long retain, the name of a nation.

In matters of State, a constitutional competence to act is in many cases the smallest part of the question. Without disputing (God forbid I should dispute) the sole competence of the King and the Parliament, each in it's province, to decide on war and peace, I venture to say, no war *can* be long carried on against the will of the people. This war, in particular, cannot be carried on unless they are enthusiastically in favour of it. Acquiescence will not do. There must be zeal. Universal zeal in such a cause, and at such a time as this is, cannot be looked for; neither is it necessary. A zeal in the larger part carries the force of the whole. Without this, no Government, certainly not our Government, is capable of a great war. None of the [49] ancient regular Governments have wherewithal to fight abroad with a foreign foe, and at home to overcome repining, reluctance, and chicane. It must be some portentous thing, like Regicide France, that can exhibit such a prodigy. Yet even she, the mother of monsters, more prolifick than the country of old called *ferax monstrorum,* shews symptoms of being almost effete already; and she will be so, unless the fallow of a peace comes to recruit her fertility. But whatever may be represented concerning the meanness of the popular spirit, I, for one, do not think so desperately of the British nation. Our minds, as I said, are light; but they are not depraved. We are dreadfully open to delusion and to dejection; but we are capable of being animated and undeceived.

It cannot be concealed—we are a divided people. But in divisions, where a part is to be taken, we are to make a muster of our strength. I have often endeavoured to compute and to class those who, in any political view, are to be called the

people. Without doing something of this sort we must proceed absurdly. We should not be much wiser, if we pretended
to very great accuracy in our estimate. But I think, in the
calculation I have made, the error cannot be very material.
In England and Scotland, I compute that those of adult age,
not declining in life, of tolerable leisure for such discussions,
and of some means of information, more or less, and who
are above menial dependence, (or what virtually is such) may
amount to about four hundred thousand. There is such a
thing as a natural representative of the people. This body is
that representative; and on this body, more than on the legal
constituent, the artificial representative depends. This is the
British publick; and it is a publick very numerous. The rest,
when feeble, are the objects of protection; when strong, the
means of force. They who [50] affect to consider that part of
us in any other light, insult while they cajole us; they do not
want us for counsellors in deliberation, but to list us as soldiers for battle.

OF THESE four hundred thousand political citizens, I look
upon one fifth, or about eighty thousand, to be pure Jacobins;
utterly incapable of amendment; objects of eternal vigilance;
and when they break out, of legal constraint. On these, no
reason, no argument, no example, no venerable authority,
can have the slightest influence. They desire a change; and
they will have it if they can. If they cannot have it by English
cabal, they will make no sort of scruple of having it by the
cabal of France, into which already they are virtually incorporated. It is only their assured and confident expectation
of the advantages of French fraternity and the approaching
blessings of Regicide intercourse, that skins over their mischievous dispositions with a momentary quiet.

This minority is great and formidable. I do not know
whether if I aimed at the total overthrow of a kingdom I
should wish to be encumbered with a larger body of partizans. They are more easily disciplined and directed than if

the number were greater. These, by their spirit of intrigue, and by their restless agitating activity, are of a force far superior to their numbers; and if times grew the least critical, have the means of debauching or intimidating many of those who are now sound, as well as of adding to their force large bodies of the more passive part of the nation. This minority is numerous enough to make a mighty cry for peace, or for war, or for any object they are led vehemently to desire. By passing from place to place with a velocity incredible, and diversifying their character and description, they are capable of mimicking the general voice. We must not always judge of the generality of the opinion by the noise of the acclamation.

[51] THE MAJORITY, the other four fifths, is perfectly sound; and of the best possible disposition to religion, to government, to the true and undivided interest of their country. Such men are naturally disposed to peace. They who are in possession of all they wish are languid and improvident. With this fault, (and I admit it's existence in all it's extent) they would not endure to hear of a peace that led to the ruin of every thing for which peace is dear to them. However, the desire of peace is essentially the weak side of that kind of men. All men that are ruined, are ruined on the side of their natural propensities. There they are unguarded. Above all, good men do not suspect that their destruction is attempted through their virtues. This their enemies are perfectly aware of: and accordingly, they, the most turbulent of mankind, who never made a scruple to shake the tranquillity of their country to its center, raise a continual cry for peace with France. Peace with Regicide, and war with the rest of the world, is their motto. From the beginning, and even whilst the French gave the blows, and we hardly opposed the *vis inertiae* to their efforts—from that day to this hour, like importunate Guinea-fowls crying one note day and night, they have called for peace.

REGICIDE PEACE I

In this they are, as I confess in all things they are, perfectly consistent. They who wish to unite themselves to your enemies, naturally desire, that you should disarm yourself by a peace with these enemies. But it passes my conception, how they, who wish well to their country on its antient system of laws and manners, come not to be doubly alarmed, when they find nothing but a clamor for peace, in the mouths of the men on earth the least disposed to it in their natural or in their habitual character.

I have a good opinion of the general abilities of the Jacobins: not that I suppose them better born than others; but strong passions awaken the faculties. They suffer not a [52] particle of the man to be lost. The spirit of enterprise gives to this description the full use of all their native energies. If I have reason to conceive that my enemy, who, as such, must have an interest in my destruction, is also a person of discernment and sagacity, then I must be quite sure that, in a contest, the object he violently pursues is the very thing by which my ruin is likely to be the most perfectly accomplished. Why do the Jacobins cry for peace? Because they know, that this point gained, the rest will follow of course. On our part, why are all the rules of prudence, as sure as the laws of material nature, to be at this time reversed? How comes it, that now for the first time, men think it right to be governed by the counsels of their enemies? Ought they not rather to tremble, when they are persuaded to travel on the same road, and to tend to the same place of rest?

The minority I speak of is not susceptible of an impression from the topics of argument to be used to the larger part of the community. I therefore do not address to them any part of what I have to say. The more forcibly I drive my arguments against their system, so as to make an impression where I wish to make it, the more strongly I rivet them in their sentiments. As for us, who compose the far larger, and what I call the far better part of the people, let me say, that we have not been quite fairly dealt with when called to this delibera-

tion. The Jacobin minority have been abundantly supplied
with stores and provisions of all kinds towards their warfare.
No sort of argumentative materials, suited to their purposes,
have been withheld. False they are, unsound, sophistical; but
they are regular in their direction. They all bear one way; and
they all go to the support of the substantial merits of their
cause. The others have not had the question so much as fairly
stated to them.

[53] THERE HAS NOT BEEN, in this century, any foreign
peace or war, in it's origin the fruit of popular desire, except
the war that was made with Spain in 1739. Sir Robert Walpole
was forced into the war by the people, who were inflamed to
this measure by the most leading politicians, by the first orators, and the greatest poets of the time. For that war, Pope
sung his dying notes. For that war, Johnson, in more energetic
strains, employed the voice of his early genius. For that war,
Glover distinguished himself in the way in which his muse
was the most natural and happy. The crowd readily followed
the politicians in the cry for a war which threatened little
bloodshed, and which promised victories that were attended
with something more solid than glory. A war with Spain was a
war of plunder. In the present conflict with Regicide, Mr. Pitt
has not hitherto had, nor will perhaps for a few days have,
many prizes to hold out in the lottery of war, to tempt the
lower part of our character. He can only maintain it by an
appeal to the higher; and to those, in whom that higher part
is the most predominant, he must look the most for his support. Whilst he holds out no inducements to the wise, nor
bribes to the avaricious, he may be forced by a vulgar cry into
a peace ten times more ruinous than the most disastrous war.
The weaker he is in the fund of motives which apply to our
avarice, to our laziness, and to our lassitude, if he means to
carry the war to any end at all, the stronger he ought to be
in his addresses to our magnanimity and to our reason.

In stating that Walpole was driven by a popular clamour

into a measure not to be justified, I do not mean wholly to
excuse his conduct. My time of observation did not exactly
coincide with that event; but I read much of the controver-
sies then carried on. Several years after the contests of parties
had ceased, the people were amused, and [54] in a degree
warmed with them. The events of that aera seemed then of
magnitude, which the revolutions of our time have reduced
to parochial importance; and the debates, which then shook
the nation, now appear of no higher moment than a discussion in a vestry. When I was very young, a general fashion told
me I was to admire some of the writings against that Minister;
a little more maturity taught me as much to despise them. I
observed one fault in his general proceeding. He never manfully put forward the entire strength of his cause. He tempo-
rized; he managed; and, adopting very nearly the sentiments
of his adversaries, he opposed their inferences. This, for a
political commander, is the choice of a weak post. His adversaries had the better of the argument, as he handled it;
not as the reason and justice of his cause enabled him to
manage it. I say this, after having seen, and with some care
examined, the original documents concerning certain important transactions of those times. They perfectly satisfied
me of the extreme injustice of that war, and of the falsehood
of the colours, which to his own ruin, and guided by a mistaken policy, he suffered to be daubed over that measure.
Some years after, it was my fortune to converse with many
of the principal actors against that Minister, and with those
who principally excited that clamour. None of them, no not
one, did in the least defend the measure, or attempt to justify their conduct. They condemned it as freely as they would
have done in commenting upon any proceeding in history,
in which they were totally unconcerned. Thus it will be. They
who stir up the people to improper desires, whether of peace
or war, will be condemned by themselves. They who weakly
yield to them will be condemned by history.

In my opinion, the present Ministry are as far from doing

full justice to their cause in this war, as Walpole was from [55] doing justice to the peace which at that time he was willing to preserve. They throw the light on one side only of their case; though it is impossible they should not observe, that the other side which is kept in the shade has it's importance too. They must know that France is formidable not only as she is France, but as she is Jacobin France. They knew from the beginning that the Jacobin party was not confined to that country. They knew, they felt, the strong disposition of the same faction in both countries to communicate and to co-operate. For some time past, these two points have been kept, and even industriously kept, out of sight. France is considered as merely a foreign Power; and the seditious English only as a domestic faction. The merits of the war with the former have been argued solely on political grounds. To prevent the mischievous doctrines of the latter from corrupting our minds, matter and argument have been supplied abundantly, and even to surfeit, on the excellency of our own government. But nothing has been done to make us feel in what manner the safety of that Government is connected with the principle and with the issue of this war. For any thing which in the late discussion has appeared, the war is entirely collateral to the state of Jacobinism; as truly a foreign war to us and to all our home concerns, as the war with Spain in 1739, about *Guarda-Costas,* the Madrid Convention, and the fable of Captain *Jenkins's* ears.

WHENEVER THE ADVERSE PARTY has raised a cry for peace with the Regicide, the answer has been little more than this, "that the Administration wished for such a peace, full as much as the Opposition; but that the time was not convenient for making it." Whatever else has been said was much in the same spirit. Reasons of this kind never touched the substantial merits of the war. They were in [56] the nature of dilatory pleas, exceptions of form, previous questions. Accordingly all the arguments against a compliance with what was represented as the popular desire, (urged on with all possible vehemence and earnestness by the Jacobins) have appeared flat and languid, feeble and evasive. They appeared to aim only at gaining time. They never entered into the peculiar and distinctive character of the war. They spoke neither to the understanding nor to the heart. Cold as ice themselves, they never could kindle in our breasts a spark of that zeal, which is necessary to a conflict with an adverse zeal; much less were they made to infuse into our minds that stubborn persevering spirit, which alone is capable of bearing up against those vicissitudes of fortune which will probably occur, and those burthens which must be inevitably borne in a long war. I speak it emphatically, and with a desire that it should be marked, in a *long* war; because, without such a war, no experience has yet told us, that a dangerous power has ever been reduced to measure or to reason. I do not throw back my view to the Peloponnesian war of twenty-seven years; nor to two of the Punic wars, the first of twenty-four, the second of eighteen; nor to the more recent war concluded by the treaty of Westphalia, which continued, I think, for thirty. I go to what is but just fallen behind living memory, and immediately touches our own country. Let the portion of our history from the year 1689 to 1713 be brought before us. We shall find, that in all that period of twenty-four years, there were hardly five that could be called a season of peace; and the interval between the two wars was in reality, nothing more than a very active preparation for renovated hostility. During that period, every one of the propositions of peace came from the enemy: the first, when they were accepted, at the peace of Ryswick; the second, when they were [57] rejected, at the congress at Gertruydenburgh; the last, when the war ended by the treaty of Utrecht. Even then, a very great part of the nation, and that which contained by far the most intelligent statesmen, was against the conclusion of the war. I do not enter into the merits of that question as between the parties. I only state the existence of that opinion as a fact, from whence you may draw such an inference as you think properly arises from it.

It is for us at present to recollect what we have been; and to consider what, if we please, we may be still. At the period of those wars, our principal strength was found in the resolution of the people; and that in the resolution of a part only of the then whole, which bore no proportion to our existing magnitude. England and Scotland were not united at the beginning of that mighty struggle. When, in the course of the contest they were conjoined, it was in a raw, an ill-cemented, an unproductive union. For the whole duration of the war, and long after, the names, and other outward and visible signs of approximation, rather augmented than diminished our insular feuds. They were rather the causes of new discontents and new troubles, than promoters of cordiality and affection. The now single and potent Great Britain was then not only two countries, but, from the party heats in both, and the divisions formed in each of them, each of the old kingdoms within itself in effect was made up of two hostile nations. Ireland, now so large a source of the common opulence and power, which wisely managed might be made much more beneficial and much more effective, was then the heaviest of the burthens. An army not much less than forty thousand men was drawn from the general effort, to keep that kingdom in a poor, unfruitful, and resourceless subjection.

[58] Such was the state of the empire. The state of our finances was worse, if possible. Every branch of the revenue became less productive after the Revolution. Silver, not as now a sort of counter, but the body of the current coin, was reduced so low as not to have above three parts in four of the value in the shilling. It required a dead expence of three mil-

lions sterling to renew the coinage. Publick credit, that great but ambiguous principle, which has so often been predicted as the cause of our certain ruin, but which for a century has been the constant companion, and often the means, of our prosperity and greatness, had it's origin, and was cradled, I may say, in bankruptcy and beggary. At this day we have seen parties contending to be admitted, at a moderate premium, to advance eighteen millions to the Exchequer. For infinitely smaller loans, the Chancellor of the Exchequer of that day, Montagu, the father of publick credit, counter-securing the State by the appearance of the city, with the Lord-Mayor of London at his side, was obliged, like an agent at an election, to go cap in hand from shop to shop, to borrow an hundred pound and even smaller sums. When made up in driblets as they could, their best securities were at an interest of 12 per cent. Even the paper of the Bank (now at par with cash, and even sometimes preferred to it) was often at a discount of twenty per cent. By this the state of the rest may be judged.

As to our commerce, the imports and exports of the nation, now six and forty million, did not then amount to ten. The inland trade, which is commonly passed by in this sort of estimates, but which, in part growing out of the foreign and connected with it, is more advantageous, and more substantially nutritive to the State, is not only grown in a proportion of near five to one as the foreign, but has been augmented, at least, in a tenfold proportion. When I came [59] to England, I remember but one river navigation, the rate of carriage on which was limited by an Act of Parliament. It was made in the reign of William the Third; I mean that of the Aire and Calder. The rate was settled at thirteen pence. So high a price demonstrated the feebleness of these beginnings of our inland intercourse. In my time, one of the longest and sharpest contests I remember in your House, and which rather resembled a violent contention amongst national parties than a local dispute, was, as well as I can recollect, to hold the price up to threepence. Even this, which a very scanty justice to the proprietors required, was done with infinite difficulty. As to private credit, there were not, as I best remember, twelve Banker's shops at that time out of London. In this their number, when I first saw the country, I cannot be quite exact; but certainly those machines of domestick credit were then very few indeed. They are now in almost every market town: and this circumstance (whether the thing be carried to an excess or not) demonstrates the astonishing encrease of private confidence, of general circulation, and of internal commerce; an encrease out of all proportion to the growth of the foreign trade. Our naval strength in the time of King William's war was nearly matched by that of France; and though conjoined with Holland, then a maritime Power hardly inferior to our own, even with that force we were not always victorious. Though finally superior, the allied fleets experienced many unpleasant reverses on their own element. In two years three thousand vessels were taken from the English trade. On the continent we lost almost every battle we fought.

In 1697, it is not quite an hundred years ago, in that state of things, amidst the general debasement of the coin, the fall of the ordinary revenue, the failure of all the extraordinary supplies, the ruin of commerce and the almost total extinction [60] of an infant credit, the Chancellor of the Exchequer himself, whom we have just seen begging from door to door, came forward to move a resolution, full of vigour, in which, far from being discouraged by the generally adverse fortune, and the long continuance of the war, the Commons agreed to address the Crown in the following manly, spirited, and truly animating style.

This is the EIGHTH year in which your Majesty's most dutiful and loyal subjects the Commons in Parliament assembled, have assisted your Majesty with large supplies for carrying on a just and necessary war, in defence of our religion, and preservation of our laws, and vindication of the rights and liberties of the people of England.

Afterwards they proceed in this manner:

> To shew to your Majesty and all Christendom, that the Commons of England will not be *amused* or diverted from their firm resolutions of obtaining by WAR, a safe and honourable peace, we do, in the name of those we represent, renew our assurances to support your Majesty and your Government against all your enemies at home and abroad; and that we will effectually assist you in carrying on the war against France.

The amusement and diversion they speak of, was the suggestion of a treaty *proposed by the enemy,* and announced from the Throne. Thus the people of England felt in the *eighth,* not in the *fourth* year of the war. No sighing or panting after negociation; no motions from the Opposition to force the Ministry into a peace; no messages from Ministers to palsy and deaden the resolution of Parliament or the spirit of the nation. They did not so much as advise the King to listen to the propositions of the enemy, nor to seek for peace but through the mediation of a vigorous war. This address was moved in an hot, a divided, a factious, and in a great part, disaffected House of Commons, and it was carried *nemine contradicente.*

[61] WHILE THAT FIRST WAR (which was ill smothered by the treaty of Ryswick) slept in the thin ashes of a seeming peace, a new conflagration was in it's immediate causes. A fresh and a far greater war was in preparation. A year had hardly elapsed when arrangements were made for renewing the contest with tenfold fury. The steps which were taken, at that time, to compose, to reconcile, to unite, and to discipline all Europe against the growth of France, certainly furnish to a statesman the finest and most interesting part in the history of that great period. It formed the master-piece of King William's policy, dexterity, and perseverance. Full of the idea

of preserving, not only a local civil liberty, united with order, to our country, but to embody it in the political liberty, the order, and the independence of nations united under a natural head, the King called upon his Parliament to put itself into a posture *to preserve to England the weight and influence it at present had on the counsels and affairs* ABROAD. "It will be requisite *Europe* should see you will not be wanting to yourselves."

Baffled as that Monarch was, and almost heart-broken at the disappointment he met with in the mode he first proposed for that great end, he held on his course. He was faithful to his object; and in councils, as in arms, over and over again repulsed, over and over again he returned to the charge. All the mortifications he had suffered from the last Parliament, and the greater he had to apprehend from that newly chosen, were not capable of relaxing the vigour of his mind. He was in Holland when he combined the vast plan of his foreign negociations. When he came to open his design to his Ministers in England, even the sober firmness of Somers, the undaunted resolution of Shrewsbury, and the adventurous spirit of Montagu and Orford, were staggered. They were not yet mounted to the elevation of the King. The Cabinet met on the subject [62] at Tunbridge Wells the 28th of August, 1698; and there, Lord Somers holding the pen, after expressing doubts on the state of the continent, which they ultimately refer to the King, as best informed, they give him a most discouraging portrait of the spirit of this nation.

"So far as relates to England," say these Ministers,

it would be want of duty not to give your Majesty this clear account, that *there* is a *deadness and want of spirit in the nation universally,* so as not to be at all disposed to *entering into a new war.* That they seem to be *tired out with taxes* to a degree beyond what was discerned, till it appeared upon occasion of the *late elections.* This is the truth of the fact upon which your Majesty will determine what resolution ought to be taken.

HIS MAJESTY DID DETERMINE; and did take and pursue his resolution. In all the tottering imbecility of a new

Government, and with Parliament totally unmanageable, he persevered. He persevered to expel the fears of his people, by his fortitude; to steady their fickleness, by his constancy; to expand their narrow prudence, by his enlarged wisdom; to sink their factious temper in his public spirit. In spite of his people, he resolved to make them great and glorious; to make England, inclined to shrink into her narrow self, the Arbitress of Europe, the tutelary Angel of the human race. In spite of the Ministers, who staggered under the weight that his mind imposed upon theirs, unsupported as they felt themselves by the popular spirit, he infused into them his own soul; he renewed in them their ancient heart; he rallied them in the same cause.

It required some time to accomplish this work. The people were first gained; and through them their distracted representatives. Under the influence of King William, Holland had resisted the allurements of every seduction, and the terrors of every menace. With Hannibal at her [63] gates, she had nobly and magnanimously refused all separate treaty, or any thing which might for a moment appear to divide her affection or her interest, or even to distinguish her in identity from England. Having settled the great point of the consolidation (which he hoped would be eternal) of the countries, made for a common interest and common sentiment, the King, in his message to both Houses, calls their attention to the affairs of the *States General.* The House of Lords was perfectly sound, and entirely impressed with the wisdom and dignity of the King's proceedings. In answer to the message, (which you will observe was narrowed to a single point, the danger of the States General) after the usual professions of zeal for his service, the Lords opened themselves at large. They go far beyond the demands of the message. They express themselves as follows:

We take this occasion *further* to assure your Majesty, that we are sensible of the *great and imminent danger to which the States General are ex-*

posed. And we perfectly agree with them in believing that their safety and ours are so inseparably united, that whatsoever is ruin to the one must be fatal to the other.

We humbly desire your Majesty will be pleased, *not only* to make good all the articles of any *former* treaties to the States General, but that you will enter into a strict league, offensive and defensive, with them, *for their common preservation: and that you will invite into it all Princes and States who are concerned in the present visible danger, arising from the union of France and Spain.*

And we further desire your Majesty, that you will be pleased to enter into such alliances with the *Emperor,* as your Majesty shall think fit, pursuant to the ends of the treaty of 1689; towards all which we assure your Majesty of our hearty and sincere assistance; not doubting, but whenever your Majesty shall be obliged to be engaged for the defence of your allies, *and securing the liberty and quiet of Europe,* Almighty God will protect your sacred person in so righteous a cause. And that the unanimity, wealth, and [64] courage of your subjects will carry your Majesty with honour and success *through all the difficulties of a* JUST WAR.

The House of Commons was more reserved; the late popular disposition was still in a great degree prevalent in the representative, after it had been made to change in the constituent body. The principle of the Grand Alliance was not directly recognized in the resolution of the Commons, nor the war announced, though they were well aware the alliance was formed for the war. However, compelled by the returning sense of the people, they went so far as to fix the three great immoveable pillars of the safety and greatness of England, as they were then, as they are now, and as they must ever be to the end of time. They asserted in general terms the necessity of supporting Holland; of keeping united with our allies; and maintaining the liberty of Europe; though they restricted their vote to the succours stipulated by actual treaty. But now they were fairly embarked; they were obliged to go with the course of the vessel; and the whole nation, split before into an hundred adverse factions, with a King at it's head evidently declining to his tomb, the whole nation, Lords, Commons, and People, proceeded as one body, informed by one soul. Under the British union, the union of Europe was consolidated; and it long held together with a degree of cohesion, firmness, and fidelity not known before or since in any political combination of that extent.

Just as the last hand was given to this immense and complicated machine, the master workman died. But the work was formed on true mechanical principles; and it was as truly wrought. It went by the impulse it had received from the first mover. The man was dead: but the grand alliance survived, in which King William lived and reigned. That heartless and dispirited people, whom Lord Somers had represented, about two years before, as dead in energy [65] and operation, continued that war to which it was supposed they were unequal in mind, and in means, for near thirteen years.

FOR WHAT HAVE I ENTERED into all this detail? To what purpose have I recalled your view to the end of the last century? It has been done to shew that the British Nation was then a great people—to point out how and by what means they came to be exalted above the vulgar level, and to take that lead which they assumed among mankind. To qualify us for that pre-eminence, we had then an high mind, and a constancy unconquerable; we were then inspired with no flashy passions; but such as were durable as well as warm; such as corresponded to the great interests we had at stake. This force of character was inspired, as all such spirit must ever be, from above. Government gave the impulse. As well may we fancy that of itself the sea will swell, and that without winds the billows will insult the adverse shore, as that the gross mass of the people will be moved, and elevated, and continue by a steady and permanent direction to bear upon one point, without the influence of superior authority, or superior mind.

This impulse ought, in my opinion, to have been given in this war; and it ought to have been continued to it at every instant. It is made, if ever war was made, to touch all the great springs of action in the human breast. It ought not to have been a war of apology. The Minister had, in this conflict, wherewithal to glory in success; to be consoled in adversity; to hold high his principle in all fortunes. If it were not given him to support the falling edifice, he ought to bury himself under the ruins of the civilized world. All the art of Greece, and all the pride and power of eastern Monarchs, never heaped upon their ashes so grand a monument.

[66] There were days when his great mind was up to the crisis of the world he is called to act in.[1] His manly eloquence was equal to the elevated wisdom of such sentiments. But the little have triumphed over the great; an unnatural, (as it should seem) not an unusual victory. I am sure you cannot forget with how much uneasiness we heard in conversation the language of more than one gentleman at the opening of this contest, "that he was willing to try the war for a year or two, and if it did not succeed, then to vote for peace." As if war was a matter of experiment! As if you could take it up or lay it down as an idle frolick! As if the dire goddess that presides over it, with her murderous spear in her hand, and her gorgon at her breast, was a coquette to be flirted with! We ought with reverence to approach that tremendous divinity, that loves courage, but commands counsel. War never leaves, where it found a nation. It is never to be entered into without a mature deliberation; not a deliberation lengthened out into a perplexing indecision, but a deliberation leading to a sure and fixed judgment. When so taken up, it is not to be abandoned without reason as valid, as fully and as extensively considered. Peace may be made as unadvisedly as war. Nothing is so rash as fear; and the counsels of pusillanimity very rarely put off, whilst they are always sure to aggravate, the evils from which they would fly.

In that great war carried on against Louis the Fourteenth,

1. See the Declaration.

for near eighteen years, Government spared no pains to satisfy the nation that, though they were to be animated by a
desire of glory, glory was not their ultimate object; but that
every thing dear to them, in religion, in law, in liberty—every
thing which as freemen, as Englishmen, and as citizens of
the great commonwealth of Christendom, they had at heart,
was then at stake. This was to know the true art of [67] gaining the affections and confidence of an high-minded people;
this was to understand human nature. A danger to avert a
danger; a present inconvenience and suffering to prevent a
foreseen future, and a worse calamity; these are the motives
that belong to an animal, who, in his constitution, is at once
adventurous and provident; circumspect and daring; whom
his Creator has made, as the Poet says, "of large discourse,
looking before and after." But never can a vehement and sustained spirit of fortitude be kindled in a people by a war
of calculation. It has nothing that can keep the mind erect
under the gusts of adversity. Even where men are willing, as
sometimes they are, to barter their blood for lucre, to hazard their safety for the gratification of their avarice, the passion which animates them to that sort of conflict, like all the
short-sighted passions, must see it's objects distinct and near
at hand. The passions of the lower order are hungry and impatient. Speculative plunder; contingent spoil; future, long
adjourned, uncertain booty; pillage which must enrich a late
posterity, and which possibly may not reach to posterity at
all; these, for any length of time, will never support a mercenary war. The people are in the right. The calculation of
profit in all such wars is false. On balancing the account of
such wars, ten thousand hogsheads of sugar are purchased
at ten thousand times their price. The blood of man should
never be shed but to redeem the blood of man. It is well shed
for our family, for our friends, for our God, for our country,
for our kind. The rest is vanity; the rest is crime.

In the war of the Grand Alliance, most of these considerations voluntarily and naturally had their part. Some were pressed into the service. The political interest easily went in the track of the natural sentiment. In the reverse course the carriage does not follow freely. I am sure the natural feeling, as I have just said, is a far more predominant [68] ingredient in this war, than in that of any other that ever was waged by this kingdom.

IF THE WAR MADE TO PREVENT the union of two crowns upon one head was a just war, this, which is made to prevent the tearing all crowns from all heads which ought to wear them, and with the crowns to smite off the sacred heads themselves, this is a just war.

IF A WAR TO PREVENT Louis the Fourteenth from imposing his religion was just, a war to prevent the murderers of Louis the Sixteenth from imposing their irreligion upon us is just; a war to prevent the operation of a system, which makes life without dignity, and death without hope, is a just war.

IF TO PRESERVE POLITICAL INDEPENDENCE and civil freedom to nations, was a just ground of war; a war to preserve national independence, property, liberty, life, and honour, from certain universal havock, is a war just, necessary, manly, pious; and we are bound to persevere in it by every principle, divine and human, as long as the system which menaces them all, and all equally, has an existence in the world.

YOU, WHO HAVE LOOKED at this matter with as fair and impartial an eye as can be united with a feeling heart, you will not think it an hardy assertion, when I affirm, that it were far better to be conquered by any other nation, than to have this faction for a neighbour. Before I felt myself authorised to say this, I considered the state of all the countries in Europe for these last three hundred years, which have been

obliged to submit to a foreign law. In most of those I found
the condition of the annexed countries even better, certainly
not worse, than the lot of those which [69] were the patrimony of the conquerour. They wanted some blessings; but
they were free from many very great evils. They were rich and
tranquil. Such was Artois, Flanders, Lorrain, Alsatia, under
the old Government of France. Such was Silesia under the
King of Prussia. They who are to live in the vicinity of this new
fabrick, are to prepare to live in perpetual conspiracies and
seditions; and to end at last in being conquered, if not to her
dominion, to her resemblance. But when we talk of conquest
by other nations, it is only to put a case. This is the only power
in Europe by which it is *possible* we should be conquered. To
live under the continual dread of such immeasurable evils is
itself a grievous calamity. To live without the dread of them is
to turn the danger into the disaster. The influence of such a
France is equal to a war; it's example, more wasting than an
hostile irruption. The hostility with any other power is sepa-
rable and accidental; this power, by the very condition of it's
existence, by it's very essential constitution, is in a state of
hostility with us, and with all civilized people.[1]

A Government of the nature of that set up at our very
door, has never been hitherto seen, or even imagined, in
Europe. What our relation to it will be cannot be judged by
other relations. It is a serious thing to have a connexion with
a people, who live only under positive, arbitrary, and changeable institutions; and those not perfected nor supplied, nor
explained, by any common acknowledged rule of moral science. I remember that in one of my last conversations with
the late Lord Camden, we were struck much in the same
manner with the abolition in France of the law, as a science
of methodized and artificial equity. France, since her Revolution, is under the sway of a sect, whose leaders have deliber-

1. See declaration, Whitehall, October 29, 1793. [Ante, p. 99.]

ately, at one stroke, demolished the [70] whole body of that jurisprudence which France had pretty nearly in common with other civilized countries. In that jurisprudence were contained the elements and principles of the law of nations, the great ligament of mankind. With the law they have of course destroyed all seminaries in which jurisprudence was taught, as well as all the corporations established for it's conservation. I have not heard of any country, whether in Europe or Asia, or even in Africa on this side of Mount Atlas, which is wholly without some such colleges and such corporations, except France. No man, in a publick or private concern, can divine by what rule or principle her judgments are to be directed; nor is there to be found a professor in any University, or a practitioner in any Court, who will hazard an opinion of what is or is not law in France, in any case whatever. They have not only annulled all their old treaties, but they have renounced the law of nations from whence treaties have their force. With a fixed design, they have outlawed themselves, and, to their power, outlawed all other nations.

Instead of the religion and the law by which they were in a great politick communion with the Christian world, they have constructed their Republick on three bases, all fundamentally opposite to those on which the communities of Europe are built. It's foundation is laid in Regicide; in Jacobinism; and in Atheism; and it has joined to those principles, a body of systematick manners which secures their operation.

If I am asked how I would be understood in the use of these terms, Regicide, Jacobinism, Atheism, and a system of correspondent manners and their establishment, I will tell you.

I call a commonwealth *Regicide,* which lays it down as a fixed law of nature, and a fundamental right of man, that all government, not being a democracy, is an usurpation;[1] [71]

1. Nothing could be more solemn than their promulgation of this principle as a preamble to the destructive code of their famous articles for the

that all Kings, as such, are usurpers, and for being Kings, may and ought to be put to death, with their wives, families, and adherents. The commonwealth which acts uniformly upon those principles; and which after abolishing every festival of religion, chooses the most flagrant act of a murderous Regicide treason for a feast of eternal commemoration, and which forces all her people to observe it—this I call *Regicide by establishment.*

Jacobinism is the revolt of the enterprising talents of a country against it's property. When private men form themselves into associations for the purpose of destroying the pre-existing laws and institutions of their country; when they secure to themselves an army by dividing amongst the people of no property, the estates of the ancient and lawful proprietors; when a state recognizes those acts; when it does not make confiscations for crimes, but makes crimes for confiscations; when it has it's principal strength, and all it's resources in such a violation of property; when it stands chiefly upon such a violation; massacring by judgments, or otherwise, those who make any struggle for their old legal government, and their legal, hereditary, or acquired possessions—I call this *Jacobinism by Establishment.*

I call it *Atheism by Establishment,* when any State, as such, shall not acknowledge the existence of God as a moral Governor of the World; when it shall offer to Him no religious or moral worship: when it shall abolish the Christian religion by a regular decree; when it shall persecute with a cold, unrelenting, steady cruelty, by every mode of confiscation, imprisonment, exile, and death, all [72] it's ministers; when it shall generally shut up, or pull down, churches; when the

---

decomposition of society into whatever country they should enter. "La Convention Nationale, après avoir entendu le rapport de ses Comités de Finances, de la Guerre, & Diplomatiques réunis, fidèle *au principe de souveraineté de peuples qui ne lui permet pas de reconnoître aucune institution qui y porte atteinte,*" &c. &c. Decrêt sur le Rapport de Cambon, Dec. 18, 1792, and see the subsequent proclamation.

few buildings which remain of this kind shall be opened only for the purpose of making a profane apotheosis of monsters whose vices and crimes have no parallel amongst men, and whom all other men consider as objects of general detestation, and the severest animadversion of law. When, in the place of that religion of social benevolence, and of individual self-denial, in mockery of all religion, they institute impious, blasphemous, indecent theatric rites, in honour of their vitiated, perverted reason, and erect altars to the personification of their own corrupted and bloody Republick; when schools and seminaries are founded at publick expence to poison mankind, from generation to generation, with the horrible maxims of this impiety; when wearied out with incessant martyrdom, and the cries of a people hungering and thirsting for religion, they permit it, only as a tolerated evil— I call this *Atheism by Establishment.*

When to these establishments of Regicide, of Jacobinism, and of Atheism, you add the *correspondent system of manners,* no doubt can be left on the mind of a thinking man, concerning their determined hostility to the human race. Manners are of more importance than laws. Upon them, in a great measure, the laws depend. The law touches us but here and there, and now and then. Manners are what vex or sooth, corrupt or purify, exalt or debase, barbarize or refine us, by a constant, steady, uniform, insensible operation, like that of the air we breathe in. They give their whole form and colour to our lives. According to their quality, they aid morals, they supply them, or they totally destroy them. Of this the new French Legislators were aware; therefore, with the same method, and under the same authority, they settled a system of manners, the most licentious, prostitute, and abandoned that ever has [73] been known, and at the same time the most coarse, rude, savage, and ferocious. Nothing in the Revolution, no, not to a phrase or a gesture, not to the fashion of a hat or a shoe, was left to accident. All has been the result of design; all has been matter of institution. No mechanical means could be devised in favour of this incredible system of wickedness and vice, that has not been employed. The noblest passions, the love of glory, the love of country, have been debauched into means of it's preservation and it's propagation. All sorts of shews and exhibitions calculated to inflame and vitiate the imagination, and pervert the moral sense, have been contrived. They have sometimes brought forth five or six hundred drunken women, calling at the bar of the Assembly for the blood of their own children, as being royalists or constitutionalists. Sometimes they have got a body of wretches, calling themselves fathers, to demand the murder of their sons; boasting that Rome had but one Brutus, but that they could shew five hundred. There were instances in which they inverted and retaliated the impiety, and produced sons, who called for the execution of their parents. The foundation of their Republick is laid in moral paradoxes. Their patriotism is always prodigy. All those instances to be found in history, whether real or fabulous, of a doubtful publick spirit, at which morality is perplexed, reason is staggered, and from which affrighted nature recoils, are their chosen, and almost sole examples for the instruction of their youth.

The whole drift of their institution is contrary to that of the wise Legislators of all countries, who aimed at improving instincts into morals, and at grafting the virtues on the stock of the natural affections. They, on the contrary, have omitted no pains to eradicate every benevolent and noble propensity in the mind of men. In their culture it is a rule always to graft virtues on vices. They think [74] everything unworthy of the name of publick virtue, unless it indicates violence on the private. All their new institutions, (and with them every thing is new,) strike at the root of our social nature. Other Legislators, knowing that marriage is the origin of all relations, and consequently the first element of all duties, have endeavoured, by every art, to make it sacred. The Christian Religion, by confining it to the pairs, and by rendering that relation indissoluble, has, by these two things, done more towards the peace, happiness, settlement, and civilization of the world, than by any other part in this whole scheme of Divine Wisdom. The direct contrary course has been taken in the Synagogue of Antichrist, I mean in that forge and manufactory of all evil, the sect which predominated in the Constituent Assembly of 1789. Those monsters employed the same, or greater industry, to desecrate and degrade that State, which other Legislators have used to render it holy and honourable. By a strange, uncalled-for declaration, they pronounced, that marriage was no better than a common civil contract. It was one of their ordinary tricks, to put their sentiments into the mouths of certain personated characters, which they theatrically exhibited at the bar of what ought to be a serious Assembly. One of these was brought out in the figure of a prostitute, whom they called by the affected name of "a mother without being a wife." This creature they made to call for a repeal of the incapacities, which in civilized States are put upon bastards. The prostitutes of the Assembly gave to this their puppet the sanction of their greater impudence. In consequence of the principles laid down, and the manners authorised, bastards were not long after put on the footing of the issue of lawful unions. Proceeding in the spirit of the first authors of their constitution, succeeding assemblies went the full length of the principle, and gave a licence to divorce at the mere [75] pleasure of either party, and at a month's notice. With them the matrimonial connexion is brought into so degraded a state of concubinage, that, I believe, none of the wretches in London, who keep warehouses of infamy, would give out one of their victims to private custody on so short and insolent a tenure. There was indeed a kind of profligate equity in thus giving to women the same licentious power. The reason they assigned was as infamous as the act; declaring that women had been too long under the tyranny of parents and of husbands. It is not necessary to observe upon the horrible consequences of taking one half of the species wholly out of the guardianship and protection of the other.

The practice of divorce, though in some countries permitted, has been discouraged in all. In the East polygamy and divorce are in discredit; and the manners correct the laws. In Rome, whilst Rome was in it's integrity, the few causes allowed for divorce amounted in effect to a prohibition. They were only three. The arbitrary was totally excluded; and accordingly some hundreds of years passed, without a single example of that kind. When manners were corrupted, the laws were relaxed; as the latter always follow the former, when they are not able to regulate them, or to vanquish them. Of this circumstance the Legislators of vice and crime were pleased to take notice, as an inducement to adopt their regulation: holding out an hope, that the permission would as rarely be made use of. They knew the contrary to be true; and they had taken good care, that the laws should be well seconded by the manners. Their law of divorce, like all their laws, had not for it's object the relief of domestick uneasiness, but the total corruption of all morals, the total disconnection of social life.

It is a matter of curiosity to observe the operation of this encouragement to disorder. I have before me the Paris paper, correspondent to the usual register of births, marriages, [76] and deaths. Divorce, happily, is no regular head of registry among civilized nations. With the Jacobins it is remarkable, that divorce is not only a regular head, but it has the post of honour. It occupies the first place in the list. In the three first months of the year 1793, the number of divorces in that city amounted to 562. The marriages were 1785; so that the proportion of divorces to marriages was not much less than one to three; a thing unexampled, I believe, among mankind. I caused an enquiry to be made at Doctor's Commons, concerning the number of divorces; and found, that all the divorces, (which, except by special Act of Parliament, are separations, and not proper divorces) did not amount in all those Courts, and in a hundred years, to much more than one fifth of those that passed, in the single city of Paris, in three months. I followed up the enquiry relative to that city through several of the subsequent months until I was tired, and found the proportions still the same. Since then I have heard that they have declared for a revisal of these laws: but I know of nothing done. It appears as if the contract that renovates the world was under no law at all. From this we may take our estimate of the havock that has been made through all the relations of life. With the Jacobins of France, vague intercourse is without reproach; marriage is reduced to the vilest concubinage; children are encouraged to cut the throats of their parents; mothers are taught that tenderness is no part of their character; and to demonstrate their attachment to their party, that they ought to make no scruple to rake with their bloody hands in the bowels of those who came from their own.

To all this let us join the practice of *cannibalism*, with which, in the proper terms, and with the greatest truth, their several factions accuse each other. By cannibalism, I mean their devouring, as a nutriment of their ferocity, some part of [77] the bodies of those they have murdered; their drinking the blood of their victims, and forcing the victims themselves to drink the blood of their kindred slaughtered before their faces. By cannibalism, I mean also to signify all their nameless, unmanly, and abominable insults on the bodies of those they slaughter.

As to those whom they suffer to die a natural death, they do not permit them to enjoy the last consolations of mankind, or those rights of sepulture, which indicate hope, and which meer nature has taught to mankind in all countries, to soothe the afflictions, and to cover the infirmity of mortal condition. They disgrace men in the entry into life; they vitiate and enslave them through the whole course of it; and they deprive them of all comfort at the conclusion of their dishonoured and depraved existence. Endeavouring to persuade the people that they are no better than beasts, the whole body of their institution tends to make them beasts of prey, furious and savage. For this purpose the active part of them is disciplined into a ferocity which has no parallel. To this ferocity there is joined not one of the rude, unfashioned virtues, which accompany the vices, where the whole are left to grow up together in the rankness of uncultivated nature. But nothing is left to nature in their systems.

The same discipline which hardens their hearts relaxes their morals. Whilst courts of justice were thrust out by revolutionary tribunals, and silent churches were only the funeral monuments of departed religion, there were no fewer than nineteen or twenty theatres, great and small, most of them kept open at the publick expence, and all of them crowded every night. Among the gaunt, haggard forms of famine and nakedness, amidst the yells of murder, the tears of affliction, and the cries of despair, the song, the dance, the mimick scene, the buffoon laughter, went on as regularly as in the gay hour of festive peace. I have it [78] from good authority, that under the scaffold of judicial murder, and the gaping planks that poured down blood on the spectators, the space was hired out for a shew of dancing dogs. I think, without concert, we have made the very same remark on reading some of their pieces, which, being written for other purposes, let us into a view of their social life. It struck us that the habits of Paris had no resemblance to the finished virtues, or to the polished vice, and elegant, though not blameless luxury, of the capital of a great empire. Their society was more like that of a den of outlaws upon a doubtful frontier; of a lewd tavern for the revels and debauches of banditti, assassins, bravos, smugglers, and their more desperate paramours, mixed with bombastick players, the refuse and rejected offal of strolling theatres, puffing out ill-sorted verses about virtue, mixed with the licentious and blasphemous songs, proper to the brutal and hardened course of life belonging to that sort of wretches. This system of manners in itself is at war with all orderly and moral society, and is in it's neighbourhood unsafe. If great bodies of that kind were any where established in a bordering territory, we should have a right to demand of their Governments the suppression of such a nuisance. What are we to do if the Government and the whole community is of the same description? Yet that Government has thought proper to invite ours to lay by its unjust hatred, and to listen to the voice of humanity as taught by their example.

The operation of dangerous and delusive first principles obliges us to have recourse to the true ones. In the intercourse between nations, we are apt to rely too much on the instrumental part. We lay too much weight upon the formality of treaties and compacts. We do not act much more wisely when we trust to the interests of men as guarantees of their engagements. The interests frequently tear to pieces [79] the engagements; and the passions trample upon both. Entirely to trust to either, is to disregard our own safety, or not to know mankind. Men are not tied to one another by papers and seals. They are led to associate by resemblances, by conformities, by sympathies. It is with nations as with individuals. Nothing is so strong a tie of amity between nation and nation as correspondence in laws, customs, manners, and habits of life. They have more than the force of treaties in themselves. They are obligations written in the heart. They approximate men to men, without their knowledge, and sometimes against their intentions. The secret, unseen, but irrefragable bond of habitual intercourse, holds them together, even when their perverse and litigious nature sets them to equivocate, scuffle, and fight about the terms of their written obligations.

As to war, if it be the means of wrong and violence, it is the sole means of justice amongst nations. Nothing can banish it from the world. They who say otherwise, intending to impose upon us, do not impose upon themselves. But it is one of the greatest objects of human wisdom to mitigate those evils which we are unable to remove. The conformity and analogy of which I speak, incapable, like every thing else, of preserving perfect trust and tranquillity among men, has a strong tendency to facilitate accommodation, and to produce a generous oblivion of the rancour of their quarrels. With this similitude, peace is more of peace, and war is less of war. I will go further. There have been periods of time in which communities, apparently in peace with each other, have been more perfectly separated than, in later times, many nations in Europe have been in the course of long and bloody wars. The cause must be sought in the similitude throughout Europe of religion, laws, and manners. At bottom, these are all the same. The writers on public law have often called this aggregate of nations [80] a Commonwealth. They had reason. It is virtually one great state having the same basis of general law; with some diversity of provincial customs and local establishments. The nations of Europe have had the very same christian religion, agreeing in the fundamental parts, varying a little in the ceremonies and in the subordinate doctrines. The whole of the polity and oeconomy of every country in Europe has been derived from the same sources. It was drawn from the old Germanic or Gothic custumary; from the feudal institutions which must be considered as an emanation from that custumary; and the whole has been improved and digested into system and discipline by the Roman law. From hence arose the several orders, with or without a Monarch, which are called States, in every European country; the strong traces of which, where Monarchy predominated, were never wholly extinguished or merged in despotism. In the few places where Monarchy was cast off, the spirit of European Monarchy was still left. Those countries still continued countries of States; that is, of classes, orders, and distinctions, such as had before subsisted, or nearly so. Indeed the force and form of the institution called States, continued in greater perfection in those republican communities than under Monarchies. From all those sources arose a system of manners and of education which was nearly similar in all this quarter of the globe; and which softened, blended, and harmonized the colours of the whole. There was little difference in the form of the Universities for the education of their youth, whether with regard to faculties, to sciences, or to the more liberal and elegant kinds of erudition. From this resemblance in the modes of intercourse, and in the whole form and fashion of life, no citizen of Europe could be altogether an exile in any part of it. There was nothing more than a pleasing variety to recreate and instruct the mind, to enrich the imagination, [81] and to meliorate the heart. When a man travelled or resided for health, pleasure, business or necessity, from his own country, he never felt himself quite abroad.

The whole body of this new scheme of manners, in support of the new scheme of politicks, I consider as a strong and decisive proof of determined ambition and systematick hostility. I defy the most refining ingenuity to invent any other cause for the total departure of the Jacobin Republick from every one of the ideas and usages, religious, legal, moral, or social, of this civilized world, and for her tearing herself from its communion with such studied violence, but from a formed resolution of keeping no terms with that world. It has not been, as has been falsely and insidiously represented, that these miscreants had only broke with their old Government. They made a schism with the whole universe; and that schism extended to almost every thing great and small. For one, I wish, since it is gone thus far, that the breach had been so compleat, as to make all intercourse impracticable; but, partly by accident, partly by design, partly from the resistance of the matter, enough is left to preserve intercourse, whilst amity is destroyed or corrupted in it's principle.

This violent breach of the community of Europe we must

conclude to have been made, (even if they had not expressly declared it over and over again) either to force mankind into an adoption of their system, or to live in perpetual enmity with a community the most potent we have ever known. Can any person imagine, that in offering to mankind this desperate alternative, there is no indication of a hostile mind, because men in possession of the ruling authority are supposed to have a right to act without coercion in their own territories? As to the right of men to act any where according to their pleasure, without any moral tie, no such right exists. Men are never in a state of *total* independence of each other. It is [82] not the condition of our nature: nor is it conceivable how any man can pursue a considerable course of action without it's having some effect upon others; or, of course, without producing some degree of responsibility for his conduct. The *situations* in which men relatively stand produce the rules and principles of that responsibility, and afford directions to prudence in exacting it.

Distance of place does not extinguish the duties or the rights of men; but it often renders their exercise impracticable. The same circumstance of distance renders the noxious effects of an evil system in any community less pernicious. But there are situations where this difficulty does not occur; and in which, therefore, these duties are obligatory, and these rights are to be asserted. It has ever been the method of publick jurists, to draw a great part of the analogies on which they form the law of nations from the principles of law which prevail in civil community. Civil laws are not all of them merely positive. Those which are rather conclusions of legal reason, than matters of statutable provision, belong to universal equity, and are universally applicable. Almost the whole praetorian law is such. There is a *Law of Neighbourhood* which does not leave a man perfect master on his own ground. When a neighbour sees a *new erection*, in the nature of a nuisance, set up at his door, he has a right to represent it to the judge; who, on his part, has a right to order the work to be staid; or if established, to be removed. On this head, the parent law is express and clear; and has made many wise provisions, which, without destroying, regulate and restrain the right of *ownership*, by the right of *vicinage*. No *innovation* is permitted that may redound, even secondarily, to the prejudice of a neighbour. The whole doctrine of that important head of praetorian law, "*De novi operis nunciatione*," is founded on the principle, that no *new* use should be made of a man's private liberty of [83] operating upon his private property, from whence a detriment may be justly apprehended by his neighbour. This law of denunciation is prospective. It is to anticipate what is called *damnum infectum*, or *damnum nondum factum*, that is a damage justly apprehended but not actually done. Even before it is clearly known whether the innovation be damageable or not, the judge is competent to issue a prohibition to innovate, until the point can be determined. This prompt interference is grounded on principles favourable to both parties. It is preventive of mischief difficult to be repaired, and of ill blood difficult to be softened. The rule of law, therefore, which comes before the evil, is amongst the very best parts of equity, and justifies the promptness of the remedy; because, as it is well observed, *Res damni infecti celeritatem desiderat et periculosa est dilatio*. This right of denunciation does not hold, when things continue, however inconveniently to the neighbourhood, according to the *antient* mode. For there is a sort of presumption against novelty, drawn out of a deep consideration of human nature and human affairs; and the maxim of jurisprudence is well laid down, *Vetustas pro lege semper habetur.*

Such is the law of civil vicinity. Now where there is no constituted judge, as between independent states there is not, the vicinage itself is the natural judge. It is, preventively, the assertor of its own rights; or remedially, their avenger. Neighbours are presumed to take cognizance of each other's acts.

Vicini vicinorum facta praesumuntur scire. This principle, which, like the rest, is as true of nations as of individual men, has bestowed on the grand vicinage of Europe a duty to know, and a right to prevent, any capital innovation which may amount to the erection of a dangerous nuisance.[1] Of [84] the importance of that innovation, and the mischief of that nuisance, they are, to be sure, bound to judge not litigiously; but it is in their competence to judge. They have uniformly acted on this right. What in civil society is a ground of action, in politick society is a ground of war. But the exercise of that competent jurisdiction is a matter of moral prudence. As suits in civil society, so war in the political, must ever be a matter of great deliberation. It is not this or that particular proceeding, picked out here or there, as a subject of quarrel, that will do. There must be an aggregate of mischief. There must be marks of deliberation; there must be traces of design; there must be indications of malice; there must be tokens of ambition. There must be force in the body where they exist; there must be energy in the mind. When all these circumstances combine, or the important parts of them, the duty of the vicinity calls for the exercise of it's competence; and the rules of prudence do not restrain, but demand it.

In describing the nuisance erected by so pestilential a manufactory, by the construction of so infamous a brothel, by digging a night-cellar for such thieves, murderers, and house-breakers, as never infested the world, I am so far from aggravating, that I have fallen infinitely short of the evil. No man who has attended to the particulars of what has been done in France, and combined them with the principles there asserted, can possibly doubt it. When I compare with this

---

1. "This state of things cannot exist in France without involving all the surrounding powers in one common danger, without giving them the right, without imposing it on them as a duty, to stop the progress of an evil which attacks the fundamental principles by which mankind is united in civil society." Declaration, 29th Oct., 1793.

great cause of nations, the trifling points of honour, the still more contemptible points of interest, the light ceremonies, the undefinable punctilios, the disputes about precedency, the lowering or the hoisting of a sail, the dealing in a hundred or two of wild-cat skins on the other side of the globe, which have often kindled up the flames of war [85] between nations, I stand astonished at those persons who do not feel a resentment, not more natural than politick, at the atrocious insults that this monstrous compound offers to the dignity of every nation, and who are not alarmed with what it threatens to their safety.

I have therefore been decidedly of opinion, with our declaration at Whitehall, in the beginning of this war, that the vicinage of Europe had not only a right, but an indispensable duty, and an exigent interest, to denunciate this new work before it had produced the danger we have so sorely felt, and which we shall long feel. The example of what is done by France is too important not to have a vast and extensive influence; and that example, backed with it's power, must bear with great force on those who are near it; especially on those who shall recognize the pretended Republick on the principle upon which it now stands. It is not an old structure which you have found as it is, and are not to dispute of the original end and design with which it had been so fashioned. It is a recent wrong, and can plead no prescription. It violates the rights upon which not only the community of France, but all communities, are founded. The principles on which they proceed are *general* principles, and are as true in England as in any other country. They who (though with the purest intentions) recognize the authority of these Regicides and robbers upon principle, justify their acts, and establish them as precedents. It is a question not between France and England. It is a question between property and force. The property claims; and it's claim has been allowed. The property of the nation is the nation. They who massacre, plunder, and expel the body of the proprietary, are murderers and robbers. The State, in it's essence, must be moral and just: and it may be so, though a tyrant or usurper should be accidentally at the head [86] of it. This is a thing to be lamented: but this notwithstanding, the body of the commonwealth may remain in all it's integrity and be perfectly sound in it's composition. The present case is different. It is not a revolution in government. It is not the victory of party over party. It is a destruction and decomposition of the whole society; which never can be made of right by any faction, however powerful, nor without terrible consequences to all about it, both in the act and in the example. This pretended Republick is founded in crimes, and exists by wrong and robbery; and wrong and robbery, far from a title to any thing, is war with mankind. To be at peace with robbery is to be an accomplice with it.

Mere locality does not constitute a body politick. Had Cade and his gang got possession of London, they would not have been the Lord-Mayor, Aldermen, and Common Council. The body politick of France existed in the majesty of it's throne; in the dignity of it's nobility; in the honour of it's gentry; in the sanctity of it's clergy; in the reverence of it's magistracy; in the weight and consideration due to it's landed property in the several bailliages; in the respect due to it's moveable substance represented by the corporations of the kingdom. All these particular *moleculae* united, form the great mass of what is truly the body politick, in all countries. They are so many deposits and receptacles of justice; because they can only exist by justice. Nation is a moral essence, not a geographical arrangement, or a denomination of the nomenclator. France, though out of her territorial possession, exists; because the sole possible claimant, I mean the proprietary, and the Government to which the proprietary adheres, exists and claims. God forbid, that if you were expelled from your house by ruffians and assassins, that I should call the material walls, doors and windows of [87] ———, the ancient and honourable family of ———. Am I to transfer to the intruders, who not content to turn you out naked to the world, would rob you of your very name, all the esteem and respect I owe to you? The Regicides in France are not France. France is out of her bounds, but the kingdom is the same.

To illustrate my opinions on this subject, let us suppose a case, which, after what has happened, we cannot think absolutely impossible, though the augury is to be abominated, and the event deprecated with our most ardent prayers. Let us suppose then, that our gracious Sovereign was sacrilegiously murdered; his exemplary Queen, at the head of the matronage of this land, murdered in the same manner: that those Princesses whose beauty and modest elegance are the ornaments of the country, and who are the leaders and patterns of the ingenuous youth of their sex, were put to a cruel and ignominious death, with hundreds of others, mothers and daughters, ladies of the first distinction; that the Prince of Wales and the Duke of York, princes the hope and pride of the nation, with all their brethren, were forced to fly from the knives of assassins; that the whole body of our excellent Clergy were either massacred or robbed of all, and transported; the Christian Religion, in all its denominations, forbidden and persecuted; the law totally, fundamentally, and in all it's parts destroyed; the judges put to death by revolutionary tribunals; the Peers and Commons robbed to the last acre of their estates; massacred if they staid, or obliged to seek life in flight, in exile, and in beggary; that the whole landed property should share the very same fate; that every military and naval officer of honour and rank, almost to a man, should be placed in the same description of confiscation and exile; that the principal merchants and bankers should be drawn out, as from an [88] hen-coop, for slaughter; that the citizens of our greatest and most flourishing cities, when the hand and the machinery of the hangman were not found sufficient, should have been collected in the publick squares, and massacred by thousands with cannon; if three hundred thousand others should have been doomed to a situation worse than death in noisome and pestilential prisons—in such a case, is it in the faction of robbers I am to look for my country? Would this be the England that you and I, and even strangers, admired, honoured, loved, and cherished? Would not the exiles of England alone be my Government and my fellow-citizens? Would not their places of refuge be my temporary country? Would not all my duties and all my affections be there and there only? Should I consider myself as a traitor to my country, and deserving of death, if I knocked at the door and heart of every potentate in Christendom to succour my friends, and to avenge them on their enemies? Could I, in any way, shew myself more a patriot? What should I think of those potentates who insulted their suffering brethren; who treated them as vagrants, or at least as mendicants; and could find no allies, no friends, but in Regicide murderers and robbers? What ought I to think and feel, if being geographers instead of Kings, they recognized the desolated cities, the wasted fields, and the rivers polluted with blood, of this geometrical measurement, as the honourable member of Europe, called England? In that condition, what should we think of Sweden, Denmark, or Holland, or whatever Power afforded us a churlish and treacherous hospitality, if they should invite us to join the standard of our King, our Laws, and our Religion, if they should give us a direct promise of protection—if after all this, taking advantage of our deplorable situation, which left us no choice, they were to treat us as the lowest and vilest of all mercenaries? If they [89] were to send us far from the aid of our King, and our suffering Country, to squander us away in the most pestilential climates for a venal enlargement of their own territories, for the purpose of trucking them, when obtained, with those very robbers and murderers they had called upon us to oppose with our blood? What would be our sentiments, if in that miserable service we were not to be considered either as English, or as Swedes, Dutch, Danes, but as outcasts of the human race? Whilst we were fighting those battles of their interest, and as their soldiers, how should we feel if we were to be excluded from all their cartels? How must we feel, if the pride and flower of the English Nobility and Gentry, who might escape the pestilential clime, and the devouring sword, should, if taken prisoners, be delivered over as rebel subjects, to be condemned as rebels, as traitors, as the vilest of all criminals, by tribunals formed of Maroon negro slaves, covered over with the blood of their masters, who were made free and organized into judges, for their robberies and murders? What should we feel under this inhuman, insulting, and barbarous protection of Muscovites, Swedes, or Hollanders? Should we not obtest Heaven, and whatever justice there is yet on earth? Oppression makes wise men mad; but the distemper is still the madness of the wise, which is better than the sobriety of fools. Their cry is the voice of sacred misery, exalted, not into wild raving, but into the sanctified phrensy of prophecy and inspiration. In that bitterness of soul, in that indignation of suffering virtue, in that exaltation of despair, would not persecuted English loyalty cry out, with an awful warning voice, and denounce the destruction that waits on Monarchs, who consider fidelity to them as the most degrading of all vices; who suffer it to be punished as the most abominable of all crimes; and who have no respect but for rebels, traitors, Regicides, and furious negro [90] slaves, whose crimes have broke their chains? Would not this warm language of high indignation have more of sound reason in it, more of real affection, more of true attachment, than all the lullabies of flatterers, who would hush Monarchs to sleep in the arms of death? Let them be well convinced, that if ever this example should prevail in it's whole extent, it will have it's full operation. Whilst Kings stand firm on their base, though under that base there is a sure-wrought mine, there will not be wanting to their levées a single person of those who are attached to their fortune, and not to their persons or cause. But hereafter none will support a tottering throne. Some will fly for fear of being crushed under the ruin; some will join in making it. They will seek in the destruction of Royalty, fame, and power, and wealth, and the homage of Kings, with *Reubel*, with *Carnot*, with *Revellière*, and with the *Merlins* and the *Talliens*, rather than suffer exile and beggary with the *Condés*, or the *Broglies*, the *Castries*, the *D'Avrais*, the *Serrents*, the *Cazalés*, and the long line of loyal, suffering Patriot Nobility, or to be butchered with the oracles and the victims of the laws, the *D'Ormestons*, the *d'Espremesnils*, and the *Malesherbes*. This example we shall give, if, instead of adhering to our fellows in a cause which is an honour to us all, we abandon the lawful Government and lawful corporate body of France, to hunt for a shameful and ruinous fraternity with this odious usurpation that disgraces civilized society and the human race.

And is then example nothing? It is every thing. Example is the school of mankind, and they will learn at no other. This war is a war against that example. It is not a war for Louis the Eighteenth, or even for the property, virtue, fidelity of France. It is a war for George the Third, for Francis the Second, and for all the dignity, property, honour, virtue, and religion of England, of Germany, and of all nations.

I know that all I have said of the systematick unsociability [91] of this new-invented species of republick, and the impossibility of preserving peace, is answered by asserting that the scheme of manners, morals, and even of maxims and principles of state, is of no weight in a question of peace or war between communities. This doctrine is supported by example. The case of Algiers is cited, with an hint, as if it were the stronger case. I should take no notice of this sort of inducement, if I had found it only where first it was. I do not want respect for those from whom I first heard it—but having no controversy at present with them, I only think it not amiss to rest on it a little, as I find it adopted with much more of the same kind, by several of those on whom such reasoning had formerly made no apparent impression. If it had no force to prevent us from submitting to this necessary war, it furnishes no better ground for our making an unnecessary and ruinous peace.

This analogical argument drawn from the case of Algiers would lead us a good way. The fact is, we ourselves with a little cover, others more directly, pay a *tribute* to the Republick of Algiers. Is it meant to reconcile us to the payment of a *tribute* to the French Republick? That this, with other things more ruinous, will be demanded hereafter, I little doubt; but for the present, this will not be avowed—though our minds are to be gradually prepared for it. In truth, the arguments from this case are worth little, even to those who approve the buying an Algerine forbearance of piracy. There are many things which men do not approve that they must do to avoid a greater evil. To argue from thence, that they are to act in the same manner in all cases, is turning necessity into a law. Upon what is matter of prudence, the argument concludes the contrary way. Because we have done one humiliating act, we ought with infinite caution to admit more acts of the same nature, lest humiliation should become our habitual state. Matters of prudence are [92] under the dominion of circumstances, and not of logical analogies. It is absurd to take it otherwise.

I, for one, do more than doubt the policy of this kind of convention with Algiers. On those who think as I do, the argument *ad hominem* can make no sort of impression. I know something of the Constitution and composition of this very extraordinary Republick. It has a Constitution, I admit, similar to the present tumultuous military tyranny of France, by which an handful of obscure ruffians domineer over a fertile country and a brave people. For the composition, too, I admit, the Algerine community resembles that of France; being formed out of the very scum, scandal, disgrace, and pest of the Turkish Asia. The grand Seignor, to disburthen the country, suffers the Dey to recruit, in his dominions, the corps of Janissaries, or Asaphs, which form the Directory and Council of Elders of the African Republick one and indivisible. But notwithstanding this resemblance, which I allow, I never shall so far injure the Janissarian Republick of Algiers, as to put it in comparison for every sort of crime, turpitude, and oppression with the Jacobin Republick of Paris. There is no question with me to which of the two I should choose to be a neighbour or a subject. But situated as I am, I am in no danger of becoming to Algiers either the one or the other. It is not so in my relation to the atheistical fanaticks of France. I *am* their neighbour; I *may* become their subject. Have the gentlemen who borrowed this happy parallel, no idea of the different conduct to be held with regard to the very same evil at an immense distance, and when it is at your door? When it's power is enormous, as when it is comparatively as feeble as it's distance is remote? When there is a barrier of language and usages, which prevents corruption through certain old correspondences and habitudes, from the contagion of the horrible novelties that are introduced into every [93] thing else? I can contemplate, without dread, a royal or a national tyger on the borders of Pegu. I can look at him, with an easy curiosity, as prisoner within bars in the menagerie of the Tower. But if, by *habeas corpus,* or otherwise, he was to come into the lobby of the House of Commons whilst your door was open, any of you would be more stout than wise, who would not gladly make your escape out of the back windows. I certainly should dread more from a wild cat in my bed-chamber, than from all the lions that roar in the deserts behind Algiers. But in this parallel it is the cat that is at a distance, and the lions and tygers that are in our ante-chambers and our lobbies. Algiers is not near; Algiers is not powerful; Algiers is not our neighbour; Algiers is not infectious. Algiers, whatever it may be, is an old creation; and we have good data to calculate all the mischief to be apprehended from it. When I find Algiers transferred to Calais, I will tell you what I think of that point. In the mean time, the case quoted from the Algerine reports, will not apply as authority. We shall put it out of court; and so far as that goes, let the counsel for the Jacobin peace take nothing by their motion.

When we voted, as you and I did, with many more whom you and I respect and love, to resist this enemy, we were providing for dangers that were direct, home, pressing, and not remote, contingent, uncertain, and formed upon loose analogies. We judged of the danger with which we were menaced by Jacobin France, from the whole tenor of it's conduct; not from one or two doubtful or detached acts or expressions. I not only concurred in the idea of combining with Europe in this war; but to the best of my power ever stimulated Ministers to that conjunction of interests and of efforts. I joined with them with all my soul, on the principles contained in that manly and masterly state-paper, which I have two or three times referred to,[1] and may still [94] more frequently hereafter. The diplomatick collection never was more enriched than with this piece. The historick facts justify every stroke of the master. "Thus painters write their names at Co."

Various persons may concur in the same measure on various grounds. They may be various, without being contrary to, or exclusive of each other. I thought the insolent, unprovoked aggression of the Regicide upon our ally of Holland, a good ground of war. I think his manifest attempt to overturn the balance of Europe, a good ground of war. As a good ground of war, I consider his declaration of war on his Majesty and his kingdom. But though I have taken all these to my aid, I consider them as nothing more than as a sort of evidence to indicate the treasonable mind within. Long before their acts of aggression, and their declaration of war, the fac-

1. Declaration, Whitehall, Oct. 29, 1793.

tion in France had assumed a form, had adopted a body of principles and maxims, and had regularly and systematically acted on them, by which she virtually had put herself in a posture, which was in itself a declaration of war against mankind.

IT IS SAID BY THE DIRECTORY in their several manifestoes, that we of the people are tumultuous for peace; and that Ministers pretend negociation to amuse us. This they have learned from the language of many amongst ourselves, whose conversations have been one main cause of whatever extent the opinion for peace with Regicide may be. But I, who think the Ministers unfortunately to be but too serious in their proceedings, find myself obliged to say a little more on this subject of the popular opinion.

Before our opinions are quoted against ourselves, it is proper that, from our serious deliberation, they may be worth quoting. It is without reason we praise the wisdom of our Constitution, in putting under the discretion of the [95] Crown the awful trust of war and peace, if the Ministers of the Crown virtually return it again into our hands. The trust was placed there as a sacred deposit, to secure us against popular rashness in plunging into wars, and against the effects of popular dismay, disgust, or lassitude in getting out of them as imprudently as we might first engage in them. To have no other measure in judging of those great objects than our momentary opinions and desires, is to throw us back upon that very democracy which, in this part, our Constitution was formed to avoid.

It is no excuse at all for a minister, who at our desire, takes a measure contrary to our safety, that it is our own act. He who does not stay the hand of suicide, is guilty of murder. On our part I say, that to be instructed, is not to be degraded or enslaved. Information is an advantage to us; and we have a right to demand it. He that is bound to act in the dark cannot be said to act freely. When it appears evident to our governors that our desires and our interests are at variance, they ought not to gratify the former at the expence of the latter. Statesmen are placed on an eminence, that they may have a larger horizon than we can possibly command. They have a whole before them, which we can contemplate only in the parts, and even without the necessary relations. Ministers are not only our natural rulers but our natural guides. Reason, clearly and manfully delivered, has in itself a mighty force: but reason in the mouth of legal authority, is, I may fairly say, irresistible.

I admit that reason of state will not, in many circumstances, permit the disclosure of the true ground of a public proceeding. In that case, silence is manly; and it is wise. It is fair to call for trust when the principle of reason itself suspends it's public use. I take the distinction to be this. The ground of a particular measure, making a part of a plan, it is rarely proper to divulge. All the broader grounds [96] of policy on which the general plan is to be adopted, ought as rarely to be concealed. They who have not the whole cause before them, call them politicians, call them people, call them what you will, are no judges. The difficulties of the case, as well as it's fair side, ought to be presented. This ought to be done: and it is all that can be done. When we have our true situation distinctly presented to us, if then we resolve, with a blind and headlong violence, to resist the admonitions of our friends, and to cast ourselves into the hands of our potent and irreconcileable foes, then, and not till then, the ministers stand acquitted before God and man, for whatever may come.

LAMENTING AS I DO, that the matter has not had so full and free a discussion as it requires, I mean to omit none of the points which seem to me necessary for consideration, previous to an arrangement which is for ever to decide the form and the fate of Europe. In the course, therefore, of what I shall have the honour to address to you, I propose the following questions to your serious thoughts. 1. Whether the present system, which stands for a Government in France, be such as in peace and war affects the neighbouring States in a manner different from the internal Government that formerly prevailed in that country? 2. Whether that system, supposing its views hostile to other nations, possesses any means of being hurtful to them peculiar to itself? 3. Whether there has been lately such a change in France, as to alter the nature of its system, or it's effect upon other Powers? 4. Whether any publick declarations or engagements exist, on the part of the allied Powers, which stand in the way of a treaty of peace, which supposes the right and confirms the power of the Regicide faction in France? 5. What the state of the other Powers of Europe will be with respect to each other, and their colonies, on the conclusion of a [97] Regicide Peace? 6. Whether we are driven to the absolute necessity of making that kind of peace?

These heads of enquiry will enable us to make the application of the several matters of fact and topicks of argument, that occur in this vast discussion, to certain fixed principles. I do not mean to confine myself to the order in which they stand. I shall discuss them in such a manner as shall appear to me the best adapted for shewing their mutual bearings and relations. Here then I close the public matter of my Letter; but before I have done, let me say one word in apology for myself.

In wishing this nominal peace not to be precipitated, I am sure no man living is less disposed to blame the present Ministry than I am. Some of my oldest friends, (and I wish I could say it of more of them) make a part in that Ministry. There are some indeed, "whom my dim eyes in vain explore." In my mind, a greater calamity could not have fallen on the publick than the exclusion of one of them. But I drive away that, with other melancholy thoughts. A great deal ought to be said upon that subject, or nothing. As to the distinguished

persons to whom my friends, who remain, are joined, if benefits, nobly and generously conferred, ought to procure good
wishes, they are intitled to my best vows; and they have them
all. They have administered to me the only consolation I am
capable of receiving, which is to know that no individual will
suffer by my thirty years' service to the publick. If things
should give us the comparative happiness of a struggle, I shall
be found, (I was going to say fighting—that would be foolish—but) dying by the side of Mr. Pitt. I must add, that if any
thing defensive in our domestick system can possibly save us
from the disasters of a Regicide peace, he is the man to save
us. If the finances in such a case can be repaired, he is the
man to repair them. [98] If I should lament any of his acts,
it is only when they appear to me to have no resemblance
to acts of his. But let him not have a confidence in himself,
which no human abilities can warrant. His abilities are fully
equal (and that is to say much for any man) to those that are
opposed to him. But if we look to him as our security against
the consequences of a Regicide Peace, let us be assured, that
a Regicide Peace and a Constitutional Ministry are terms that
will not agree. With a Regicide Peace the King cannot long
have a Minister to serve him, nor the Minister a King to serve.
If the Great Disposer, in reward of the royal and the private
virtues of our Sovereign, should call him from the calamitous
spectacles, which will attend a state of amity with Regicide,
his successor will surely see them, unless the same providence
greatly anticipates the course of nature. Thinking thus, (and
not, as I conceive, on light grounds) I dare not flatter the
reigning Sovereign, nor any Minister he has or can have, nor
his Successor Apparent, nor any of those who may be called
to serve him, with what appears to me a false state of their
situation. We cannot have them and that Peace together.

I do not forget that there had been a considerable difference between several of our friends, with my insignificant
self, and the great man at the head of Ministry, in an early

REGICIDE PEACE I

stage of these discussions. But I am sure there was a period in which we agreed better in the danger of a Jacobin existence in France. At one time, he and all Europe seemed to feel it. But why am not I converted with so many great Powers, and so many great Ministers? It is because I am old and slow. I am in this year, 1796, only where all the powers of Europe were in 1793. I cannot move with this procession of the Equinoxes, which is preparing for us the return of some very old, I am afraid no golden aera, or the commencement of some new aera that [99] must be denominated from some new metal. In this crisis I must hold my tongue, or I must speak with freedom. Falsehood and delusion are allowed in no case whatever: but, as in the exercise of all the virtues, there is an oeconomy of truth. It is a sort of temperance, by which a man speaks truth with measure that he may speak it the longer. But, as the same rules do not hold in all cases, what would be right for you, who may presume on a series of years before you, would have no sense for me, who cannot, without absurdity, calculate on six months of life. What I say, I *must* say at once. Whatever I write is in it's nature testamentary. It may have the weakness, but it has the sincerity of a dying declaration. For the few days I have to linger here, I am removed completely from the busy scene of the world; but I hold myself to be still responsible for every thing that I have done whilst I continued on the place of action. If the rawest tyro in politicks has been influenced by the authority of my grey hairs, and led by any thing in my speeches, or my writings, to enter into this war, he has a right to call upon me to know why I have changed my opinions, or why, when those I voted with, have adopted better notions, I persevere in exploded errour.

When I seem not to acquiesce in the acts of those I respect in every degree short of superstition, I am obliged to give my reasons fully. I cannot set my authority against their authority. But to exert reason is not to revolt against authority. Reason and authority do not move in the same parallel. That reason is an *amicus curiae* who speaks *de plano*, not *pro tribunali*. It is a friend who makes an useful suggestion to the Court, without questioning it's jurisdiction. Whilst he acknowledges it's competence, he promotes it's efficiency. I shall pursue the plan I have chalked out in my Letters that follow this.

LETTER II

On the Genius and Character of the French Revolution as it regards other Nations

[Argument

INTRODUCTION, p. 154. The complete transformation of France by its New Government leads the writer to enquire into the nature of the governing faction.

PART I, pp. 155–68

(1) Great Diffusion, (2) Great Abilities, and (3) Great Successes of the Jacobin Party

(1) Not a local party, p. 155, though their centre is in France: this illustrated by the action of the Allies, p. 155, which was (2) paralysed by the intrigues of the Jacobins, p. 156. Their easy triumph over the routine politicians of Europe, p. 157, and over the ridiculous "centrifugal war" waged against France, p. 159. (3) False policy pursued in the war, p. 159, and impossibility now of compensating the successes of the French, without which they are not likely to make peace, unless "by giving up Europe, bound hand and foot, to France," p. 161.

PART II, pp. 168–89

Jacobinism implies the Repudiation of the Ordinary Relations of France with the rest of Europe

Jacobinism alien from ordinary European relations, p. 168. Two classes of Jacobins, philosophers and politicians; character of the former, p. 170, of the latter, p. 171. Ambition of French politicians, p. 172. Divided into the Anti-Anglican and Anti-Continental factions, p. 173, the existence of which is traced to the reign of Louis XV, p. 174. Causes of discontent on the part of the politicians, and their [101] ready conversion to Republicanism, as a more powerful system for aggression,

p. 175. Their intrigues in Holland, Austria, and America, before the Revolution, p. 178. Essential antagonism between France since the Revolution, and the rest of Europe, especially England, p. 180. And the only safety for Europe the destruction of the new system in France, illustrated by the fate of Louis XVI, p. 184].

M Y DEAR SIR,

I CLOSED MY FIRST LETTER with serious matter; and I hope it has employed your thoughts. The system of peace must have a reference to the system of the war. On that ground, I must therefore again recal your mind to our original opinions, which time and events have not taught me to vary.

My ideas and my principles led me, in this contest, to encounter France, not as a State, but as a Faction. The vast territorial extent of that country, it's immense population, it's riches of production, it's riches of commerce and convention—the whole aggregate mass of what, in ordinary cases, constitutes the force of a State, to me were but objects of secondary consideration. They might be balanced; and they have been often more than balanced. Great as these things are, they are not what make the faction formidable. It is the faction that makes them truly dreadful. The faction is the evil spirit that possesses the body of France; that informs it as a soul; that stamps upon it's ambition, and upon all it's pursuits, a characteristic mark, which strongly distinguishes them from the same general passions, and the same general views, in other men and in other communities. It is that spirit which inspires into them a new, a pernicious, and desolating activity. Constituted as France was ten years ago, it was not in that [102] France to shake, to shatter, and to overwhelm Europe in the manner that we behold. A sure destruction impends over those infatuated Princes, who, in the conflict with this new and unheard-of power, proceed as if they were

REGICIDE PEACE II

engaged in a war that bore a resemblance to their former contests; or that they can make peace in the spirit of their former arrangements or pacification. Here the beaten path is the very reverse of the safe road.

As to me, I was always steadily of opinion that this disorder was not in it's nature intermittent. I conceived that the contest, once begun, could not be laid down again to be resumed at our discretion; but that our first struggle with this evil would also be our last. I never thought we could make peace with the system; because it was not for the sake of an object we pursued in rivalry with each other, but with the system itself, that we were at war. As I understood the matter, we were at war, not with it's conduct, but with it's existence; convinced that it's existence and it's hostility were the same.

THE FACTION IS NOT LOCAL or territorial. It is a general evil. Where it least appears in action, it is still full of life. In it's sleep it recruits it's strength, and prepares it's exertion. It's spirit lies deep in the corruptions of our common nature. The social order which restrains it, feeds it. It exists in every country in Europe; and among all orders of men in every country, who look up to France as to a common head. The centre is there. The circumference is the world of Europe wherever the race of Europe may be settled. Everywhere else the faction is militant; in France it is triumphant. In France is the bank of deposit, and the bank of circulation, of all the pernicious principles that are forming in every State. It will be a folly scarcely deserving of pity, and too mischievous for contempt, to think of restraining [103] it in any other country whilst it is predominant there. War, instead of being the cause of it's force, has suspended it's operation. It has given a reprieve, at least, to the Christian World.

THE TRUE NATURE of a Jacobin war, in the beginning, was, by most of the Christian Powers, felt, acknowledged, and even in the most precise manner declared. In the joint manifesto, published by the Emperor and the King of Prussia, on the 4th of August 1792, it is expressed in the clearest terms, and on principles which could not fail, if they had adhered to them, of classing those monarchs with the first benefactors of mankind. This manifesto was published, as they themselves express it, "to lay open to the present generation, as well as to posterity, their motives, their intentions, and the *disinterestedness* of their personal views; taking up arms for the purpose of preserving social and political order amongst all civilized nations, and to secure to *each* state its religion, happiness, independence, territories, and real constitution." "On this ground, they hoped that all Empires, and all States, ought to be unanimous; and becoming the firm guardians of the happiness of mankind, that they cannot fail to unite their efforts to rescue a numerous nation from it's own fury, to preserve Europe from the return of barbarism, and the Universe from the subversion and anarchy with which it was threatened." The whole of that noble performance ought to be read at the first meeting of any Congress which may assemble for the purpose of pacification. In that piece "these Powers expressly renounce all views of personal aggrandizement," and confine themselves to objects worthy of so generous, so heroic, and so perfectly wise and politick an enterprise. It was to the principles of this consideration, and to no other, that we wished our Sovereign and our Country to accede, as a part of the [104] commonwealth of Europe. To these principles, with some trifling exceptions and limitations, they did fully accede.[1] And all our friends who did take office acceded to the Ministry (whether wisely or not) as I always understood the matter, on the faith and on the principles of that declaration.

As LONG AS THESE POWERS flattered themselves that the menace of force would produce the effect of force, they acted

1. See Declaration. Whitehall, Oct. 29, 1793.

on those declarations: but when their menaces failed of success, their efforts took a new direction. It did not appear to them that virtue and heroism ought to be purchased by millions of rix-dollars. It is a dreadful truth, but it is a truth that cannot be concealed; in ability, in dexterity, in the distinctness of their views, the Jacobins are our superiors. They saw the thing right from the very beginning. Whatever were the first motives to the war among politicians, they saw that it is in it's spirit, and for it's objects, a *civil war;* and as such they pursued it. It is a war between the partizans of the ancient, civil, moral, and political order of Europe against a sect of fanatical and ambitious atheists which means to change them all. It is not France extending a foreign empire over other nations: it is a sect aiming at universal empire, and beginning with the conquest of France. The leaders of that sect secured the *centre of Europe;* and that secured, they knew, that whatever might be the event of battles and sieges, their *cause* was victorious. Whether it's territory had a little more or a little less peeled from it's surface, or whether an island or two was detached from it's commerce, to them was of little moment. The conquest of France was a glorious acquisition. That once well laid as a basis of empire, opportunities never could be wanting to regain or to replace what had been lost, and [105] dreadfully to avenge themselves on the faction of their adversaries.

THEY SAW IT WAS a *civil war.* It was their business to persuade their adversaries that it ought to be a *foreign* war. The Jacobins every where set up a cry against the new crusade; and they intrigued with effect in the cabinet, in the field, and in every private society in Europe. Their talk was not difficult. The condition of Princes, and sometimes of first Ministers too, is to be pitied. The creatures of the desk, and the creatures of favour, had no relish for the principles of the manifestoes. They promised no governments, no regiments, no revenues from whence emoluments might arise, by perquisite or by grant. In truth, the tribe of vulgar politicians are the lowest of our species. There is no trade so vile and mechanical as government in their hands. Virtue is not their habit. They are out of themselves in any course of conduct recommended only by conscience and glory. A large, liberal and prospective view of the interests of States passes with them for romance; and the principles that recommend it for the wanderings of a disordered imagination. The calculators compute them out of their senses. The jesters and buffoons shame them out of every thing grand and elevated. Littleness, in object and in means, to them appears soundness and sobriety. They think there is nothing worth pursuit, but that which they can handle; which they can measure with a two-foot rule; which they can tell upon ten fingers.

Without the principles of the Jacobins, perhaps without any principles at all, they played the game of that faction. There was a beaten road before them. The Powers of Europe were armed; France had always appeared dangerous; the war was easily diverted from France as a faction, to France as a state. The Princes were easily taught to [106] slide back into their old habitual course of politicks. They were easily led to consider the flames that were consuming France, not as a warning to protect their own buildings, (which were without any party wall, and linked by a contignation into the edifice of France,) but as an happy occasion for pillaging the goods, and for carrying off the materials of their neighbour's house. Their provident fears were changed into avaricious hopes. They carried on their new designs without seeming to abandon the principles of their old policy. They pretended to seek, or they flattered themselves that they sought, in the accession of new fortresses, and new territories, a *defensive* security. But the security wanted was against a kind of power, which was not so truly dangerous in it's fortresses nor in it's territories, as in it's spirit and it's principles. They aimed, or pretended to aim, at *defending* themselves against a danger, from which there can be no security in any *defensive* plan. If armies and fortresses were a defence against Jacobinism, Louis the Sixteenth would this day reign a powerful monarch over an happy people.

THIS ERROR OBLIGED THEM, even in their offensive operations, to adopt a plan of war, against the success of which there was something little short of mathematical demonstration. They refused to take any step which might strike at the heart of affairs. They seemed unwilling to wound the enemy in any vital part. They acted through the whole, as if they really wished the conservation of the Jacobin power; as what might be more favourable than the lawful Government to the attainment of the petty objects they looked for. They always kept on the circumference; and the wider and remoter the circle was, the more eagerly they chose it as their sphere of action in this centrifugal war. The plan they pursued, in it's nature, demanded great length of time. [107] In it's execution, they, who went the nearest way to work, were obliged to cover an incredible extent of country. It left to the enemy every means of destroying this extended line of weakness. Ill success in any part was sure to defeat the effect of the whole. This is true of Austria. It is still more true of England. On this false plan, even good fortune, by further weakening the victor, put him but the further off from his object.

As long as there was any appearance of success, the spirit of aggrandizement, and consequently the spirit of mutual jealousy seized upon all the coalesced Powers. Some sought an accession of territory at the expence of France, some at the expence of each other; some at the expence of third parties; and when the vicissitude of disaster took it's turn, they found common distress a treacherous bond of faith and friendship.

The greatest skill conducting the greatest military apparatus has been employed; but it has been worse than uselessly employed, through the false policy of the war. The operations of the field suffered by the errors of the Cabinet. If the same spirit continues when peace is made, the peace will fix and perpetuate all the errors of the war; because it will be made upon the same false principle. What has been lost in the field, in the field may be regained. An arrangement of peace in it's nature is a permanent settlement; it is the effect of counsel and deliberation, and not of fortuitous events. If built upon a basis fundamentally erroneous, it can only be retrieved by some of those unforeseen dispositions, which the all-wise but mysterious Governor of the World sometimes interposes, to snatch nations from ruin. It would not be pious error, but mad and impious presumption, for any one to trust in an unknown order of dispensations, in defiance of the rules of prudence, which are formed upon the known march of the ordinary providence of God.

[108] IT WAS not of that sort of war that I was amongst the least considerable, but amongst the most zealous advisers; and it is not by the sort of peace now talked of, that I wish it concluded. It would answer no great purpose to enter into the particular errours of the war. The whole has been but one errour. It was but nominally a war of alliance. As the combined powers pursued it, there was nothing to hold an alliance together. There could be no tie of *honour*, in a society for pillage. There could be no tie of a common *interest* where the object did not offer such a division amongst the parties, as could well give them a warm concern in the gains of each other, or could indeed form such a body of equivalents, as might make one of them willing to abandon a separate object of his ambition for the justification of any other member of the alliance. The partition of Poland offered an object of spoil in which the parties *might* agree. They were circumjacent; and each might take a portion convenient to his own territory. They might dispute about the value of their several shares: but the contiguity to each of the demandants

always furnished the means of an adjustment. Though hereafter the world will have cause to rue this iniquitous measure,
and they most who were most concerned in it, for the moment there was wherewithal in the object to preserve peace
amongst confederates in wrong. But the spoil of France did
not afford the same facilities for accommodation. What might
satisfy the House of Austria in a Flemish frontier afforded no
equivalent to tempt the cupidity of the King of Prussia. What
might be desired by Great Britain in the West-Indies, must
be coldly and remotely, if at all, felt as an interest at Vienna;
and it would be felt as something worse than a negative interest at Madrid. Austria, long possessed with unwise and dangerous designs on Italy, could not be very much in earnest
about the conservation of the old patrimony of the House
of Savoy: [109] and Sardinia, who owed to an Italian force
all her means of shutting out France from Italy, of which she
has been supposed to hold the key, would not purchase the
means of strength upon one side by yielding it on the other.
She would not readily give the possession of Novara for the
hope of Savoy. No continental Power was willing to lose any
of it's continental objects for the encrease of the naval power
of Great Britain; and Great Britain would not give up any of
the objects she sought for as the means of an encrease to her
naval power, to further their aggrandizement.

The moment this war came to be considered as a war
merely of profit, the actual circumstances are such, that it
never could become really a war of alliance. Nor can the
peace be a peace of alliance, until things are put upon their
right bottom.

I DON'T FIND IT DENIED, that when a treaty is entered
into for peace, a demand will be made on the Regicides to
surrender a great part of their conquests on the Continent.
Will they, in the present state of the war, make that surrender without an equivalent? This continental cession must of

course be made in favour of that party in the alliance, that has suffered losses. That party has nothing to furnish towards an equivalent. What equivalent, for instance, has Holland to offer, who has lost her all? What equivalent can come from the Emperor, every part of whose territories contiguous to France, is already within the pale of the Regicide dominion? What equivalent has Sardinia to offer for Savoy and for Nice, I may say for her whole being? What has she taken from the faction of France? She has lost very nearly her all; and she has gained nothing. What equivalent has Spain to give? Alas! she has already paid for her own ransom the fund of equivalent, and a dreadful equivalent it is, to England and to herself. But I put Spain [110] out of the question. She is a province of the Jacobin Empire, and she must make peace or war according to the orders she receives from the Directory of Assassins. In effect and substance, her Crown is a fief of Regicide.

Whence then can the compensation be demanded? Undoubtedly from that power which alone has made some conquests. That power is England. Will the allies then give away their ancient patrimony, that England may keep Islands in the West-Indies? They never can protract the war in good earnest for that object; nor can they act in concert with us, in our refusal to grant any thing towards their redemption. In that case we are thus situated. Either we must give Europe, bound hand and foot, to France; or we must quit the West Indies without any one object, great or small, towards indemnity and security. I repeat it—without any advantage whatever: because, supposing that our conquest could comprize all that France ever possessed in the tropical America, it never can amount, in any fair estimation, to a fair equivalent for Holland, for the Austrian Netherlands, for the lower Germany, that is, for the whole antient kingdom or circle of Burgundy, now under the yoke of Regicide, to say nothing of almost all Italy under the same barbarous domination. If we treat in the present situation of things, we have nothing in our hands that can redeem Europe. Nor is the Emperor, as I have observed, more rich in the fund of equivalents.

If we look to our stock in the Eastern world, our most valuable and systematick acquisitions are made in that quarter. Is it from France they are made? France has but one or two contemptible factories, subsisting by the offal of the private fortunes of English individuals to support them, in any part of India. I look on the taking of the Cape of Good Hope as the securing of a post of great moment. It does honour to those who planned, and to those who [111] executed that enterprize: but I speak of it always as *comparatively* good; as good as any thing can be in a scheme of war that repels us from a center, and employs all our forces where nothing can be finally decisive. But giving, as I freely give, every possible credit to these eastern conquests, I ask one question—On whom are they made? It is evident, that if we can keep our eastern conquests, we keep them not at the expence of France, but at the expence of Holland, our *ally;* of Holland, the immediate cause of the war, the nation whom we had undertaken to protect; and not of the Republic which it was our business to destroy. If we return the African and the Asiatick conquests, we put them into the hands of a nominal State, (to that Holland is reduced) unable to retain them; and which will virtually leave them under the direction of France. If we withhold them, Holland declines still more as a State; and she loses so much carrying trade and that means of keeping up the small degree of naval power she holds; for which policy, and not for any commercial gain, she maintains the Cape, or any settlement beyond it. In that case, resentment, faction, and even necessity will throw her more and more into the power of the new mischievous Republick. But on the probable state of Holland, I shall say more, when in this correspondence I come to talk over with you the state in which any sort of Jacobin peace will leave all Europe. So far as to the East Indies.

As to the West Indies, indeed as to either, if we look for

matter of exchange in order to ransom Europe, it is easy to shew that we have taken a terrible roundabout road. I cannot conceive, even if, for the sake of holding conquests there, we should refuse to redeem Holland, and the Austrian Netherlands, and the hither Germany, that Spain, merely as she is Spain, (and forgetting that the Regicide Ambassador governs at Madrid) will see with perfect satisfaction [112] Great Britain sole mistress of the Isles. In truth it appears to me, that, when we come to balance our account, we shall find in the proposed peace only the pure, simple, and unendowed charms of Jacobin amity. We shall have the satisfaction of knowing that no blood or treasure has been spared by the allies for support of the Regicide system. We shall reflect at leisure on one great truth, that it was ten times more easy totally to destroy the system itself, than when established, it would be to reduce it's power: and that this Republick, most formidable abroad, was, of all things, the weakest at home. That her frontier was terrible, her interior feeble; that it was matter of choice to attack her where she is invincible, and to spare her where she was ready to dissolve by her own internal disorders. We shall reflect, that our plan was good neither for offence nor defence.

It would not be at all difficult to prove that an army of a hundred thousand men, horse, foot, and artillery, might have been employed against the enemy on the very soil which he has usurped, at a far less expense than has been squandered away upon tropical adventures. In these adventures it was not an enemy we had to vanquish, but a cemetery to conquer. In carrying on the war in the West Indies, the hostile sword is merciful: the country in which we engage is the dreadful enemy. There the European conqueror finds a cruel defeat in the very fruits of his success. Every advantage is but a new demand on England for recruits to the West Indian grave. In a West India war, the Regicides have for their troops a race of fierce barbarians, to whom the poisoned air, in which our youth inhale certain death, is salubrity and life. To them the climate is the surest and most faithful of allies.

Had we carried on the war on the side of France which looks towards the Channel or the Atlantick, we should have [113] attacked our enemy on his weak and unarmed side. We should not have to reckon on the loss of a man, who did not fall in battle. We should have an ally in the heart of the country, who to our hundred thousand, would at one time have added eighty thousand men at the least, and all animated by principle, by enthusiasm, and by vengeance: motives which secured them to the cause in a very different manner from some of our allies whom we subsidized with millions. This ally, or rather this principal in the war, by the confession of the Regicide himself, was more formidable to him than all his other foes united. Warring there, we should have led our arms to the capital of Wrong. Defeated, we could not fail (proper precautions taken) of a sure retreat. Stationary, and only supporting the Royalists, an impenetrable barrier, an impregnable rampart, would have been formed between the enemy and his naval power. We are probably the only nation who have declined to act against an enemy, when it might have been done in his own country; and who having an armed, a powerful, and a long victorious ally in that country, declined all effectual cooperation, and suffered him to perish for want of support. On the plan of a war in France, every advantage that our allies might gain would be doubled in its effect. Disasters on the one side might have a fair chance of being compensated by victories on the other. Had we brought the main of our force to bear upon that quarter, all the operations of the British and Imperial crowns would have been combined. The war would have had system, correspondence, and a certain direction. But as the war has been pursued, the operations of the two crowns have not the smallest degree of mutual bearing or relation.

Had acquisitions in the West Indies been our object, or

success in France, every thing reasonable in those remote parts might be demanded with decorum, and justice, and [114] a sure effect. Well might we call for a recompense in America for those services to which Europe owed its safety. Having abandoned this obvious policy connected with principle, we have seen the Regicide power taking the reverse course, and making real conquests in the West Indies, to which all our dear-bought advantages, if we could hold them, are mean and contemptible. The noblest island within the tropicks, worth all that we possess put together, is by the vassal Spaniard delivered into her hands. The island of Hispaniola, of which we have but one poor corner, by a slippery hold, is perhaps equal to England in extent, and in fertility is far superior. The part possessed by Spain of that great island, made for the seat and center of a tropical empire, was not improved, to be sure, as the French division had been, before it was systematically destroyed by the cannibal republick: but it is not only the far larger, but the far more salubrious and more fertile part.

It was delivered into the hands of the barbarians without, as I can find, any public reclamation on our part, not only in contravention of one of the fundamental treaties that compose the public law of Europe, but in defiance of the fundamental colonial policy of Spain herself. This part of the Treaty of Utrecht was made for great general ends, unquestionably: but whilst it provided for those general ends, it was an affirmance of that particular policy. It was not to injure but to save Spain, by making a settlement of her estate which prohibited her to alienate it to France. It is her policy not to see the balance of West Indian power overturned, by France or by Great Britain. Whilst the monarchies subsisted, this unprincipled cession was what the influence of the elder branch of the House of Bourbon never dared attempt on the younger. But cannibal terror has been more powerful than family influence. The Bourbon [115] monarchy of Spain is united to the republic of France by what may be truly called the ties of *blood*.

By this measure the balance of power in the West Indies is totally destroyed. It has followed the balance of power in Europe. It is not alone what shall be left nominally to the assassins, that is theirs. Theirs is the whole empire of Spain in America. That stroke finishes all. I should be glad to see our suppliant negotiator in the act of putting his feather to the ear of the Directory; and by his tickling, to charm that rich prize out of the iron gripe of robbery and ambition! It does not require much sagacity to discern that no power wholly baffled and defeated in Europe can flatter itself with conquests in the West Indies. In that state of things it can neither keep nor hold. No! It cannot even long make war, if the grand bank and deposit of its force is at all in the West Indies. But here a scene opens to my view too important to pass by, perhaps too critical to touch. Is it possible that it should not present itself, in all its relations, to a mind habituated to consider either war or peace on a large scale, or as one whole?

Unfortunately other ideas have prevailed. A remote, an expensive, a murderous, and in the end, an unproductive adventure, carried on upon ideas of mercantile knight-errantry, without any of the generous wildness of Quixotism, is considered as sound, solid sense: and a war in a wholesome climate, a war at our door, a war directly on the enemy, a war in the heart of his country, a war in concert with an internal ally, and in combination with the external, is regarded as folly and romance.

My dear Friend, I hold it impossible that these considerations should have escaped the Statesmen on both sides of the water, and on both sides of the house of Commons. How a question of peace can be discussed without having them in view, I cannot imagine. If you or others see a way [116] out of these difficulties I am happy. I see indeed a fund from whence equivalents will be proposed. I see it. But I cannot

just now touch it. It is a question of high moment. It opens
another Iliad of woes to Europe.

Such is the time proposed for making *a common political
peace,* to which no one circumstance is propitious. As to the
grand principle of the peace, it is left, as if by common consent, wholly out of the question.

Viewing things in this light, I have frequently sunk
into a degree of despondency and dejection hardly to be described: yet out of the profoundest depths of this despair, an
impulse which I have in vain endeavoured to resist has urged
me to raise one feeble cry against this unfortunate coalition
which is formed at home, in order to make a coalition with
France, subversive of the whole ancient order of the world.
No disaster of war, no calamity of season, could ever strike
me with half the horror which I felt from what is introduced
to us by this junction of parties, under the soothing name of
peace. We are apt to speak of a low and pusillanimous spirit
as the ordinary cause by which dubious wars terminate in humiliating treaties. It is here the direct contrary. I am perfectly
astonished at the boldness of character, at the intrepidity of
mind, the firmness of nerve, in those who are able with deliberation to face the perils of Jacobin fraternity.

This fraternity is indeed so terrible in it's nature, and
in it's manifest consequences, that there is no way of quieting our apprehensions about it, but by totally putting it out
of sight, by substituting for it, through a sort of periphra-
sis, something of an ambiguous quality, and describing such
a connection under the terms of *"the usual relations of peace
and amity."* By this means the proposed fraternity is hustled
in the crowd of those treaties, which imply no [117] change
in the public law of Europe, and which do not upon system affect the interior condition of nations. It is confounded
with those conventions in which matters of dispute among
sovereign powers are compromised, by the taking off a duty

more or less, by the surrender of a frontier town, or a disputed district on the one side or the other; by pactions in
which the pretensions of families are settled, (as by a convey-
ancer, making family substitutions and successions), without
any alteration in the laws, manners, religion, privileges and
customs of the cities or territories which are the subject of
such arrangements.

All this body of old conventions, composing the vast and
voluminous collection called the *corps diplomatique,* forms the
code or statute law, as the methodized reasonings of the
great publicists and jurists form the digest and jurisprudence,
of the Christian world. In these treasures are to be found
the *usual* relations of peace and amity in civilized Europe;
and there the relations of ancient France were to be found
amongst the rest.

The present system in France is not the ancient France.
It is not the ancient France with ordinary ambition and ordinary means. It is not a new power of an old kind. It is a new
power of a new species. When such a questionable shape is to
be admitted for the first time into the brotherhood of Christendom, it is not a mere matter of idle curiosity to consider
how far it is, in it's nature, alliable with the rest, or whether
"the relations of peace and amity" with this new State are
likely to be of the same nature with the *usual* relations of the
States of Europe.

The Revolution in France had the relation of France to
other nations as one of it's principal objects. The changes
made by that Revolution were not the better to accommo-
date her to the old and usual relations, but to produce new
ones. The Revolution was made, not to make France free,
but to [118] make her formidable; not to make her a neighbour, but a mistress; not to make her more observant of
laws, but to put her in a condition to impose them. To make
France truly formidable it was necessary that France should
be new-modelled. They who have not followed the train of

the late proceedings, have been led by deceitful representations (which deceit made a part in the plan) to conceive that
this totally new model of a state in which nothing escaped a
change, was made with a view to it's internal relations only.

IN THE REVOLUTION OF FRANCE two sorts of men were
principally concerned in giving a character and determination to it's pursuits; the philosophers and the politicians. They
took different ways: but they met in the same end. The philosophers had one predominant object, which they pursued
with a fanatical fury, that is, the utter extirpation of religion. To that every question of empire was subordinate. They
had rather domineer in a parish of Atheists, than rule over
a Christian world. Their temporal ambition was wholly subservient to their proselytizing spirit, in which they were not
exceeded by Mahomet himself.

They who have made but superficial studies in the Natural History of the human mind, have been taught to look
on religious opinions as the only cause of enthusiastick zeal,
and sectarian propagation. But there is no doctrine whatever, on which men can warm, that is not capable of the very
same effect. The social nature of man impels him to propagate his principles, as much as physical impulses urge him to
propagate his kind. The passions give zeal and vehemence.
The understanding bestows design and system. The whole
man moves under the discipline of his opinions. Religion is
among the most powerful causes of enthusiasm. When any
thing concerning it becomes an object of much meditation,
it cannot be indifferent to the [119] mind. They who do not
love religion, hate it. The rebels to God perfectly abhor the
Author of their being. They hate him "with all their heart,
with all their mind, with all their soul, and with all their
strength." He never presents himself to their thoughts but to
menace and alarm them. They cannot strike the Sun out of
Heaven, but they are able to raise a smouldering smoke that

obscures him from their own eyes. Not being able to revenge themselves on God, they have a delight in vicariously defacing, degrading, torturing, and tearing in pieces his image in man. Let no one judge of them by what he has conceived of them, when they were not incorporated, and had no lead. They were then only passengers in a common vehicle. They were then carried along with the general motion of religion in the community, and without being aware of it, partook of it's influence. In that situation, at worst, their nature was left free to counterwork their principles. They despaired of giving any very general currency to their opinions. They considered them as a reserved privilege for the chosen few. But when the possibility of dominion, lead, and propagation presented themselves, and that the ambition, which before had so often made them hypocrites, might rather gain than lose by a daring avowal of their sentiments, then the nature of this infernal spirit, which has "evil for it's good," appeared in it's full perfection. Nothing, indeed, but the possession of some power, can with any certainty discover what at the bottom is the true character of any man. Without reading the speeches of Vergniaux, Français of Nantz, Isnard, and some others of that sort, it would not be easy to conceive the passion, rancour, and malice of their tongues and hearts. They worked themselves up to a perfect phrenzy against religion and all it's professors. They tore the reputation of the Clergy to pieces by their infuriated declamations and invectives, before they lacerated their bodies by their [120] massacres. This fanatical atheism left out, we omit the principal feature in the French Revolution, and a principal consideration with regard to the effects to be expected from a peace with it.

THE OTHER SORT OF MEN were the politicians. To them who had little or not at all reflected on the subject, religion was in itself no object of love or hatred. They disbelieved it, and that was all. Neutral with regard to that object, they took the side which in the present state of things might best answer their purposes. They soon found that they could not do without the philosophers; and the philosophers soon made them sensible that the destruction of religion was to supply them with means of conquest, first at home, and then abroad. The philosophers were the active internal agitators, and supplied the spirit and principles: the second gave the practical direction. Sometimes the one predominated in the composition, sometimes the other. The only difference between them was in the necessity of concealing the general design for a time, and in their dealing with foreign nations; the fanaticks going strait forward and openly, the politicians by the surer mode of zigzag. In the course of events this, among other causes, produced fierce and bloody contentions between them. But at the bottom they thoroughly agreed in all the objects of ambition and irreligion, and substantially in all the means of promoting these ends.

WITHOUT QUESTION, to bring about the unexampled event of the French Revolution, the concurrence of a very great number of views and passions was necessary. In that stupendous work, no one principle by which the human mind may have it's faculties at once invigorated and depraved, was left unemployed: but I can speak it to a certainty, and support it by undoubted proofs, that the ruling [121] principle of those who acted in the Revolution *as statesmen,* had the exterior aggrandizement of France as their ultimate end, in the most minute part of the internal changes that were made. We, who of late years have been drawn from an attention to foreign affairs by the importance of our domestic discussions, cannot easily form a conception of the general eagerness of the active and energetick part of the French nation itself, the most active and energetick of all nations previous to it's Revolution, upon that subject. I am convinced that the foreign speculators in France, under the old Government, were twenty to one of the same description then or now in England; and few of that description there were, who did not emulously set forward the Revolution. The whole official system, particularly in the diplomatic part, the regulars, the irregulars, down to the clerks in office, (a corps, without all comparison, more numerous than the same amongst us) co-operated in it. All the intriguers in foreign politicks, all the spies, all the intelligencers, actually or late in function, all the candidates for that sort of employment, acted solely upon that principle.

ON THAT SYSTEM of aggrandizement there was but one mind: but two violent factions arose about the means. The first wished France, diverted from the politicks of the continent, to attend solely to her marine, to feed it by an encrease of commerce, and thereby to overpower England on her own element. They contended, that if England were disabled, the Powers on the continent would fall into their proper subordination; that it was England which deranged the whole continental system of Europe. The others, who were by far the more numerous, though not the most outwardly prevalent at Court, considered this plan for France as contrary to her genius, her situation, and her natural means. They agreed as to the ultimate object, the reduction [122] of the British power, and if possible, it's naval power; but they considered an ascendancy on the continent as a necessary preliminary to that undertaking. They argued that the proceedings of England herself had proved the soundness of this policy. That her greatest and ablest Statesmen had not considered the support of a continental balance against France as a deviation from the principle of her naval power, but as one of the most effectual modes of carrying it into effect. That such had been her policy ever since the Revolution; during which period the naval strength of Great Britain had gone on encreasing in the direct ratio of her interference in the politicks of the continent. With much stronger reason ought the politicks of France to take the same direction; as well for pursuing objects which her situation would dictate to her, though England had no existence, as for counteracting the politicks of that nation; to France continental politicks are primary; they looked on them only of secondary consideration to England, and however necessary, but as means necessary to an end.

WHAT IS TRULY ASTONISHING, the partizans of those two opposite systems were at once prevalent, and at once employed, and in the very same transactions, the one ostensibly, the other secretly, during the latter part of the reign of Lewis XV. Nor was there one Court in which an Ambassador resided on the part of the Ministers, in which another as a spy on him did not also reside on the part of the King: they who pursued the scheme for keeping peace on the continent, and particularly with Austria, acting officially and publickly, the other faction counteracting and opposing them. These private agents were continually going from their function to the Bastille, and from the Bastille to employment, and favour again. An inextricable cabal was formed, some of persons of rank, others of subordinates. [123] But by this means the corps of politicians was augmented in number, and the whole formed a body of active, adventuring, ambitious, discontented people, despising the regular Ministry, despising the Courts at which they were employed, despising the Court which employed them.

The unfortunate Louis the Sixteenth[1] was not the first

---

1. It may be right to do justice to Louis XVI. He did what he could to destroy the double diplomacy of France. He had all his secret correspondence burnt, except one piece, which was called, *Conjectures raisonnées sur la Situation de la France dans le Système Politique de l'Europe;* a work executed by M. Favier, under the direction of Count Broglie. A single copy of this was said to have been found in the Cabinet of Louis XVI. It was published with some subsequent state papers of Vergennes, Turgot, and others, as, "A new Benefit of the

cause of the evil by which he suffered. He came to it, as to a sort of inheritance, by the false politicks of his immediate predecessor. This system of dark and perplexed intrigue had come to it's perfection before he came to the throne: and even then the Revolution strongly operated in all it's causes.

THERE WAS NO POINT ON WHICH the discontented diplomatic politicians so bitterly arraigned their Cabinet, as for the decay of French influence in all others. From quarrelling with the Court, they began to complain of Monarchy itself; as a system of Government too variable for any regular plan of national aggrandizement. They observed, that in that sort of regimen too much depended on the personal character of the Prince; that the vicissitudes produced by the succession of Princes of a different character, and even the [124] vicissitudes produced in the same man, by the different views and inclinations belonging to youth, manhood, and age, disturbed and distracted the policy of a country made by nature for extensive empire, or what was still more to their taste, for that sort of general over-ruling influence which prepared empire or supplied the place of it. They had continually in their hands the observations of *Machiavel* on *Livy*. They had *Montesquieu's Grandeur & Décadence des Romains* as a manual; and they compared with mortification the systematic proceedings of a Roman senate with the fluctuations of a Monarchy. They observed the very small additions of territory which all the power of France, actuated by all the ambition of France, had acquired in two centuries. The Romans had frequently

---

Revolution"; and the advertisement to the publication ends with the following words. "*Il sera facile de se convaincre, qu'*Y COMPRIS MÊME LA RÉVOLUTION, *en grande partie,* ON TROUVE DANS CES MÉMOIRES ET SES CONJECTURES LE GERME DE TOUT CE QU'ARRIVA AUJOURD'HUI, *& qu'on ne peut pas sans les avoir lus, être bien au fait des intérêts, & même des vues actuelles des diverses puissances de l'Europe.*" The book is entitled, *Politique de tous les Cabinets de l'Europe pendant les règnes de Louis XV. & Louis XVI.* It is altogether very curious, and worth reading.

acquired more in a single year. They severely and in every part of it criticised the reign of Louis the XIVth, whose irregular and desultory ambition had more provoked than endangered Europe. Indeed, they who will be at the pains of seriously considering the history of that period will see, that those French politicians had some reason. They who will not take the trouble of reviewing it through all it's wars and all it's negociations, will consult the short but judicious criticism of the Marquis de Montalembert on that subject. It may be read separately from his ingenious system of fortification and military defence, on the practical merit of which I am unable to form a judgment.

The diplomatick politicians of whom I speak, and who formed by far the majority in that class, made disadvantageous comparisons even between their more legal and formalising Monarchy, and the monarchies of other states, as a system of power and influence. They observed, that France not only lost ground herself, but through the languor and unsteadiness of her pursuits, and from her aiming through commerce at naval force which she never could [125] attain without losing more on one side than she could gain on the other, three great powers, each of them (as military states) capable of balancing her, had grown up on the continent. Russia and Prussia had been created almost within memory; and Austria, though not a new power, and even curtailed in territory, was by the very collision in which she lost that territory, greatly improved in her military discipline and force. During the reign of Maria Theresa the interior oeconomy of the country was made more to correspond with the support of great armies than formerly it had been. As to Prussia, a merely military power, they observed that one war had enriched her with as considerable a conquest as France had acquired in centuries. Russia had broken the Turkish power by which Austria might be, as formerly she had been, balanced in favour of France. They felt it with pain, that the two northern powers of Sweden and Denmark were in general under the sway of Russia; or that at best, France kept up a very doubtful conflict, with many fluctuations of fortune, and at an enormous expence, in Sweden. In Holland, the French party seemed, if not extinguished, at least utterly obscured, and kept under by a Stadtholder, sometimes leaning for support on Great Britain, sometimes on Prussia, sometimes on both, never on France. Even the spreading of the Bourbon family had become merely a family accommodation; and had little effect on the national politicks. This alliance, they said, extinguished Spain by destroying all it's energy, without adding any thing to the real power of France in the accession of the forces of it's great rival. In Italy, the same family accommodation, the same national insignificance, were equally visible. What cure for the radical weakness of the French Monarchy, to which all the means which wit could devise, or nature and fortune could bestow, towards universal empire, was not of force to give [126] life, or vigour, or consistency, but in a republick? Out the word came; and it never went back.

Whether they reasoned right or wrong, or that there was some mixture of right and wrong in their reasoning, I am sure, that in this manner they felt and reasoned. The different effects of a great military and ambitious republick, and of a monarchy of the same description were constantly in their mouths. The principle was ready to operate when opportunities should offer, which few of them indeed foresaw in the extent in which they were afterwards presented; but these opportunities, in some degree or other, they all ardently wished for.

When I was in Paris in 1773, the treaty of 1756 between Austria and France was deplored as a national calamity; because it united France in friendship with a Power, at whose expence alone they could hope any continental aggrandizement. When the first partition of Poland was made, in which France had no share, and which had farther aggrandized every one of the three Powers of which they were most jealous, I found them in a perfect phrenzy of rage and indignation. Not that they were hurt at the shocking and uncoloured violence and injustice of that partition; but at the debility, improvidence, and want of activity in their Government, in not preventing it as a means of aggrandizement to their rivals, or in not contriving, by exchanges of some kind or other, to obtain their share of advantage from that robbery.

In that or nearly in that state of things and of opinions, came the Austrian match; which promised to draw the knot, as afterwards in effect it did, still more closely between the old rival houses. This added exceedingly to their hatred and contempt of their monarchy. It was for this reason that the late glorious Queen, who on all accounts was formed to produce general love and admiration, and whose life was [127] as mild and beneficent as her death was beyond example great and heroic, became so very soon and so very much the object of an implacable rancour, never to be extinguished but in her blood. When I wrote my letter in answer to M. de Menonville, in the beginning of January, 1791, I had good reason for thinking that this description of revolutionists did not so early nor so steadily point their murderous designs at the martyr King as at the Royal Heroine. It was accident, and the momentary depression of that part of the faction, that gave to the husband the happy priority in death.

FROM THIS THEIR RESTLESS DESIRE of an over-ruling influence, they bent a very great part of their designs and efforts to revive the old French party, which was a democratick party, in Holland, and to make a revolution there. They were happy at the troubles which the singular imprudence of Joseph the Second had stirred up in the Austrian Netherlands. They rejoiced, when they saw him irritate his subjects, profess philosophy, send away the Dutch garrisons, and dismantle his fortifications. As to Holland, they never forgave either the King or the Ministry, for suffering that object, which they justly looked on as principal in their design of reducing the power of England, to escape out of their hands. This was the true secret of the commercial treaty, made, on their part, against all the old rules and principles of commerce, with a view of diverting the English nation, by a pursuit of immediate profit, from an attention to the progress of France in it's designs upon that Republic. The system of the oeconomists, which led to the general opening of commerce, facilitated that treaty, but did not produce it. They were in despair when they found that by the vigour of Mr. Pitt, supported in this point by Mr. Fox and the opposition, the object, to which they had sacrificed their manufactures, was lost to their ambition. This eager desire of raising [128] France from the condition into which she had fallen, as they conceived, from her monarchical imbecility, had been the main spring of their precedent interference in that unhappy American quarrel, the bad effects of which to this nation have not, as yet, fully disclosed themselves.

These sentiments had been long lurking in their breasts, though their views were only discovered now and then, in heat and as by escapes; but on this occasion they exploded suddenly. They were professed with ostentation, and propagated with zeal. These sentiments were not produced, as some think, by their American alliance. The American alliance was produced by their republican principles and republican policy. This new relation undoubtedly did much. The discourses and cabals that it produced, the intercourse that it established, and above all, the example, which made it seem practicable to establish a Republick in a great extent of country, finished the work, and gave to that part of the Revolutionary faction a degree of strength, which required other energies than the late King possessed, to resist, or even to restrain. It spread every where; but it was no where more prevalent than in the heart of the Court. The palace of Versailles, by it's language, seemed a forum of democracy. To have pointed out to most of those politicians, from their dispositions and movements, what has since happened, the fall of their own Monarchy, of their own Laws, of their own Religion, would have been to furnish a motive the more for pushing forward a system on which they considered all these things as incumbrances. Such in truth they were. And we have seen them succeed, not only in the destruction of their monarchy, but in all the objects of ambition that they proposed from that destruction.

WHEN I CONTEMPLATE the scheme on which France is formed, and when I compare it with these systems, with which it is, [129] and ever must be, in conflict, those things which seem as defects in her polity are the very things which make me tremble. The States of the Christian World have grown up to their present magnitude in a great length of time, and by a great variety of accidents. They have been improved to what we see them with greater or less degrees of felicity and skill. Not one of them has been formed upon a regular plan or with any unity of design. As their Constitutions are not systematical, they have not been directed to any *peculiar* end, eminently distinguished, and superseding every other. The objects which they embrace are of the greatest possible variety, and have become in a manner infinite. In all these old countries the state has been made to the people, and not the people conformed to the state. Every state has pursued, not only every sort of social advantage, but it has cultivated the welfare of every individual. His wants, his wishes, even his tastes have been consulted. This comprehensive scheme virtually produced a degree of personal liberty in forms the most adverse to it. That liberty was found, under monarchies stiled absolute, in a degree unknown to the ancient commonwealths. From hence the powers of all our modern states meet in all their movements with some obstruction. It is therefore no wonder, that when these states are to be considered as machines to operate for some one great end, that this dissipated and balanced force is not easily concentered, or made to bear with the whole nation upon one point.

The British State is, without question, that which pursues the greatest variety of ends, and is the least disposed to sacrifice any one of them to another, or to the whole. It aims at taking in the entire circle of human desires, and securing for them their fair enjoyment. Our legislature has been ever closely connected, in it's most efficient part, with individual feeling and individual interest. Personal liberty, the most [130] lively of these feelings and the most important of these interests, which in other European countries has rather arisen from the system of manners and the habitudes of life, than from the laws of the state, (in which it flourished more from neglect than attention) in England has been a direct object of Government.

On this principle England would be the weakest power in the whole system. Fortunately, however, the great riches of this kingdom, arising from a variety of causes, and the disposition of the people, which is as great to spend as to accumulate, has easily afforded a disposeable surplus that gives a mighty momentum to the state. This difficulty, with these advantages to overcome it, has called forth the talents of the English financiers, who, by the surplus of industry poured out by prodigality, have outdone every thing which has been accomplished in other nations. The present Minister has outdone his predecessors; and as a Minister of revenue, is far above my power of praise. But still there are cases in which England feels more than several others, (though they all feel) the perplexity of an immense body of balanced advantages, and of individual demands, and of some irregularity in the whole mass.

France differs essentially from all those Governments which are formed without system, which exist by habit, and which are confused with the multitude, and with the complexity of their pursuits. What now stands as Government in France is struck out at a heat. The design is wicked, immoral, impious, oppressive; but it is spirited and daring: it is systematick; it is simple in it's principle; it has unity and consistency in perfection. In that country entirely to cut off a branch of commerce, to extinguish a manufacture, to destroy the circulation of money, to violate credit, to suspend the course of agriculture, even to burn a city, or to lay waste a province of their own, does not cost them a [131] moment's anxiety. To them, the will, the wish, the want, the liberty, the toil, the blood of individuals is as nothing. Individuality is left out of their scheme of Government. The state is all in all. Every thing is referred to the production of force; afterwards every thing is trusted to the use of it. It is military in it's principle, in it's maxims, in it's spirit, and in all it's movements. The state has dominion and conquest for it's sole objects; dominion over minds by proselytism, over bodies by arms.

Thus constituted with an immense body of natural means, which are lessened in their amount only to be increased in their effect, France has, since the accomplishment of the Revolution, a complete unity in it's direction. It has destroyed every resource of the State which depends upon opinion and the good-will of individuals. The riches of convention disappear. The advantages of nature in some measure remain; even these, I admit, are astonishingly lessened; the command over what remains is complete and absolute. We go about asking when *assignats* will expire, and we laugh at the last price of them. But what signifies the fate of those tickets of despotism? The despotism will find despotick means of supply. They have found the short cut to the productions of Nature, while others, in pursuit of them, are obliged to wind through the labyrinth of a very intricate state of society. They seize upon the fruit of the labour; they seize upon the labourer himself. Were France but half of what it is in population, in compactness, in applicability of it's force, situated as it is, and being what it is, it would be too strong for most of the States of Europe, constituted as they are, and proceeding as they proceed. Would it be wise to estimate what the world of Europe, as well as the world of Asia, had to dread from Jinghiz Khân, upon a contemplation of the resources of the cold and barren spot in the remotest Tartary, from [132] whence first issued that scourge of the human race? Ought we to judge from the excise and stamp duties of the rocks, or from the paper circulation of the sands of Arabia, the power by which Mahomet and his tribes laid hold at once on the two most powerful Empires of the world; beat one of them totally to the ground, broke to pieces the other, and, in not much longer space of time than I have lived, overturned governments, laws, manners, religion, and extended an empire from the Indus to the Pyrenees?

Material resources never have supplied, nor ever can supply, the want of unity in design and constancy in pursuit. But unity in design, and perseverance, and boldness in pursuit, have never wanted resources, and never will. We have not considered as we ought the dreadful energy of a State, in which the property has nothing to do with the Government. Reflect, my dear Sir, reflect again and again on a Government, in which the property is in complete subjection, and where nothing rules but the mind of desperate men. The condition of a commonwealth not governed by it's property was a combination of things, which the learned and ingenious speculator Harrington, who has tossed about society into all forms, never could imagine to be possible. We have seen it; the world has felt it; and if the world will shut their eyes to this state of things, they will feel it more. The rulers there have found their resources in crimes. The discovery is dreadful: the mine exhaustless. They have every thing to gain, and they have nothing to lose. They have a boundless inheritance in hope; and there is no medium for them, betwixt the highest elevation, and death with infamy. Never can they who from the miserable servitude of the desk have been raised to Empire, again submit to the bondage of a starving bureau, or the profit of copying music, or writing plaidoyers by the sheet. It has made me often smile in bitterness, when I have heard [133] talk of an indemnity to such men, provided they returned to their allegiance.

FROM ALL THIS, what is my inference? It is, that this new system of robbery in France, cannot be rendered safe by any art; that it *must* be destroyed, or that it will destroy all Europe; that to destroy that enemy, by some means or other, the force opposed to it should be made to bear some analogy and resemblance to the force and spirit which that system exerts; that war ought to be made against it in its vulnerable parts. These are my inferences. In one word, with this Republick nothing independent can co-exist. The errors of Louis the XVIth. were more pardonable to prudence, than any of those of the same kind into which the Allied Courts may fall. They have the benefit of his dreadful example.

The unhappy Louis XVI. was a man of the best intentions that probably ever reigned. He was by no means deficient in talents. He had a most laudable desire to supply by general reading, and even by the acquisition of elemental knowledge, an education in all points originally defective; but nobody told him (and it was no wonder he should not himself divine it) that the world of which he read, and the world in which he lived, were no longer the same. Desirous of doing every thing for the best, fearful of cabal, distrusting his own judgment, he sought his Ministers of all kinds upon public testimony. But as Courts are the field for caballers, the publick is the theatre for mountebanks and impostors. The cure for both those evils is in the discernment of the Prince. But an accurate and penetrating discernment is what in a young Prince could not be looked for.

REGICIDE PEACE II

His conduct in it's principle was not unwise; but, like most other of his well-meant designs, it failed in his hands. It failed partly from mere ill fortune, to which speculators [134] are rarely pleased to assign that very large share to which she is justly entitled in all human affairs. The failure, perhaps, in part was owing to his suffering his system to be vitiated and disturbed by those intrigues, which it is, humanly speaking, impossible wholly to prevent in Courts, or indeed under any form of Government. However, with these aberrations, he gave himself over to a succession of the statesmen of publick opinion. In other things he thought that he might be a King on the terms of his predecessors. He was conscious of the purity of his heart and the general good tendency of his Government. He flattered himself, as most men in his situation will, that he might consult his ease without danger to his safety. It is not at all wonderful that both he and his Ministers, giving way abundantly in other respects to innovation, should take up in policy with the tradition of their monarchy. Under his ancestors the Monarchy had subsisted, and even been strengthened by the generation or support of Republicks. First, the Swiss Republicks grew under the guardianship of the French Monarchy. The Dutch Republicks were hatched and cherished under the same incubation. Afterwards, a Republican constitution was under it's influence established in the Empire against the pretensions of it's chief. Even whilst the Monarchy of France, by a series of wars and negotiations, and lastly by the treaties of Westphalia, had obtained the establishment of the Protestants in Germany as a law of the Empire, the same Monarchy under Louis the XIIIth. had force enough to destroy the Republican system of the Protestants at home.

Louis the XVIth. was a diligent reader of history. But the very lamp of prudence blinded him. The guide of human life led him astray. A silent revolution in the moral world preceded the political, and prepared it. It became of more importance than ever what examples [135] were given, and what measures were adopted. Their causes no longer lurked in the recesses of cabinets, or in the private conspiracies of the factious. They were no longer to be controlled by the force and influence of the grandees, who formerly had been able to stir up troubles by their discontents, and to quiet them by their corruption. The chain of subordination, even in cabal and sedition, was broken in it's most important links. It was no longer the great and the populace. Other interests were formed, other dependencies, other connexions, other communications. The middle classes had swelled far beyond their former proportion. Like whatever is the most effectively rich and great in society, these classes became the seat of all the active politicks; and the preponderating weight to decide on them. There were all the energies by which fortune is acquired; there the consequence of their success. There were all the talents which assert their pretensions, and are impatient of the place which settled society prescribes to them. These descriptions had got between the great and the populace; and the influence on the lower classes was with them. The spirit of ambition had taken possession of this class as violently as ever it had done of any other. They felt the importance of this situation. The correspondence of the monied and the mercantile world, the literary intercourse of academies, but, above all, the press, of which they had in a manner, entire possession, made a kind of electrick communication every where. The press, in reality, has made every Government, in it's spirit, almost democratick. Without the great, the first movements in this revolution could not, perhaps, have been given. But the spirit of ambition, now for the first time connected with the spirit of speculation, was not to be restrained at will. There was no longer any means of arresting a principle in it's course. [136] When Louis the XVIth. under the influence of the enemies to Monarchy, meant to found but one Republic, he set up two. When he meant to take away half the crown of his neighbour, he lost the whole of his own. Louis the XVIth. could not with impunity countenance a new Republick: yet between his throne and that dangerous lodgment for an enemy, which he had erected, he had the whole Atlantick for a ditch. He had for an out-work the English nation itself, friendly to liberty, adverse to that mode of it. He was surrounded by a rampart of Monarchies, most of them allied to him, and generally under his influence. Yet even thus secured, a Republick erected under his auspices, and dependent on his power, became fatal to his throne. The very money which he had lent to support this Republick, by a good faith, which to him operated as perfidy, was punctually paid to his enemies, and became a resource in the hands of his assassins.

With this example before their eyes, do any Ministers in England, do any Ministers in Austria, really flatter themselves, that they can erect, not on the remote shores of the Atlantick, but in their view, in their vicinity, in absolute contact with one of them, not a commercial but a martial Republick — a Republick not of simple husbandmen or fishermen, but of intriguers, and of warriors — a Republick of a character the most restless, the most enterprizing, the most impious, the most fierce and bloody, the most hypocritical and perfidious, the most bold and daring that ever has been seen, or indeed that can be conceived to exist, without bringing on their own certain ruin?

Such is the Republick to which we are going to give a place in civilized fellowship. The Republick, which with joint consent we are going to establish in the center of Europe, in a post that overlooks and commands every [137] other State, and which eminently confronts and menaces this kingdom.

You cannot fail to observe, that I speak as if the allied powers were actually consenting, and not compelled by events to the establishment of this faction in France. The words have not escaped me. You will hereafter naturally expect that I should make them good. But whether in adopting this measure we are madly active, or weakly passive, or pusillanimously panick-struck, the effects will be the same. You may call this faction, which has eradicated the monarchy—expelled the proprietary, persecuted religion, and trampled upon law[1]—you may call this France if you please: but of the ancient France nothing remains but it's central geography; it's iron frontier; it's spirit of ambition; it's audacity of enterprize; it's perplexing intrigue. These and these alone remain; and they remain heightened in their principle and augmented in their means. All the former correctives, whether of virtue or of weakness, which existed in the old Monarchy, are gone. No single new corrective is to be found in the whole body of the new institutions. How should such a thing be found there, when every thing has been chosen with care and selection to forward all those ambitious designs and dispositions, not to controul them? The whole is a body of ways and means for the supply of dominion, without one heterogeneous particle in it.

Here I suffer you to breathe, and leave to your meditation what has occurred to me on the *genius and character* of the French Revolution. From having this before us, we may be better able to determine on the first question I proposed, that is, how far nations, called foreign, are likely to be affected with the system established within that territory? [138] I intended to proceed next on the question of her facilities, from *the internal state of other nations, and particularly of this,* for obtaining her ends: but I ought to be aware, that my notions are controverted. I mean, therefore, in my next letter, to take notice of what, in that way, has been recommended to me as the most deserving of notice. In the examination of those pieces, I shall have occasion to discuss some others of the topics I have recommended to your attention. You know, that the Letters which I now send to the press, as well as a part

1. See our declaration.

of what is to follow, have been long since written. A circumstance which your partiality alone could make of importance to you, but which to the publick is of no importance at all, retarded their appearance. The late events which press upon us obliged me to make some few additions; but no substantial change in the matter.

This discussion, my Friend, will be long. But the matter is serious; and if ever the fate of the world could be truly said to depend on a particular measure, it is upon this peace. For the present, farewell.

A Third Letter
to a Member of
the Present Parliament,
on the
Proposals for Peace
with the
Regicide Directory of France
by the late right honourable
Edmund Burke

[Third Edition. Rivingtons, 1797.]

ADVERTISEMENT

In the conclusion of Mr. Burke's second Letter on the Proposals of Peace, he threw out some intimation of the plan which he meant to adopt in the sequel. A third Letter was mentioned by him, as having been then in part written. "He intended to proceed next on the question of the facilities possessed by the French Republick, *from the internal State of other Nations, and particularly of this,* for obtaining her ends; and, as his notions were controverted, to take notice of what, in that way, had been recommended to him."

But the abrupt and unprecedented conclusion of Lord Malmesbury's first negociation induced him to make some change in the arrangement of his matter. He took up the question of his Lordship's mission, as stated in the papers laid before Parliament, his Majesty's Declaration, and in the publick comments upon it; he thought it necessary to examine the new basis of compensation proposed for this treaty; and having heard it currently whispered about, that the foundation of all his opinions failed in this essential point, that he had not shewn what means and resources we possessed to carry them into effect, he also determined to bring forward the consideration of the "absolute necessity of peace," which he had postponed at the end of his first letter. This was the origin of the letter now offered to the Publick.

[140] The greater part of this pamphlet was actually revised in print by the Author himself, but not in the exact order of the pages. He enlarged his first draft, and separated one great member of his subject for the purpose of introducing some other matter between. Two separate parcels of manuscript, designed to intervene, were found among his papers. One of them he seemed to have gone over himself, and to have improved and augmented. The other (fortunately the smaller) was much more imperfect, just as it was taken from his mouth by dictation. Of course it was necessary to use a more ample discretion in preparing that part for the press.

There is, however, still a very considerable member, or rather there are large fragments and pieces of a considerable member, to which the candour and indulgence of the Publick must be respectfully intreated. Mr. Burke had himself chalked out an accurate outline. There were loose papers found, containing a summary and conclusion of the whole. He had preserved some scattered hints, documents, and parts of a correspondence on the state of the country. He had been long anxiously waiting for some authentick and official information, which he wanted, to ascertain to the Publick, what with his usual sagacity he had fully anticipated from his own observation to his own conviction. When the first Reports of the Finance Committee of the House of Commons, and the Great Reports of the Secret Committee of both Houses, were procured and were printed, he read them with much avidity; but the Supreme Disposer of all, in his inscrutable counsels, did not permit the complete execution of the task which he meditated.

Under these circumstances his friends originally inclined to lop off altogether that member which he had left so lame and mutilated; but from a consideration how much the ultimate credit of all his opinions might possibly depend on that main branch of his question not being wholly suppressed, it was thought best that some use should be made of the important materials which he had so far in readiness. It was then conceived that it might in some degree answer the purpose, to draw out mere tables of figures, with short observations under each of them; and they were actually printed in that form. These would still however have remained an unseemly chasm, very incoherently and aukwardly filled. At length, therefore, it was resolved, after much hesitation, and under a very unpleasant responsibility, to make a humble attempt at supplying the void with some continued explanation and illustration of the documents, agreeably to Mr. Burke's own Sketch. In performing with reverential diffidence that duty of friendship, no one sentiment has been attributed to Mr. Burke, which is not most explicitly known, from repeated conversations and from correspondence, to have been entertained by that illustrious man. Some passages from his own private letters, and some from letters to him, which he was pleased to commend and to preserve, have been interwoven.

From what has been thus fairly submitted, it will be seen, that it is impossible to indicate every period or sentence in the latter part of this letter, which is, and which is not, from the hand of Mr. Burke. It would swell this advertisement to a long preface. In general, the style will too surely declare the author. Not only his friends, but his bitterest [141] enemies (if he now has any enemies) will agree, that he is not to be imitated: he is, as Cowley says, "a vast species alone."

The fourth Letter, which was originally designed for the first, has been found complete, as it was first written. The friends of the Author trust that they shall be able to present it to the Publick nearly as it came from his pen, with little more than some trifling alterations of temporary allusions to things now past, and in this eventful crisis already obsolete.

SECOND ADVERTISEMENT

In the Advertisement originally prefixed to this Publication, it was supposed that enough had been said to point out generally the only part of the Letter, in which any considerable additions had been made by another hand. The attention of the Reader was directed to the last member of it, especially to the arrangement and illustrations of the documents there inserted, as having been supplied agreeably to an outline marked out by Mr. Burke himself. Strange mistakes, however, have been committed by some of our Criticks in the Publick Prints.

One of them, wholly forgetting how large a proportion of the work was stated to have been given untouched to the Publick, and applying to the whole what was expressly limited to pieces and fragments of one considerable member, was pleased to represent the Advertisement as giving notice of "a manufactory for pamphlets under the *title* of Edmund Burke." A second more handsomely selected the supplement alone for observation, and gave it distinguished praise, as being written with all Mr. Burke's "depth of research." A third pronounced the Letter to be "evidently a work of shreds and patches," and then sagaciously produced, as perhaps "the most curious part" of the whole, what was in reality a shred from the most imperfect parcel of the authentick Manuscript; and he crowned all by speaking in the same handsome manner with the former, of the supplement, to which he ascribed Mr. Burke's "usual superiority." Some have levelled innocent pleasantries at a wrong mark, and others have bestowed commendation on detached sentiments and phrases, under the influence of similar errour. No deception of this kind was intended; but what has happened seems to indicate that some further explanation may be acceptable.

All the beginning, nearly down to the end of the fifty-sixth page * was revised in print by the illustrious Authour. What follows to the end of the seventy-fourth page,† is printed from a parcel of manuscript, which appeared to have been re-considered, and in part re-written. Very little alteration was made in those eighteen pages, except of a mere mechanical kind, in re-modelling two or three sentences, which, having been much interlined, were in consequence rather clogged and embarrassed in their movement; a sort of correction, which the Authour himself was accustomed to postpone, till he saw and read the proof-sheets. The succeeding twelve pages and a half, to the end of the paragraph in page eighty-seven,‡ are all that rest on the authority of the more imperfect [142] manuscript. The true order was ascertained by the circumstance, that full two pages at the beginning of the latter contained a rude and meagre draft of the same subject with the concluding pages of the former parcel; to the head of which it was necessary, on the other hand, to transfer a single short paragraph of six lines and a half, which is to be found in the fifty-sixth and fifty-seventh pages.§ In the more imperfect parcel, a blank was left in

---

* P. 234, l. 23, of the present Edition.

† P. 246, l. 10, of the present Edition.

‡ P. 251, l. 20, of the present Edition.

§ It begins p. 234, l. 24, of the present Edition.

the middle of one sentence, which was filled up from conjecture, and several other sentences were a little dilated and rounded, but without any change in the sentiment.

All the first part of the great member which follows, on the question of necessity, was revised in print by Mr. Burke, down to the middle of the hundred and tenth page.* The brilliancy and solidity of the oeconomical and moral philosophy, with which those pages abound, manifest at once the inimitable Authour. His Friends at first thought of supplying a short conclusion at the end of the hundred and second page,† but in addition to the reasons formerly mentioned, a desire to preserve the beautiful and truly philanthropick branch of the argument, which relates to the condition of the poor, induced the attempt to complete, what the great master had left unfinished.

It is the enquiry into the condition of the higher classes, which was principally meant to be submitted to the candour and indulgence of the Publick. The summary of the whole topick indeed, nearly as it stands in the hundred and sixty-first and hundred and sixty-second pages,‡ contains the substance of all the preceding details: and that, with a marginal reference to the bankrupt list, was found in Mr. Burke's own hand-writing. The censure of our defensive system, in page a hundred and fourteen§ and the two following pages, is taken from a letter, of which he never wrote more than the introduction. He intended to have comprised in it the short results of his opinions, when he despaired of living to proceed with his original plan; but he abandoned it, when his health for a short time seemed to improve, about two months before his death. The actual conclusion of the present Pamphlet is also from his dictation. But for some intermediate passages, which were indispensably requisite to connect and introduce these noble fragments, and for the execution of the details produced to prove the flourishing state of the higher classes, and the general prosperity of the country, his reputation is not responsible. The Publick have been already informed, with all humility, upon what ground they stand.

⁎ An errour of some magnitude has been discovered at the end of the note in page 123.‖ The money actually received into the Exche-

* P. 268, l. 21, of the present Edition.

† P. 262, l. 30, of the present Edition.

‡ Pp. 304 and 305 of the present Edition.

§ P. 270 of the present Edition.

‖ P. 277 of the present Edition.

quer on the new assessed takes of 1796 has been deducted instead of the gross assessment, which is £401,652; leaving still an increase of upwards of one fourth more than the whole increase of the preceding three years, notwithstanding so heavy an additional burthen.

[143] # LETTER III

[Argument

INTRODUCTION, pp. 198–214. Lord Malmesbury's mission to Paris having ended in failure and insult, the British Ministry, on Dec. 27, 1796, published a long Declaration explaining the circumstances, but expressing an intention to renew the negotiations whenever the Directory might see fit. Burke comments bitterly on the spirit shown by the Ministry (p. 203), and declares the Ministry and the Opposition to be equally wanting to the national dignity (p. 205). After characterising the Jacobin tone of the Opposition (p. 207), and comparing their action in the two cases of the imprisonment of Lafayette (p. 210) and of Sir Sydney Smith (p. 212), he proceeds to examine the Declaration itself.

PART I, pp. 214–34.

On the Declaration of Dec. 27, 1796

The natural and proper conclusion from the facts which it recites, p. 214. Contrast of this with the conclusion as it stands, p. 218. This conclusion for the first time assumed the French government to be a lawful one, leaving them, as it did, the initiative in future negotiations (p. 219), while on the very day of its issue a hostile French fleet was quitting the shelter of a British port, p. 220. Burke enquires, *What can have been the motive of the Ministry in making this un-English declaration* (p. 222)? (1) It is said to be "a pledge to Europe" (p. 224): but the absurdity of supposing that it can meet with the approval of Europe is shown by going through the nations of Europe *seriatim*. It must therefore be (2) a concession to some party at home (p. 232): and, after observing that the old Tory and Whig parties have been extinguished, leaving a Conservative and a Jacobin party in their stead, he concludes it to be a concession to the latter.

REGICIDE PEACE III

PART II, pp. 234-54

On the Futile Negotiations which preceded the Declaration.

1. The *futility of the negotiations* confessed in the Lords by Lord Auckland, and the embassy described as an *experiment*, p. 234. This degrading experiment not demanded by the country, but the sole work of the Ministry, to satisfy the leaders of the Jacobin [144] Opposition, p. 236. Proofs of this from Lord Auckland's Pamphlet, ministerial newspapers, &c. p. 238. The country disgraced by the negotiation (p. 240) in the person of the Ambassador (p. 241), and of the King himself (p. 242). 2. The *false basis chosen for the negotiations* ensured their failure, p. 243. The Ministry instructed Lord Malmesbury to abandon that great principle of the maintenance of a Balance of Power in Europe which England has always hitherto insisted on, p. 244. Proofs of this from the Treaties of Paris of 1783 and 1763, and the Treaty of Aix-la-Chapelle, p. 245. This principle now for the first time treated as obsolete, and France allowed to claim universal empire through the means of universal revolution, p. 247. Absurdity of the proposed principle of "mutual compensation," p. 249. As if Martinique, England's only conquest of any value to France, could be compared with the Netherlands, which is what England expected France to resign! (p. 249). Having learned from Lord Malmesbury the nature of the absurd settlement expected by England, the Directory most naturally declined it, and drove him from Paris, p. 252. Futility of further negotiations proved from the character of the Directory, and the absence of any public opinion in France, p. 253. The allegation that these humiliating negotiations were a "necessity" for England is now disproved in a third and concluding part.

PART III, pp. 254-304

On the Ability of England to maintain the War

Nothing remains but to prosecute the war vigorously: and the ability of England to do this is proved (1) by the readiness with which the open loan of £18,000,000 has been raised (p. 255). This indicates three facts: that England is perfectly *able* to maintain the Balance of Power, has *spirit* enough for the task, and *confidence* in the Ministry whose duty it is to execute it (p. 256). The principle of this loan jus-

LETTERS ON A REGICIDE PEACE

tified against its assailants (p. 256), and that of "patriotic contributions" refuted, p. 260. English resources proved (2) by the abundance of labour, p. 263, and the high wages it commands, p. 265. The high price of provisions produced by other causes than the war, p. 266. English resources proved (3) by the enthusiasm of the upper classes for the war, p. 268 (though this has not yet produced its due effect), and by their obvious material prosperity, p. 272, which is placed beyond a doubt by the three recent enquiries into the financial condition of the country before Committees of the House of Commons, p. 273, and by external evidence, p. 286. The accumulation of Capital [145] (contrary to the presages of ignorance, p. 287) proved by the increased number of Inclosure (p. 289) and Canal (p. 290) Acts, all attributable to the vitality of the landed interest, p. 291. The increase in the Post-Horse duty, and in the revenue of the Post Office (p. 293), the low average of Bankruptcies (p. 294), and the growth of retail trade, as shewn by the duties on Licences (p. 295), all point the same way: and the whole argument is crowned by the proofs of the prosperity of the Port of London (p. 298), and by the evidence of the Inspector-General, as given in the report of the Secret Committee of the House of Lords, drawn up by Lord Auckland himself, p. 301.

CONCLUSION, pp. 304–6.

DEAR SIR,

I THANK YOU FOR THE BUNDLE of State-papers, which I received yesterday. I have travelled through the Negotiation; and a sad, founderous road it is. There is a sort of standing jest against my countrymen, that one of them on his journey having found a piece of pleasant road, he proposed to his companion to go over it again. This proposal, with regard to the worthy traveller's final destination, was certainly a blunder. It was no blunder as to his immediate satisfaction; for the way was pleasant. In the irksome journey of the Regicide negotiations, it is otherwise: our "paths are not paths of pleasantness, nor our ways the ways to peace." All our mistakes (if such they are) like those of our Hibernian traveller, are mistakes of repetition; and they will be full as far from bringing us to our place of rest, as his well considered project was from forwarding him to his inn. Yet I see we persevere. Fatigued with our former course; too listless to explore a new one; kept in action by inertness; moving only because we have been in motion; with a sort of plodding perseverance, we resolve to measure back again the very same joyless, hopeless, and inglorious track. Backward [146] and forward; oscillation not progression; much going in a scanty space; the travels of a postillion, miles enough to circle the globe in one short stage; we have been, and we are yet to be jolted and rattled over the loose, misplaced stones, and the treacherous hollows, of this rough, ill kept, broken up, treacherous French causeway!

The Declaration, which brings up the rear of the papers laid before Parliament, contains a review and a reasoned summary of all our attempts, and all our failures; a concise but correct narrative of the painful steps taken to bring on the essay of a treaty at Paris; a clear exposure of all the rebuffs we received in the progress of that experiment; an honest confession of our departure from all the rules and all the principles of political negotiation, and of common prudence, in the conduct of it; and to crown the whole, a fair account of the atrocious manner in which the Regicide enemies had broken up what had been so inauspiciously begun and so feebly carried on, by finally, and with all scorn, driving our suppliant Ambassador out of the limits of their usurpation.

Even after all that I have lately seen, I was a little surprized at this exposure. A minute display of hopes formed without foundation, and of labours pursued without fruit, is a thing not very flattering to self-estimation. But truth has it's rights; and it will assert them. The Declaration, after doing all this with a mortifying candour, concludes the whole recapitulation with an engagement still more extraordinary than all the unusual matter it contains. It says, "That his Majesty, who had entered into this negotiation with *good faith*, who has suffered *no* impediment to prevent his prose, cuting it with *earnestness and sincerity*, has now *only to lament* it's abrupt termination, and to renew *in the face of all Europe the solemn declaration*, that whenever his enemies shall be *disposed* to enter upon the work of a general pacification in [147] a spirit of conciliation and equity, nothing shall be wanting on his part to contribute to the accomplishment of that great object."

If the disgusting detail of the accumulated insults we have received, in what we have very properly called our "solicitation," to a gang of felons and murderers, had been produced as a proof of the utter inefficacy of that mode of proceeding with that description of persons, I should have nothing at all to object to it. It might furnish matter conclusive in argument, and instructive in policy: but with all due submission to high authority, and with all decent deference to superiour lights, it does not seem quite clear to a discernment no better than mine, that the premises in that piece conduct irresistibly to the conclusion. A laboured display of the ill consequences which have attended an uniform course of submission to every mode of contumelious insult, with which the despotism of a proud, capricious, insulting and implacable foe has chosen to buffet our patience, does not appear, to my poor thoughts, to be properly brought forth as a preliminary to justify a resolution of persevering in the very same kind of conduct, towards the very same sort of person, and on the very same principles. We state our experience, and then we come to the manly resolution of acting in contradiction to it. All that has passed at Paris, to the moment of our being shamefully hissed off that stage, has been nothing but a more solemn representation, on the theatre of the nation, of what had been before in rehearsal at Basle. As it is not only confessed by us, but made a matter of charge on the enemy, that he had given us no encouragement to believe there was a change in his disposition, or in his policy at any time subsequent to the period of his rejecting our first overtures, there seems to have been no assignable motive for sending Lord Malmesbury to Paris, except to expose his humbled country to the worst indignities and [148] the first of the kind, as the Declaration very truly observes, that have been known in the world of negotiation.

An honest neighbour of mine is not altogether unhappy in the application of an old common story to a present occasion. It may be said of my friend, what Horace says of a neighbour of his, "*garrit aniles ex re fabellas.*" Conversing on this strange subject, he told me a current story of a simple English country 'Squire, who was persuaded by certain *dilettanti* of his acquaintance to see the world, and to become knowing in men and manners. Among other celebrated places, it was recommended to him to visit Constantinople. He took their advice. After various adventures, not to our purpose to dwell upon, he happily arrived at that famous city. As soon as he had a little reposed himself from his fatigue, he took a walk into the streets; but he had not gone far, before a "malignant and a turban'd Turk" had his choler roused by the careless and assured air with which this infidel strutted about in the metropolis of true believers. In this temper, he lost no time in doing to our traveller the honours of the place. The Turk crossed over the way, and with perfect good-will gave him two or three lusty kicks on the seat of honour. To resent, or to return the compliment in Turkey, was quite out of the question. Our traveller, since he could not otherwise acknowledge this kind of favour, received it with the best grace in the world—he made one of his most ceremonious bows, and begged the kicking Mussulman "to accept his perfect assurances of high consideration." Our countryman was too wise to imitate Othello in the use of the dagger. He thought it better, as better it was, to assuage his bruised dignity with half a yard square of balmy diplomatick diachylon. In the disasters of their friends, people are seldom wanting in a laudable patience. When they are such as do not threaten to end fatally, they become even matter of pleasantry. The English [149] fellow-travellers of our sufferer, finding him a little out of spirits, entreated him not to take so slight a business so very seriously. They told him it was the custom of the country; that every country had its customs; that the Turkish manners were a little rough; but that in the main the Turks were a good-natured people; that what would have been a deadly affront any where else, was only a little freedom there; in short, they told him to think no more of the matter, and to try his fortune in another *promenade*. But the 'Squire, though a little clownish, had some homebred sense. What! have I come, at all this expence and trouble, all the way to Constantinople only to be kicked? Without going beyond my own stable, my groom, for half a crown, would have kicked me to my heart's content. I don't mean to stay in Constantinople eight and forty hours, nor ever to return to this rough, good-natured people, that have their own customs.

In my opinion the 'Squire was in the right. He was satisfied with his first ramble and his first injuries. But reason of state and common-sense are two things. If it were not for this difference, it might not appear of absolute necessity, after having received a certain quantity of buffetings by advance, that we should send a Peer of the realm to the scum of the earth, to collect the debt to the last farthing; and to receive, with infinite aggravation, the same scorns which had been paid to our supplication through a Commoner. But it was proper, I suppose, that the whole of our country, in all its orders, should have a share of the indignity; and, as in reason, that the higher orders should touch the larger proportion.

This business was not ended, because our dignity was wounded, or because our patience was worn out with contumely and scorn. We had not disgorged one particle of the nauseous doses with which we were so liberally crammed [150] by the mountebanks of Paris, in order to drug and diet us into perfect tameness. No; we waited, till the morbid strength of our *boulimia* for their physick had exhausted the well-stored dispensary of their empiricism. It is impossible to guess at the term to which our forbearance would have extended. The Regicides were more fatigued with giving blows than the callous cheek of British Diplomacy was hurt in receiving them. They had no way left for getting rid of this mendicant perseverance, but by sending for the Beadle, and forcibly driving our Embassy "of shreds and patches," with all it's mumping cant, from the inhospitable door of Cannibal Castle—

Where the gaunt mastiff, growling at the gate,
Affrights the beggar whom he longs to eat.

I think we might have found, before the rude hand of insolent office was on our shoulder, and the staff of usurped authority brandished over our heads, that contempt of the suppliant is not the best forwarder of a suit; that national disgrace is not the high road to security, much less to power and greatness. Patience, indeed, strongly indicates the love of peace. But mere love does not always lead to enjoyment. It is the power of winning that palm which insures our wearing it. Virtues have their place; and out of their place they hardly deserve the name. They pass into the neighbouring vice. The patience of fortitude, and the endurance of pusillanimity, are things very different, as in their principle, so in their effects.

IN TRUTH THIS DECLARATION, containing a narrative of the first transaction of the kind (and I hope it will be the last) in the intercourse of nations, as a composition, is ably drawn. It does credit to our official style. The report of the Speech of the Minister in a great Assembly, which I have read, is a [151] comment upon the Declaration. Without enquiry how far that report is exact, (inferior I believe it may be to what it would represent,) yet still it reads as a most eloquent and finished performance. Hardly one galling circumstance of the indignities offered by the Directory of Regicide, to the supplications made to that junto in his Majesty's name, has been spared. Every one of the aggravations attendant on these acts of outrage is, with wonderful perspicuity and order, brought forward in it's place, and in the manner most fitted to produce it's effect. They are turned to every point of view in which they can be seen to the best advantage. All the parts are so arranged as to point out their relation, and to furnish a true idea of the spirit of the whole transaction.

This Speech may stand for a model. Never, for the triumphal decoration of any theatre, not for the decoration of those of Athens and Rome, or even of this theatre of Paris, from the embroideries of Babylon or from the loom of the Gobelins, has there been sent any historick tissue so truly drawn, so closely and so finely wrought, or in which the forms are brought out in the rich purple of such glowing and blushing colours. It puts me in mind of the piece of tapestry, with which Virgil proposed to adorn the theatre he was to erect to Augustus, upon the banks of the Mincio, who now hides his head in his reeds, and leads his slow and melancholy windings through banks wasted by the barbarians of Gaul. He supposes that the artifice is such, that the figures of the conquered nations in his tapestry are made to play their part, and are confounded in the machine:

> Utque
> Purpurea intexti tollant aulaea Britanni;

Or as Dryden translates it somewhat paraphrastically, but not less in the spirit of the Prophet than of the Poet,

[152] Where the proud theatres disclose the scene,
Which, interwoven, Britons seem to raise,
And show the triumph which their shame displays.

It is something wonderful, that the sagacity shown in the Declaration and the Speech (and, so far as it goes, greater was never shown) should have failed to discover to the writer and to the speaker the inseparable relation between the parties to this transaction; and that nothing can be said to display the imperious arrogance of a base enemy, which does not describe with equal force and equal truth the contemptible figure of an abject embassy to that imperious Power.

IT IS NO LESS STRIKING, that the same obvious reflexion should not occur to those gentlemen who conducted the opposition to Government. But their thoughts were turned another way. They seem to have been so entirely occupied with the defence of the French Directory, so very eager in finding recriminatory precedents to justify every act of it's intolerable insolence, so animated in their accusations of Ministry for not having, at the very outset, made concessions proportioned to the dignity of the great victorious Power we had offended, that every thing concerning the sacrifice in this business of national honour, and of the most fundamental principles in the policy of negotiation, seemed wholly to have escaped them. To this fatal hour, the contention in Parliament appeared in another form, and was animated by another spirit. For three hundred years and more, we have had wars with what stood as Government in France. In all that period the language of Ministers, whether of boast or of apology, was, that they had left nothing undone for the assertion of the national honour; the Opposition, whether patriotically or factiously, contending that the Ministers had been oblivious of the national glory, and had made improper sacrifices of that publick interest, which they were [153] bound not only to preserve, but by all fair methods to augment. This total change of tone on both sides of your house, forms itself no inconsiderable revolution; and I am afraid it prognosticates others of still greater importance. The Ministers exhausted the stores of their eloquence in demonstrating, that they had quitted the safe, beaten high-way of treaty between independent Powers; that to pacify the enemy they had made every sacrifice of the national dignity; and that they had offered to immolate at the same shrine the most valuable of the national acquisitions. The Opposition insisted, that the victims were not fat nor fair enough to be offered on the altars of blasphemed Regicide; and it was inferred from thence, that the sacrifical ministers, (who were a sort of intruders in the worship of the new divinity) in their schismatical devotion, had discovered more of hypocrisy than zeal. They charged them with a concealed resolution to persevere in what these gentlemen have (in perfect consistency, indeed, with themselves, but most irreconcileably with fact and reason) called an unjust and impolitick war.

That day was, I fear, the fatal term of *local* patriotism. On that day, I fear, there was an end of that narrow scheme of relations called our country, with all it's pride, it's prejudices, and it's partial affections. All the little quiet rivulets that watered an humble, a contracted, but not an unfruitful field, are to be lost in the waste expanse, and boundless, barren ocean of the homicide philanthropy of France. It is no longer an object of terror, the aggrandizement of a new power, which teaches as a professor that philanthropy in the chair; whilst it propagates by arms, and establishes by conquest, the comprehensive system of universal fraternity. In what light is all this viewed in a great assembly? The party which takes the lead there has no longer any apprehensions, except those that arise [154] from not being admitted to the closest and most confidential connexions with the metropolis of that fraternity. That reigning party no longer touches on it's favourite subject, the display of those horrours that must attend the existence of a power, with such dispositions and principles, seated in the heart of Europe. It is satisfied to find some loose, ambiguous expressions in it's former declarations, which may set it free from it's professions and engagements. It always speaks of peace with the Regicides as a great and an undoubted blessing; and such a blessing, as if obtained, promises, as much as any human disposition of things can promise, security and permanence. It holds out nothing at all definite towards this security. It only seeks, by a restoration, to some of their former owners, of some fragments of the general wreck of Europe, to find a plausible plea for a present retreat from an embarrassing position. As to the future, that party is content to leave it covered in a night of the most palpable obscurity. It never once has entered into a particle of detail of what our own situation, or that of other powers must be, under the blessings of the peace we seek. This defect, to my power, I mean to supply; that if any persons should still continue to think an attempt at foresight is any part of the duty of a Statesman, I may contribute my trifle to the materials of his speculation.

As to the other party, the minority of to-day, possibly the majority of to-morrow, small in number, but full of talents and every species of energy, which, upon the avowed ground of being more acceptable to France, is a candidate for the helm of this kingdom, it has never changed from the beginning. It has preserved a perennial consistency. This would be a never-failing source of true glory, if springing from just and right; but it is truly dreadful if it be an arm of Styx, which springs out of the profoundest [155] depths of a poisoned soil. The French maxims were by these gentlemen at no time condemned. I speak of their language in the most moderate terms. There are many who think that they have gone much further; that they have always magnified and extolled the French maxims; that not in the least disgusted or discouraged by the monstrous evils, which have attended these maxims from the moment of their adoption, both at home and abroad, they still continue to predict, that in due time they must produce the greatest good to the poor human race. They obstinately persist in stating those evils as matter of accident; as things wholly collateral to the system.

It is observed, that this party has never spoken of an ally

of Great Britain with the smallest degree of respect or regard; on the contrary, it has generally mentioned them under opprobrious appellations, and in such terms of contempt or execration, as never had been heard before, because no such would have formerly been permitted in our public assemblies. The moment, however, that any of those allies quitted this obnoxious connexion, the party has instantly passed an act of indemnity and oblivion in their favour. After this, no sort of censure on their conduct; no imputation on their character! From that moment their pardon was sealed in a reverential and mysterious silence. With the Gentlemen of this minority, there is no ally, from one end of Europe to the other, with whom we ought not to be ashamed to act. The whole College of the States of Europe is no better than a gang of tyrants. With them all our connexions were broken off at once. We ought to have cultivated France, and France alone, from the moment of her Revolution. On that happy change, all our dread of that nation as a power was to cease. She became in an instant dear to our affections, and one with our interests. All other nations we ought to have commanded not to trouble her sacred [156] throes, whilst in labour to bring into an happy birth her abundant litter of constitutions. We ought to have acted under her auspices, in extending her salutary influence upon every side. From that moment England and France were become natural allies, and all the other States natural enemies. The whole face of the world was changed. What was it to us if she acquired Holland and the Austrian Netherlands? By her conquests she only enlarged the sphere of her beneficence; she only extended the blessings of liberty to so many more foolishly reluctant nations. What was it to England, if by adding these, among the richest and most peopled countries of the world, to her territories, she thereby left no possible link of communication between us and any other Power with whom we could act against her? On this new system of optimism, it is so much the better—so much the further are we removed from the contact with infectious despotism. No longer a thought of a barrier in the Netherlands to Holland against France. All that is obsolete policy. It is fit that France should have both Holland and the Austrian Netherlands too, as a barrier to her against the attacks of despotism. She cannot multiply her securities too much; and as to our security, it is to be found in her's. Had we cherished her from the beginning, and felt for her when attacked, she, poor good soul, would never have invaded any foreign nation; never have murdered her Sovereign and his family; never proscribed, never exiled, never imprisoned, never been guilty of extrajudicial massacre, or of legal murder. All would have been a golden age, full of peace, order, and liberty! and philosophy, raying out from Europe, would have warmed and enlightened the universe: but unluckily, irritable philosophy, the most irritable of all things, was put into a passion, and provoked into ambition abroad and tyranny at home. They find all this very natural and very justifiable. They [157] chuse to forget, that other nations struggling for freedom, have been attacked by their neighbours; or that their neighbours have otherwise interfered in their affairs. Often have neighbours interfered in favour of Princes against their rebellious subjects; and often in favour of subjects against their Prince. Such cases fill half the pages of history, yet never were they used as an apology, much less as a justification, for atrocious cruelty in Princes, or for general massacre and confiscation on the part of revolted subjects; never as a politick cause for suffering any such powers to aggrandize themselves without limit and without measure. A thousand times have we seen it asserted in publick prints and pamphlets, that if the nobility and priesthood of France had staid at home, their property never would have been confiscated. One would think that none of the clergy had been robbed previous to their deportation, or that their deportation had, on their part, been a voluntary act. One would think that the nobility and gentry, and merchants and bankers, who staid at home, had enjoyed their property in security and repose. The assertors of these positions well know, that the lot of thousands who remained at home was far more terrible; that the most cruel imprisonment was only a harbinger of a cruel and ignominious death; and that in this mother country of freedom, there were no less than *Three Hundred Thousand* at one time in prison. I go no further. I instance only these representations of the party as staring indications of partiality to that sect, to whose dominion they would have left this country nothing to oppose but her own naked force, and consequently subjected us, on every reverse of fortune, to the imminent danger of falling under those very evils in that very system, which are attributed, not to it's own nature, but to the perverseness of others. There is nothing in the world so difficult as to put [158] men in a state of judicial neutrality. A leaning there must ever be, and it is of the first importance to any nation to observe to what side that leaning inclines—whether to our own community, or to one with which it is in a state of hostility.

MEN ARE RARELY without some sympathy in the sufferings of others; but in the immense and diversified mass of human misery, which may be pitied, but cannot be relieved, in the gross, the mind must make a choice. Our sympathy is always more forcibly attracted towards the misfortunes of certain persons, and in certain descriptions: and this sympathetic attraction discovers, beyond a possibility of mistake, our mental affinities, and elective affections. It is a much surer proof, than the strongest declaration, of a real connexion and of an over-ruling bias in the mind. I am told that the active sympathies of this party have been chiefly, if not wholly attracted to the sufferings of the patriarchal rebels, who were amongst the promulgators of the maxims of the French Revolution, and who have suffered, from their apt and forward scholars, some part of the evils, which they had themselves so liberally distributed to all the other parts of the community. Some of these men, flying from the knives which they had sharpened against their country and it's laws, rebelling against the very powers they had set over themselves by their rebellion against their Sovereign, given up by those very armies to whose faithful attachment they trusted for their safety and support, after they had compleatly debauched all military fidelity in it's source—some of these men, I say, had fallen into the hands of the head of that family, the most illustrious person of which they had three times cruelly imprisoned, and delivered in that state of captivity to those hands, from which they were able to relieve, neither her, nor their own nearest and most venerable kindred. One of these men connected with [159] this country by no circumstance of birth; not related to any distinguished families here; recommended by no service; endeared to this nation by no act or even expression of kindness; comprehended in no league or common cause; embraced by no laws of publick hospitality; this man was the only one to be found in Europe, in whose favour the British nation, passing judgment, without hearing, on it's almost only ally, was to force, (and that not by soothing interposition, but with every reproach for inhumanity, cruelty, and breach of the laws of war,) from prison. We were to release him from that prison out of which, in abuse of the lenity of Government amidst it's rigour, and in violation of at least an understood parole, he had attempted an escape; an escape excuseable if you will, but naturally productive of strict and vigilant confinement. The earnestness of gentlemen to free this person was the more extraordinary, because there was full as little in him to raise admiration, from any eminent qualities he possessed, as there was to excite an interest, from any that were amiable. A person, not only of no real civil or literary talents, but of no specious appearance of either; and in his military profession, not marked as a leader in any one act of able or successful enterprize—unless his leading on (or his following) the allied army of Amazonian and male cannibal Parisians to Versailles, on the famous fifth of October, 1789, is to make his glory. Any other exploit of his, as a General, I never heard of. But the triumph of general fraternity was but the more signalized by the total want of particular claims in that case; and by postponing all such claims, in a case where they really existed, where they stood embossed, and in a manner forced themselves on the view of common short-sighted benevolence. Whilst, for its improvement, the humanity of these gentlemen was thus on it's travels, and had got as far off as Olmutz, they never thought of a place and a [160] person much nearer to them, or of moving an instruction to Lord Malmesbury in favour of their own suffering countryman, Sir Sydney Smith.

This officer, having attempted, with great gallantry, to cut out a vessel from one of the enemy's harbours, was taken after an obstinate resistance; such as obtained him the marked respect of those who were witnesses of his valour, and knew the circumstances in which it was displayed. Upon his arrival at Paris, he was instantly thrown into prison; where the nature of his situation will best be understood, by knowing, that amongst its *mitigations,* was the permission to walk occasionally in the court, and to enjoy the privilege of shaving himself. On the old system of feelings and principles, his sufferings might have been entitled to consideration, and even in a comparison with those of Citizen la Fayette, to a priority in the order of compassion. If the Ministers had neglected to take any steps in his favour, a declaration of the sense of the House of Commons would have stimulated them to their duty. If they had caused a representation to be made, such a proceeding would have added force to it. If reprisal should be thought adviseable, the address of the House would have given an additional sanction to a measure, which would have been, indeed, justifiable without any other sanction than it's

own reason. But no. Nothing at all like it. In fact, the merit of
Sir Sydney Smith, and his claim on British compassion, was
of a kind altogether different from that which interested so
deeply the authors of the motion in favour of Citizen la Fayette. In my humble opinion, Captain Sir Sydney Smith has
another sort of merit with the British nation, and something
of a higher claim on British humanity than Citizen de la Fayette. Faithful, zealous, and ardent in the service of his King
and Country; full of spirit; full of resources; going [161] out
of the beaten road, but going right, because his uncommon
enterprize was not conducted by a vulgar judgment—in his
profession, Sir Sydney Smith might be considered as a distinguished person, if any person could well be distinguished in
a service in which scarce a Commander can be named without putting you in mind of some action of intrepidity, skill,
and vigilance, that has given them a fair title to contend with
any men and in any age. But I will say nothing farther of the
merits of Sir Sydney Smith. The mortal animosity of the Regicide enemy supersedes all other panegyrick. Their hatred is
a judgment in his favour without appeal. At present he is
lodged in the tower of the Temple, the last prison of Louis the
Sixteenth, and the last but one of Maria Antonietta of Austria; the prison of Louis the Seventeenth; the prison of Elizabeth of Bourbon. There he lies, unpitied by the grand philanthropy, to meditate upon the fate of those who are faithful to
their King and Country. Whilst this prisoner, secluded from
intercourse, was indulging in these cheering reflections, he
might possibly have had the further consolation of learning
(by means of the insolent exultation of his guards) that there
was an English Ambassador at Paris; he might have had the
proud comfort of hearing, that this Ambassador had the honour of passing his mornings in respectful attendance at the
office of a Regicide pettifogger; and that in the evening he
relaxed in the amusements of the opera, and in the spectacle
of an audience totally new; an audience in which he had the
pleasure of seeing about him not a single face that he could

formerly have known in Paris; but in the place of that company, one indeed more than equal to it in display of gaiety, splendour and luxury; a set of abandoned wretches, squandering in insolent riot the spoils of their bleeding country. A subject of profound reflection both to the prisoner and to the Ambassador.

[162] Whether all the matter upon which I have grounded my opinion of this last party be fully authenticated or not, must be left to those who have had the opportunity of a nearer view of it's conduct, and who have been more attentive in their perusal of the writings, which have appeared in it's favour. But for my part, I have never heard the gross facts on which I ground my idea of their marked partiality to the reigning Tyranny in France, in any part, denied. I am not surprized at all this. Opinions, as they sometimes follow, so they frequently guide and direct the affections; and men may become more attached to the country of their principles, than to the country of their birth. What I have stated here is only to mark the spirit which seems to me, though in somewhat different ways, to actuate our great party-leaders; and to trace this first pattern of a negotiation to it's true source.

Such is the present state of our publick councils. Well might I be ashamed of what seems to be a censure of two great factions, with the two most eloquent men, which this country ever saw, at the head of them, if I had found that either of them could support their conduct by any example in the history of their country. I should very much prefer their judgment to my own, if I were not obliged, by an infinitely overbalancing weight of authority, to prefer the collected wisdom of ages to the abilities of any two men living. I return to the Declaration, with which the history of the abortion of a treaty with the Regicides is closed.

AFTER SUCH AN ELABORATE DISPLAY had been made of the injustice and insolence of an enemy, who seems to have been irritated by every one of the means which had been commonly used with effect to soothe the rage of intemperate power, the natural result would be, that the scabbard, in which we in vain attempted to plunge our sword, should [163] have been thrown away with scorn. It would have been natural, that, rising in the fulness of their might, insulted majesty, despised dignity, violated justice, rejected supplication, patience goaded into fury, would have poured out all the length of the reins upon all the wrath which they had so long restrained. It might have been expected, that, emulous of the glory of the youthful hero[1] in alliance with him, touched by the example of what one man, well formed and well placed, may do in the most desperate state of affairs, convinced there is a courage of the Cabinet full as powerful, and far less vulgar than that of the field, our Minister would have changed the whole line of that unprosperous prudence, which hitherto had produced all the effects of the blindest temerity. If he found his situation full of danger, (and I do not deny that it is perilous in the extreme) he must feel that it is also full of glory; and that he is placed on a stage, than which no Muse of fire that had ascended the highest heaven of invention, could imagine any thing more awful and august. It was hoped, that in this swelling scene, in which he moved with some of the first Potentates of Europe for his fellow actors, and with so many of the rest for the anxious spectators of a part, which, as he plays it, determines for ever their destiny and his own, like Ulysses, in the unravelling point of the epic story, he would have thrown off his patience and his rags together; and stripped of unworthy disguises, he would have stood forth in the form, and in the attitude of an hero. On that day, it was thought he would have assumed the port of Mars; that he would bid to be brought forth from their hideous kennel (where his scrupulous tenderness had too long immured

1. The Archduke Charles of Austria.

them) those impatient dogs of war, whose fierce regards affright even the Minister of Vengeance that feeds them; that he would let them loose, in famine, fever, plagues, [164] and death, upon a guilty race, to whose frame, and to all whose habit, order, peace, religion, and virtue, are alien and abhorrent. It was expected that he would at last have thought of active and effectual war; that he would no longer amuse the British Lion in the chace of mice and rats; that he would no longer employ the whole naval power of Great Britain, once the terrour of the world, to prey upon the miserable remains of a pedling commerce, which the enemy did not regard, and from which none could profit. It was expected that he would have re-asserted the justice of his cause; that he would have re-animated whatever remained to him of his allies, and endeavoured to recover those whom their fears had led astray; that he would have re-kindled the martial ardour of his citizens; that he would have held out to them the example of their ancestry, the assertor of Europe, and the scourge of French ambition; that he would have reminded them of a posterity, which if this nefarious robbery, under the fraudulent name and false colour of a government, should in full power be seated in the heart of Europe, must for ever be consigned to vice, impiety, barbarism, and the most ignominious slavery of body and mind. In so holy a cause it was presumed, that he would, (as in the beginning of the war he did) have opened all the temples; and with prayer, with fasting, and with supplication, better directed than to the grim Moloch of Regicide in France, have called upon us to raise that united cry, which has so often stormed Heaven, and with a pious violence forced down blessings upon a repentant people. It was hoped that when he had invoked upon his endeavours the favourable regard of the Protector of the human race, it would be seen that his menaces to the enemy, and his prayers to the Almighty, were, not followed, but accompanied, with correspondent action. It was hoped that his shrilling trumpet should be heard, not to announce a shew, but to sound a charge.

[165] Such a conclusion to such a Declaration and such a Speech, would have been a thing of course; so much a thing of course, that I will be bold to say, if in any ancient history, the Roman for instance, (supposing that in Rome the matter of such a detail could have been furnished) a Consul had gone through such a long train of proceedings, and that there was a chasm in the manuscripts by which we had lost the conclusion of the speech and the subsequent part of the narrative, all criticks would agree, that a *Freinshemius* would have been thought to have managed the supplementary business of a continuator most unskilfully, and to have supplied the hiatus most improbably, if he had not filled up the gaping space, in a manner somewhat similar (though better executed) to what I have imagined. But too often different is rational conjecture from melancholy fact. This exordium, as contrary to all the rules of rhetorick, as to those more essential rules of policy which our situation would dictate, is intended as a prelude to a deadening and disheartening proposition; as if all that a Minister had to fear in a war of his own conducting, was, that the people should pursue it with too ardent a zeal. Such a tone as I guessed the Minister would have taken, I am very sure, is the true, unsuborned, unsophisticated language of genuine natural feeling under the smart of patience exhausted and abused. Such a conduct as the facts stated in the Declaration gave room to expect, is that which true wisdom would have dictated under the impression of those genuine feelings. Never was there a jar or discord, between genuine sentiment and sound policy. Never, no, never, did Nature say one thing and Wisdom say another. Nor are sentiments of elevation in themselves turgid and unnatural. Nature is never more truly herself, than in her grandest forms. The Apollo of Belvedere (if the universal robber has yet left him at Belvedere) is as much in Nature, as any figure from [166] the pencil of Rembrandt, or any clown in the rustic revels of Teniers. Indeed it is when a great nation is in great difficulties, that minds must exalt themselves to

the occasion, or all is lost. Strong passion under the direction of a feeble reason feeds a low fever, which serves only to destroy the body that entertains it. But vehement passion does not always indicate an infirm judgment. It often accompanies, and actuates, and is even auxiliary to a powerful understanding; and when they both conspire and act harmoniously, their force is great to destroy disorder within, and to repel injury from abroad. If ever there was a time that calls on us for no vulgar conception of things, and for exertions in no vulgar strain, it is the awful hour that Providence has now appointed to this nation. Every little measure is a great errour; and every great errour will bring on no small ruin. Nothing can be directed above the mark that we must aim at. Every thing below it is absolutely thrown away.

EXCEPT WITH THE ADDITION of the unheard-of insult offered to our Ambassador by his rude expulsion, we are never to forget that the point on which the negotiation with De la Croix broke off, was exactly that which had stifled in it's cradle the negotiation we had attempted with Barthélémy. Each of these transactions concluded with a manifesto upon our part: but the last of our manifestoes very materially differed from the first. The first Declaration stated, that "*nothing was left* but to prosecute a war *equally just and necessary.*" In the second, the justice and necessity of the war is dropped: The sentence importing that nothing was left but the prosecution of such a war, disappears also. Instead of this resolution to prosecute the war, we sink into a whining lamentation on the abrupt termination of the treaty. We have nothing left but the last resource of female weakness, [167] of helpless infancy, of doting decrepitude—wailing and lamentation. We cannot even utter a sentiment of vigour. "His Majesty has only to lament." A poor possession, to be left to a great Monarch! Mark the effect produced on our councils by continued insolence, and inveterate hostility. We grow more malleable under their blows. In reverential silence, we smother the cause and origin of the war. On that fundamental article of faith, we leave every one to abound in his own sense. In the Minister's speech, glossing on the Declaration, it is indeed mentioned; but very feebly. The lines are so faintly drawn as hardly to be traced. They only make a part of our *consolation* in the circumstances which we so dolefully lament. We rest our merits on the humility, the earnestness of solicitation, and the perfect good faith of those submissions, which have been used to persuade our Regicide enemies to grant us some sort of peace. Not a word is said, which might not have been full as well said, and much better too, if the British nation had appeared in the simple character of a penitent convinced of his errours and offences, and offering, by penances, by pilgrimages, and by all the modes of expiation ever devised by anxious, restless guilt, to make all the atonement in his miserable power.

THE DECLARATION ENDS as I have before quoted it, with a solemn voluntary pledge, the most full and the most solemn that ever was given, of our resolution (if so it may be called) to enter again into the very same course. It requires nothing more of the Regicides, than to furnish some sort of excuse, some sort of colourable pretext, for our renewing the supplications of innocence at the feet of guilt. It leaves the moment of negotiation, (a most important moment,) to the choice of the enemy. He is to regulate it according to the convenience of his affairs. He is to bring it forward at that [168] time when it may best serve to establish his authority at home, and to extend his power abroad. A dangerous assurance for this nation to give, whether it is broken or whether it is kept. As all treaty was broken off, and broken off in the manner we have seen, the field of future conduct ought to be reserved free and unincumbered to our future discretion. As to the sort of condition prefixed to the pledge, namely, "that the enemy should be disposed to enter into the work of general pacification with the spirit of reconciliation and equity," this phraseology cannot possibly be considered otherwise than as so many words thrown in to fill the sentence, and to round it to the ear. We prefixed the same plausible conditions to any renewal of the negotiation, in our manifesto on the rejection of our proposals at Basle. We did not consider those conditions as binding. We opened a much more serious negotiation without any sort of regard to them; and there is no new negotiation, which we can possibly open upon fewer indications of conciliation and equity, than were to be discovered, when we entered into our last at Paris. Any of the slightest pretences, any of the most loose, formal, equivocating expressions, would justify us, under the peroration of this piece, in again sending the last, or some other Lord Malmesbury to Paris.

I hope I misunderstand this pledge; or, that we shall shew no more regard to it, than we have done to all the faith that we have plighted to vigour and resolution in our former declaration. If I am to understand the conclusion of the declaration to be what unfortunately it seems to me, we make an engagement with the enemy, without any correspondent engagement on his side. We seem to have cut ourselves off from any benefit which an intermediate state of things might furnish to enable us totally to overturn that power, so little connected with moderation and justice. By holding out no hope, either to the justly discontented in [169] France, or to any foreign power, and leaving the re-commencement of all treaty to this identical junto of assassins, we do in effect assure and guarantee to them the full possession of the rich fruits of their confiscations, of their murders of men, women, and children, and of all the multiplied, endless, nameless iniquities by which they have obtained their power. We guarantee to them the possession of a country, such and so situated as France, round, entire, immensely perhaps augmented.

WELL! SOME WILL SAY, in this case we have only submitted to the nature of things. The nature of things is, I admit, a sturdy adversary. This might be alleged as a plea for our attempt at a treaty. But what plea of that kind can be alleged, after the treaty was dead and gone, in favour of this posthumous declaration? No necessity has driven us to *that* pledge. It is without a counterpart even in expectation. And what can be stated to obviate the evil which that solitary engagement must produce on the understandings or the fears of men? I ask, what have the Regicides promised you in return, in case *you* should shew what *they* would call dispositions to conciliation and equity, whilst you are giving that pledge from the throne, and engaging Parliament to counter-secure it? It is an awful consideration. It was on the very day of the date of this wonderful pledge,* in which we assumed the directorial Government as lawful, and in which we engaged ourselves to treat with them whenever they pleased; it was on that very day, the Regicide fleet was weighing anchor from one of your harbours, where it had remained four days in perfect quiet. These harbours of the British dominions are the ports of France. They are of no use, but to protect an enemy from your best Allies, [170] the storms of Heaven, and his own rashness. Had the West of Ireland been an unportuous coast, the French naval power would have been undone. The enemy uses the moment for hostility, without the least regard to your future dispositions of equity and conciliation. They go out of what were once your harbours, and they return to them at their pleasure. Eleven days they had the full use of Bantry Bay, and at length their fleet returns from their harbour of Bantry to their harbour of Brest. Whilst you are invoking the propitious spirit of Regicide equity and conciliation, they answer you with an attack. They turn out the pacifick bearer of your "how-do-you-do's," Lord Malmesbury; and they return your visit, and their "thanks for your obliging enquiries," by their old practised assassin *Hoche.* They come to attack—What? A town, a fort, a naval station? They

* Dec. 27, 1796.

come to attack your King, your Constitution, and the very being of that Parliament, which was holding out to them these pledges, together with the entireness of the Empire, the Laws, Liberties, and Properties of all the people. We know that they meditated the very same invasion, and for the very same purposes, upon this Kingdom; and had the coast been as opportune, would have effected it.

Whilst *you* are in vain torturing your invention to assure them of *your* sincerity and good faith, they have left no doubt concerning *their* good faith, and *their* sincerity towards those to whom they have engaged their honour. To their power they have been true to the only pledge they have ever yet given to you, or to any of yours; I mean the solemn engagement which they entered into with the deputation of traitors who appeared at their bar, from England and from Ireland, in 1792. They have been true and faithful to the engagement which they had made more largely; that is, their engagement to give effectual aid to insurrection and treason, wherever they might appear in the world. We have [171] seen the British Declaration. This is the counter-declaration of the Directory. This is the reciprocal pledge which Regicide amity gives to the conciliatory pledges of Kings! But, thank God, such pledges cannot exist single. They have no counterpart; and if they had, the enemy's conduct cancels such declarations; and I trust, along with them, cancels every thing of mischief and dishonour that they contain.

THERE IS ONE THING in this business which appears to be wholly unaccountable, or accountable on a supposition I dare not entertain for a moment. I cannot help asking, Why all this pains to clear the British Nation of ambition, perfidy, and the insatiate thirst of war? At what period of time was it that our country has deserved that load of infamy, of which nothing but preternatural humiliation in language and conduct can serve to clear us? If we have deserved this kind of evil fame from any thing we have done in a state of prosperity, I am sure, that it is not an abject conduct in adversity that can clear our reputation. Well is it known that ambition can creep as well as soar. The pride of no person in a flourishing condition is more justly to be dreaded, than that of him who is mean and cringing under a doubtful and unprosperous fortune. But it seems it was thought necessary to give some out-of-the-way proofs of our sincerity, as well as of our freedom from ambition. Is then fraud and falsehood become the distinctive character of Englishmen? Whenever your enemy chooses to accuse you of perfidy and ill faith, will you put it into his power to throw you into the purgatory of self-humiliation? Is his charge equal to the finding of the grand jury of Europe, and sufficient to put you upon your trial? But on that trial I will defend the English Ministry. I am sorry that on some points I have, on the principles I have always opposed, so good a defence [172] to make. They were not the first to begin the war. They did not excite the general confederacy in Europe, which was so properly formed on the alarm given by the Jacobinism of France. They did not begin with an hostile aggression on the Regicides or any of their allies. These parricides of their own country, disciplining themselves for foreign by domestick violence, were the first to attack a power that was our ally, by nature, by habit, and by the sanction of multiplied treaties. Is it not true, that they were the first to declare war upon this kingdom? Is every word in the declaration from Downing-Street, concerning their conduct, and concerning ours and that of our allies, so obviously false, that it is necessary to give some new invented proofs of our good faith, in order to expunge the memory of all this perfidy?

We know that over-labouring a point of this kind, has the direct contrary effect from what we wish. We know that there is a legal presumption against men *quando se nimis purgitant;* and if a charge of ambition is not refuted by an affected humility, certainly the character of fraud and perfidy is still less to be washed away by indications of meanness. Fraud and pre-varication are servile vices. They sometimes grow out of the necessities, always out of the habits of slavish and degenerate spirits: and on the theatre of the world, it is not by assuming the mask of a Davus or a Geta that an actor will obtain credit for manly simplicity and a liberal openness of proceeding. It is an erect countenance: it is a firm adherence to principle; it is a power of resisting false shame and frivolous fear, that assert our good faith and honour, and assure to us the confidence of mankind. Therefore all these Negotiations, and all the Declarations with which they were preceded and followed, can only serve to raise presumptions against that good faith and public integrity, the fame of which to preserve inviolate is so much the interest and duty of every nation.

[173] THE PLEDGE IS AN ENGAGEMENT "to all Europe." This is the more extraordinary, because it is a pledge, which no power in Europe, whom I have yet heard of, has thought proper to require at our hands. I am not in the secrets of office; and therefore I may be excused for proceeding upon probabilities and exteriour indications. I have surveyed all Europe from the east to the west, from the north to the south, in search of this call upon us to purge ourselves of "subtle *duplicity* and a *Punick* style" in our proceedings. I have not heard that his Excellency the Ottoman Ambassador has expressed his doubts of the British sincerity in our Negotiation with the most unchristian Republic lately set up at our door. What sympathy, in that quarter, may have introduced a remonstrance upon the want of faith in this nation, I cannot positively say. If it exists, it is in Turkish or Arabick, and possibly is not yet translated. But none of the nations which compose the old Christian world have I yet heard as calling upon us for those judicial purgations and ordeals, by fire and water, which we have chosen to go through; for the other great proof, by battle, we seem to decline.

REGICIDE PEACE III

For whose use, entertainment, or instruction, are all those over-strained and over-laboured proceedings in Council, in Negotiation, and in Speeches in Parliament, intended? What Royal Cabinet is to be enriched with these high-finished pictures of the arrogance of the sworn enemies of Kings, and the meek patience of a British Administration? In what heart is it intended to kindle pity towards our multiplied mortifications and disgraces? At best it is superfluous. What nation is unacquainted with the haughty disposition of the common enemy of all nations? It has been more than seen, it has been felt; not only by those who have been the victims of their imperious rapacity, but, in a degree, by those very powers who have consented to establish this robbery, that they might be able to copy it, and with impunity [174] to make new usurpations of their own. The King of Prussia has hypothecated in trust to the Regicides his rich and fertile territories on the Rhine, as a pledge of his zeal and affection to the cause of liberty and equality. He has seen them robbed with unbounded liberty, and with the most levelling equality. The woods are wasted; the country is ravaged; property is confiscated; and the people are put to bear a double yoke, in the exactions of a tyrannical Government and in the contributions of an hostile irruption. Is it to satisfy the Court of Berlin, that the Court of London is to give the same sort of pledge of it's sincerity and good faith to the French Directory? It is not that heart full of sensibility—it is not Luchesini, the Minister of his Prussian Majesty, the late ally of England, and the present ally of it's enemy, who has demanded this pledge of our sincerity, as the price of the renewal of the long lease of his sincere friendship to this kingdom.

It is not to our enemy, the now faithful ally of Regicide, late the faithful ally of Great Britain, the Catholick King, that we address our doleful lamentation. It is not to the *Prince of Peace,* whose declaration of war was one of the first auspicious omens of general tranquillity, which our dove-like Ambassador, with the olive branch in his beak, was saluted with at his entrance into the ark of clean birds at Paris.

Surely it is not to the Tetrarch of Sardinia, now the faithful ally of a power who has seized upon all his fortresses, and confiscated the oldest dominions of his house; it is not to this once powerful, once respected, and once cherished ally of Great Britain, that we mean to prove the sincerity of the peace which we offered to make at his expence. Or is it to him we are to prove the arrogance of the power who, under the name of friend, oppresses him, and the poor remains of his subjects, with all the ferocity of the most cruel enemy?

[175] It is not to Holland, under the name of an ally laid under a permanent military contribution, filled with their double garrison of barbarous Jacobin troops and ten times more barbarous Jacobin clubs and assemblies, that we find ourselves obliged to give this pledge.

Is it to Genoa, that we make this kind promise; a state which the Regicides were to defend in a favourable neutrality, but whose neutrality has been, by the gentle influence of Jacobin authority, forced into the trammels of an alliance; whose alliance has been secured by the admission of French garrisons; and whose peace has been for ever ratified by a forced declaration of war against ourselves?

It is not the Grand Duke of Tuscany who claims this Declaration; not the Grand Duke, who for his early sincerity, for his love of peace, and for his entire confidence in the amity of the assassins of his House, has been complimented in the British Parliament with the name of "*the wisest Sovereign in Europe*"—it is not this pacifick Solomon, or his philosophick cudgelled Ministry, cudgelled by English and by French, whose wisdom and philosophy between them, have placed Leghorn in the hands of the enemy of the Austrian family, and driven the only profitable commerce of Tuscany from its only port. It is not this Sovereign, a far more able Statesman than any of the *Medici* in whose chair he sits; it is not the philosopher *Carletti,* more ably speculative than *Galileo,* more profoundly politick than *Machiavel,* that call upon us so loudly to give the same happy proofs of the same good faith to the Republick, always the same, always one and indivisible.

It is not Venice, whose principal cities the enemy has appropriated to himself, and scornfully desired the State to indemnify itself from the Emperor, that we wish to convince of the pride and the despotism of an enemy, who loads us with his scoffs and buffets.

[176] It is not for his Holiness we intend this consolatory declaration of our own weakness and of the tyrannous temper of his grand enemy. That Prince has known both the one and the other from the beginning. The artists of the French Revolution, had given their very first essays and sketches of robbery and desolation against his territories, in a far more cruel "murdering piece" than had ever entered into the imagination of painter or poet. Without ceremony, they tore from his cherishing arms the possessions which he held for five hundred years, undisturbed by all the ambition of all the ambitious Monarchs who, during that period, have reigned in France. Is it to him, in whose wrong we have in our late negotiation ceded his now unhappy countries near the Rhone, lately amongst the most flourishing (perhaps the most flourishing for their extent) of all the countries upon earth, that we are to prove the sincerity of our resolution to make peace with the Republick of barbarism? That venerable Potentate and Pontiff is sunk deep into the vale of years; he is half disarmed by his peaceful character; his dominions are more than half disarmed by a peace of two hundred years, defended, as they were, not by force but by reverence; yet in all these straits, we see him display, amidst the recent ruins and the new defacements of his plundered capital, along with the mild and decorated piety of the modern, all the spirit and magnanimity of ancient Rome. Does he, who, though himself unable to defend them, nobly refused to re-

LETTERS ON A REGICIDE PEACE

ceive pecuniary compensations for the protection he owed to his people of Avignon, Carpentras, and the Venaissin—does he want proofs of our good disposition to deliver over that people, without any security for them, or any compensation to their Sovereign, to this cruel enemy? Does he want to be satisfied of the sincerity of our humiliation to France, who has seen his free, fertile and happy city and state of Bologna, the cradle of regenerated law, the seat [177] of sciences and of arts, so hideously metamorphosed, whilst he was crying to Great Britain for aid, and offering to purchase that aid at any price? Is it him, who sees that chosen spot of plenty and delight converted into a Jacobin ferocious Republick, dependent on the homicides of France—is it him, who, from the miracles of his beneficent industry, has done a work which defied the power of the Roman Emperors, though with an enthralled world to labour for them, is it him, who has drained and cultivated the *Pontine Marshes,* that we are to satisfy of our cordial spirit of conciliation, with those who, in their equity, are restoring Holland again to the seas, whose maxims poison more than the exhalations of the most deadly fens, and who turn all the fertilities of nature and of art into an howling desert? Is it to him, that we are to demonstrate the good faith of our submissions to the cannibal Republick; to him who is commanded to deliver up into their hands Ancona and Civita Vecchia, seats of commerce, raised by the wise and liberal labours and expences of the present and late Pontiffs—ports not more belonging to the Ecclesiastical State than to the commerce of Great Britain—thus wresting from his hands the power of the keys of the centre of Italy, as before they had taken possession of the keys of the northern part from the hands of the unhappy King of Sardinia, the natural ally of England? Is it to him we are to prove our good faith in the peace which we are soliciting to receive from the hands of his and our robbers, the enemies of all arts, all sciences, all civilization, and all commerce?

Regicide Peace III

Is it to the Cispadane or to the Transpadane Republicks, which have been forced to bow under the galling yoke of French liberty, that we address all these pledges of our sincerity and love of peace with their unnatural parents?

Are we by this declaration to satisfy the King of Naples, whom we have left to struggle as he can, after our abdication [178] of Corsica, and the flight of the whole naval force of England out of the whole circuit of the Mediterranean, abandoning our allies, our commerce, and the honour of a nation, once the protectress of all other nations, because strengthened by the independence, and enriched by the commerce of them all? By the express provisions of a recent treaty, we had engaged with the King of Naples to keep a naval force in the Mediterranean. But, good God! was a treaty at all necessary for this? The uniform policy of this kingdom as a state, and eminently so as a commercial State, has at all times led us to keep a powerful squadron and a commodious naval station in that central sea, which borders upon, and which connects, a far greater number and variety of States, European, Asiatick, and African, than any other. Without such a naval force, France must become despotick mistress of that sea, and of all the countries whose shores it washes. Our commerce must become vassal to her, and dependent on her will. Since we are come no longer to trust to our force in arms, but to our dexterity in negotiation, and begin to pay a desperate court to a proud and coy usurpation, and have finally sent an Ambassador to the Bourbon Regicides at Paris; the King of Naples, who saw that no reliance was to be placed on our engagements, or on any pledge of our adherence to our nearest and dearest interests, has been obliged to send his Ambassador also to join the rest of the squalid tribe of the representatives of degraded Kings. This Monarch, surely, does not want any proof of the sincerity of our amicable dispositions to that amicable Republick, into whose arms he has been given by our desertion of him.

To look to the powers of the North, it is not to the Danish Ambassador, insolently treated, in his own character and in ours, that we are to give proofs of the Regicide arrogance, and of our disposition to submit to it.

[179] With regard to Sweden, I cannot say much. The French influence is struggling with her independence; and they who consider the manner in which the Ambassador of that Power was treated not long since at Paris, and the manner in which the father of the present King of Sweden (himself the victim of Regicide principles and passions) would have looked on the present assassins of France, will not be very prompt to believe that the young King of Sweden has made this kind of requisition to the King of Great Britain, and has given this kind of auspice of his new government.

I speak last of the most important of all. It certainly was not the late Empress of Russia at whose instance we have given this pledge. It is not the new Emperour, the inheritour of so much glory, and placed in a situation of so much delicacy and difficulty for the preservation of that inheritance—who calls on England, the natural ally of his dominions, to deprive herself of her power of action, and to bind herself to France. France at no time, and in none of it's fashions, least of all in it's last, has been ever looked upon as the friend either of Russia or of Great Britain. Every thing good, I trust, is to be expected from this Prince, whatever may be, without authority, given out of an influence over his mind possessed by that only Potentate from whom he has any thing to apprehend, or with whom he has much even to discuss.

This Sovereign knows, I have no doubt, and feels, on what sort of bottom is to be laid the foundation of a Russian throne. He knows what a rock of native granite is to form the pedestal of his statue, who is to emulate Peter the Great. His renown will be in continuing with ease and safety, what his predecessor was obliged to atchieve through mighty struggles. He is sensible that his business is not to innovate,

but to secure and to establish; that reformations at this day
are attempts at best of ambiguous utility. He will revere [180]
his father with the piety of a son; but in his government he
will imitate the policy of his mother. His father, with many
excellent qualities, had a short reign; because, being a native
Russian, he was unfortunately advised to act in the spirit of
a foreigner. His mother reigned over Russia three and thirty
years with the greatest glory; because, with the disadvan-
tage of being a foreigner born, she made herself a Russian.
A wise Prince like the present will improve his country; but
it will be cautiously and progressively, upon it's own native
ground-work of religion, manners, habitudes, and alliances.
If I prognosticate right, it is not the Emperour of Russia that
ever will call for extravagant proofs of our desire to reconcile
ourselves to the irreconcileable enemy of all Thrones.

I do not know why I should not include America among
the European Powers; because she is of European origin, and
has not yet, like France, destroyed all traces of manners, laws,
opinions, and usages which she drew from Europe. As long
as that Europe shall have any possessions either in the south-
ern or the northern parts of that America, even separated
as it is by the ocean, it must be considered as a part of the
European system. It is not America, menaced with internal
ruin from the attempts to plant Jacobinism instead of Liberty in that country; it is not America, whose independence
is directly attacked by the French, the enemies of the independence of all nations, that calls upon us to give security by
disarming ourselves in a treacherous peace. By such a peace,
we shall deliver the Americans, their liberty, and their order,
without resource, to the mercy of their imperious allies, who
will have peace or neutrality with no state which is not ready
to join her in war against England.

Having run round the whole circle of the European system wherever it acts, I must affirm, that all the foreign powers
[181] who are not leagued with France for the utter de-

struction of all balance through Europe and throughout the world, demand other assurances from this kingdom than are given in that Declaration. They require assurances, not of the sincerity of our good dispositions towards the usurpation in France, but of our affection towards the College of the ancient States of Europe, and pledges of our constancy, of our fidelity, and of our fortitude in resisting to the last the power that menaces them all. The apprehension from which they wish to be delivered cannot be from any thing they dread in the ambition of England. Our power must be their strength. They hope more from us than they fear. I am sure the only ground of their hope, and of our hope, is in the greatness of mind hitherto shewn by the people of this nation, and it's adherence to the unalterable principles of it's antient policy, whatever Government may finally prevail in France. I have entered into this detail of the wishes and expectations of the European Powers, in order to point out more clearly, not so much what their disposition, as (a consideration of far greater importance) what their situation demands, according as that situation is related to the Regicide Republick and to this Kingdom.

THEN IF IT IS NOT TO SATISFY the foreign Powers we make this assurance, to what Power at home is it that we pay all this humiliating court? Not to the old Whigs or to the antient Tories of this Kingdom; if any memory of such antient divisions still exists amongst us. To which of the principles of these parties is this assurance agreeable? Is it to the Whigs we are to recommend the aggrandisement of France, and the subversion of the balance of power? Is it to the Tories we are to recommend our eagerness to cement ourselves with the enemies of Royalty and Religion? But if these parties, which by their dissensions have so often [182] distracted the Kingdom, which by their union have once saved it, and which by their collision and mutual resistance, have preserved the variety of this Constitution in it's unity, be (as I believe they are) nearly extinct by the growth of new ones, which have their roots in the present circumstances of the times—I wish to know, to which of these new descriptions this Declaration is addressed? It can hardly be to those persons, who, in the new distribution of parties, consider the conservation in England of the antient order of things, as necessary to preserve order every where else, and who regard the general conservation of order in other countries, as reciprocally necessary to preserve the same state of things in those Islands. That party never can wish to see Great Britain pledge herself to give the lead and the ground of advantage and superiority to the France of to-day, in any treaty which is to settle Europe. I insist upon it, that so far from expecting such an engagement, they are generally stupefied and confounded with it. That the other party which demands great changes here, and is so pleased to see them every where else, which party I call Jacobin, that this faction does from the bottom of it's heart, approve the declaration, and does erect it's crest upon the engagement, there can be little doubt. To them it may be addressed with propriety, for it answers their purposes in every point.

The party in Opposition within the House of Lords and Commons, it is irreverent, and half a breach of privilege, (far from my thoughts) to consider as Jacobin. This party has always denied the existence of such a faction; and has treated the machinations of those, whom you and I call Jacobins, as so many forgeries and fictions of the Minister and his adherents, to find a pretext for destroying freedom, and setting up an arbitrary power in this Kingdom. However, whether this Minority has a leaning towards the [183] French system, or only a charitable toleration of those who lean that way, it is certain that they have always attacked the sincerity of the Minister in the same modes, and on the very same grounds, and nearly in the same terms, with the Directory. It must, therefore, be at the tribunal of the Minority, (from the whole tenour of the speech) that the Minister appeared to consider himself obliged to purge himself of duplicity. It was at their bar that he held up his hand. It was on their *sellette* that he seemed to answer interrogatories; it was on their principles that he defended his whole conduct. They certainly take what the French call the *haute du pavé*. They have loudly called for the negotiation. It was accorded to them. They engaged their support of the war with vigour, in case Peace was not granted on honourable terms. Peace was not granted on any terms, honourable or shameful. Whether these judges, few in number but powerful in jurisdiction, are satisfied; whether they to whom this new pledge is hypothecated, have redeemed their own; whether they have given one particle more of their support to Ministry, or even favoured them with their good opinion, or their candid construction, I leave it to those, who recollect that memorable debate, to determine.

The fact is, that neither this Declaration, nor the negotiation which is it's subject, could serve any one good purpose, foreign or domestick; it could conduce to no end either with regard to allies or neutrals. It tends neither to bring back the misled; nor to give courage to the fearful; nor to animate and confirm those, who are hearty and zealous in the cause.

I HEAR IT HAS BEEN SAID (though I can scarcely believe it) that a distinguished person in an Assembly, where if there be less of the torrent and tempest of eloquence, more [184] guarded expression is to be expected, that, indeed, there was no just ground of hope in this business from the beginning.

It is plain that this noble person, however conversant in negotiation, having been employed in no less than four embassies, and in two hemispheres, and in one of those negotiations having fully experienced what it was to proceed to treaty without previous encouragement, was not at all consulted in this experiment. For his Majesty's principal Minister declared, on the very same day, in another House, "his Majesty's deep and sincere regret at it's unfortunate and abrupt termination, so different from the wishes and *hopes* that were entertained"; and in other parts of the speech speaks of this abrupt termination as a great disappointment, and as a fall from sincere endeavours and sanguine expectation. Here are, indeed, sentiments diametrically opposite, as to the hopes with which the negotiation was commenced and carried on, and what is curious is, the grounds of the hopes on the one side and the despair on the other are exactly the same. The logical conclusion from the common premises is indeed in favour of the noble Lord, for they are agreed that the enemy was far from giving the least degree of countenance to any such hopes; and that they proceeded in spite of every discouragement which the enemy had thrown in their way. But there is another material point in which they do not seem to differ; that is to say, the result of the desperate experiment of the noble Lord, and of the promising attempt of the Great Minister, in satisfying the people of England, and in causing discontent to the people of France; or, as the Minister expresses it, "in uniting England and in dividing France."

For my own part, though I perfectly agreed with the noble Lord that the attempt was desperate, so desperate indeed, as to deserve his name of an *experiment,* yet no fair man can possibly doubt that the Minister was perfectly [185] sincere in his proceeding, and that, from his ardent wishes for peace with the Regicides, he was led to conceive hopes which were founded rather in his vehement desires than in any rational ground of political speculation. Convinced as I am of this, it had been better, in my humble opinion, that persons of great name and authority had abstained from those topics which had been used to call the Minister's sincerity into doubt, and had not adopted the sentiments of the Directory upon the subject of all our negotiations; for the noble Lord expressly says that the experiment was made for the satisfaction of the country. The Directory says exactly the same thing. Upon granting, in consequence of our supplications, the passport to Lord Malmesbury, in order to remove all sort of hope from it's success, they charged all our previous steps, even to that moment of submissive demand to be admitted to their presence, on duplicity and perfidy; and assumed that the object of all the steps we had taken was that "of justifying the continuance of the war in the eyes of the English nation, and of throwing all the odium of it upon the French": "The English nation (said they) supports impatiently the continuance of the war, and a *reply must be made to it's complaints and it's reproaches;* the Parliament is about to be opened, *and the mouths of the orators who will declaim against the war must be shut; the demands for new taxes must be justified; and to obtain these results, it is necessary to be able to advance, that the French Government refuses every reasonable proposition for peace.*" I am sorry that the language of the friends to Ministry and the enemies to mankind should be so much in unison.

As to the fact in which these parties are so well agreed, that the *experiment* ought to have been made for the satisfaction of this country, (meaning the country of [186] England) it were well to be wished, that persons of eminence would cease to make themselves representatives of the people of England without a letter of attorney, or any other act of procuration. In legal construction, the sense of the people of England is to be collected from the House of Commons; and, though I do not deny the possibility of an abuse of this trust as well as any other, yet I think, without the most weighty reasons, and in the most urgent exigencies, it is highly dangerous to suppose that the House speaks any thing contrary to the sense of the people, or that the representative is silent when the sense of the constituent strongly, decidedly, and upon long deliberation, speaks audibly upon any topic of moment. If there is a doubt whether the House of Commons represents perfectly the whole Commons of Great Britain, (I think there is none) there can be no question but that the Lords and the Commons together represent the sense of the whole people to the Crown, and to the world. Thus it is, when we speak legally and constitutionally. In a great measure, it is equally true, when we speak prudentially; but I do not pretend to assert, that there are no other principles to guide discretion than those which are or can be fixed by some law, or some constitution; yet before the legally presumed sense of the people should be superseded by a supposition of one more real (as in all cases, where a legal presumption is to be ascertained) some strong proofs ought to exist of a contrary disposition in the people at large, and some decisive indications of their desire upon this subject. There can be no question, that, previously to a direct message from the Crown, neither House of Parliament did indicate any thing like a wish for such advances as we have made, or such negotiations as we have carried on. The Parliament has assented to Ministry; it is not Ministry that has obeyed the impulse of Parliament. The people at large [187] have their organs through which they can speak to Parliament and to the Crown by a respectful petition, and, though not with absolute authority, yet with weight, they can instruct their Representatives. The freeholders and other electors in this kingdom have another, and a surer mode of expressing their sentiments concerning the conduct which is held by Members of Parliament. In the middle of these transactions, this last opportunity has been held out to them. In all these points of view, I positively assert, that the people have no where, and in no way, expressed their wish of throwing themselves and their Sovereign at the feet of a wicked and rancorous foe, to supplicate mercy, which, from the nature of that foe, and from the circumstances of affairs, we had no sort of ground to expect. It is undoubtedly the business of Ministers very much to consult the inclinations of the people, but they ought to take great care that they do not receive that inclination from the few persons who may happen to approach them. The petty interests of such gentlemen, their low conceptions of things, their fears arising from the danger to which the very arduous and critical situation of publick affairs may expose their places; their apprehensions from the hazards to which the discontents of a few popular men at elections may expose their seats in Parliament—all these causes trouble and confuse the representations which they make to Ministers of the real temper of the nation. If Ministers, instead of following the great indications of the Constitution, proceed on such reports, they will take the whispers of a cabal for the voice of the people, and the counsels of imprudent timidity for the wisdom of a nation.

I well remember, that when the fortune of the war began, and it began pretty early, to turn, as it is common and natural, we were dejected by the losses that had been sustained, and with the doubtful issue of the contests that were foreseen. But not a word was uttered that supposed [188] peace upon any proper terms, was in our power, or therefore that it should be in our desire. As usual, with or without reason, we criticised the conduct of the war, and compared our fortunes with our measures. The mass of the nation went no further. For I suppose that you always understood me as speaking of that very preponderating part of the nation, which had always been equally adverse to the French principles, and to the general progress of their Revolution throughout Europe; considering the final success of their arms and the triumph of their principles as one and the same thing.

THE FIRST MEANS that were used, by any one professing our principles, to change the minds of this party upon that subject, appeared in a small pamphlet circulated with considerable industry. It was commonly given to the noble person himself, who has passed judgment upon all hopes of negotiation, and justified our late abortive attempt only as an *experiment* made to satisfy the country; and yet that pamphlet led the way in endeavouring to dissatisfy that very country with the continuance of the war, and to raise in the people the most sanguine expectations from some such course of nego-tiation as has been fatally pursued. This leads me to suppose (and I am glad to have reason for supposing) that there was no foundation for attributing the performance in question to that authour; but without mentioning his name in the title-page, it passed for his, and does still pass uncontradicted. It was entitled "Remarks on the apparent Circumstances of the War in the fourth Week of October, 1795."

This sanguine little king's-fisher (not prescient of the storm, as by his instinct he ought to be) appearing at that uncertain season, before the riggs of old Michaelmas were yet well composed, and when the inclement storms of [189] winter were approaching, began to flicker over the seas, and was busy in building it's halcyon nest, as if the angry ocean had been soothed by the genial breath of May. Very unfor-tunately this auspice was instantly followed by a speech from the Throne, in the very spirit and principles of that pamphlet.

I say nothing of the newspapers, which are undoubtedly in the interest, and which are supposed by some to be directly or indirectly under the influence of Ministers, and which, with less authority than the pamphlet I speak of, had indeed for some time before held a similar language, in direct contra-diction to their more early tone: in so much, that I can speak it with a certain assurance, that very many who wished to Ad-ministration as well as you and I do, thought that in giving their opinion in favour of this peace, they followed the opin-ion of Ministry—they were conscious that they did not lead it. My inference therefore is this, that the negotiation, what-ever it's merits may be, in the general principle and policy of undertaking it, is, what every political measure in general ought to be, the sole work of Administration; and that if it was an experiment to satisfy any body, it was to satisfy those, whom the Ministers were in the daily habit of condemning, and by whom they were daily condemned; I mean, *the Leaders of the Opposition in Parliament.* I am certain that the Ministers were then, and are now, invested with the fullest confidence of the major part of the nation, to pursue such measures of peace or war as the nature of things shall suggest as most adapted to the publick safety. It is in this light therefore, as a measure which ought to have been avoided, and ought not to be repeated, that I take the liberty of discussing the merits of this system of Regicide Negotiations. It is not a matter of light experiment, that leaves us where it found us. Peace or war are the great [190] hinges upon which the very being of nations turns. Negotiations are the means of making peace or preventing war, and are therefore of more serious importance than almost any single event of war can possibly be.

AT THE VERY OUTSET I do not hesitate to affirm, that this country in particular, and the publick law in general, have suffered more by this negotiation of experiment, than by all the battles together that we have lost from the commencement of this century to this time, when it touches so nearly to it's close. I therefore have the misfortune not to coincide in opinion with the great Statesman who set on foot a negotiation, as he said, "in spite of the constant opposition he had met with from France." He admits, "that the difficulty in this negotiation became most seriously increased indeed, by the situation in which we were placed, and the manner in which alone the enemy would *admit* of a negotiation." This situation so described, and so truly described, rendered our solicitation not only degrading, but from the very outset evidently hopeless.

I find it asserted, and even a merit taken for it, "that this country surmounted every difficulty of form and etiquette which the enemy had thrown in our way." An odd way of surmounting a difficulty by cowering under it! I find it asserted that an heroick resolution had been taken, and avowed in Parliament, previous to this negotiation, "that no consideration of etiquette should stand in the way of it."

Etiquette, if I understand rightly the term, which in any extent is of modern usage, had it's original application to those ceremonial and formal observances practised at Courts, which had been established by long usage, in order to preserve the sovereign power from the rude intrusion of licentious familiarity, as well as to preserve Majesty itself from a disposition to consult it's ease at the expence of [191] it's dignity. The term came afterwards to have a greater latitude, and to be employed to signify certain formal methods used in the transactions between sovereign States.

In the more limited as well as in the larger sense of the term, without knowing what the etiquette is, it is impossible to determine whether it is a vain and captious punctilio, or a form necessary to preserve decorum in character and order in business. I readily admit, that nothing tends to facilitate the issue of all public transactions more than a mutual disposition, in the parties treating, to waive all ceremony. But the use of this temporary suspension of the recognised modes of respect consists in it's being mutual, and in the spirit of conciliation in which all ceremony is laid aside. On the contrary, when one of the parties to a treaty intrenches himself up to the chin in these ceremonies, and will not, on his side, abate a single punctilio, and that all the concessions are upon one side only, the part so conceding does by this act place himself in a relation of inferiority, and thereby fundamentally subverts that equality which is of the very essence of all treaty.

AFTER THIS FORMAL ACT of degradation, it was but a matter of course, that gross insult should be offered to our Ambassador, and that he should tamely submit to it. He found himself provoked to complain of the atrocious libels against his publick character and his person, which appeared in a paper under the avowed patronage of that Government. The Regicide Directory, on this complaint, did not recognise the paper; and that was all. They did not punish, they did not dismiss, they did not even reprimand the writer. As to our Ambassador, this total want of reparation for the injury was passed by under the pretence of despising it.

In this but too serious business, it is not possible here to avoid a smile. Contempt is not a thing to be despised. [192] It may be borne with a calm and equal mind, but no man by lifting his head high can pretend that he does not perceive the scorns that are poured down upon him from above. All these sudden complaints of injury, and all these deliberate submissions to it, are the inevitable consequences of the situation in which we had placed ourselves; a situation wherein the insults were such as nature would not enable us to bear, and circumstances would not permit us to resent.

IT WAS NOT LONG, however, after this contempt of contempt upon the part of our Ambassador (who by the way represented his Sovereign) that a new object was furnished for displaying sentiments of the same kind, though the case was infinitely aggravated. Not the Ambassador, but the King himself was libelled and insulted; libelled, not by a creature of the Directory, but by the Directory itself. At least so Lord Malmesbury understood it, and so he answered it in his note of the 12th December, 1796, in which he says, "With regard to the *offensive and injurious* insinuations which are contained in that paper, and which are only calculated to throw new obstacles in the way of that accommodation, which the French Government profess to desire, THE KING HAS DEEMED IT FAR BENEATH HIS DIGNITY to permit an answer to be made to them on his part, in any manner whatsoever."

I am of opinion, that if his Majesty had kept aloof from that wash and off-scouring of every thing that is low and barbarous in the world, it might be well thought unworthy of his dignity to take notice of such scurrilities. They must be considered as much the natural expression of that kind of animal, as it is the expression of the feelings of a dog to bark; but when the King had been advised to recognise not only the monstrous composition as a Sovereign Power, but, in conduct, to admit something in it like a superiority—[193] when the Bench of Regicide was made, at least, co-ordinate with his Throne, and raised upon a platform full as elevated—this treatment could not be passed by under the appearance of despising it. It would not, indeed, have been proper to keep up a war of the same kind, but an immediate, manly, and decided resentment ought to have been the consequence. We ought not to have waited for the disgraceful dismissal of our Ambassador. There are cases in which we may pretend to sleep: but the wittol rule has some sense in it, *Non omnibus dormio*. We might, however, have seemed ignorant of the affront; but what was the fact? Did we dissemble or pass it by in silence? When dignity is talked of, (a language which I did not expect to hear in such a transaction,) I must say what all the world must feel, that it was not for the King's dignity to notice this insult, and not to resent it. This mode of proceeding is formed on new ideas of the correspondence between Sovereign Powers.

THIS WAS FAR from the only ill effect of the policy of degradation. The state of inferiority in which we were placed in this vain attempt at treaty, drove us headlong from errour into errour, and led us to wander far away, not only from all the paths which have been beaten in the old course of political communication between mankind, but out of the ways even of the most common prudence. Against all rules, after we had met nothing but rebuffs in return to all our proposals, we made *two confidential communications* to those in whom we had no confidence, and who reposed no confidence in us. What was worse, we were fully aware of the madness of the step we were taking. Ambassadors are not sent to a hostile power, persevering in sentiments of hostility, to make candid, confidential, and amicable communications. Hitherto the world has considered it as the duty of an Ambassador in such a situation to be cautious, [194] guarded, dexterous, and circumspect. It is true that mutual confidence and common interest dispense with all rules, smooth the rugged way, remove every obstacle, and make all things plain and level. When, in the last century, *Temple* and *De Witt* negotiated the famous Triple Alliance, their candour, their freedom, and the most *confidential* disclosures, were the result of true policy. Accordingly, in spite of all the dilatory forms of the complex Government of the United Provinces, the treaty was concluded in three days. It did not take a much longer time to bring the same State (that of Holland) through a still more complicated transaction, that of the *Grand Alliance*. But in the present case, this unparalleled candour, this unpardonable want of reserve, produced what might have been expected from it, the most serious evils. It instructed the enemy in the whole plan of our demands and concessions. It made the most fatal discoveries.

AND FIRST, IT INDUCED US to lay down the basis of a treaty which itself had nothing to rest upon; it seems, we thought we had gained a great point in getting this basis admitted — that is, a basis of mutual compensation and exchange of conquests. If a disposition to peace, and with any reasonable assurance, had been previously indicated, such a plan of arrangement might with propriety and safety be proposed, because these arrangements were not, in effect, to make the basis, but a part of the superstructure, of the fabrick of pacification. The order of things would thus be reversed. The mutual disposition to peace would form the reasonable base upon which the scheme of compensation, upon one side or the other, might be constructed. This truly fundamental base being once laid, all differences arising from the spirit of huckstering and barter might be easily adjusted. If the restoration of peace, with a view to the establishment [195] of a fair balance of power in Europe, had been made the real basis of the treaty, the reciprocal value of the compensations could not be estimated according to their proportion to each other, but according to their proportionate relation to that end: to that great end the whole would be subservient. The effect of the treaty would be in a manner secured before the detail of particulars was begun, and for a plain reason, because the hostile spirit on both sides had been conjured down. But if in the full fury, and unappeased rancour of war, a little traffick is attempted, it is easy to divine what must be the consequence to those who endeavour to open that kind of petty commerce.

To ILLUSTRATE what I have said, I go back no further than to the two last Treaties of Paris, and to the Treaty of Aix-la-Chapelle, which preceded the first of these two Treaties of Paris by about fourteen or fifteen years. I do not mean here to criticise any of them. My opinions upon some particulars of the Treaty of Paris in 1763, are published in a pamphlet,* which your recollection will readily bring into your view. I recur to them only to shew that their basis had not been, and never could have been a mere dealing of truck and barter, but that the parties being willing, from common fatigue or common suffering, to put an end to a war, the first object of which had either been obtained or despaired of, the lesser objects were not thought worth the price of further contest. The parties understanding one another, so much was given away without considering from whose budget it came, not as the value of the objects, but as the value of peace to the parties might require. At the last treaty of Paris, the subjugation of America being despaired of on the part of Great Brit-

* Observations on a late State of the Nation.

ain, and the independence of America being looked upon as secure upon the part of [196] France, the main cause of the war was removed; and then the conquests which France had made upon us (for we had made none of importance upon her) were surrendered with sufficient facility. Peace was restored as peace. In America the parties stood as they were possessed. A limit was to be settled, but settled as a limit to secure that peace, and not at all on a system of equivalents, for which, as we then stood with the United States, there were little or no materials.

At the preceding treaty of Paris, I mean that of 1763, there was nothing at all on which to fix a basis of compensation from reciprocal cession of conquests. They were all on one side. The question with us was not what we were to receive, and on what consideration, but what we were to keep for indemnity or to cede for peace. Accordingly no place being left for barter, sacrifices were made on our side to peace; and we surrendered to the French their most valuable possessions in the West Indies without any equivalent. The rest of Europe fell soon after into it's antient order; and the German war ended exactly where it had begun.

The treaty of Aix-la-Chapelle was built upon a similar basis. All the conquests in Europe had been made by France. She had subdued the Austrian Netherlands, and broken open the gates of Holland. We had taken nothing in the West Indies, and Cape Breton was a trifling business indeed. France gave up all for peace. The allies had given up all that was ceded at Utrecht. Louis the Fourteenth made all, or nearly all, the cessions at Ryswick, and at Nimeguen. In all those treaties, and in all the preceding, as well as in the others which intervened, the question never had been that of barter. The balance of power had been ever assumed as the known common law of Europe at all times, and by all powers: the question had only been (as [197] it must happen) on the more or less inclination of that balance.

This general balance was regarded in four principal

points of view: the GREAT MIDDLE BALANCE, which comprehended Great Britain, France, and Spain; the BALANCE OF
THE NORTH; the BALANCE, external and internal, of GER-
MANY; and the BALANCE OF ITALY. In all those systems of balance, England was the power to whose custody it was thought
it might be most safely committed.

France, as she happened to stand, secured the balance, or
endangered it. Without question she had been long the security for the balance of Germany, and under her auspices the
system, if not formed, had been at least perfected. She was
so in some measure with regard to Italy, more than occasionally. She had a clear interest in the balance of the North, and
had endeavoured to preserve it. But when we began to treat
with the present France, or more properly to prostrate ourselves to her, and to try if we should be admitted to ransom
our allies, upon a system of mutual concession and compensation, we had not one of the usual facilities. For first, we had
not the smallest indication of a desire for peace on the part of
the enemy; but rather the direct contrary. Men do not make
sacrifices to obtain what they do not desire: and as for the
balance of power, it was so far from being admitted by France
either on the general system, or with regard to the particular systems that I have mentioned, that, in the whole body
of their authorized or encouraged reports and discussions
upon the theory of the diplomatic system, they constantly rejected the very idea of the balance of power, and treated it
as the true cause of all the wars and calamities that had afflicted Europe: and their practice was correspondent to the
dogmatick positions they had laid down. The Empire and
the Papacy it was their great object to destroy, and this, now
openly avowed and [198] stedfastly acted upon, might have
been discerned with very little acuteness of sight, from the
very first dawnings of the Revolution, to be the main drift of
their policy. For they professed a resolution to destroy every
thing which can hold States together by the tie of opinion.

Exploding, therefore, all sorts of balances, they avow

their design to erect themselves into a new description of Empire, which is not grounded on any balance, but forms a sort of impious hierarchy, of which France is to be the head and the guardian. The law of this their Empire is any thing rather than the publick law of Europe, the antient conventions of it's several States, or the antient opinions which assign to them superiority or pre-eminence of any sort, or any other kind of connexion in virtue of antient relations. They permit, and that is all, the temporary existence of some of the old communities; but whilst they give to these tolerated States this temporary respite in order to secure them in a condition of real dependence on themselves, they invest them on every side by a body of Republicks, formed on the model, and dependent ostensibly, as well as substantially, on the will, of the mother Republick to which they owe their origin. These are to be so many garrisons to check and controul the States which are to be permitted to remain on the old model, until they are ripe for a change. It is in this manner that France, on her new system, means to form an universal empire, by producing an universal revolution. By this means, forming a new code of communities according to what she calls the natural rights of man and of States, she pretends to secure eternal peace to the world, guaranteed by her generosity and justice, which are to grow with the extent of her power. To talk of the balance of power to the governors of such a country, was a jargon which they could not understand even through an interpreter. Before men can transact any affair, they must have a common language [199] to speak, and some common recognised principles on which they can argue. Otherwise, all is cross-purpose and confusion. It was, therefore, an essential preliminary to the whole proceeding, to fix, whether the balance of power, the liberties and laws of the Empire, and the treaties of different belligerent powers in past times, when they put an end to hostilities, were to be considered as the basis of the present negotiation.

The whole of the enemy's plan was known when Lord
Malmesbury was sent with his scrap of equivalents to Paris.
Yet, in this unfortunate attempt at negotiation, instead of fixing these points, and assuming the balance of power and the
peace of Europe as the basis to which all cessions on all sides
were to be subservient, our solicitor for peace was directed
to reverse that order. He was directed to make mutual concessions, on a mere comparison of their marketable value,
the base of treaty. The balance of power was to be thrown in
as an inducement, and a sort of make-weight, to supply the
manifest deficiency which must stare him and the world in
the face, between those objects which he was to require the
enemy to surrender, and those which he had to offer as a fair
equivalent.

To GIVE ANY FORCE to this inducement, and to make it
answer even the secondary purpose of equalizing equivalents
having in themselves no natural proportionate value, it supposed, that the enemy, contrary to the most notorious fact,
did admit this balance of power to be of some value, great
or small; whereas it is plain, that in the enemy's estimate of
things, the consideration of the balance of power, as we have
said before, was so far from going in diminution of the value
of what the Directory was desired to surrender, or of giving
an additional price to our objects offered in exchange, that
the hope of the utter destruction of that balance became a
[200] new motive to the junto of Regicides for preserving,
as a means for realizing that hope, what we wished them to
abandon.

THUS STOOD THE BASIS of the treaty on laying the first
stone of the foundation. At the very best, upon our side, the
question stood upon a mere naked bargain and sale. Unthinking people here triumphed when they thought they had obtained it, whereas when obtained as a basis of a treaty, it was

just the worst we could possibly have chosen. As to our offer to cede a most unprofitable, and, indeed, beggarly, chargeable counting-house or two in the East-Indies, we ought not to presume that they would consider this as any thing else than a mockery. As to any thing of real value, we had nothing under Heaven to offer (for which we were not ourselves in a very dubious struggle) except the Island of Martinico only. When this object was to be weighed against the directorial conquests, merely as an object of a value at market, the principle of barter became perfectly ridiculous. A single quarter in the single city of Amsterdam was worth ten Martinicos; and would have sold for many more years' purchase in any market overt in Europe. How was this gross and glaring defect in the objects of exchange to be supplied? It was to be made up by argument. And what was that argument? The extreme utility of possessions in the West-Indies to the augmentation of the naval power of France. A very curious topick of argument to be proposed and insisted on by an Ambassador of Great Britain. It is directly and plainly this—"Come, we know that of all things you wish a naval power, and it is natural you should, who wish to destroy the very sources of the British greatness, to overpower our marine, to destroy our commerce, to eradicate our foreign influence, and to lay us open to an invasion, which, at one stroke, may complete our servitude [201] and ruin, and expunge us from among the nations of the earth. Here I have it in my budget, the infallible arcanum for that purpose. You are but novices in the art of naval resources. Let you have the West-Indies back, and your maritime preponderance is secured, for which you would do well to be moderate in your demands upon the Austrian Netherlands."

Under any circumstances, this is a most extraordinary topick of argument; but it is rendered by much the more unaccountable, when we are told, that, if the war has been diverted from the great object of establishing society and good order in Europe by destroying the usurpation in France, this diversion was made to increase the naval resources and power of Great-Britain, and to lower, if not annihilate, those of the marine of France. I leave all this to the very serious reflexion of every Englishman.

This basis was no sooner admitted, than the rejection of a treaty upon that sole foundation was a thing of course. The enemy did not think it worthy of a discussion, as in truth it was not; and immediately, as usual, they began, in the most opprobrious and most insolent manner, to question our sincerity and good faith. Whereas, in truth, there was no one symptom wanting of openness and fair dealing. What could be more fair than to lay open to an enemy all that you wished to obtain, and the price you meant to pay for it, and to desire him to imitate your ingenuous proceeding, and in the same manner to open his honest heart to you? Here was no want of fair dealing: but there was too evidently a fault of another kind. There was much weakness; there was an eager and impotent desire of associating with this unsocial power, and of attempting the connexion by any means, however manifestly feeble and ineffectual. The event was committed to chance; that is, to such a manifestation of the desire of France for peace, as would [202] induce the Directory to forget the advantages they had in the system of barter. Accordingly, the general desire for such a peace was triumphantly reported from the moment that Lord Malmesbury had set his foot on shore at Calais.

It has been said, that the Directory was compelled against it's will to accept the basis of barter (as if that had tended to accelerate the work of pacification!) by the voice of all France. Had this been the case, the Directors would have continued to listen to that voice to which it seems they were so obedient: they would have proceeded with the negotiation upon that basis. But the fact is, that they instantly broke up the negotiation, as soon as they had obliged our Ambassador to violate all the principles of treaty, and weakly, rashly, and unguardedly, to expose, without any counter-proposition, the whole of our project with regard to ourselves and our allies, and without holding out the smallest hope that they would admit the smallest part of our pretensions.

When they had thus drawn from us all that they could draw out, they expelled Lord Malmesbury, and they appealed for the propriety of their conduct, to that very France which, we thought proper to suppose, had driven them to this fine concession; and I do not find, that in either division of the family of thieves, the younger branch, or the elder, or in any other body whatsoever, there was any indignation excited, or any tumult raised; or any thing like the virulence of opposition which was shewn to the King's Ministers here, on account of that transaction.

NOTWITHSTANDING ALL THIS, it seems a hope is still entertained, that the Directory will have that tenderness for the carcase of their country, by whose very distemper, and on whose festering wounds, like vermin, they are fed; that these pious patriots will of themselves come into a more moderate [203] and reasonable way of thinking and acting. In the name of wonder, what has inspired our Ministry with this hope any more than with their former expectations?

Do these hopes only arise from continual disappointment? Do they grow out of the usual grounds of despair? What is there to encourage them, in the conduct, or even in the declarations of the Ruling Powers in France, from the first formation of their mischievous Republic to the hour in which I write? Is not the Directory composed of the same junto? Are they not the identical men, who, from the base and sordid vices which belonged to their original place and situation, aspired to the dignity of crimes; and from the dirtiest, lowest, most fraudulent, and most knavish of chicaners, ascended in the scale of robbery, sacrilege, and assassination in all it's forms, till at last they had imbrued their impious hands in the blood of their Sovereign? Is it from these men that we are to hope for this paternal tenderness to their country, and this sacred regard for the peace and happiness of all nations?

BUT IT SEEMS there is still another lurking hope, akin to that which duped us so egregiously before, when our delightful basis was accepted: we still flatter ourselves that the publick voice of France will compel this Directory to more moderation. Whence does this hope arise? What publick voice is there in France? There are, indeed, some writers, who, since this monster of a Directory has obtained a great regular military force to guard them, are indulged in a sufficient liberty of writing, and some of them write well undoubtedly. But the world knows that in France there is no publick, that the country is composed but of two descriptions; audacious tyrants and trembling slaves. The contest between the tyrants is the only vital principle that can be discerned in France. The only thing which there [204] appears like spirit, is amongst the late associates, and fastest friends of the Directory, the more furious and untameable part of the Jacobins. This discontented member of the faction does almost balance the reigning divisions; and it threatens every moment to predominate. For the present, however, the dread of their fury forms some sort of security to their fellows, who now exercise a more regular, and therefore a somewhat less ferocious tyranny. Most of the slaves chuse a quiet, however reluctant, submission to those who are somewhat satiated with blood, and who, like wolves, are a little more tame from being a little less hungry, in preference to an irruption of the famished devourers who are prowling and howling about the fold.

This circumstance assures some degree of permanence to the power of those, whom we know to be permanently our rancourous and implacable enemies. But to those very enemies, who have sworn our destruction, we have ourselves given a further and far better security by rendering the cause of the Royalists desperate. Those brave and virtuous, but unfortunate adherents to the ancient constitution of their country, after the miserable slaughters which have been made in that body, after all their losses by emigration, are still numerous, but unable to exert themselves against the force of the usurpation, evidently countenanced and upheld by those very Princes who had called them to arm for the support of the legal Monarchy. Where then, after chasing these fleeting hopes of ours from point to point of the political horizon, are they at last really found? Not where, under Providence, the hopes of Englishmen used to be placed—in our own courage and in our own virtues, but in the moderation and virtue of the most atrocious monsters that have ever disgraced and plagued mankind.

THE ONLY EXCUSE TO BE MADE for all our mendicant diplomacy [205] is the same as in the case of all other mendicancy—namely, that it has been founded on absolute necessity. This deserves consideration. Necessity, as it has no law, so it has no shame; but moral necessity is not like metaphysical, or even physical. In that category, it is a word of loose signification, and conveys different ideas to different minds. To the low-minded, the slightest necessity becomes an invincible necessity. "The slothful man saith, There is a lion in the way, and I shall be devoured in the streets." But when the necessity pleaded is not in the nature of things, but in the vices of him who alleges it, the whining tones of commonplace beggarly rhetorick produce nothing but indignation; because they indicate a desire of keeping up a dishonourable existence, without utility to others, and without dignity to itself; because they aim at obtaining the dues of labour without industry; and by frauds would draw from the compassion of others, what men ought to owe to their own spirit and their own exertions.

I am thoroughly satisfied that if we degrade ourselves, it

is the degradation which will subject us to the yoke of necessity, and, not that it is necessity which has brought on our
degradation. In this same chaos, where light and darkness are
struggling together, the open subscription of last year, with
all it's circumstances, must have given us no little glimmering
of hope; not (as I have heard, it was vainly discoursed) that
the loan could prove a crutch to a lame negotiation abroad;
and that the whiff and wind of it must at once have disposed
the enemies of all tranquillity to a desire for peace. Judging
on the face of facts, if on them it had any effect at all, it had
the direct contrary effect; for very soon after the loan became
publick at Paris, the negotiation ended, and our Ambassador
was ignominiously expelled. My view of this was different: I
liked the loan, not from the influence which it might have
on the enemy, but on account [206] of the temper which it
indicated in our own people. This alone is a consideration of
any importance; because all calculation, formed upon a supposed relation of the habitudes of others to our own, under
the present circumstances, is weak and fallacious. The adversary must be judged, not by what we are, or by what we
wish him to be, but by what we must know he actually is; unless we choose to shut our eyes and our ears to the uniform
tenour of all his discourses, and to his uniform course in all
his actions. We may be deluded; but we cannot pretend that
we have been disappointed. The old rule of *Ne te quaesiveris
extra,* is a precept as available in policy as it is in morals. Let
us leave off speculating upon the disposition and the wants
of the enemy. Let us descend into our own bosoms; let us
ask ourselves what are our duties, and what are our means
of discharging them. In what heart are you at home? How
far may an English Minister confide in the affections, in the
confidence, in the force of an English people? What does he
find us when he puts us to the proof of what English interest
and English honour demand? It is as furnishing an answer to
these questions that I consider the circumstances of the loan.

The effect on the enemy is not in what he may speculate on our resources, but in what he shall feel from our arms.

The circumstances of the loan have proved beyond a doubt three capital points, which, if they are properly used, may be advantageous to the future liberty and happiness of mankind. In the first place, the loan demonstrates, in regard to instrumental resources, the competency of this kingdom to the assertion of the common cause, and to the maintenance and superintendance of that, which it is it's duty and it's glory to hold, and to watch over—the balance of power throughout the Christian World. Secondly, it brings to light what, under the most discouraging appearances, [207] I always reckoned on; that with it's ancient physical force, not only unimpaired, but augmented, it's ancient spirit is still alive in the British nation. It proves, that for their application there is a spirit equal to the resources, for it's energy above them. It proves that there exists, though not always visible, a spirit which never fails to come forth whenever it is ritually invoked; a spirit which will give no equivocal response, but such as will hearten the timidity, and fix the irresolution, of hesitating prudence; a spirit which will be ready to perform all the tasks that shall be imposed upon it by publick honour. Thirdly, the loan displays an abundant confidence in his Majesty's Government, as administered by his present servants, in the prosecution of a war which the people consider, not as a war made on the suggestion of Ministers, and to answer the purposes of the ambition or pride of statesmen, but as a war of their own, and in defence of that very property which they expend for it's support; a war for that order of things, from which every thing valuable that they possess is derived, and in which order alone it can possibly be maintained.

I HEAR IN DEROGATION of the value of the fact, from which I draw inferences so favourable to the spirit of the people, and to it's just expectation from Ministers, that the eighteen million loan is to be considered in no other light, than as taking advantage of a very lucrative bargain held out to the subscribers. I do not in truth believe it. All the circumstances which attended the subscription strongly spoke a different language. Be it, however, as these detractors say. This with me derogates little, or rather nothing at all, from the political value and importance of the fact. I should be very sorry if the transaction was not such a bargain, otherwise it would not have been a fair one. A corrupt and improvident loan, like every thing else corrupt or prodigal, [208] cannot be too much condemned: but there is a shortsighted parsimony still more fatal than an unforeseeing expence. The value of money must be judged, like every thing else, from it's rate at market. To force that market, or any market, is of all things the most dangerous. For a small temporary benefit, the spring of all public credit might be relaxed for ever. The monied men have a right to look to advantage in the investment of their property. To advance their money, they risk it; and the risk is to be included in the price. If they were to incur a loss, that loss would amount to a tax on that peculiar species of property. In effect, it would be the most unjust and impolitick of all things, unequal taxation. It would throw upon one description of persons in the community, that burthen which ought by fair and equitable distribution to rest upon the whole. None on account of their dignity should be exempt; none (preserving due proportion) on account of the scantiness of their means. The moment a man is exempted from the maintenance of the community, he is in a sort separated from it. He loses the place of a citizen.

So it is in all *taxation;* but in a *bargain,* when terms of loss are looked for by the borrower from the lender, compulsion, or what virtually is compulsion, introduces itself into the place of treaty. When compulsion may be at all used by a State in borrowing, the occasion must determine. But the compulsion ought to be known, and well defined, and well distinguished: for otherwise treaty only weakens the energy of compulsion, while compulsion destroys the freedom of a bargain. The advantage of both is lost by the confusion of things in their nature utterly unsociable. It would be to introduce compulsion into that in which freedom and existence are the same; I mean credit. The moment that shame, or fear, or force, are directly or indirectly applied to a loan, credit perishes.

[209] There must be some impulse besides public spirit, to put private interest into motion along with it. Monied men ought to be allowed to set a value on their money; if they did not, there could be no monied men. This desire of accumulation is a principle without which the means of their service to the State could not exist. The love of lucre, though sometimes carried to a ridiculous, sometimes to a vicious excess, is the grand cause of prosperity to all States. In this natural, this reasonable, this powerful, this prolifick principle, it is for the satyrist to expose the ridiculous; it is for the moralist to censure the vicious; it is for the sympathetick heart to reprobate the hard and cruel; it is for the Judge to animadvert on the fraud, the extortion, and the oppression: but it is for the Statesman to employ it as he finds it, with all it's concomitant excellencies, with all it's imperfections on it's head. It is his part, in this case, as it is in all other cases, where he is to make use of the general energies of nature, to take them as he finds them.

After all, it is a great mistake to imagine, as too commonly, almost indeed generally, it is imagined, that the publick borrower and the private lender are two adverse parties with different and contending interests, and that what is given to the one, is wholly taken from the other. Constituted as our system of finance and taxation is, the interests of the contracting parties cannot well be separated, whatever they may reciprocally intend. He who is the hard lender of to-day, to-morrow is the generous contributor to his own payment. For example,

the last loan is raised on publick taxes, which are designed
to produce annually two millions sterling. At first view, this
is an annuity of two millions dead charge upon the publick
in favour of certain monied men. But inspect the thing more
nearly, follow the stream in it's meanders; and you will find
that there is a good deal of fallacy in this state of things.

[210] I take it, that whoever considers any man's expenditure of his income, old or new (I speak of certain classes in
life) will find a full third of it to go in taxes, direct or indirect.
If so, this new-created income of two millions will probably
furnish 665,000*l*. (I avoid broken numbers) towards the payment of it's own interest, or to the sinking of it's own capital.
So it is with the whole of the publick debt. Suppose it any
given sum, it is a fallacious estimate of the affairs of a nation
to consider it as a mere burthen; to a degree it is so without question, but not wholly so, nor any thing like it. If the
income from the interest be spent, the above proportion returns again into the publick stock: insomuch, that taking the
interest of the whole debt to be twelve million, three hundred thousand pound, (it is something more) not less than
a sum of four million one hundred thousand pound comes
back again to the publick through the channel of imposition.
If the whole, or any part, of that income be saved, so much
new capital is generated; the infallible operation of which is
to lower the value of money, and consequently to conduce
towards the improvement of publick credit.

I take the expenditure of the *capitalist,* not the value of
the capital, as my standard; because it is the standard upon
which, amongst us, property as an object of taxation is rated.
In this country, land and offices only excepted, we raise no
faculty tax. We preserve the faculty from the expence. Our
taxes, for the far greater portion, fly over the heads of the
lowest classes. They escape too who, with better ability, voluntarily subject themselves to the harsh discipline of a rigid
necessity. With us, labour and frugality, the parents of riches,

are spread, and wisely too. The moment men cease to augment the common stock, the moment they no longer enrich it by their industry or their self-denial, their luxury and even their ease are obliged to [211] pay contribution to the publick; not because they are vicious principles, but because they are unproductive. If, in fact, the interest paid by the publick had not thus revolved again into it's own fund; if this secretion had not again been absorbed into the mass of blood, it would have been impossible for the nation to have existed to this time under such a debt. But under the debt it does exist and flourish; and this flourishing state of existence in no small degree is owing to the contribution from the debt to the payment. Whatever, therefore, is taken from that capital by too close a bargain, is but a delusive advantage; it is so much lost to the publick in another way. This matter cannot, on the one side or the other, be metaphysically pursued to the extreme, but it is a consideration of which, in all discussions of this kind, we ought never wholly to lose sight.

IT IS NEVER, THEREFORE, wise to quarrel with the interested views of men, whilst they are combined with the publick interest and promote it: it is our business to tie the knot, if possible, closer. Resources that are derived from extraordinary virtues, as such virtues are rare, so they must be unproductive. It is a good thing for a monied man to pledge his property on the welfare of his country; he shews that he places his treasure where his heart is; and, revolving in this circle, we know that "wherever a man's treasure is, there his heart will be also." For these reasons and on these principles, I have been sorry to see the attempts which have been made, with more good meaning than foresight and consideration, towards raising the annual interest of this loan by private contributions. Wherever a regular revenue is established, there voluntary contribution can answer no purpose, but to disorder and disturb it in it's course. To recur to such aids is, for so much, to dissolve the community, and to return to a state of unconnected nature. And even if [212] such a supply should be productive in a degree commensurate to its object, it must also be productive of much vexation, and much oppression. Either the citizens, by the proposed duties, pay their proportion according to some rate made by public authority, or they do not. If the law be well made, and the contributions founded on just proportions, every thing superadded by something that is not as regular as law, and as uniform in it's operation, will become more or less out of proportion. If, on the contrary, the law be not made upon proper calculation, it is a disgrace to the publick wisdom, which fails in skill to assess the citizen in just measure, and according to his means. But the hand of authority is not always the most heavy hand. It is obvious that men may be oppressed by many ways, besides those which take their course from the supreme power of the State. Suppose the payment to be wholly discretionary. Whatever has it's origin in caprice, is sure not to improve in it's progress, nor to end in reason. It is impossible for each private individual to have any measure conformable to the particular condition of each of his fellow-citizens, or to the general exigencies of his country. 'Tis a random shot at best.

When men proceed in this irregular mode, the first contributor is apt to grow peevish with his neighbours. He is but too well disposed to measure their means by his own envy, and not by the real state of their fortunes, which he can rarely know, and which it may in them be an act of the grossest imprudence to reveal. Hence the odium and lassitude, with which people will look upon a provision for the publick which is bought by discord at the expence of social quiet. Hence the bitter heartburnings, and the war of tongues which is so often the prelude to other wars. Nor is it every contribution, called voluntary, which is according to the free will of the giver. A false shame, or a false glory, against his feelings, and [213] his judgment, may tax an individual to the detriment of his family, and in wrong of his creditors. A pretence of publick spirit may disable him from the performance of his private duties. It may disable him even from paying the legitimate contributions which he is to furnish according to the prescript of law; but what is the most dangerous of all is, that malignant disposition to which this mode of contribution evidently tends, and which at length leaves the comparatively indigent, to judge of the wealth, and to prescribe to the opulent, or those whom they conceive to be such, the use they are to make of their fortunes. From thence it is but one step to the subversion of all property.

Far, very far am I from supposing that such things enter into the purposes of those excellent persons whose zeal has led them to this kind of measure; but the measure itself will lead them beyond their intention, and what is begun with the best designs, bad men will perversely improve to the worst of their purposes. An ill-founded plausibility in great affairs is a real evil. In France we have seen the wickedest and most foolish of men, the Constitution-mongers of 1789, pursuing this very course, and ending in this very event. These projectors of deception set on foot two modes of voluntary contribution to the state. The first, they called patriotick gifts. These, for the greater part were not more ridiculous in the mode, than contemptible in the project. The other, which they called the patriotick contribution, was expected to amount to a fourth of the fortunes of individuals, but at their own will and on their own estimate; but this contribution threatening to fall infinitely short of their hopes, they soon made it compulsory, both in the rate and in the levy, beginning in fraud, and ending, as all the frauds of power end, in plain violence. All these devices to produce an involuntary will, were under the pretext of relieving the more indigent [214] classes. But the principle of voluntary contribution, however delusive, being once established, these lower classes first, and then all classes, were encouraged to throw off the regular methodical

Regicide Peace III

payments to the State as so many badges of slavery. Thus all regular revenue failing, these impostors, raising the superstructure on the same cheats with which they had laid the foundation of their greatness, and not content with a portion of the possessions of the rich, confiscated the whole, and to prevent them from reclaiming their rights, murdered the proprietors. The whole of the process has passed before our eyes, and been conducted indeed with a greater degree of rapidity than could be expected.

My opinion then is, that publick contributions ought only to be raised by the publick will. By the judicious form of our constitution, the publick contribution is in it's name and substance a grant. In it's origin it is truly voluntary; not voluntary according to the irregular, unsteady, capricious will of individuals, but according to the will and wisdom of the whole popular mass, in the only way in which will and wisdom can go together. This voluntary grant obtaining in it's progress the force of a law, a general necessity which takes away all merit, and consequently all jealousy from individuals, compresses, equalizes, and satisfies the whole; suffering no man to judge of his neighbour, or to arrogate any thing to himself. If their will complies with their obligation, the great end is answered in the happiest mode; if the will resists the burthen, every one loses a great part of his own will as a common lot. After all, perhaps contributions raised by a charge on luxury, or that degree of convenience which approaches so near as to be confounded with luxury, is the only mode of contribution which may be with truth termed voluntary.

I MIGHT REST HERE, and take the loan I speak of as leading [215] to a solution of that question, which I proposed in my first letter: "Whether the inability of the country to prosecute the war did necessitate a submission to the indignities and the calamities of a Peace with the Regicide power." But give me leave to pursue this point a little further.

I know that it has been a cry usual on this occasion, as it has been upon occasions where such a cry could have less apparent justification, that great distress and misery have been the consequence of this war, by the burthens brought and laid upon the people. But to know where the burthen really lies, and where it presses, we must divide the people. As to the common people, their stock is in their persons and in their earnings. I deny that the stock of their persons is diminished in a greater proportion than the common sources of populousness abundantly fill up—I mean, constant employment; proportioned pay according to the produce of the soil, and where the soil fails, according to the operation of the general capital; plentiful nourishment to vigorous labour; comfortable provision to decrepid age, to orphan infancy, and to accidental malady. I say nothing to the *policy* of the provision for the poor, in all the variety of faces under which it presents itself. This is the matter of another enquiry. I only just speak of it as of a fact, taken with others, to support me in my denial that hitherto any one of the ordinary sources of the increase of mankind is dried up by this war. I affirm, what I can well prove, that the waste has been less than the supply. To say that in war no man must be killed, is to say that there ought to be no war. This they may say, who wish to talk idly, and who would display their humanity at the expence of their honesty, or their understanding. If more lives are lost in this war than necessity requires, they are lost by misconduct or mistake. But if the hostility be just, the errour is to be corrected: the war is not to be abandoned.

[216] That the stock of the common people, in numbers is not lessened, any more than the causes are impaired, is manifest, without being at the pains of an actual numeration. An improved and improving agriculture, which implies a great augmentation of labour, has not yet found itself at a stand, no, not for a single moment, for want of the necessary hands, either in the settled progress of husbandry, or in the occasional pressure of harvests. I have even reason to believe that

there has been a much smaller importation, or the demand of it, from a neighbouring kingdom than in former times, when agriculture was more limited in it's extent and it's means, and when the time was a season of profound peace. On the contrary, the prolifick fertility of country life has poured it's superfluity of population into the canals, and into other publick works which of late years have been undertaken to so amazing an extent, and which have not only not been discontinued, but beyond all expectation pushed on with redoubled vigour, in a war that calls for so many of our men, and so much of our riches. An increasing capital calls for labour: and an increasing population answers to the call. Our manufactures, augmented both for the supply of foreign and domestick consumption, reproducing with the means of life the multitudes which they use and waste, (and which many of them devour much more surely and much more largely than the war) have always found the laborious hand ready for the liberal pay. That the price of the soldier is highly raised is true. In part this rise may be owing to some measures not so well considered in the beginning of this war; but the grand cause has been the reluctance of that class of people from whom the soldiery is taken, to enter into a military life — not that but once entered into, it has it's conveniences, and even it's pleasures. I have seldom known a soldier who, at the intercession of his friends, [217] and at their no small charge, had been redeemed from that discipline, that in a short time was not eager to return to it again. But the true reason is the abundant occupation, and the augmented stipend found in towns, and villages, and farms, which leaves a smaller number of persons to be disposed of. The price of men for new and untried ways of life must bear a proportion to the profits of that mode of existence from whence they are to be bought.

So far as to the stock of the common people, as it consists in their persons. As to the other part, which consists in their earnings, I have to say, that the rates of wages are very greatly augmented almost through the kingdom. In the parish where I live, it has been raised from seven to nine shillings in the week for the same labourer, performing the same task, and no greater. Except something in the malt taxes, and the duties upon sugars, I do not know any one tax imposed for very many years past which affects the labourer in any degree whatsoever; while on the other hand, the tax upon houses not having more than seven windows (that is, upon cottages) was repealed the very year before the commencement of the present war. On the whole, I am satisfied, that the humblest class, and that class which touches the most nearly on the lowest, out of which it is continually emerging, and to which it is continually falling, receives far more from publick impositions than it pays. That class receives two million sterling annually from the classes above it. It pays to no such amount towards any publick contribution.

I HOPE IT IS NOT NECESSARY for me to take notice of that language, so ill suited to the persons to whom it has been attributed, and so unbecoming the place in which it is said [218] to have been uttered, concerning the present war as the cause of the high price of provisions during the greater part of the year 1796. I presume it is only to be ascribed to the intolerable licence with which the newspapers break not only the rules of decorum in real life, but even the dramatick decorum, when they personate great men, and, like bad poets, make the heroes of the piece talk more like us Grub-street scribblers, than in a style consonant to persons of gravity and importance in the State. It was easy to demonstrate the cause, and the sole cause, of that rise in the grand article and first necessary of life. It would appear that it had no more connexion with the war, than the moderate price to which all sorts of grain were reduced, soon after the return of Lord Malmesbury, had with the state of politicks and the fate of his Lordship's treaty. I have quite as good reason (that is, no reason at all) to attribute this abundance to the longer continuance of the war, as the gentlemen who personate leading Members of Parliament, have had for giving the enhanced price to that war, at a more early period of it's duration. Oh, the folly of us poor creatures, who, in the midst of our distresses, or our escapes, are ready to claw or caress one another, upon matters that so seldom depend on our wisdom or our weakness, on our good or evil conduct towards each other!

An untimely shower, or an unseasonable drought; a frost too long continued, or too suddenly broken up, with rain and tempest; the blight of the spring, or the smut of the harvest; will do more to cause the distress of the belly, than all the contrivances of all Statesmen can do to relieve it. Let Government protect and encourage industry, secure property, repress violence, and discountenance fraud, it is all that they have to do. In other respects, the less they meddle in these affairs the better; the rest is in the hands [219] of our Master and theirs. We are in a constitution of things wherein "*Modo sol nimius, modo corripit imber.*" But I will push this matter no further. As I have said a good deal upon it at various times during my publick service, and have lately written something on it, which may yet see the light, I shall content myself now with observing, that the vigorous and laborious class of life has lately got from the *bon ton* of the humanity of this day, the name of the "*labouring poor.*" We have heard many plans for the relief of the "*Labouring Poor.*" This puling jargon is not as innocent as it is foolish. In meddling with great affairs, weakness is never innoxious. Hitherto the name of Poor (in the sense in which it is used to excite compassion) has not been used for those who can, but for those who cannot labour — for the sick and infirm; for orphan infancy; for languishing and decrepid age: but when we affect to pity as poor, those who must labour or the world cannot exist, we are trifling with the condition of mankind. It is the common doom of man that he must eat his bread by the sweat of his brow, that is, by the sweat of his body, or the sweat of his mind. If this toil was inflicted as a curse, it is as might be expected from the curses of the Father of all Blessings—it is tempered with many alleviations, many comforts. Every attempt to fly from it, and to refuse the very terms of our existence, becomes much more truly a curse, and heavier pains and penalties fall upon those who would elude the tasks which are put upon them by the great Master Workman of the World, who in his dealings with his creatures sympathizes with their weakness, and speaking of a creation wrought by mere will out of nothing, speaks of six days of *labour* and one of *rest*. I do not call a healthy young man, chearful in his mind, and vigorous in his arms—I cannot call such a man, *poor;* I cannot pity my [220] kind as a kind, merely because they are men. This affected pity only tends to dissatisfy them with their condition, and to teach them to seek resources where no resources are to be found—in something else than their own industry, and frugality, and sobriety. Whatever may be the intention (which, because I do not know, I cannot dispute) of those who would discontent mankind by this strange pity, they act towards us, in the consequences, as if they were our worst enemies.

IN TURNING OUR VIEW from the lower to the higher classes, it will not be necessary for me to shew at any length that the stock of the latter, as it consists in their numbers, has not yet suffered any material diminution. I have not seen, or heard it asserted: I have no reason to believe it. There is no want of officers, that I have ever understood, for the new ships which we commission, or the new regiments which we raise. In the nature of things it is not with their persons that the higher classes principally pay their contingent to the demands of war. There is another, and not less important, part which rests with almost exclusive weight upon them. They furnish the means,

REGICIDE PEACE III

How war may best upheld,
Move by her two main nerves, iron and gold,
In all her equipage.

Not that they are exempt from contributing also by their personal service in the fleets and armies of their country. They do contribute, and in their full and fair proportion, according to the relative proportion of their numbers in the community. They contribute all the mind that actuates the whole machine. The fortitude required of them is very different from the unthinking alacrity of the common soldier, or common sailor in the face of danger and death. It is not a passion, it is not an impulse, it is not a sentiment. It is a cool, steady, [221] deliberate principle, always present, always equable; having no connexion with anger; tempering honour with prudence; incited, invigorated, and sustained by a generous love of fame; informed, moderated and directed by an enlarged knowledge of it's own great publick ends; flowing in one blended stream from the opposite sources of the heart and the head; carrying in itself it's own commission, and proving it's title to every other command, by the first and most difficult command, that of the bosom in which it resides. It is a fortitude, which unites with the courage of the field the more exalted and refined courage of the council; which knows as well to retreat as to advance; which can conquer as well by delay, as by the rapidity of a march, or the impetuosity of an attack; which can be, with Fabius, the black cloud that lowers on the tops of the mountains, or with Scipio, the thunderbolt of war; which, undismayed by false shame, can patiently endure the severest trial that a gallant spirit can undergo, in the taunts and provocations of the enemy, the suspicions, the cold respect, and "mouth-honour" of those, from whom it should meet a cheerful obedience; which, undisturbed by false humanity, can calmly assume that most awful moral responsibility of deciding when victory may be too dearly purchased by the loss of a single life, and when the safety and glory of their country may demand the certain sacrifice of thousands. Different stations of command may call for different modifications of this fortitude, but the character ought to be the same in all. And never, in the most "palmy state" of our martial renown, did it shine with brighter lustre than in the present sanguinary and ferocious hostilities, wherever the British arms have been carried. But, in this most arduous, and momentous conflict, which from it's nature should have roused us to new and unexampled efforts, I know not how it has been, that we have never put forth half the strength, which we have exerted in ordinary [222] wars. In the fatal battles which have drenched the Continent with blood, and shaken the system of Europe to pieces, we have never had any considerable army of a magnitude to be compared to the least of those by which, in former times, we so gloriously asserted our place as protectors, not oppressors, at the head of the great Commonwealth of Europe. We have never manfully met the danger in front: and when the enemy, resigning to us our natural dominion of the ocean, and abandoning the defence of his distant possessions to the infernal energy of the destroying principles which he had planted there for the subversion of the neighbouring Colonies, drove forth, by one sweeping law of unprecedented despotism, his armed multitudes on every side, to overwhelm the Countries and States, which had for centuries stood the firm barriers against the ambition of France; we drew back the arm of our military force, which had never been more than half raised to oppose him. From that time we have been combating only with the other arm of our naval power; the right arm of England I admit; but which struck almost unresisted, with blows that could never reach the heart of the hostile mischief. From that time, without a single effort to regain those outworks, which ever till now we so strenuously maintained, as the strong frontier of our own dignity and safety, no less than the liberties of

Europe; with but one feeble attempt to succour those brave, faithful, and numerous allies, whom for the first time since the days of our Edwards and Henrys, we now have in the bosom of France itself; we have been intrenching, and fortifying, and garrisoning ourselves at home: we have been redoubling security on security, to protect ourselves from invasion, which has now first become to us a serious object of alarm and terrour. Alas! the few of us, who have protracted life in any measure near to the extreme limits of our short period, have been condemned to see strange things; [223] new systems of policy, new principles, and not only new men, but what might appear a new species of men! I believe that any person who was of age to take a part in publick affairs forty years ago, if the intermediate space of time were expunged from his memory, would hardly credit his senses, when he should hear from the highest authority, that an army of two hundred thousand men was kept up in this island, and that in the neighbouring island there were at least fourscore thousand more. But when he had recovered from his surprise on being told of this army, which has not it's parallel, what must be his astonishment to be told again, that this mighty force was kept up for the mere purpose of an inert and passive defence, and that, in it's far greater part, it was disabled by it's constitution and very essence, from defending us against an enemy by any one preventive stroke, or any one operation of active hostility? What must his reflexions be, on learning further, that a fleet of five hundred men of war, the best appointed, and to the full as ably commanded as this country ever had upon the sea, was for the greater part employed in carrying on the same system of unenterprising defence? What must be the sentiments and feelings of one, who remembers the former energy of England, when he is given to understand, that these two islands, with their extensive, and every where vulnerable coast, should be considered as a garrisoned sea-town; what would such a man, what would any man think, if the garrison of so strange a fortress should be such, and so feebly commanded, as never to make a sally; and that, contrary to all which has hitherto been seen in war, an infinitely inferiour army, with the shattered relicks of an almost annihilated navy, ill found, and ill manned, may with safety besiege this superiour garrison, and without hazarding the life of a man, ruin the place, merely by the menaces and false appearances of an attack? Indeed, indeed, my dear [224] friend, I look upon this matter of our defensive system as much the most important of all considerations at this moment. It has oppressed me with many anxious thoughts, which, more than any bodily distemper, have sunk me to the condition, in which you know that I am. Should it please Providence to restore to me even the late weak remains of my strength, I propose to make this matter the subject of a particular discussion. I only mean here to argue, that the mode of conducting the war on our part, be it good or bad, has prevented even the common havock of war in our population, and especially among that class, whose duty and privilege of superiority it is, to lead the way amidst the perils and slaughter of the field of battle.

The other causes, which sometimes affect the numbers of the lower classes, but which I have shewn not to have existed to any such degree during this war—penury, cold, hunger, nakedness, do not easily reach the higher orders of society. I do not dread for them the slightest taste of these calamities from the distress and pressure of the war. They have much more to dread in that way from the confiscations, the rapines, the burnings, and the massacres, that may follow in the train of a peace, which shall establish the devastating and depopulating principles and example of the French Regicides, in security, and triumph and dominion. In the ordinary course of human affairs, any check to population among men in ease and opulence, is less to be apprehended from what they may suffer, than from what they enjoy. Peace is more likely to be injurious to them in that respect than war. The excesses of delicacy, repose, and satiety, are as unfavourable as the extremes of hardship, toil, and want, to the increase and multiplication of our kind. Indeed, the abuse of the bounties of Nature, much more surely than any partial privation of them, tends to intercept [225] that precious boon of a second and dearer life in our progeny, which was bestowed in the first great command to man from the All-gracious Giver of all, whose name be blessed, whether he gives or takes away. His hand, in every page of his book, has written the lesson of moderation. Our physical well-being, our moral worth, our social happiness, our political tranquillity, all depend on that controul of all our appetites and passions, which the ancients designed by the cardinal virtue of Temperance.

The only real question to our present purpose, with regard to the higher classes, is, how stands the account of their stock, as it consists in wealth of every description? Have the burthens of the war compelled them to curtail any part of their former expenditure; which, I have before observed, affords the only standard of estimating property as an object of taxation? Do they enjoy all the same conveniencies, the same comforts, the same elegancies, the same luxuries, in the same, or in as many different modes as they did before the war?

IN THE LAST ELEVEN YEARS, there have been no less than three solemn enquiries into the finances of the kingdom, by three different Committees of your House. The first was in the year 1786. On that occasion, I remember, the Report of the Committee was examined, and sifted, and bolted to the bran, by a gentleman whose keen and powerful talents I have ever admired. He thought there was not sufficient evidence to warrant the pleasing representation, which the Committee had made, of our national prosperity. He did not believe that our publick revenue could continue to be so productive as they had assumed. He even went the length of recording his own inferences of doubt, in a set of resolutions, which now stand upon your Journals. And perhaps the retrospect, on which the Report proceeded, did not go far [226] enough back, to allow any sure and satisfactory average for a ground of solid calculation. But what was the event? When the next Committee sate in 1791, they found, that, on an average of the last four years, their predecessors had fallen short in their estimate of the permanent taxes, by more than three hundred and forty thousand pounds a year. Surely then, if I can show that in the produce of those same taxes, and more particularly of such as affect articles of luxurious use and consumption, the four years of the war have equalled those four years of peace, flourishing, as they were, beyond the most sanguine speculations, I may expect to hear no more of the distress occasioned by the war.

The additional burdens which have been laid on some of those same articles, might reasonably claim some allowance to be made. Every new advance of the price to the consumer, is a new incentive to him to retrench the quantity of his consumption; and if, upon the whole, he pays the same, his property, computed by the standard of what he voluntarily pays, must remain the same. But I am willing to forego that fair advantage in the enquiry. I am willing that the receipts of the permanent taxes which existed before January 1793, should be compared during the war, and during the period of peace which I have mentioned. I will go further. Complete accounts of the year 1791 were separately laid before your House. I am ready to stand by a comparison of the produce of four years up to the beginning of the year 1792, with that of the war. Of the year immediately previous to hostilities, I have not been able to obtain any perfect documents; but I have seen enough to satisfy me, that although a comparison including that year might be less favourable, yet it would not essentially injure my argument.

REGICIDE PEACE III

You will always bear in mind, my dear Sir, that I am not considering whether, if the common enemy of the quiet of [227] Europe had not forced us to take up arms in our own defence, the spring-tide of our prosperity might not have flowed higher than the mark at which it now stands. That consideration is connected with the question of the justice and the necessity of the war. It is a question which I have long since discussed. I am now endeavouring to ascertain whether there exists, in fact, any such necessity as we hear every day asserted, to furnish a miserable pretext for counselling us to surrender, at discretion, our conquests, our honour, our dignity, our very independence, and, with it, all that is dear to man. It will be more than sufficient for that purpose, if I can make it appear that we have been stationary during the war. What then will be said, if, in reality, it shall be proved that there is every indication of increased and increasing wealth, not only poured into the grand reservoir of the national capital, but diffused through all the channels of all the higher classes, and giving life and activity, as it passes, to the agriculture, the manufactures, the commerce, and the navigation of the country?

The Finance Committee, which has been appointed in this Session, has already made two reports. Every conclusion that I had before drawn, as you know, from my own observation, I have the satisfaction of seeing there confirmed by their authority. Large as was the sum, by which the Committee of 1791 found the estimate of 1786 to have been exceeded in the actual produce of four years of peace, their own estimate has been exceeded, during the war, by a sum more than one-third larger. The same taxes have yielded more than half a million beyond their calculation. They yielded this, notwithstanding the stoppage of the distilleries, against which you may remember that I privately remonstrated. With an allowance for that defalcation, they have yielded sixty thousand pounds annually above the actual average of the preceding four years of peace. I believe this [228] to have been without parallel in all former wars. If regard be had to the great and unavoidable burthens of the present war, I am confident of the fact.

But let us descend to particulars. The taxes, which go by the general name of assessed taxes, comprehend the whole, or nearly the whole domestick establishment of the rich. They include some things, which belong to the middling, and even to all but the very lowest, classes. They now consist of the duties on houses and windows, on male servants, horses, and carriages. They did also extend to cottages, to female servants, waggons, and carts used in husbandry, previous to the year 1792; when, with more enlightened policy, at the moment that the possibility of war could not be out of the contemplation of any statesman, the wisdom of Parliament confined them to their present objects. I shall give the gross assessment for five years, as I find it in the Appendix to the second Report of your Committee:

1791	ending 5th April	1792	£1,706,334
1792	"	"	1793	1,585,991
1793	"	"	1794	1,597,623
1794	"	"	1795	1,608,196
1795	"	"	1796	1,625,874

Here will be seen a gradual increase during the whole progress of the war: and if[1] I am correctly informed, the rise

1. The account given above is from the appendix B to the second Report. Since Mr. Burke's death, a fourth Report has come out, which very fully substantiates his information. There is a table, containing *a view of the Land Tax, and Assessed Taxes*, blended together. The amount of the Assessed Taxes may be easily found (except an occasional difference in the last figure, from the omission of the shillings and pence) by deducting the sum of £2,037,627, which is the gross charge of the Land-Tax, according to the Report of the Committee in 1791.

1789	ending 5th April	1790	£3,572,434
1790	"	"	1791	3,741,222
1791	"	"	1792	3,743,961

REGICIDE PEACE III

in [229] the last year, after every deduction that can be made, almost surpasses belief. It is enormously out of all proportion to the increase, not of any single year, but of all the years put together, since the time that the duties, which I have mentioned above, were repealed.

There are some other taxes, which seem to have a reference to the same general head. The present Minister, many years ago, subjected bricks and tiles to a duty under the excise. It is of little consequence to our present consideration, whether these materials have been employed in building more commodious, more elegant, and more magnificent habitations, or in enlarging, decorating, and remodelling those, which sufficed for our plainer ancestors. During the first two years of the war, they paid so largely to the publick revenue, that in 1794 a new duty was laid upon them, which was equal to one half of the old, and which has produced upwards of £165,000 in the last three years. Yet notwithstanding the pressure of this additional weight,[1] there has been

1792	"	"	1793	3,623,619
1793	"	"	1794	3,635,250
1794	"	"	1795	3,645,824
1795	"	"	1796	3,663,501
1796	"	"	1797	4,101,869

A ten per cent. was laid upon the Assessed Taxes in 1791, to commence from October, 1790. In 1796 were laid, a new tax on Horses not before included, an additional tax of 2s. and a new ten per cent. These produced in that year altogether £84,232, which being deducted, will still leave an actual increase in that one year of £354,130.

1. This and the following tables on the same construction are compiled from the Reports of the Finance Committee in 1791 and 1797, with the addition of the separate paper laid before the House of Commons, and ordered to be printed on the 7th of February, 1792.

BRICKS AND TILES

YEARS OF PEACE	£	YEARS OF WAR	£
1787	94,521	1793	122,975
1788	96,278	1794	106,811

an actual augmentation in the [230] consumption. The only two other articles which come under this description, are, the stamp-duty on gold and silver plate, and the Customs on glass-plates. This latter is now, I believe, the single instance of costly furniture to be found in the catalogue of our imports. If it were wholly to vanish, I should not think we were ruined. Both the duties have risen, during the war, very considerably in proportion to the total of their produce.

We have no tax among us on the great necessaries of life with regard to food. The receipts of our Custom-House, under the head of Groceries, afford us, however, some means of calculating our luxuries of the table. The articles of Tea, Coffee, and Cocoa-Nuts, I would propose to omit, and to take

BRICKS AND TILES

YEARS OF PEACE	£	YEARS OF WAR	£	
1789	91,773	1795	83,804	
1790	104,409	1796	94,668	Increase to 1790
	£386,981		£408,258	£21,277
				Increase to 1791
1791	115,382	4 Years to 1791	407,842	£416

PLATE

1787	22,707	1793	25,920	
1788	23,295	1794	23,637	
1789	22,453	1795	25,607	
1790	18,483	1796	28,513	Increase to 1790
	£86,888		£103,677	£16,789
				Increase to 1791
1791	31,523	4 Years to 1791	95,754	£7,923

GLASS PLATES

1787	—	1793	5,655	
1788	5,496	1794	5,456	
1789	4,686	1795	5,839	
1790	6,008	1796	8,871	
	£16,190		£25,821	Increase to 1791
1791	7,880	4 Years to 1791	24,070	£1,721

them instead from the Excise, as best showing what is consumed at home. Upon this principle, adding them altogether (with the exception of Sugar, for a reason which I shall afterwards mention) I find that they have produced, in one mode of comparison, upwards of £272,000, and in the other mode, upwards of £165,000, [231] more, during the war than in peace.[1] An additional duty was also laid in 1795 on Tea,

1.

GROCERIES

YEARS OF PEACE	£	YEARS OF WAR	£	
1787	167,389	1793	124,655	
1788	133,191	1794	195,840	
1789	142,871	1795	208,242	
1790	156,311	1796	159,826	Increase to 1790
	£599,762		£688,563	£88,801
				Increase to 1791
1791	236,727	4 Years to 1791	669,100	£19,463

TEA

1787	424,144	1793	477,644	
1788	426,660	1794	467,132	
1789	539,575	1795	507,518	
1790	417,736	1796	526,307	Increase to 1790
	£1,808,115		£1,978,601	£170,486
				Increase to 1791
1791	448,709	4 Years to 1791	1,832,680	£145,921

The additional duty imposed in 1795, produced in that year £137,656, and in 1796 £200,107.

COFFEE AND COCOA NUTS

1787	17,006	1793	36,846	
1788	30,217	1794	49,177	
1789	34,784	1795	27,913	
1790	38,647	1796	19,711	Increase to 1790
	£120,654		£133,647	£12,993
				Decrease to 1791
1791	41,194	4 Years to 1791	144,842	£11,195

The additional duty of 1795 in that year gave £16,775, and in 1796 £15,319.

another on Coffee, and a third on Raisins; an article, together with currants, of much more extensive use than would readily be imagined. The balance in favour of our argument would have been much enhanced, if our Coffee and fruit-ships from the Mediterranean had arrived, last year, at their usual season. [232] They do not appear in these accounts. This was one consequence arising (would to God, that none more afflicting to Italy, to Europe, and the whole civilized world had arisen!) from our impolitick and precipitate desertion of that important maritime station. As to Sugar,[1] I have excluded it from the Groceries, because the account of the Customs is not a perfect criterion of the consumption, much having been re-exported to the north of Europe, which used to be supplied by France; and there are no materials to furnish grounds for computing this re-exportation. The increase on the face of our entries is immense during the four years of war—little short of thirteen hundred thousand pounds.

The encrease of the duties on Beer has been regularly progressive, or nearly so, to a very large amount.[2] It is a good

1.

SUGAR

YEARS OF PEACE	£	YEARS OF WAR	£	
1787	1,065,109	1793	1,473,139	
1788	1,184,458	1794	1,392,965	
1789	1,095,106	1795	1,338,246	
1790	1,069,108	1796	1,474,899	Increase to 1790
	£4,413,781		£5,679,249	£1,265,468
				Increase to 1791
1791	1,044,053	4 Years to 1791	4,392,725	£1,286,524

There was a new duty on *Sugar* in 1791, which produced in 1794 £234,292, in 1795 £206,932, and in 1796 £245,024. It is not clear from the Report of the Committee, whether the additional duty is included in the account given above.

2.

BEER, &c

1787	1,761,429	1793	2,043,902

REGICIDE PEACE III

BEER, &c

YEARS OF PEACE	£	YEARS OF WAR	£	
1788	1,705,199	1794	2,082,053	
1789	1,742,514	1795	1,931,101	
1790	1,858,043	1796	2,294,377	Increase to 1790
	£7,067,185		£8,351,433	£1,284,248
				Increase to 1791
1791	1,880,478	4 Years to 1791	7,186,234	£1,165,199

WINE

1787	219,934	1793	222,887	
1788	215,578	1794	283,644	
1789	252,649	1795	317,072	
1790	308,624	1796	187,818	Increase to 1790
	£996,785		£1,011,421	£14,638
				Decrease to 1791
1791	336,549	4 Years to 1791	1,113,400	£101,979

QUANTITY IMPORTED

	TONS		TONS
1787	29,978	1793	22,788
1788	25,442	1794	27,868
1789	27,414	1795	32,033
1790	29,182	1796	19,079

The additional duty of 1795 produced that year £730,871, and in 1796 £394,686. A second additional duty which produced £98,165 was laid in 1796.

SWEETS

	£		£	
1787	11,167	1793	11,016	
1788	7,375	1794	10,612	
1789	7,202	1795	13,321	
1790	4,953	1796	15,050	Increase to 1790
	£30,697		£49,990	£19,302
				Increase to 1791
1791	13,282	4 Years to 1791	32,812	£17,178

In 1795, an additional duty was laid on this article, which produced that year £5,679, and in 1796 £9,443, and in 1796 a second to commence on the 20th of June; it's produce in that year was £2,325.

deal above a million, and is more than equal to [233] one-eighth of the whole produce. Under this general head, some other liquors are included—Cyder, Perry, and Mead, as well as Vinegar, and Verjuice; but these are of very trifling consideration. The Excise-Duties on Wine, having sunk a little during the first two years of the war, were rapidly recovering their level again. In 1795, a heavy additional duty was imposed upon them, and a second in the following year; yet being compared with four years of peace to the end of 1790, they actually exhibit a small gain [234] to the revenue. And low as the importation may seem in 1796, when contrasted with any year since the French Treaty in 1787, it is still more than 3000 tons above the average importation for three years previous to that period. I have added Sweets, from which our factitious Wines are made; and I would have added Spirits, but that the total alteration of the duties in 1789 and the recent interruption of our Distilleries, rendered any comparison impracticable.

The ancient staple of our island, in which we are clothed, is very imperfectly to be traced on the books of the Custom-House: but I know, that our Woollen Manufactures flourish. I recollect to have seen that fact very fully established, last year, from the registers kept in the West-Riding of Yorkshire. This year, in the west of England I received a similar account, on the authority of a respectable clothier, in that quarter, whose testimony can less be questioned, because, in his political opinions, he is adverse, as I understand, to the continuance of the war. The principal articles of female dress, for some time past, have been Muslins and Callicoes.[1] These elegant

1.

MUSLINS AND CALLICOES

YEARS OF PEACE	£	YEARS OF WAR	£
1788	129,297	1793	173,050
1789	138,660	1794	104,902

fabricks of our own looms in the East, which serve for the remittance of our own revenues, have lately been imitated at home, with improving success, by the ingenious and enterprising manufacturers of Manchester, Paisley, and Glasgow. At the same time the importation from Bengal has kept pace with the extension [235] of our own dexterity and industry; while the sale of our printed goods,[1] of both kinds, has been with equal steadiness advanced, by the taste and execution of our designers and artists. Our Woollens and Cottons, it is true, are not all for the home market. They do not distinctly prove, what is my present point, our own wealth by our own expence. I admit it: we export them in great and growing quantities: and they, who croak themselves hoarse about the decay of our trade, may put as much of this account, as they chuse, to the creditor side of money received

MUSLINS AND CALLICOES

YEARS OF PEACE	£	YEARS OF WAR	£	
1790	126,267	1795	103,856	
1791	128,364	1796	272,544	Increase to 1791
	£522,588		£654,352	£131,764

This table begins with 1788. The net produce of the preceding year is not in the Report, whence the table is taken.

1.

PRINTED GOODS

1787	142,000	1793	191,566	
1788	154,486	1794	190,554	
1789	153,202	1795	197,416	
1790	167,156	1796	230,530	Increase to 1790
	£616,844		£810,066	£193,222
1791	191,489	4 Years to 1791	666,333	Increase to 1791 £143,733

These duties for 1787, are blended with several others. The proportion of printed goods to the other articles for four years, was found to be one-fourth. That proportion is here taken.

LETTERS ON A REGICIDE PEACE

from other countries in payment for British skill and labour. They may settle the items to their own liking, where all goes to demonstrate our riches. I shall be contented here with whatever they will have the goodness to leave me, and pass to another entry, which is less ambiguous—I mean that of Silk.[1] The manufactory itself is a forced [236] plant. We have been obliged to guard it from foreign competition by very strict prohibitory laws. What we import, is the raw and prepared material, which is worked up in various ways, and worn in various shapes by both sexes. After what we have just seen, you will probably be surprised to learn, that the quantity of silk, imported during the war, has been much greater, than it was previously in peace; and yet we must all remember to our mortification, that several of our silk ships fell a prey to Citizen Admiral Richery. You will hardly expect me to go through the tape and thread, and all the other small wares of haberdashery and millinery to be gleaned up among our imports. But I shall make one observation, and with great satisfaction, respecting them. They gradually diminish, as our own manufactures of the same description spread into their places; while the account of ornamental articles which our country does not produce, and we cannot wish it to produce, continues, upon the whole, to rise, in spite of all the caprices

1.

SILK

YEARS OF PEACE	£	YEARS OF WAR	£	
1787	159,912	1793	209,915	
1788	123,998	1794	221,306	
1789	157,730	1795	210,725	
1790	212,522	1796	221,007	Increase to 1790
	£634,162		£862,955	£208,793
				Increase to 1791
1791	279,128	4 Years to 1791	773,378	£89,577

of fancy and fashion. Of this kind are the different furs[1] used for muffs, trimmings, and linings, which, as the chief of the kind, I shall particularize. You will find them below.

The diversions of the higher classes form another, and the only remaining, head of enquiry into their expences. I mean those diversions which distinguish the country and [237] the town life; which are visible and tangible to the Statesman; which have some publick measure and standard. And here, when I look to the report of your Committee, I, for the first time, perceive a failure. It is clearly so. Whichever way I reckon the four years of peace, the old tax on the sports of the field has certainly proved deficient since the war. The same money, however, or nearly the same, has been paid to Government; though the same number of individuals have not contributed to the payment. An additional tax was laid in 1791, and, during the war, has produced upwards of £61,000; which is about £4000 more than the decrease of the old tax, in one scheme of comparison; and about £4000 less, in the other scheme. I might remark that the amount of the new tax, in the several years of the war, by no means bears the proportion, which it ought, to the old. There seems to be some great irregularity or other in the receipt: but I do

1.

FURS

YEARS OF PEACE	£	YEARS OF WAR	£	
1787	3,463	1793	2,829	
1788	2,957	1794	3,353	
1789	1,151	1795	3,266	
1790	3,328	1796	6,138	Increase to 1790
	£10,899		£15,586	£4,687
				Increase to 1791
1791	5,731	4 Years to 1791	13,167	£2,419

The skins here selected from the Custom-House Accounts are, *Black Bear, Ordinary Fox, Marten, Mink, Musquash, Otter, Raccoon,* and *Wolf.*

not think it worth while to examine into the argument. I am willing to suppose that many, who, in the idleness of peace, made war upon partridges, hares, and pheasants, may now carry more noble arms against the enemies of their country. Our political adversaries may do what they please with that concession. They are welcome to make the most of it. I am sure of a very handsome set-off in the other branch of expence; the amusements of a town-life.

THERE IS MUCH GAIETY, and dissipation, and profusion, which must escape and disappoint all the arithmetick of political oeconomy. But the Theatres are a prominent feature. They are established through every part of the kingdom, at a cost unknown till our days. There is hardly a provincial capital, which does not possess, or which does not aspire to possess, a Theatre-Royal. Most of them engage for a short time, at a vast price, every actor or actress [238] of name in the metropolis; a distinction, which, in the reign of my old friend Garrick, was confined to very few. The dresses, the scenes, the decorations of every kind, I am told, are in a new style of splendour and magnificence; whether to the advantage of our dramatick taste, upon the whole, I very much doubt. It is a shew, and a spectacle, not a play, that is exhibited. This is undoubtedly in the genuine manner of the Augustan age, but in a manner, which was censured by one of the best Poets and Criticks of that or any age:

Migravit ab aure voluptas
Omnis ad incertos oculos, et gaudia vana:
Quatuor aut plures aulaea premuntur in horas,
Dum fugiunt equitum turmae, peditumque catervae —

I must interrupt the passage, most fervently to deprecate and abominate the sequel,

Mox trahitur manibus Regum fortuna retortis.

I hope, that no French fraternization, which the relations of peace and amity with systematized Regicide, would assuredly, sooner or later, draw after them, even if it should overturn our happy constitution itself, could so change the hearts of Englishmen, as to make them delight in representations and processions, which have no other merit than that of degrading and insulting the name of Royalty. But good taste, manners, morals, religion, all fly, wherever the principles of Jacobinism enter: and we have no safety against them but in arms.

The Proprietors, whether in this they follow or lead what is called the town, to furnish out these gaudy and pompous entertainments, must collect so much more from the Publick. It was just before the breaking out of hostilities, that they levied for themselves the very tax, which, at the close of the American war, they represented to Lord North, as certain ruin to their affairs to demand for the State. The [239] example has since been imitated by the Managers of our Italian Opera. Once during the war, if not twice (I would not willingly misstate any thing, but I am not very accurate on these subjects) they have raised the price of their subscription. Yet I have never heard, that any lasting dissatisfaction has been manifested, or that their houses have been unusually and constantly thin. On the contrary, all the three theatres have been repeatedly altered, and refitted, and enlarged, to make them capacious of the crowds that nightly flock to them; and one of those huge and lofty piles, which lifts its broad shoulders in gigantick pride, almost emulous of the temples of God, has been reared from the foundation at a charge of more than fourscore thousand pounds, and yet remains a naked, rough, unsightly heap.

I am afraid, my dear Sir, that I have tired you with these dull, though important details. But we are upon a subject, which, like some of a higher nature, refuses ornament, and is contented with conveying instruction. I know too the obstinacy of unbelief, in those perverted minds, which have no delight, but in contemplating the supposed distress, and predicting the immediate ruin, of their country. These birds of evil presage, at all times, have grated our ears with their melancholy song; and, by some strange fatality or other, it has generally happened, that they have poured forth their loudest and deepest lamentations, at the periods of our most abundant prosperity. Very early in my publick life, I had occasion to make myself a little acquainted with their natural history. My first political tract in the collection, which a friend has made of my publications, is an answer to a very gloomy picture of the state of the nation, which was thought to have been drawn by a statesman of some eminence in his time. That was no more than the common spleen of disappointed ambition: in the present day, I fear, [240] that too many are actuated by a more malignant and dangerous spirit. They hope, by depressing our minds with a despair of our means and resources, to drive us, trembling and unresisting, into the toils of our enemies, with whom, from the beginning of the Revolution in France, they have ever moved in strict concert and co-operation. If, with the report of your Finance Committee in their hands, they can still affect to despond, and can still succeed, as they do, in spreading the contagion of their pretended fears, among well-disposed, though weak men; there is no way of counteracting them, but by fixing them down to particulars. Nor must we forget, that they are unwearied agitators, bold assertors, dextrous sophisters. Proof must be accumulated upon proof, to silence them. With this view, I shall now direct your attention to some other striking and unerring indications of our flourishing condition; and they will in general be derived from other sources, but equally authentick; from other reports and proceedings of both Houses of Parliament, all which unite with wonderful force of consent in the same general result. Hitherto we have seen the superfluity of our capital discovering itself only in procuring superfluous accommodation and enjoyment, in our houses, in our furniture, in our establishments, in our eating and drinking, our clothing, and our publick diversions. We shall now see it more beneficially employed in improving our territory itself. We shall see part of our present opulence, with provident care, put out to usury for posterity.

To WHAT ULTIMATE EXTENT it may be wise or practicable to push inclosures of common and waste lands, may be a question of doubt, in some points of view. But no person thinks them already carried to excess; and the relative magnitude of the sums laid out upon them gives us a standard of estimating the comparative situation of the [241] landed interest. Your House, this Session, appointed a Committee on Waste Lands, and they have made a Report by their chairman, an Honourable Baronet, for whom the Minister the other day, (with very good intentions, I believe, but with little real profit to the publick) thought fit to erect a Board of Agriculture. The account, as it stands there, appears sufficiently favourable. The greatest number of inclosing bills, passed in any one year of the last peace, does not equal the smallest annual number in the war; and those of the last year exceed, by more than one half, the highest year of peace. But what was my surprise, on looking into the late report of the Secret Committee of the Lords, to find a list of these Bills during the war, differing in every year, and larger on the whole, by nearly one third![1] I have checked this account by the Statute-

1. Report of the Lords Committee of Secrecy, ordered to be printed, 28th April, 1797, Appendix 44.

INCLOSURE BILLS

	4 YEARS OF PEACE		4 YEARS OF WAR
1789	33	1793	60
1790	25	1794	73
1791	40	1795	77

Book, and find it to be correct. What new brilliancy then does it throw over the prospect, bright as it was before! The number during the last four years, has more than doubled that of the four years immediately preceding; it has surpassed the five years of peace, beyond which the Lords Committees have not gone; it has even surpassed (I have verified the fact) the whole ten years of peace. I cannot stop here. I cannot advance a single step in this enquiry, without being obliged to cast my eyes back to the period when I first knew the country. These Bills, which had begun in the [242] reign of Queen Anne, had passed every year in greater or less numbers from the year 1723; yet in all that space of time, they had not reached the amount of any two years during the present war; and though soon after that time they rapidly increased, still, at the accession of his present Majesty, they were very far short of the number passed in the four years of hostilities.

IN MY FIRST LETTER I mentioned the state of our inland navigation, neglected as it had been from the reign of King William to the time of my observation. It was not till the present reign, that the Duke of Bridgwater's canal first excited a spirit of speculation and adventure in this way. This spirit shewed itself, but necessarily made no great progress, in the American war. When peace was restored, it began of course to work with more sensible effect; yet in ten years from that event, the Bills passed on that subject were not so many as from the year 1793 to the present Session of Parliament. From what I can trace on the Statute-Book, I am confident that all the capital expended in these projects during

INCLOSURE BILLS

	4 YEARS OF PEACE		4 YEARS OF WAR
1792	40	1796	72
	138		283

the peace, bore no degree of proportion, (I doubt on very grave consideration whether all that was ever so expended was equal) to the money which has been raised for the same purposes, since the war.[1] I know, that in the last four years of peace, when [243] they rose regularly, and rapidly, the sums specified in the acts were not near one-third of the subsequent amount. In the last Session of Parliament, the Grand Junction Company, as it is called, having sunk half a million, (of which I feel the good effects at my own door) applied to your House, for permission to subscribe half as much more, among themselves. This Grand Junction is an inoculation of the Grand Trunk: and in the present Session, the latter Company has obtained the authority of Parliament, to float two hundred acres of land, for the purpose of forming a reservoir, thirty feet deep, two hundred yards wide at the head, and two miles in length; a lake which may almost vie with that which feeds, what once was the (now obliterated) canal of Languedoc.

THE PRESENT WAR IS, above all others of which we have heard or read, a war against landed property. That description of property is in it's nature the firm base of every stable government; and has been so considered, by all the wisest writers of the old philosophy, from the time of the Stagyrite, who observes that the agricultural class of all others

1.

NAVIGATION AND CANAL BILLS

	4 YEARS OF PEACE		4 YEARS OF WAR
1789	3	1793	28
1790	8	1794	18
1791	10	1795	11
1792	9	1796	12
	30		69
Money raised	£2,377,200		£7,415,100

is the least inclined to sedition. We find it to have been so regarded in the practical politicks of antiquity, where they are brought more directly home to our understandings and bosoms, in the History of Rome, and above all, in the writings of Cicero. The country tribes were always thought more respectable, than those of the City. And if in our own history, there is any one circumstance to which, under God, are to be attributed the steady resistance, the fortunate issue, and sober settlement, of all our struggles for liberty, it is, that while the landed interest, instead of forming a separate body, as in other countries, has, at all times, been in close connexion and union with the other great interests of the country, it has been spontaneously [244] allowed to lead and direct, and moderate all the rest. I cannot, therefore, but see with singular gratification that during a war which has been eminently made for the destruction of the landed proprietors, as well as of Priests and Kings, as much has been done, by publick works, for the permanent benefit of their stake in this country, as in all the rest of the current century, which now touches to it's close. Perhaps, after this, it may not be necessary to refer to private observation; but I am satisfied, that in general, the rents of lands have been considerably increased: they are increased very considerably indeed, if I may draw any conclusion from my own little property of that kind. I am not ignorant, however, where our publick burdens are most galling. But all of this class will consider, who they are, that are principally menaced; how little the men of their description in other countries, where this revolutionary fury has but touched, have been found equal to their own protection; how tardy, and unprovided, and full of anguish in their flight, chained down as they are by every tie to the soil; how helpless they are, above all other men, in exile, in poverty, in need, in all the varieties of wretchedness; and then let them well weigh what are the burdens to which they ought not to submit for their own salvation.

REGICIDE PEACE III

MANY OF THE AUTHORITIES, which I have already ad-
duced, or to which I have referred, may convey a competent
notion of some of our principal manufactures. Their general
state will be clear from that of our external and internal commerce, through which they circulate, and of which they are
at once the cause and effect. But the communication of the
several parts of the kingdom with each other, and with foreign countries, has always been regarded as one of the most
certain tests to evince the prosperous or adverse state of our
trade in all it's branches. Recourse has usually been [245]
had to the revenue of the Post-office with this view. I shall include the product of the Tax which was laid in the last war,
and which will make the evidence more conclusive, if it shall
afford the same inference—I allude to the Post-Horse duty,
which shews the personal intercourse within the Kingdom, as
the Post-office shews the intercourse by letters, both within
and without. The first of these standards, then, exhibits an
increase, according to my former schemes of comparison,
from an eleventh to a twentieth part of the whole duty.[1] The
Post-office gives still less consolation to those who are miserable, in proportion as the country feels no misery. From the
commencement of the war, to the month of April, 1796, the
gross produce had increased by nearly one sixth of the whole
sum which the state now derives from that fund. I find that
the year ending 5th of April, 1793, gave £627,592, and the

1.

POST HORSE DUTY

YEARS OF PEACE	£	YEARS OF WAR	£	
1787	169,410	1793	191,488	
1788	204,659	1794	202,884	
1789	170,554	1795	196,691	
1790	181,155	1796	204,061	Increase 1790
	£725,778		£795,124	£69,346 to 1791
1791	198,634	4 Years to 1791	755,002	£40,122

LETTERS ON A REGICIDE PEACE

year ending at the same quarter in 1796, £750,637, after a fair deduction having been made for the alteration (which, you know, on grounds of policy I never approved) in your privilege of franking. I have seen no formal document subsequent to that period, but I have been credibly informed, there is very good ground to believe, that the revenue of the Post-office[1] still continues to be regularly and largely upon the rise.

[246] WHAT IS THE TRUE INFERENCE to be drawn from the annual number of bankruptcies, has been the occasion of much dispute. On one side, it has been confidently urged

1. The above account is taken from a paper which was ordered by the House of Commons to be printed, 8th December, 1796. From the gross produce of the year ending 5th April, 1796, there has been deducted in that statement the sum of £36,666, in consequence of the regulation on franking, which took place on the 5th May, 1795, and was computed at £40,000 per annum. To shew an equal number of years, both of peace and war, the accounts of two preceding years are given in the following table, from a Report made since Mr. Burke's death by a Committee of the House of Commons appointed to consider the claims of Mr. Palmer, the late Comptroller General; and for still greater satisfaction, the number of letters, inwards and outwards, have been added, except for the year 1790–1791. The letter-book for that year is not to be found.

POST OFFICE

| | GROSS REVENUE | NUMBER OF LETTERS | |
	£	INWARDS	OUTWARDS
April 1790–1791	575,079	—	—
1791–1792	585,432	6,391,149	5,081,344
1792–1793	627,592	6,584,867	5,041,137
1793–1794	691,268	7,094,777	6,537,234
1794–1795	705,319	7,071,029	7,473,626
1795–1796	750,637	7,641,077	8,597,167

From the last mentioned Report it appears that the accounts have not been completely and authentically made up, for the years ending 5th April, 1796 and 1797, but on the Receiver-General's books there is an increase of the latter year over the former, equal to something more than 5 per cent.

as a sure symptom of decaying trade: on the other side, it has been insisted, that it is a circumstance attendant upon a thriving trade; for that the greater is the whole quantity of trade, the greater of course must be the positive number of failures, while the aggregate success is still in the same proportion. In truth, the increase of the number may arise from either of those causes. But all must agree in one conclusion, that, if the number diminishes, and at the same time, every other sort of evidence tends to shew an augmentation of trade, there can be no better indication. We have already had very ample means of gathering that the year 1796 was a very favourable year of trade; and in that year the number of Bankruptcies was at least one-fifth below [247] the usual average. I take this from the Declaration of the Lord Chancellor in the House of Lords.[1] He professed to speak from the records of Chancery; and he added another very striking fact—that on the property actually paid into his Court (a very small part, indeed, of the whole property of the kingdom) there had accrued in that year a nett surplus of eight hundred thousand pounds, which was so much new capital.

BUT THE REAL SITUATION of our trade, during the whole of this war, deserves more minute investigation. I shall begin with that, which, though the least in consequence, makes perhaps the most impression on our senses, because it meets our eyes in our daily walks—I mean our retail trade. The exuberant display of wealth in our shops was the sight which most amazed a learned foreigner of distinction who lately resided among us. His expression, I remember, was, that "*they seemed to be bursting with opulence into the streets.*" The documents which throw light on this subject are not many; but

---

1. In a debate, 30th December, 1796, on the return of Lord Malmesbury. See Woodfall's Parliamentary Debates, vol. xiii. page 591.

they all meet in the same point: all concur in exhibiting an increase. The most material are the General Licences[1] which the law requires to be taken out by all dealers in exciseable commodities. These seem to be subject to considerable fluctuations. They have not been so [248] low in any year of the war, as in the years 1788 and 1789, nor ever so high in peace, as in the first year of the war. I should next state the licences to dealers in Spirits and Wine, but the change in them which took place in 1789 would give an unfair advantage to my argument. I shall therefore content myself with remarking, that from the date of that change the spirit licences kept nearly the same level till the stoppage of the Distilleries in 1795. If they dropped a little, and it was but little, the Wine Licences during the same time more than countervailed that loss to the revenue; and it is remarkable with regard to the latter, that in the year 1796, which was the lowest in the excise duties on wine itself, as well as in the quantity imported, more dealers in wine appear to have been licenced, than in any former year, excepting the first year of the war. This fact may raise some doubt, whether the consumption has been lessened so much, as (I believe) is commonly imagined. The only other retail-traders, whom I found so entered as to admit of being selected, are Tea-dealers, and sellers of Gold and Silver Plate; both of whom seem to have multiplied very much in propor-

1.

GENERAL LICENCES

YEARS OF PEACE	£	YEARS OF WAR	£	
1787	44,030	1793	45,568	
1788	40,882	1794	42,129	
1789	39,917	1795	43,350	
1790	41,970	1796	41,190	Increase to 1790
	£166,799		£170,237	£3,438
				Increase to 1791
1791	44,240	4 Years to 1791	167,009	£3,228

tion to their aggregate number.[1] I have kept apart one set of licensed sellers, because I am aware that our antagonists may be inclined to triumph a little, when I name Auctioneers and Auctions. They may be disposed to consider it as a sort of trade which thrives [249] by the distress of others. But if they will look at it a little more attentively, they will find their gloomy comfort vanish. The publick income from these licences has risen with very great regularity, through a series of years which all must admit to have been years of prosperity. It is remarkable too, that in the year 1793, which was the great year of Bankruptcies, these duties on Auctioneers and Auctions,[2] fell below the mark of 1791; and in 1796,

1.

DEALERS IN TEA

YEARS OF PEACE	£	YEARS OF WAR	£	
1787	10,934	1793	13,939	
1788	11,949	1794	14,315	
1789	12,501	1795	13,956	
1790	13,126	1796	14,830	Increase to 1790
	£48,510		£57,040	£8,530
				Increase to 1791
1791	13,921	4 Years to 1791	51,497	£5,543

SELLERS OF PLATE

1787	6,593	1793	8,178	
1788	7,953	1794	8,296	
1789	7,348	1795	8,128	
1790	7,988	1796	8,835	Increase to 1790
	£29,882		£33,437	£3,555
				Increase to 1791
1791	8,327	4 Years to 1791	31,616	£1,821

2.

AUCTIONS AND AUCTIONEERS

1787	48,964	1793	70,004
1788	53,993	1794	82,659
1789	52,024	1795	86,890

which year had one fifth less than the accustomed average of Bankruptcies, they mounted at once beyond all former examples. In concluding this general head, will you permit me, my dear Sir, to bring to your notice an humble, but industrious and laborious set of chapmen against whom the vengeance of your House has sometimes been levelled, with what policy I need not stay to enquire, as they have escaped without much injury? The Hawkers and Pedlars,[1] [250] I am assured, are still doing well, though from some new arrangements respecting them made in 1789, it would be difficult to trace their proceedings in any satisfactory manner.

WHEN SUCH IS THE VIGOUR of our traffick in it's minutest ramifications, we may be persuaded that the root and the trunk are sound. When we see the life-blood of the State circulate so freely through the capillary vessels of the system, we scarcely need enquire, if the heart performs its functions

AUCTIONS AND AUCTIONEERS

YEARS OF PEACE	£	YEARS OF WAR	£	
1790	53,156	1796	109,594	Increase to 1790
	£208,137		£349,147	£141,010
				Increase to 1791
1791	70,973	4 Years to 1791	230,146	£119,001

1. Since Mr. Burke's death a fourth Report of the Committee of Finance has made its appearance. An account is there given from the Stamp-office of the gross produce of duties on Hawkers and Pedlars for four years of peace and four of war. It is therefore added in the manner of the other tables.

HAWKERS AND PEDLARS

1789	6,132	1793	6,042
1790	6,708	1794	6,104
1791	6,482	1795	6,795
1792	6,008	1796	7,882
	£25,330		£26,823
	Increase in 4 Years of War		£1,493

aright. But let us approach it; let us lay it bare, and watch the systole and diastole, as it now receives, and now pours forth the vital stream through all the members. The port of London has always supplied the main evidence of the state of our commerce. I know, that amidst all the difficulties and embarrassments of the year 1793, from causes unconnected with and prior to the war, the tonnage of ships in the Thames actually rose. But I shall not go through a detail of official papers on this point. There is evidence which has appeared this very session before your House, infinitely more forcible and impressive to my apprehension, than all the journals and ledgers of all the Inspectors General from the days of Davenant. It is such as cannot carry with [251] it any sort of fallacy. It comes, not from one set, but from many opposite sets of witnesses, who all agree in nothing else; witnesses of the gravest and most unexceptionable character, and who confirm what they say, in the surest manner, by their conduct. Two different bills have been brought in for improving the port of London. I have it from very good intelligence, that when the project was first suggested from necessity, there were no less than eight different plans, supported by eight different bodies of subscribers. The cost of the least was estimated at two hundred thousand pounds, and of the most extensive, at twelve hundred thousand. The two between which the contest now lies, substantially agree (as all the others must have done) in the motives and reasons of the preamble: but I shall confine myself to that bill which is proposed on the part of the Mayor, Aldermen, and Common Council, because I regard them as the best authority, and their language in itself is fuller and more precise. I certainly see them complain of the "great delays, accidents, damages, losses, and extraordinary expences, which are almost continually sustained, to the hindrance and discouragement of commerce, and the great injury of the publick revenues." But what are the causes to which they attribute their complaints? The first

is, "THAT FROM THE VERY GREAT AND PROGRESSIVE IN-
CREASE OF THE NUMBER AND SIZE OF SHIPS AND OTHER
VESSELS, TRADING TO THE PORT OF LONDON; the River
Thames is, in general, so much crowded that the navigation
of a considerable part of the river is rendered tedious and
dangerous; and there is much want of room for the safe and
convenient mooring of vessels, and constant access to them."
The second is of the same nature. It is the want of regulations
and arrangements, never before found necessary, for expedition and facility. The third is of another kind, but to the
same effect: "that the legal quays are [252] too confined, and
there is not sufficient accommodation for the landing and
shipping of cargoes." And the fourth and last is still different;
they describe "the avenues to the legal quays," (which little
more than a century since, the great fire of London opened
and dilated beyond the measure of our then circumstances)
to be now "much too narrow, and incommodious, for the
great concourse of carts and other carriages usually passing
and repassing there." Thus, our trade has grown too big for
the ancient limits of art and nature. Our streets, our lanes,
our shores, the river itself, which has so long been our pride,
are impeded, and obstructed, and choaked up by our riches.
They are like our shops, "bursting with opulence." To these
misfortunes, to these distresses and grievances alone, we are
told, it is to be imputed that still more of our capital has
not been pushed into the channel of our commerce, to roll
back in it's reflux still more abundant capital, and fructify the
national treasury in it's course. Indeed, my dear Sir, when I
have before my eyes this consentient testimony of the Corporation of the City of London, the West-India Merchants,
and all the other Merchants who promoted the other plans,
struggling and contending, which of them shall be permitted
to lay out their money in consonance with their testimony; I
cannot turn aside to examine what one or two violent petitions, tumultuously voted by real or pretended Liverymen of

London, may have said of the utter destruction and annihilation of trade.

This opens a subject, on which every true lover of his country, and at this crisis, every friend to the liberties of Europe, and of social order in every country, must dwell and expatiate with delight. I mean to wind up all my proofs of our astonishing and almost incredible prosperity, with the valuable information given to the Secret Committee of the [253] Lords by the Inspector-General. And here I am happy that I can administer an antidote to all despondence, from the same dispensary from which the first dose of poison was supposed to have come. The Report of that Committee is generally believed to have been drawn up, (and it is certainly done with great ability) by the same noble Lord, who was said, as the author of the pamphlet of 1795, to have led the way in teaching us to place all our hope on that very *experiment*, which he afterwards declared in his place to have been from the beginning utterly without hope. We have now his authority to say, that as far as our resources were concerned, the experiment was equally without necessity.

"It appears," as he has very justly and satisfactorily observed, "by the accounts of the value of the imports and exports for the last twenty years, produced by Mr. Irving, that the demand for cash to be sent abroad" (which by the way, including the loan to the Emperor, was nearly one third less sent to the Continent of Europe, than in the seven years war) "was greatly compensated by a very large balance of commerce in favour of this kingdom; greater than was ever known in any preceding period. The value of the exports of the last year amounted, according to the valuation on which the accounts of the Inspector General are founded, to £30,424,184; which is more than double what it was in any year of the American war, and one third more than it was on the average during the last peace, previous to the year 1792;

and though the value of the imports to this country has, during the same peace, greatly increased, the excess of the value of the exports above that of the imports, which constitutes the balance of trade, has augmented even in a greater proportion." These observations might perhaps be branched out into other points of view, but I shall leave them to your own active and ingenious mind. There is another and still more important light in which the Inspector [254] General's information may be seen; and that is, as affording a comparison of some circumstances in this war, with the commercial history of all our other wars in the present century.

In all former hostilities, our exports gradually declined in value, and then (with one single exception) ascended again, till they reached and passed the level of the preceding peace. But this was a work of time, sometimes more, sometimes less slow. In Queen Anne's war, which began in 1702, it was an interval of ten years, before this was effected. Nine years only were necessary in the war of 1739, for the same operation. The Seven Years' war saw the period much shortened: hostilities began in 1755, and in 1758, the fourth year of the war, the exports mounted above the peace-mark. There was, however, a distinguishing feature of that war, that our tonnage, to the very last moment, was in a state of great depression, while our commerce was chiefly carried on by foreign vessels. The American war was darkened with singular and peculiar adversity. Our exports never came near to their peaceful elevation, and our tonnage continued, with very little fluctuation, to subside lower and lower.[1] On the other hand, the present war, with regard to our commerce, has the white mark of a singular felicity. If from internal causes, as well as the consequence of hostilities, the tide ebbed in 1793, it rushed back

1. This account is extracted from different parts of Mr. Chalmers' Estimate. It is but just to mention, that in Mr. Chalmers' Estimate, the sums are uniformly lower, than those of the same year in Mr. Irving's account.

again with a bore in the following year; and from that time
has continued to swell, and run, every successive year, higher
and higher into all our ports. The value of our exports last
year above the year 1792 (the mere increase of our commerce during the war) is equal to the average value of all the
exports during the wars of William and Anne.

[255] It has been already pointed out, that our imports
have not kept pace with our exports; of course, on the face of
the account, the balance of trade, both positively and comparatively considered, must have been much more than ever
in our favour. In that early little tract of mine, to which I have
already more than once referred, I made many observations
on the usual method of computing that balance, as well as the
usual objection to it, that the entries at the Custom-House
were not always true. As you probably remember them, I
shall not repeat them here. On the one hand, I am not surprised that the same trite objection is perpetually renewed
by the detractors of our national affluence; and on the other
hand I am gratified in perceiving, that the balance of trade
seems to be now computed in a manner much clearer, than
it used to be, from those errors which I formerly noticed.
The Inspector-General appears to have made his estimate
with every possible guard and caution. His opinion is entitled to the greatest respect. It was in substance (I shall again
use the words of the noble Reporter, as much better than
my own) "That the true balance of our trade amounted, on
a medium of the four years preceding January 1796, to upwards of £6,500,000 per annum, exclusive of the profits arising from our East and West India trade, which he estimates
at upwards of £4,000,000 per annum; exclusive of the profits
derived from our fisheries." So that including the fisheries,
and making a moderate allowance for the exceedings, which
Mr. Irving himself supposes, beyond his calculation; without
reckoning, what the public creditors themselves pay to themselves, and without taking one shilling from the stock of the

landed interest; our colonies, our oriental possessions, our skill and industry, our commerce, and navigation, at the commencement of this year, were pouring a new annual capital into the kingdom hardly half a million short of the whole interest of that [256] tremendous debt, from which we are taught to shrink in dismay, as from an overwhelming and intolerable oppression.

IF THEN THE REAL STATE of this nation is such as I have described, and I am only apprehensive that you may think I have taken too much pains to exclude all doubt on this question—if no class is lessened in it's numbers, or in it's stock, or in it's conveniencies, or even it's luxuries; if they build as many habitations, and as elegant and as commodious as ever, and furnish them with every chargeable decoration, and every prodigality of ingenious invention, that can be thought of by those who even encumber their necessities with superfluous accommodation; if they are as numerously attended; if their equipages are as splendid; if they regale at table with as much or more variety of plenty than ever; if they are clad in as expensive and changeful a diversity according to their tastes and modes; if they are not deterred from the pleasures of the field by the charges, which Government has wisely turned from the culture to the sports of the field; if the theatres are as rich and as well filled, and greater, and at a higher price than ever; and, what is more important than all, if it is plain from the treasures which are spread over the soil, or confided to the winds and the seas, that there are as many who are indulgent to their propensities of parsimony, as others to their voluptuous desires, and that the pecuniary capital grows instead of diminishing; on what ground are we authorized to say that a nation gambolling in an ocean of superfluity is undone by want? With what face can we pretend, that they who have not denied any one gratification to any one appetite, have a right to plead poverty in order to famish their virtues, and to put their duties on short allowance? That they are to take the law from an imperious enemy, and can contribute no longer to the honour of their king, to the support of the independence [257] of their country, to the salvation of that Europe, which, if it falls, must crush them with its gigantick ruins? How can they affect to sweat, and stagger, and groan under their burthens, to whom the mines of Newfoundland, richer than those of Mexico and Peru, are now thrown in as a make-weight in the scale of their exorbitant opulence? What excuse can they have to faint, and creep, and cringe, and prostrate themselves at the footstool of ambition and crime, who, during a short though violent struggle, which they have never supported with the energy of men, have amassed more to their annual accumulation, than all the well-husbanded capital that enabled their ancestors by long, and doubtful, and obstinate conflicts to defend, and liberate, and vindicate the civilized world? But I do not accuse the People of England. As to the great majority of the nation, they have done whatever in their several ranks, and conditions, and descriptions, was required of them by their relative situations in society; and from those the great mass of mankind cannot depart, without the subversion of all publick order. They look up to that Government, which they obey that they may be protected. They ask to be led and directed by those rulers, whom Providence and the laws of their country have set over them, and under their guidance to walk in the ways of safety and honour. They have again delegated the greatest trust which they have to bestow, to those faithful representatives who made their true voice heard against the disturbers and destroyers of Europe. They suffered, with unapproving acquiescence, solicitations, which they had in no shape desired, to an unjust and usurping Power, whom they had never provoked, and whose hostile menaces they did not dread. When the exigencies of the publick service could only be met by their voluntary zeal, they started forth with an ardour which outstripped the wishes of those, who had injured them by doubting, whether [258] it might not be necessary to have recourse to compulsion. They have, in all things, reposed an enduring, but not an unreflecting confidence. That confidence demands a full return; and fixes a responsibility on the Ministers entire and undivided. The People stands acquitted, if the war is not carried on in a manner suited to it's objects. If the publick honour is tarnished; if the publick safety suffers any detriment; they, not the People, are to answer it, and they alone. It's armies, it's navies, are given to them without stint or restriction. It's treasures are poured out at their feet. It's constancy is ready to second all their efforts. They are not to fear a responsibility for acts of manly adventure. The responsibility which they are to dread, is, lest they should shew themselves unequal to the expectation of a brave people. The more doubtful may be the constitutional and oeconomical questions, upon which they have received so marked a support, the more loudly they are called upon to support this great war, for the success of which their country is willing to supersede considerations of no slight importance. Where I speak of responsibility, I do not mean to exclude that species of it, which the legal powers of the country have a right finally to exact from those who abuse a public trust; but high as this is, there is a responsibility which attaches on them, from which the whole legitimate power of the kingdom cannot absolve them; there is a responsibility to conscience and to glory; a responsibility to the existing world, and to that posterity, which men of their eminence cannot avoid for glory or for shame; a responsibility to a tribunal, at which, not only Ministers, but Kings and Parliaments, but even Nations themselves, must one day answer.

LETTER IV

To the Earl Fitzwilliam

[Christmas, 1795. First printed by Bishop King, from Burke's Manuscript, in vol. v. of the 4to ed. of Burke's Works, 1812.]

[Argument

PART I, pp. 308–76

Lord Auckland's Pamphlet criticised

General purpose of the pamphlet, p. 308. Particular positions contro-verted. 1. That the Jacobin Faction is France, p. 314. Contrast of this with the Whitehall Declaration of 1793, p. 318. 2. That France will fall by the weight of her own conquests, and crumble into separate repub-lics, p. 321. Contrast of this with the reality—the indivisible republic growing daily in force and dimensions, p. 326. 3. That the reaction in England against French ideas may encourage despotic policy, p. 328. This illustrated by the large seditious meetings advocating his views, held while Lord Auckland's pamphlet was in the press, ibid. 4. That the Revolution has been a wholesome lesson to sovereigns, p. 330, and to the higher classes generally, p. 333. 5. That the Jacobins are mending their ways, p. 337. This answered by the proceedings at the inauguration of the last Constitution, p. 341, including their insults to England p. 345. That this new Constitution is a good one—not unlike that of England, p. 350, that Robespierre, the incarnation of the old vices of the Revolution has perished, p. 353, that the constitution will be stable, and that its stability will extend to the peace to be made with it, p. 355. But England cannot possibly suffer, even for an "adequate compensation," what Lord Auckland himself describes as "The aban-donment of the Independence of Europe," p. 363. This illustrated by

the certain ruin to Britain in the West Indies which must result from
the relations at present subsisting between France and Spain, p. 368.
After this digression, Burke returns to the allegation that the Jacobins
are mending their ways, p. 373, which he denies, and [260] alleges
that this is only said with the purpose of deluding England into amity
with them. The fatal consequences of such amity are demonstrated in
the next Part.

PART II, pp. 376–94

Consequences in England itself of a Regicide Peace

The Jacobin Faction will become dominant, p. 375. Comparison of
the British Parliament and the Greek Divines, p. 381. Invasion of foreign Jacobinism, p. 382. Ancient character and decayed condition of
the British Constitution, p. 384. Picture of the French Jacobins teaching the lessons of their experience in England, p. 385. Its effect on
education, p. 389, on legislature and judicature, p. 390. The end of all
will be the destruction of monarchy and religion. All this may actually
come about, and at short notice, p. 393.]

MY DEAR LORD,

I AM not sure, that the best way of discussing any subject, except those that concern the abstracted sciences, is not somewhat in the way of dialogue. To this mode, however, there are
two objections. The first, that it happens, as in the puppet-
show, one man speaks for all the personages. An unnatural
uniformity of tone is in a manner unavoidable. The other, and
more serious objection is, that as the author (if not an absolute sceptick) must have some opinion of his own to enforce,
he will be continually tempted to enervate the arguments he
puts into the mouth of his adversary, or to place them in a
point of view most commodious for their refutation. There
is, however, a sort of dialogue not quite so liable to these

objections, because it approaches more nearly to truth and nature: it is called CONTROVERSY. Here the parties speak for themselves. If the writer, who attacks another's notions, does not deal fairly with his adversary, the diligent reader has it always in his power, by resorting to the work examined, to do justice to the original author and to himself. For this reason you will not blame me, if, in my discussion of the merits of a Regicide Peace, I do [261] not choose to trust to my own statements, but to bring forward along with them the arguments of the advocates for that measure. If I choose puny adversaries, writers of no estimation or authority, then you will justly blame me. I might as well bring in at once a fictitious speaker, and thus fall into all the inconveniences of an imaginary dialogue. This I shall avoid; and I shall take no notice of any author, who, my friends in town do not tell me, is in estimation with those whose opinions he supports.

A piece has been sent to me, called "Remarks on the apparent Circumstances of the War in the fourth week of October, 1795," with a French motto, *Que faire encore une fois dans une telle nuit?—Attendre le jour.* The very title seemed to me striking and peculiar, and to announce something uncommon. In the time I have lived to, I always seem to walk on enchanted ground. Every thing is new, and according to the fashionable phrase, revolutionary. In former days, authors valued themselves upon the maturity and fulness of their deliberations. Accordingly they predicted (perhaps with more arrogance than reason) an eternal duration to their works. Quite the contrary is our present fashion. Writers value themselves now on the instability of their opinions, and the transitory life of their productions. On this kind of credit the modern institutors open their schools. They write for youth; and it is sufficient if the instruction lasts as long as a present love, or as the painted silks and cottons of the season.

The doctrines in this work are applied, for their standard, with great exactness, to the shortest possible periods both of conception and duration. The title is "Some Remarks on the *Apparent* circumstances of the War *in the fourth week of October, 1795.*" The time is critically chosen. A month or so earlier would have made it the anniversary of a bloody Parisian September, when the French massacre one another. [262] A day or two later would have carried it into a London November, the gloomy month in which it is said by a pleasant author that Englishmen hang and drown themselves. In truth, this work has a tendency to alarm us with symptoms of publick suicide. However, there is one comfort to be taken even from the gloomy time of year. It is a rotting season. If what is brought to market is not good, it is not likely to keep long. Even buildings run up in haste with untempered mortar in that humid weather, if they are ill-contrived tenements, do not threaten long to encumber the earth. The Author tells us (and I believe he is the very first Author that ever told such a thing to his readers) "that the *entire fabrick* of his speculations might be overset by unforeseen vicissitudes"; and what is far more extraordinary, "that even the *whole* consideration might be *varied whilst he was writing those pages.*" Truly, in my poor judgement, this circumstance formed a very substantial motive for his not publishing those ill-considered considerations at all. He ought to have followed the good advice of his motto; Que faire encore dans une telle nuit? Attendre le jour. He ought to have waited till he had got a little more day-light on this subject. Night itself is hardly darker than the fogs of that time.

Finding the *last week in October* so particularly referred to, and not perceiving any particular event relative to the War, which happened on any of the days in that week, I thought it possible that they were marked by some astrological superstition, to which the greatest politicians have been subject. I therefore had recourse to my Rider's Almanack. There I found indeed something that characterized the work, and that gave directions concerning the sudden political and natural variations, and for eschewing the maladies that are most prevalent in that aguish intermittent season, "the last week of October." On that week the sagacious astrologer, [263] Rider, in his note on the third column of the calendar side, teaches us to expect "*variable and cold weather*"; but instead of encouraging us to trust ourselves to the haze and mist and doubtful lights of that changeable week, on the answerable part of the opposite page, he gives us a salutary caution, (indeed it is very nearly in the words of the author's motto): "*Avoid* (says he) *being out late at night, and in foggy weather, for a cold now caught may last the whole winter.*"[1] This ingenious author, who disdained the prudence of the almanack, walked out in the very fog he complains of, and has led us to a very unseasonable airing at that time. Whilst this noble writer, by the vigour of an excellent constitution, formed for the violent changes he prognosticates, may shake off the importunate rheum and malignant influenza of this disagreeable week, a whole Parliament may go on spitting and snivelling, and wheezing and coughing, during a whole session. All this from listening to variable, hebdomadal politicians, who run away from their opinions without giving us a month's warning; and for not listening to the wise and friendly admonitions of Dr. Cardanus Rider, who never apprehends he may change his opinions before his pen is out of his hand, but always enables us to lay in, at least, a year's stock of useful information.

At first I took comfort. I said to myself, that if I should, as I fear I must, oppose the doctrines of the last week of October, it is probable that, by this time, they are no longer those of the eminent writer, to whom they are attributed. He gives us hopes that long before this he may have embraced the direct contrary sentiments. If I am found [264] in a conflict with those of the last week of October, I may be

1. Here I have fallen into an unintentional mistake. Rider's Almanack for 1794 lay before me; and, in truth, I then had no other. For variety that sage astrologer has made some small changes on the weather side of 1795; but the caution is the same on the opposite page of instruction.

in full agreement with those of the last week in December, or the first week in January 1796. But a second edition, and a French translation (for the benefit, I must suppose, of the new Regicide Directory) have let down a little of these flattering hopes. We and the Directory know, that the author, whatever changes his works seemed made to indicate, like a weather-cock grown rusty, remains just where he was in the last week of last October. It is true, that his protest against binding him to his opinions, and his reservation of a right to whatever opinions he pleases, remain in their full force. This variability is pleasant, and shews a fertility of fancy;

Qualis in aethereo felix Vertumnus Olympo
  Mille habet ornatus, mille decenter habet.

Yet, doing all justice to the sportive variability of these weekly, daily, or hourly speculators, shall I be pardoned, if I attempt a word on the part of us simple country folk? It is not good for *us,* however it may be so for great statesmen, that we should be treated with variable politicks. I consider different relations as prescribing a different conduct. I allow, that in transactions with an enemy, a Minister may, and often must, vary his demands with the day, possibly with the hour. With an enemy, a fixed plan, variable arrangements. This is the rule the nature of the transaction prescribes. But all this belongs to treaty. All these shiftings and changes are a sort of secret amongst the parties, till a definite settlement is brought about. Such is the spirit of the proceedings in the doubtful and transitory state of things between enmity and friendship. In this change the subjects of the transformation are by nature carefully wrapt up in their cocoons. The gay ornament of summer is not seemly in his aurelia state. This mutability is allowed to [265] a foreign negociator. But when a great politician condescends publickly to instruct his own countrymen on a matter, which may fix their fate for ever, his opinions ought not to be diurnal, or even weekly.

These ephemerides of politicks are not made for our slow and coarse understandings. Our appetite demands a *piece of resistance*. We require some food that will stick to the ribs. We call for sentiments, to which we can attach ourselves; sentiments, in which we can take an interest; sentiments, on which we can warm, on which we can ground some confidence in ourselves or in others. We do not want a largess of inconstancy. Poor souls, we have enough of that sort of poverty at home. There is a difference too between deliberation and doctrine: a man ought to be decided in his opinions before he attempts to teach. His fugitive lights may serve himself in some unknown region, but they can not free us from the effects of the error, into which we have been betrayed. His active Will-o'-the-Whisp may be gone nobody can guess where, whilst he leaves us bemired and benighted in the bog.

Having premised these few reflections upon this new mode of teaching a lesson, which whilst the scholar is getting by heart the master forgets, I come to the lesson itself. On the fullest consideration of it, I am utterly incapable of saying with any great certainty what it is, in the detail, that the author means to affirm or deny, to dissuade or recommend. His march is mostly oblique, and his doctrine rather in the way of insinuation than a dogmatick assertion. It is not only fugitive in its duration, but is slippery, in the extreme, whilst it lasts. Examining it part by part, it seems almost every where to contradict itself; and the author, who claims the privilege of varying his opinions, has exercised this privilege in every section of his remarks. For this reason, amongst others, I follow the advice which the able [266] writer gives in his last page, which is "to consider the *impression* of what he has urged, taken from the *whole*, and not from detached paragraphs." That caution was not absolutely necessary. I should think it unfair to the author and to myself, to have proceeded otherwise. The author's *whole*, however, like every other whole, can not be so well comprehended without some reference to the parts; but they shall be again referred to the whole. Without this latter attention, several of the passages would certainly remain covered with an impenetrable and truly oracular obscurity.

The great general pervading purpose of the whole pamphlet is to reconcile us to peace with the present usurpation in France. In this general drift of the author I can hardly be mistaken. The other purposes, less general, and subservient to the preceding scheme, are to show, first, that the time of the remarks was the favourable time for making that peace upon our side; secondly, that on the enemy's side their disposition towards the acceptance of such terms as he is pleased to offer, was rationally to be expected; the third purpose was to make some sort of disclosure of the terms, which, if the Regicides are pleased to grant them, this nation ought to be contented to accept: these form the basis of the negociation, which the author, whoever he is, proposes to open.

Before I consider these Remarks along with the other reasonings which I hear on the same subject, I beg leave to recal to your mind the observation I made early in our correspondence, and which ought to attend us quite through the discussion of this proposed peace, amity, or fraternity, or whatever you may call it; that is, the real quality and character of the party you have to deal with. This, I find, as a thing of no importance, has every where escaped the author of the October Remarks. That hostile power to the [267] period of the fourth week in that month has been ever called and considered as an usurpation. In that week, for the first time, it changed its name of an usurped power, and took the simple name of *France.* The word France is slipped in just as if the government stood exactly as before that revolution which has astonished, terrified, and almost overpowered Europe. "France," says the author, "will do this"; "it is the interest of France"; "the returning honour and generosity of France," &c. &c. Always merely France; just as if we were in a common

political war with an old recognized member of the commonwealth of Christian Europe; and as if our dispute had turned
upon a mere matter of territorial or commercial controversy,
which a peace might settle by the imposition or the taking off
a duty, with the gain or the loss of a remote island or a frontier
town or two, on the one side or the other. This shifting of persons could not be done without the hocus-pocus of *abstraction.*
We have been in a grievous error. We thought that we had
been at war with *rebels* against the lawful government, but that
we were friends and allies of what is properly France; friends
and allies to the legal body politick of France. But by sleight
of hand the Jacobins are clean vanished, and it is France we
have got under our cup. Blessings on his soul that first invented sleep, said Don Sancho Panza the wise! All those blessings, and ten thousand times more, on him who found out abstraction, personification, and impersonals! In certain cases
they are the first of all soporificks. Terribly alarmed we should
be if things were proposed to us in the *concrete;* and if fraternity was held out to us with the individuals, who compose this
France, by their proper names and descriptions: if we were
told that it was very proper to enter into the closest bonds
of amity and good correspondence with the devout, pacifick, and tender-hearted Syeyes, with the all-accomplished
Rewbel, with the humane [268] guillotinists of Bourdeaux,
Tallien and Isabeau; with the meek butcher Legendre, and
with "the returned humanity and generosity" (that had been
only on a visit abroad) of the virtuous regicide brewer Santerre. This would seem at the outset a very strange scheme of
amity and concord; nay, though we had held out to us, as an
additional douceur, an assurance of the cordial fraternal embrace of our pious and patriotic countryman Thomas Paine.
But plain truth would here be shocking and absurd; therefore comes in *abstraction* and personification. "Make your
Peace with France." That word *France* sounds quite as well as
any other, and it conveys no idea but that of a very pleas-

ant country and very hospitable inhabitants. Nothing absurd and shocking in amity and good correspondence with *France.* Permit me to say, that I am not yet well acquainted with this new-coined France, and, without a careful assay, I am not willing to receive it in currency in place of the old Louis d'or.

Having therefore slipped the persons, with whom we are to treat, out of view, we are next to be satisfied, that the French Revolution, which this peace is to fix and consolidate, ought to give us no just cause of apprehension. Though the Author labours this point, yet he confesses a fact, (indeed he could not conceal it) which renders all his labours utterly fruitless. He confesses, that the Regicide means to *dictate* a pacification, and that this pacification, according to their decree passed but a very few days before his publication appeared, is to "unite to their Empire, either in possession or dependence, new barriers, many frontier places of strength, a large sea-coast, and many sea-ports." He ought to have stated it, that they would annex to their territory a country about a third as large as France, and much more than half as rich; and in a situation the most important, for command, that it would be possible for her any where to possess.

[269] To remove this terror, (if the Regicides should carry their point) and to give us perfect repose with regard to their Empire, whatever they may acquire, or whomsoever they might destroy, he raises a doubt "whether France will not be ruined by *retaining* these conquests, and whether she will not wholly lose that preponderance, which she has held in the scale of European powers, and will not eventually be destroyed by the effect of her present successes; or, at least, whether, so far as the *political interests of England are concerned,* she [France] will remain an object of *as much jealousy and alarm, as she was under the reign of a Monarch.*" Here, indeed, is a paragraph full of meaning! It gives matter for meditation almost in every word of it. The secret of the pacifick politicians is out. This Republick, at all hazards, is to be main-

tained. It is to be confined within some bounds, if we can; if not, with every possible acquisition of power, it is still to be cherished and supported. It is the return of the Monarchy we are to dread, and therefore we ought to pray for the permanence of the Regicide authority. *Esto perpetua* is the devout ejaculation of our Fra Paolo for the Republick one and indivisible! It was the Monarchy that rendered France dangerous; Regicide neutralizes all the acrimony of that power and renders it safe and social. The October speculator is of opinion, that Monarchy is of so poisonous a quality, that a moderate territorial power is far more dangerous to its neighbours under that abominable regimen, than the greatest Empire in the hands of a Republick. This is Jacobinism sublimed and exalted into most pure and perfect essence. It is a doctrine, I admit, made to allure and captivate, if any thing in the world can, the Jacobin directory, to mollify the ferocity of Regicide, and to persuade those patriotick Hangmen, after their reiterated oaths for our extirpation, to admit this well humbled nation to the fraternal embrace. I do not wonder that this tub of [270] October has been racked off into a French cask. It must make its fortune at Paris. That translation seems the language the most suited to these sentiments. Our author tells the French Jacobins that the political interests of Great Britain are in perfect unison with the principles of their government; that they may take and keep the keys of the civilized world, for they are safe in their unambitious and faithful custody. We say to them, "We may, indeed, wish you to be a little less murderous, wicked and atheistical, for the sake of morals: we may think it were better you were less new-fangled in your speech, for the sake of grammar: but, as *politicians*, provided you keep clear of Monarchy, all our fears, alarms and jealousies are at an end: at least they sink into nothing in comparison with our dread of your detestable Royalty." A flatterer of Cardinal Mazarin said, when that Minister had just settled the match between the young Louis the 14th and a daughter of Spain, that this alliance had the effect of Faith, and removed Mountains—that the Pyrenees were levelled by that marriage. You may now compliment Rewbel in the same spirit on the miracles of Regicide, and tell him, that the guillotine of Louis the 16th had consummated a marriage between Great Britain and France, which dried up the Channel, and restored the two countries to the unity, which, it is said, they had before the unnatural rage of seas and earthquakes had broke off their happy junction. It will be a fine subject for the Poets, who are to prophecy the blessings of this peace.

I am now convinced, that the Remarks of the last week of October cannot come from the author, to whom they are given; they are such a direct contradiction to the style of manly indignation, with which he spoke of those miscreants and murderers in his excellent Memorial to the States of Holland—to that very State, which the Author, who presumes to personate him, does not find it contrary to the [271] political interests of England to leave in the hands of these very miscreants, against whom on the part of England he took so much pains to animate their Republick. This cannot be; and, if this argument wanted any thing to give it new force, it is strengthened by an additional reason that is irresistible. Knowing that Noble person, as well as myself, to be under very great obligations to the Crown, I am confident he would not so very directly contradict, even in the paroxysm of zeal against monarchy, the declarations made in the name and with the fullest approbation of our Sovereign, his Master, and our common benefactor. In those declarations you will see, that the King, instead of being sensible of greater alarm and jealousy from a neighbouring crowned head, than from these Regicides, attributes all the dangers of Europe to the latter. Let this writer hear the description given in the Royal Declaration of the scheme of power of these Miscreants, as "*a system destructive of all publick order; maintained by proscriptions, exiles, and confiscations without number; by arbitrary impris-*

*onments; by massacres which cannot be remembered without horrour;
and at length by the execrable murder of a just and beneficent Sovereign, and of the illustrious princess, who with an unshaken firmness
has shared all the misfortunes of her Royal consort, his protracted sufferings, his cruel captivity, and his ignominious death."* After thus
describing, with an eloquence and energy equalled only by
its truth, the means, by which this usurped power had been
acquired and maintained, that government is characterized
with equal force. His Majesty, far from thinking Monarchy in
France to be a greater object of jealousy, than the Regicide
usurpation, calls upon the French to re-establish *"a monarchical government"* for the purpose of shaking off *"the yoke of
a sanguinary anarchy; of that anarchy, which has broken the most
sacred bonds of Society, dissolved all the relations of civil life, violated
every right, confounded* [272] *every duty; which uses the name of
liberty to exercise the most cruel tyranny, to annihilate all property, to
seize on all possessions; which founds its power on the pretended consent of the people, and itself carries fire and sword through extensive
provinces for having demanded their laws, their religion and their
rightful Sovereign."*

"That strain I heard was of an higher mood." That declaration of our Sovereign was worthy of his throne. It is in
a style, which neither the pen of the writer of October, nor
such a poor crow-quill as mine can ever hope to equal. I am
happy to enrich my letter with this fragment of nervous and
manly eloquence, which if it had not emanated from the awful authority of a throne, if it were not recorded amongst the
most valuable monuments of history, and consecrated in the
archives of States, would be worthy as a private composition
to live for ever in the memory of men.

In those admirable pieces, does his Majesty discover this
new opinion of his political security in having the chair of
the Scorner, that is, the discipline of Atheism and the block
of Regicide, set up by his side, elevated on the same platform, and shouldering, with the vile image of their grim

and bloody idol, the inviolable majesty of his throne? The sentiments of these declarations are the very reverse: they could not be other. Speaking of the spirit of that usurpation the Royal manifesto describes with perfect truth its internal tyranny to have been established as the very means of shaking the security of all other States; as *"disposing arbitrarily of the property and blood of the inhabitants of France, in order to disturb the tranquillity of other nations, and to render all Europe the theatre of the same crimes and the same misfortunes."* It was but a natural inference from this fact, that the Royal manifesto does not at all rest the justification of this war on common principles: *"that it was not only to defend his own rights, and those of his Allies,"* but *"that* [273] *all the dearest interests of his people imposed upon him a Duty still more important—that of exerting his efforts for the preservation of civil society itself, as happily established among the nations of Europe."* On that ground the protection offered is to those, who by "declaring for a *Monarchical government* shall shake off the yoke of a sanguinary Anarchy." It is for that purpose the Declaration calls on them to join the standard of an *"hereditary Monarchy"*; and declaring, that the *safety and peace* of this Kingdom and the powers of Europe *"materially depend upon the re-establishment of order in France,"* his Majesty does not hesitate to declare, that *"the re-establishment of Monarchy in the person of Louis the 17th and the lawful heirs of his crown appears to him* [his Majesty] *the best mode of accomplishing these just and salutary views."*

This is what his Majesty does not hesitate to declare relative to the political safety and peace of his Kingdom and of Europe, and with regard to France under her ancient hereditary Monarchy in the course and order of legal succession. But in comes a gentleman in the fag end of October, dripping with the fogs of that humid and uncertain season, and does not hesitate in Diameter to contradict this wise and just Royal declaration; and stoutly, on his part, to make a counter-declaration, that France, so far as the political interests of

England are concerned, will not remain, under the despotism of Regicide and with the better part of Europe in her hands, so much an object of jealousy and alarm, as she was under the reign of a Monarch. When I hear the Master and reason on one side, and the Servant and his single and unsupported assertion on the other, my part is taken.

This is what the Octobrist says of the political interests of England, which it looks as if he completely disconnected with those of all other nations. But not quite so; he just allows it possible (with an "at least") that the other powers [274] may not find it quite their interest, that their Territories should be conquered and their Subjects tyrannized over by the Regicides. No fewer than ten Sovereign Princes had, some the whole, all a very considerable part, of their Dominions, under the yoke of that dreadful faction. Amongst these was to be reckoned the first Republick in the World, and the closest Ally of this Kingdom, which, under the insulting name of an independency, is under her iron yoke; and, as long as a faction averse to the old government is suffered there to domineer, cannot be otherwise. I say nothing of the Austrian Netherlands, countries of a vast extent, and amongst the most fertile and populous of Europe; and with regard to us most critically situated. The rest will readily occur to you.

But if there are yet existing any people, like me, old fashioned enough to consider, that we have an important part of our very existence beyond our limits, and who therefore stretch their thoughts beyond the *Pomoerium* of England, for them too he has a comfort, which will remove all their jealousies and alarms about the extent of the Empire of Regicide. "*These conquests eventually will be the cause of her destruction.*" So that they, who hate the cause of usurpation and dread the power of France under any form, are to wish her to be a conqueror, in order to accelerate her ruin. A little more conquest would be still better. Will he tell us what dose of Dominion is to be the *quantum sufficit* for her destruction, for she seems very voracious of the food of her distemper? To be sure she is ready to perish with repletion; she has a *Boulimia,* and hardly has bolted down one State, than she calls for two or three more. There is a good deal of wit in all this; but it seems to me (with all respect to the Author) to be carrying the joke a great deal too far. I cannot yet think, that the Armies of the Allies were of this way of thinking; and that, when they evacuated [275] all these countries, it was a stratagem of war to decoy France into ruin; or that, if in a Treaty we should surrender them for ever into the hands of the usurpation (the lease, the author supposes) it is a master-stroke of policy to effect the destruction of a formidable rival, and to render her no longer an object of jealousy and alarm. This, I assure the Author, will infinitely facilitate the Treaty. The usurpers will catch at this bait, without minding the hook, which this crafty angler for the Jacobin gudgeons of the New Directory has so dexterously placed under it.

Every symptom of the exacerbation of the publick malady is with him (as with the Doctor in Molière) a happy prognostick of recovery. Flanders gone! — *tant mieux.* Holland subdued! — charming! Spain beaten, and all the hither Germany conquered! — Bravo! Better and better still! But they will retain all their conquests on a Treaty! Best of all! What a delightful thing it is to have a gay physician who sees all things, as the French express it, *couleur de rose!* What an escape we have had, that we and our Allies were not the Conquerors! By these conquests, previous to her utter destruction, she is "wholly to lose that preponderance, which she held in the scale of the European Powers." Bless me! This new system of France, after changing all other laws, reverses the law of gravitation. By throwing in weight after weight her scale rises, and will by and by kick the beam! Certainly there is one sense in which she loses her preponderance: that is she is no longer preponderant against the Countries she has conquered. They are part of herself. But I beg the Author to keep his eyes fixed on the scales for a moment longer, and then to tell me in downright earnest, whether he sees hitherto any signs of her losing preponderance by an augmentation of weight and power. Has she lost her preponderance over Spain, by her influence in Spain? Are there any signs, that the conquest [276] of Savoy and Nice begins to lessen her preponderance over Switzerland and the Italian States—or that the Canton of Berne, Genoa and Tuscany, for example, have taken arms against her, or, that Sardinia is more adverse than ever to a treacherous pacification? Was it in the last week of October, that the German States shewed that Jacobin France was losing her preponderance? Did the King of Prussia, when he delivered into her safe custody his territories on this side of the Rhine, manifest any tokens of his opinion of her loss of preponderance? Look on Sweden and on Denmark: is her preponderance less visible there?

It is true, that in a course of ages Empires have fallen, and, in the opinion of some, not in mine, by their own weight. Sometimes they have been unquestionably embarrassed in their movements by the dissociated situation of their Dominions. Such was the case of the empire of Charles the Fifth and of his successor. It might be so of others. But so compact a body of empire; so fitted in all the parts for mutual support; with a Frontier by nature and art so impenetrable; with such facility of breaking out with irresistible force, from every quarter, was never seen in such an extent of territory from the beginning of time, as in that empire, which the Jacobins possessed in October 1795, and which Boissy d'Anglas, in his Report, settled as the Law for Europe, and the Dominion assigned by Nature for the Republick of Regicide. But this Empire is to be her ruin, and to take away all alarm and jealousy on the part of England, and to destroy her preponderance over the miserable remains of Europe!

These are choice speculations, with which the Author amuses himself, and tries to divert us, in the blackest hours of the dismay, defeat and calamity of all civilized nations. They have but one fault, that they are directly contrary to the common sense and common feeling of mankind. If I [277] had but one hour to live, I would employ it in decrying this wretched system, and die with my pen in my hand to mark out the dreadful consequences of receiving an arrangement of Empire dictated by the despotism of Regicide to my own Country, and to the lawful Sovereigns of the Christian World.

I trust I shall hardly be told, in palliation of this shameful system of politicks, that the Author expresses his sentiments only as doubts. In such things it may be truly said that "once to doubt is once to be resolved." It would be a strange reason for wasting the treasures and shedding the blood of our country to prevent arrangements on the part of another power, of which we were doubtful, whether they might not be even to our advantage and render our neighbour less than before the object of our jealousy and alarm. In this doubt there is much decision. No nation would consent to carry on a war of scepticism. But the fact is, this expression of doubt is only a mode of putting an opinion when it is not the drift of the Author to overturn the doubt. Otherwise, the doubt is never stated as the Author's own, nor left, as here it is, unanswered. Indeed, the mode of stating the most decided opinions in the form of questions is so little uncommon, particularly since the excellent queries of the excellent Berkeley, that it became for a good while a fashionable mode of composition.

Here then the Author of the fourth week of October is ready for the worst, and would strike the bargain of peace on these conditions. I must leave it to you and to every considerate man to reflect upon the effect of this on any Continental alliances present or future, and whether it would be possible (if this book was thought of the least authority) that its maxims with regard to our political interest must not naturally push them to be beforehand with us in the fraternity with Regicide, and thus not only strip us of any [278] steady alliance at present, but leave us without any of that communion of interest which could produce alliances in future. Indeed, with these maxims, we should be well divided from the World.

Notwithstanding this new kind of barrier and security that is found against her ambition in her conquests, yet in the very same paragraph he admits that "for the *present* at least it is subversive of the balance of power." This, I confess, is not a direct contradiction, because the benefits which he promises himself from it, according to his hypothesis are future and more remote.

So disposed is this Author to peace, that, having laid a comfortable foundation of *our* security in the greatness of *her* Empire, he has another in reserve if that should fail, upon quite a contrary ground; that is, a speculation of her crumbling to pieces and being thrown into a number of little separate Republicks. After paying the tribute of humanity to those who will be ruined by all these changes, on the whole he is of opinion that "the change might be compatible with general tranquillity, and with the establishment of a peaceful and prosperous commerce among nations." Whether France be great or small, firm and entire, or dissipated and divided, all is well; provided we can have peace with her.

But, without entering into speculations about her dismemberment whilst she is adding great nations to her empire, is it then quite so certain, that the dissipation of France into such a cluster of petty Republicks would be so very favourable to the true balance of power in Europe, as this Author imagines it would be, and to the commerce of Nations? I greatly differ from him. I perhaps shall prove in a future letter, with the political map of Europe before my eye, that the general liberty and independence of the great Christian commonwealth could not exist with such a dismemberment; [279] unless it were followed (as probably enough it would) by the dismemberment of every other considerable country in Europe: and what convulsions would arise in the constitution of every state in Europe, it is not easy to conjecture in the mode, impossible not to foresee in the mass. Speculate on, good my Lord! provided you ground no part of your politicks on such unsteady speculations. But, as to any practice to ensue, are we not yet cured of the malady of speculating on the circumstances of things totally different from those in which we live and move? Five years has this Monster continued whole and entire in all its members. Far from falling into a division within itself, it is augmented by tremendous additions. We cannot bear to look that frightful form in the face as it is and in its own actual shape. We dare not be wise. We have not the fortitude of rational fear. We will not provide for our future safety; but we endeavour to hush the cries of present timidity by guesses at what may be hereafter. "To-morrow, and to-morrow, and to-morrow"—is this our style of talk, when "all our yesterdays have lighted fools the way to dusty death?" Talk not to me of what swarms of Republicks may come from this carcass! It is no carcass. Now, now, whilst we are talking, it is full of life and action. What say you to the Regicide Empire of to-day? Tell me, my friend, do its terrors appal you into an abject submission, or rouse you to a vigorous defence? But do—I no longer prevent it—do go on—look into futurity. Has this Empire nothing to alarm you when all struggle against it is over, when Mankind shall be silent before it, when all nations shall be disarmed, disheartened and *truly divided* by a treacherous peace? Its malignity towards humankind will subsist with undiminished heat, whilst the means of giving it effect must proceed, and every means of resisting it must inevitably and rapidly decline.

Against alarm on their politick and military empire these [280] are the writer's sedative remedies. But he leaves us sadly in the dark with regard to the moral consequences which he states have threatened to demolish a system of civilization under which his Country enjoys a prosperity unparalleled in the history of Man. We had emerged from our first terrors. But here we sink into them again; however, only to shake them off upon the credit of his being a Man of very sanguine hopes.

Against the moral terrors of this successful empire of barbarism, though he has given us no consolation here, in another place he has formed other securities; securities, indeed, which will make even the enormity of the crimes and atrocities of France a benefit to the world. We are to be cured by her diseases. We are to grow proud of our Constitution upon the distempers of theirs. Governments throughout all Europe are to become much stronger by this event. This too comes in the favourite mode of *doubt,* and *perhaps.* "To those," he says, "who meditate on the workings of the human mind, a doubt may perhaps arise, whether the effects, which I have described [namely the change he supposes to be wrought on the publick mind with regard to the French doctrines] "though *at present* a salutary check to the dangerous spirit of innovation, may not prove favourable to abuses of power, by creating a timidity in the just cause of liberty." Here the current of our apprehensions takes a contrary course. Instead of trembling for the existence of our government from the spirit of licentiousness and anarchy, the author would make us believe we are to tremble for our liberties from the great accession of power which is to accrue to government.

I believe I have read in some author who criticised the productions of the famous Jurieu, that it is not very wise in people, who dash away in prophecy, to fix the time of accomplishment at too short a period. Mr. Brothers may [281] meditate upon this at his leisure. He was a melancholy prognosticator, and has had the fate of melancholy men. But they who prophecy pleasant things get great present applause; and in days of calamity people have something else to think of—they lose in their feeling of their distress all memory of those who flattered them in their prosperity. But, merely for the credit of the prediction, nothing could have happened more unluckily for the Noble Lord's sanguine expectations of the amendment of the publick mind and the consequent greater security to government from the examples in France, than what happened in the week after the publication of his hebdomadal system. I am not sure it was not in the very week, one of the most violent and dangerous seditions broke out, that we have seen in several years. This sedition, menacing to the publick security, endangering the sacred person of the King, and violating in the most audacious manner the authority of Parliament, surrounded our sovereign with a murderous yell and war whoop for that peace, which the Noble Lord considers as a cure for all domestick disturbances and dissatisfactions.

So far as to this general cure for popular disorders. As for Government, the two Houses of Parliament, instead of being guided by the speculations of the fourth week in October, and throwing up new barriers against the dangerous power of the crown, which the Noble Lord considered as no unplausible subject of apprehension—the two Houses of Parliament thought fit to pass two Acts for the further strengthening of that very government against a most dangerous and wide spread faction.

Unluckily too for this kind of sanguine speculation, on the very first day of the ever famed "last week of October," a large, daring, and seditious meeting was publickly held, from which meeting this atrocious attempt against the Sovereign publickly originated.

[282] No wonder, that the Author should tell us, that the whole consideration might be varied *whilst he was writing those pages.* In one, and that the most material, instance, his speculations not only might be, but were at that very time, entirely overset. Their war-cry for peace with France was the same with that of this gentle Author, but in a different note. His is the *gemitus columbae,* cooing and wooing fraternity: theirs the

funereal screams of birds of night calling for their ill-omened paramours. But they are both songs of courtship. These Regicides considered a regicide peace as a cure for all their evils; and, so far as I can find, they showed nothing at all of the timidity which the Noble Lord apprehends in what *they* call the "just cause of liberty."

However, it seems, that notwithstanding these awkward appearances with regard to the strength of government, he has still his fears and doubts about our liberties. To a free people this would be a matter of alarm, but this Physician of October has in his shop all sorts of salves for all sorts of sores. It is curious, that they all come from the inexhaustible Drug Shop of the Regicide Dispensary. It costs him nothing to excite terror, because he lays it at his pleasure. He finds a security for this danger to liberty from the wonderful wisdom to be taught to Kings, to Nobility, and even to the lowest of the people, by the late transactions.

I confess I was always blind enough to regard the French Revolution, in the act and much more in the example, as one of the greatest calamities that had ever fallen upon mankind. I now find, that in its effects it is to be the greatest of all blessings. If so, we owe *amende honorable* to the Jacobins. They, it seems, were right—and if they were right a little earlier than we are, it only shews that they exceeded us in sagacity. If they brought out their [283] right ideas somewhat in a disorderly manner, it must be remembered that great zeal produces some irregularity; but, when greatly in the right, it must be pardoned by those, who are very regularly and temperately in the wrong. The Master Jacobins had told me this a thousand times. I never believed the Masters; nor do I now find myself disposed to give credit to the Disciple. I will not much dispute with our Author, which party has the best of this Revolution —that, which is from thence to learn wisdom, or that, which from the same event has obtained power. The dispute on the preference of strength to wisdom may perhaps be decided as Horace has decided the Controversy between Art and Nature. I do not like to leave all the power to my adversary, and to secure nothing to myself but the untimely wisdom that is taught by the consequences of folly. I do not like my share in the partition, because to his strength my adversary may possibly add a good deal of cunning, whereas my wisdom may totally fail in producing to me the same degree of strength. But to descend from the Author's generalities a little nearer to meaning, the security given to Liberty is this, "that Governments will have learned not to precipitate themselves into embarrassments by speculative wars. Sovereigns and Princes will not forget that steadiness, moderation and economy are the best supports of the eminence on which they stand. There seems to me a good deal of oblique reflexion in this lesson. As to the lesson itself, it is at all times a good one. One would think however, by this formal introduction of it, as a recommendation of the arrangements proposed by the Author, it had never been taught before, either by precept or by experience; and that these maxims are discoveries reserved for a Regicide peace. But is it permitted to ask, what security it affords to the liberty of the subject, that the Prince is pacifick or frugal? The very contrary has happened in our history. Our best [284] securities for freedom have been obtained from Princes who were either warlike, or prodigal, or both.

Although the amendment of Princes, in these points, can have no effect in quieting our apprehensions for Liberty on account of the strength to be acquired to government by a Regicide peace, I allow, that the avoiding of speculative wars may possibly be an advantage; provided I well understand, what the Author means by a speculative war. I suppose he means a war grounded on speculative advantages, and not wars founded on a just speculation of danger. Does he mean to include this war, which we are now carrying on, amongst those speculative wars, which this Jacobin peace is to teach Sovereigns to avoid hereafter? If so, it is doing the Party an important service. Does he mean that we are to avoid such wars as that of the grand Alliance, made on a speculation of danger to the independence of Europe? I suspect he has a sort of retrospective view to the American war, as a speculative war, carried on by England upon one side, and by Lewis the 16th on the other. As to our share of that war, let reverence to the dead and respect to the living prevent us from reading lessons of this kind at their expence. I don't know how far the Author may find himself at liberty to wanton on that subject, but, for my part, I entered into a coalition, which, when I had no longer a duty relative to that business, made me think myself bound in honour not to call it up without necessity. But if he puts England out of the question and reflects only on Louis the 16th, I have only to say "Dearly has he answered it." I will not defend him. But all those, who pushed on the Revolution, by which he was deposed, were much more in fault, than he was. They have murdered him, and have divided his Kingdom as a spoil; but they, who are the guilty, are not they, who furnish the example. They, who reign through his fault, are not among those Sovereigns, who are [285] likely to be taught to avoid speculative wars by the murder of their master. I think the Author will not be hardy enough to assert, that they have shown less disposition to meddle in the concerns of that very America, than he did, and in a way not less likely to kindle the flame of speculative war. Here is one Sovereign not yet reclaimed by these healing examples. Will he point out the other Sovereigns, who are to be reformed by this peace? Their wars may not be speculative. But the world will not be much mended by turning wars from unprofitable and speculative to practical and lucrative, whether the liberty or the repose of mankind is regarded. If the Author's new Sovereign in France is not reformed by the example of his own Revolution, that Revolution has not added much to the security and repose of Poland, for instance, or taught the three great partitioning powers more moderation in their second, than they had shewn in their first division of that devoted Country. The first division, which preceded these destructive examples, was moderation itself in comparison of what has been done since the period of the Author's amendment.

This Paragraph is written with something of a studied obscurity. If it means any thing, it seems to hint as if Sovereigns were to learn moderation, and an attention to the Liberties of their people, from *the fate of the Sovereigns who have suffered in this war,* and eminently of Louis the XVIth.

Will he say, whether the King of Sardinia's horrible tyranny was the cause of the loss of Savoy and of Nice? What lesson of moderation does it teach the Pope? I desire to know, whether his Holiness is to learn not to massacre his subjects, nor to waste and destroy such beautiful countries, as that of Avignon, lest he should call to their assistance that great deliverer of nations, *Jourdan Coupe-tête?* What lesson does it give of moderation to the Emperor, whose [286] Predecessor never put one man to death after a general rebellion of the Low Countries, that the Regicides never spared man, woman, or child, whom they but suspected of dislike to their usurpations? What, then, are all these lessons about the *softening* the character of Sovereigns by this Regicide peace? On reading this section one would imagine, that the poor tame Sovereigns of Europe had been a sort of furious wild beasts, that stood in need of some uncommonly rough discipline to subdue the ferocity of their savage nature!

As to the example to be learnt from the murder of Louis the 16th, if a lesson to Kings is not derived from his fate, I do not know whence it can come. The Author, however, ought not to have left us in the dark upon that subject, to break our shins over hints and insinuations. Is it, then, true, that this unfortunate monarch drew his punishment upon himself by his want of moderation, and his oppressing the liberties, of which he had found his people in possession? Is not the direct contrary the fact? And is not the example of this Revolution the very reverse of any thing, which can lead to that *softening* of character in Princes, which the Author supposes as a security to the people, and has brought forward as a recommendation to fraternity with those, who have administered that happy emollient in the murder of their King and the slavery and desolation of their Country?

But the Author does not confine the benefit of the Regicide lesson to Kings alone. He has a diffusive bounty. Nobles, and men of property will likewise be greatly reformed. They too will be led to a review of their social situation and duties, "and will reflect, that their large allotment of worldly advantages is for the aid and benefit of the whole." Is it then from the fate of Juignie, Archbishop of Paris, or of the Cardinal de Rochefoucault, and of so many [287] others, who gave their fortunes, and, I may say, their very beings to the poor, that the rich are to learn, that their "fortunes are for the aid and benefit of the whole?" I say nothing of the liberal persons of great rank and property, lay and ecclesiastick, men and women, to whom we have had the honour and happiness of affording an asylum—I pass by these, lest I should never have done, or lest I should omit some as deserving as any I might mention. Why will the Author then suppose, that the Nobles and men of property in France have been banished, confiscated and murdered, on account of the savageness and ferocity of their character, and their being tainted with vices beyond those of the same order and description in other countries? No Judge of a Revolutionary tribunal, with his hands dipped in their blood, and his maw gorged with their property, has yet dared to assert what this Author has been pleased, by way of a moral lesson, to insinuate.

Their Nobility and their men of property, in a mass, had the very same virtues and the very same vices, and in the very same proportions, with the same description of men in this and in other nations. I must do justice to suffering honour, generosity, and integrity. I do not know that any time or any country has furnished more splendid examples of every virtue, domestick and publick. I do not enter into the councils of Providence: but humanly speaking, many of these Nobles and men of property, from whose disastrous fate we are, it seems, to learn a general softening of character, and a revision of our social situations and duties, appear to me full as little deserving of that fate, as the Author, whoever he is, can be. Many of them, I am sure, were such as I should be proud indeed to be able to compare myself with, in knowledge, in integrity, and in every other virtue. My feeble nature might shrink, though theirs did not, from the proof; but my reason and my ambition tell me, that it [288] would be a good bargain to purchase their merits with their fate.

For which of his vices did that great magistrate, D'Espremenil, lose his fortune and his head? What were the abominations of Malesherbes, that other excellent magistrate, whose sixty years of uniform virtue was acknowledged, in the very act of his murder, by the judicial butchers who condemned him? On account of what misdemeanours was he robbed of his property, and slaughtered with two generations of his offspring; and the remains of the third race, with a refinement of cruelty, and lest they should appear to reclaim the property forfeited by the virtues of their ancestor, confounded in an Hospital with the thousands of those unhappy foundling infants, who are abandoned, without relation and without name, by the wretchedness or by the profligacy of their parents?

Is the fate of the Queen of France to produce this softening of character? Was she a person so very ferocious and cruel as, by the example of her death, to frighten us into common humanity? Is there no way to teach the Emperor a *softening* of character and a review of his social situation and duty, but his consent, by an infamous accord with regicide, to drive a second coach with the Austrian Arms through the

streets of Paris, along which, after a series of preparatory horrors exceeding the atrocities of the bloody execution itself,
the glory of the Imperial Race had been carried to an ignominious death? Is this a lesson of *moderation* to a descendant
of Maria Theresa, drawn from the fate of the daughter of that
incomparable woman and sovereign? If he learns this lesson
from such an object and from such teachers, the man may
remain, but the King is deposed. If he does not carry quite
another memory of that transaction in the inmost recesses
of his heart, he is unworthy to reign; he is unworthy to live.
In the chronicle [289] of disgrace he will have but this short
tale told of him, "he was the first Emperor, of his house, that
embraced a regicide: He was the last, that wore the imperial
purple." Far am I from thinking so ill of this august Sovereign, who is at the head of the Monarchies of Europe, and
who is the trustee of their dignities and his own.

What ferocity of character drew on the fate of Elizabeth,
the sister of King Lewis the 16th? For which of the vices of
that pattern of benevolence, of piety, and of all the virtues,
did they put her to death? For which of her vices did they
put to death the mildest of all human creatures, the Duchess
of Biron? What were the crimes of those crowds of Matrons
and Virgins of condition, whom they massacred, with their
juries of blood, in prisons and on scaffolds? What were the
enormities of the Infant King, whom they caused by linger-
ing tortures to perish in their dungeon, and whom if at last
they despatched by poison, it was in that detestable crime
the only act of mercy they have ever shewn?

What softening of character is to be had, what review of
their social situations and duties is to be taught by these examples, to Kings, to Nobles, to Men of Property, to Women,
and to Infants? The Royal Family perished, because it was
royal. The Nobles perished, because they were noble. The
Men, Women and Children, who had property, because they
had property to be robbed of. The Priests were punished,

after they had been robbed of their all, not for their vices, but for their virtues and their piety, which made them an honour to their sacred profession, and to that nature, of which we ought to be proud, since they belong to it. My Lord, nothing can be learned from such examples, except the danger of being Kings, Queens, Nobles, Priests, and Children to be butchered on account of their inheritance. These are things, at which not Vice, not Crime, not Folly, but Wisdom, Goodness, Learning, [290] Justice, Probity, Beneficence stand aghast. By these examples our reason and our moral sense are not enlightened, but confounded; and there is no refuge for astonished and affrighted virtue, but being annihilated in humility and submission, sinking into a silent adoration of the inscrutable dispensations of Providence, and flying with trembling wings from this world of daring crimes, and feeble, pusillanimous, half-bred, bastard Justice, to the asylum of another order of things, in an unknown form, but in a better life.

Whatever the Politician or Preacher of September or of October may think of the matter, it is a most comfortless, disheartening, desolating example. Dreadful is the example of ruined innocence and virtue, and the compleatest triumph of the compleatest villainy, that ever vexed and disgraced mankind! The example is ruinous in every point of view, religious, moral, civil, political. It establishes that dreadful maxim of Machiavel, that in great affairs men are not to be wicked by halves. This maxim is not made for a middle sort of beings, who, because they cannot be Angels, ought to thwart their ambition and not endeavour to become infernal spirits. It is too well exemplified in the present time, where the faults and errours of humanity, checked by the imperfect timorous virtues, have been overpowered by those, who have stopped at no crime. It is a dreadful part of the example, that infernal malevolence has had pious apologists, who read their lectures on frailties in favour of crimes; who abandoned the weak, and court the friendship of the wicked. To root out these maxims, and the examples that support them, is a wise object of years of war. This is that war. This is that moral war. It was said by old Trivulzio, that the battle of Marignan was the battle of the Giants, that all the rest of the many he had seen were those of the Cranes and Pygmies. This is true of the objects, at least, of the contest. For the greater part of those, which we have [291] hitherto contended for, in comparison, were the toys of children.

The October Politician is so full of charity and good nature, that he supposes, that these very robbers and murderers themselves are in a course of amelioration; on what ground I cannot conceive, except on the long practice of every crime, and by its complete success. He is an Origenist, and believes in the conversion of the Devil. All that runs in the place of blood in his veins, is nothing but the milk of human kindness. He is as soft as a curd, though, as a politician, he might be supposed to be made of sterner stuff. He supposes (to use his own expression) "that the salutary truths which he inculcates, are making their way into their bosoms." Their bosom is a rock of granite, on which falsehood has long since built her strong hold. Poor Truth has had a hard work of it with her little pickaxe. Nothing but gunpowder will do.

As a proof, however, of the progress of this sap of Truth, he gives us a confession they had made not long before he wrote. "Their fraternity" (as was lately stated by themselves in a solemn report) "has been the brotherhood of Cain and Abel, and they have organized nothing but Bankruptcy and Famine." A very honest confession truly; and much in the spirit of their oracle, Rousseau. Yet, what is still more marvellous than the confession, this is the very fraternity, to which our author gives us such an obliging invitation to accede. There is, indeed, a vacancy in the fraternal corps; a brother and a partner is wanted. If we please, we may fill up the place of the butchered Abel; and whilst we wait the destiny of the

departed brother, we may enjoy the advantages of the partnership, by entering without delay into a shop of ready-made
Bankruptcy and Famine. These are the *Douceurs,* by which we
are invited to regicide fraternity and friendship. But still our
Author considers the confession as [292] a proof, that "truth
is making its way into their bosoms." No! it is not making its
way into their bosoms. It has forced its way into their mouths!
The evil spirit, by which they are possessed, though essentially a liar, is forced, by the tortures of conscience, to confess
the truth; to confess enough for their condemnation, but not
for their amendment. Shakespeare very aptly expresses this
kind of confession, devoid of repentance, from the mouth of
an usurper, a murderer, and a regicide —

> We ourselves compelled
> Even to the teeth and forehead of our faults,
> To give in evidence.

Whence is their amendment? Why, the Author writes,
that on their murderous insurrectionary system their own
lives are not sure for an hour; nor has their power a greater
stability. True. They are convinced of it, and accordingly the
wretches have done all they can to preserve their lives and
to secure their power; but not one step have they taken to
amend the one, or to make a more just use of the other.
Their wicked policy has obliged them to make a pause in
the only massacres, in which their treachery and cruelty had
operated as a kind of savage justice, that is, the massacre of
the accomplices of their crimes. They have ceased to shed
the inhuman blood of their fellow murderers; but when they
take any of those persons, who contend for their lawful government, their property, and their religion, notwithstanding
the truth, which this author says is making its way into their
bosoms, it has not taught them the least tincture of mercy.
This we plainly see by their massacre at Quiberon, where they
put to death, with every species of contumely, and without

any exception, every prisoner of war who did not escape out of their hands. To have had property, to have been robbed of it, and to endeavour to regain it—these are crimes irremissible, to which every man, who regards his [293] property or his life, in every country, ought well to look in all connexion with those, with whom, to have had property was an offence, to endeavour to keep it, a second offence, to attempt to regain it, a crime that puts the offender out of all the laws of peace or war. You cannot see one of those wretches without an alarm for your life as well as your goods. They are like the worst of the French and Italian banditti, who, whenever they robbed, were sure to murder.

Are they not the very same Ruffians, Thieves, Assassins, and Regicides, that they were from the beginning? Have they diversified the scene by the least variety, or produced the face of a single new villainy? *Taedet harum quotidianarum formarum.* Oh! but I shall be answered, it is now quite another thing— they are all changed—you have not seen them in their state dresses. This makes an amazing difference. The new Habit of the Directory is so charmingly fancied, that it is impossible not to fall in love with so well-dressed a Constitution. The *Costume* of the Sansculotte Constitution of 1793 was absolutely insufferable. The Committee for Foreign Affairs were such slovens, and stunk so abominably, that no *Muscadin* Ambassador of the smallest degree of delicacy of nerves could come within ten yards of them: but now they are so powdered and perfumed and ribbanded and sashed and plumed, that, though they are grown infinitely more insolent in their fine cloaths, even than they were in their rags (and that was enough), as they now appear, there is something in it more grand and noble, something more suitable to an awful Roman Senate, receiving the homage of dependent Tetrarchs. Like that Senate (their perpetual model for conduct towards other nations) they permit their vassals, during their good pleasure, to assume the name of Kings, in order to bestow more dignity on the suite and retinue of the Sovereign Republick by the nominal rank of their slaves — *Ut habeant instrumenta servitutis* [294] *et reges.* All this is very fine, undoubtedly; and Ambassadors, whose hands are almost out for want of employment, may long to have their part in this august ceremony of the Republick one and indivisible. But, with great deference to the new diplomatic taste, we old people must retain some square-toed predilection for the fashions of our youth. I am afraid you will find me, my Lord, again falling into my usual vanity, in valuing myself on the eminent Men whose society I once enjoyed. I remember in a conversation I once had with my ever dear friend Garrick, who was the first of Actors, because he was the most acute observer of nature I ever knew, I asked him, how it happened that whenever a Senate appeared on the Stage, the Audience seemed always disposed to laughter? He said the reason was plain; the Audience was well acquainted with the faces of most of the Senators. They knew, that they were no other than candle-snuffers, revolutionary scene-shifters, second and third mob, prompters, clerks, executioners, who stand with their axe on their shoulders by the wheel, grinners in the Pantomime, murderers in Tragedies, who make ugly faces under black wigs; in short, the very scum and refuse of the Theatre; and it was of course, that the contrast of the vileness of the Actors with the pomp of their Habits naturally excited ideas of contempt and ridicule.

So it was at Paris on the inaugural day of the Constitution for the present year. The foreign Ministers were ordered to attend at this investiture of the *Directory*—for so they call the managers of their burlesque Government. The Diplomacy, who were a sort of strangers, were quite awe struck with "the pride, pomp, and circumstance" of this majestick Senate; whilst the Sansculotte Gallery instantly recognized their old insurrectionary acquaintance, burst out into a horse laugh at their absurd finery, and held them in infinitely greater contempt, than whilst they prowled about [295] the streets in the pantaloons of the last year's Constitution, when their Legislators appeared honestly, with their daggers in their belts and their pistols peeping out of their side pocket holes, like a bold brave Banditti, as they are. The Parisians, (and I am much of their mind) think that a thief with a crape on his visage, is much worse than a bare-faced knave; and that such robbers richly deserve all the penalties of all the Black Acts. In this their thin disguise, their comrades of the late abdicated Sovereign Canaille hooted and hissed them; and from that day have no other name for them, than what is not quite so easy to render into English, impossible to make it very civil English. It belongs indeed to the language of the *Halles;* but, without being instructed in that dialect, it was the opinion of the polite Lord Chesterfield, that no man could be a compleat master of French. Their Parisian brethren called them *Gueux plumés,* which, though not elegant, is expressive and characteristic—"*feathered scoundrels*" I think comes the nearest to it in that kind of English. But we are now to understand, that these *Gueux,* for no other reason, that I can divine, except their red and white cloaths, form at last a State, with which we may cultivate amity, and have a prospect of the blessings of a secure and permanent peace. In effect then, it was not with the men, or their principles, or their politicks, that we quarrelled. Our sole dislike was to the cut of their cloaths.

But to pass over *their* dresses—Good God! in what habits did the Representatives of the crowned heads of Europe appear, when they came to swell the pomp of their humiliation, and attended in solemn function this inauguration of Regicide? That would be the curiosity. Under what robes did they cover the disgrace and degradation of the whole College of Kings? What warehouses of masks and dominos furnished a cover to the nakedness of their shame? The [296] shop ought to be known; it will soon have a good trade. Were the dresses of the Ministers of those lately called Potentates, who attended on that occasion, taken from the wardrobe of that property man at the Opera, from whence my old acquaintance *Anacharsis Cloots,* some years ago, equipped a body of Ambassadors, whom he conducted, as from all the Nations of the World, to the bar of what was called the Constituent Assembly? Among those mock Ministers, one of the most conspicuous figures was the Representative of the British Nation, who unluckily was wanting at the late ceremony. In the face of all the real Ambassadors of the Sovereigns of Europe was this ludicrous representation of their several Subjects, under the name of *oppressed Sovereigns,*[1] exhibited to the Assembly; that Assembly received an harangue in the name of those Sovereigns against their Kings, delivered by this Cloots, actually a subject of Prussia, under the name of Ambassador of the Human Race. At that time there was only a feeble reclamation from one of the Ambassadors of these tyrants and oppressors. A most gracious answer was given to the Ministers of the oppressed Sovereigns; and they went so far on that occasion as to assign them, in that assumed character, a box at one of their festivals.

I was willing to indulge myself in an hope that this second appearance of Ambassadors was only an insolent mummery of the same kind. But alas! Anacharsis himself, all fanatic as he was, could not have imagined, that his Opera procession should have been the prototype of the real appearance of the Representatives of all the Sovereigns of Europe, themselves to make the same prostration that was made by those who dared to represent their people in a complaint against them. But in this the French Republick [297] has followed, as they always affect to do and have hitherto done with success, the example of the ancient Romans, who shook all Governments by listening to the complaints of their subjects, and soon after brought the Kings themselves to answer at their bar. At this

---

1. *Souverains Opprimés*—See the whole proceeding in the Process Verbal of the National Assembly.

last ceremony the Ambassadors had not Cloots for their Cotterel. Pity that Cloots had not had a reprieve from the Guillotine 'till he had compleated his work! But that engine fell before the curtain had fallen upon all the dignity of the earth.

On this their gaudy day the new Regicide Directory sent for that diplomatic rabble, as bad as themselves in principle, but infinitely worse in degradation. They called them out by a sort of roll of their Nations, one after another, much in the manner, in which they called wretches out of their prison to the guillotine. When these Ambassadors of Infamy appeared before them, the chief Director, in the name of the rest, treated each of them with a short, affected, pedantic, insolent, theatric *laconium;* a sort of epigram of contempt. When they had thus insulted them in a style and language which never before was heard, and which no Sovereign would for a moment endure from another, supposing any of them frantic enough to use it, to finish their outrage, they drummed and trumpeted the wretches out of their Hall of Audience.

Among the objects of this insolent buffoonery was a person supposed to represent the King of Prussia. To this worthy Representative they did not so much as condescend to mention his Master; they did not seem to know, that he had one; they addressed themselves solely to Prussia in the abstract, notwithstanding the infinite obligation they owed to their early protector for their first recognition and alliance, and for the part of his territory he gave into their hands for the first-fruits of his homage. None but dead Monarchs are so much as mentioned by them, and those only to insult the [298] living by an invidious comparison. They told the Prussians, they ought to learn, after the example of Frederic the Great, a love for France. What a pity it is, that he, who loved France so well as to chastise it, was not now alive, by an unsparing use of the rod (which indeed he would have spared little) to give them another instance of his paternal affection!

But the Directory were mistaken. These are not days in which Monarchs value themselves upon the title of *great*. They are grown *philosophick:* they are satisfied to be good.

Your Lordship will pardon me for this no very long reflexion on the short but excellent speech of the Plumed Director to the Ambassador of Cappadocia. The Imperial Ambassador was not in waiting, but they found for Austria a good Judean representation. With great judgement his Highness, the Grand Duke, had sent the most atheistick coxcomb to be found in Florence, to represent, at the bar of impiety, the House of Apostolic Majesty, and the descendants of the pious though high-minded Maria Theresa. He was sent to humble the whole race of Austria before those grim assassins, reeking with the blood of the Daughter of Maria Theresa, whom they sent half dead in a dung cart to a cruel execution; and this true born son of apostacy and infidelity, this Renegado from the faith and from all honour and all humanity, drove an Austrian coach over the stones which were yet wet with her blood—with that blood, which dropped every step through her tumbrel, all the way she was drawn from the horrid prison, in which they had finished all the cruelty and horrors not executed in the face of the sun! The Hungarian subjects of Maria Theresa, when they drew their swords to defend her rights against France, called her, with correctness of truth, though not with the same correctness, perhaps, of Grammar, a King; *Moriamur pro Rege nostro Maria Theresa.* SHE lived and [299] died a King, and others will have Subjects ready to make the same vow, when, in either sex, they shew themselves real Kings.

When the Directory came to this miserable fop, they bestowed a compliment on his matriculation into *their* Philosophy; but as to his Master, they made to him, as was reasonable, a reprimand, not without a pardon, and an oblique hint at the whole family. What indignities have been offered through this wretch to his Master, and how well borne, it is not necessary that I should dwell on at present. I hope that those who yet wear Royal Imperial and Ducal Crowns, will learn to feel as Men and as Kings; if not, I predict to them, they will not long exist as Kings, or as Men.

Great Britain was not there. Almost in despair, I hope she will never, in any rags and *coversluts* of Infamy, be seen at such an exhibition. The hour of her final degradation is not yet come; she did not herself appear in the Regicide presence, to be the sport and mockery of those bloody buffoons, who, in the merriment of their pride, were insulting with every species of contumely the fallen dignity of the rest of Europe. But Britain, though not personally appearing to bear her part in this monstrous Tragi-comedy, was very far from being forgotten. The new-robed Regicides found a representative for her. And who was this Representative? Without a previous knowledge any one would have given a thousand guesses, before he could arrive at a tolerable divination of their rancorous insolence. They chose to address what they had to say concerning this Nation to the Ambassador of America. They did not apply to this Ambassador for a Mediation. That, indeed, would have indicated a want of every kind of decency; but it would have indicated nothing more. But, in this their American apostrophe, your Lordship will observe, they did not so [300] much as pretend to hold out to us directly, or through any Mediator, though in the most humiliating manner, any idea whatsoever of Peace, or the smallest desire of reconciliation. To the States of America themselves they paid no compliment. They paid their compliment to Washington solely; and on what ground? This most respectable Commander and Magistrate might deserve commendation on very many of those qualities, which they, who most disapprove some part of his proceedings, not more justly, than freely, attribute to him; but they found nothing to commend in him, "*but the hatred he bore to Great Britain.*" I verily believe that in the whole history of our European wars, there never was such a compliment paid from the Sovereign of one State to a great Chief of another. Not one Ambassador from any one of those Powers, who pretend to live in amity with this Kingdom, took the least notice of that unheard-of declaration; nor will Great Britain, till she is known with certainty to be true to her own dignity, find any one disposed to feel for the indignities that are offered to her. To say the truth, those miserable creatures were all silent under the insults that were offered to themselves. They pocketed their epigrams, as Ambassadors formerly took the gold boxes, and miniature pictures set in diamonds, presented them by Sovereigns, at whose courts they had resided. It is to be presumed that by the next post they faithfully and promptly transmitted to their Masters the honours they had received. I can easily conceive the epigram, which will be presented to Lord Auckland or to the Duke of Bedford, as hereafter, according to circumstances, they may happen to represent this Kingdom. Few can have so little imagination, as not readily to conceive the nature of the boxes of epigrammatick lozenges, that will be presented to them.

But, *hae nugae seria ducunt in mala.* The conduct of the Regicide Faction is perfectly systematick in every particular, [301] and it appears absurd only as it is strange and uncouth; not as it has an application to the ends and objects of their Policy. When by insult after insult they have rendered the character of Sovereigns vile in the eyes of their subjects, they know there is but one step more to their utter destruction. All authority, in a great degree, exists in opinion: royal authority most of all. The supreme majesty of a Monarch cannot be allied with contempt. Men would reason not unplausibly, that it would be better to get rid of the Monarchy at once, than to suffer that which was instituted, and well instituted, to support the glory of the Nation, to become the instrument of its degradation and disgrace.

A good many reflexions will arise in your Lordship's mind

upon the time and circumstances of that most insulting and atrocious declaration of hostility against this Kingdom. The declaration was made subsequent to the noble Lord's Encomium on the new Regicide Constitution; after the Pamphlet had made something more than advances towards a reconciliation with that ungracious race, and had directly disowned all those who adhered to the original declaration in favour of Monarchy. It was even subsequent to the unfortunate declaration in the Speech from the Throne (which this Pamphlet but too truly announced) of the readiness of our Government to enter into connexions of friendship with that Faction. Here was the answer, from the Throne of Regicide, to the Speech from the Throne of Great Britain. They go out of their way to compliment General Washington on the supposed rancour of his heart towards this Country. It is very remarkable, that they make this compliment of malice to the Chief of the United States, who had first signed a treaty of peace, amity and commerce with this Kingdom. This radical hatred, according to their way of thinking, the most recent, solemn compacts of friendship [302] cannot or ought not to remove. In this malice to England, as in the one great comprehensive virtue, all other merits of this illustrious person are entirely merged. For my part, I do not believe the fact to be so, as they represent it. Certainly it is not for Mr. Washington's honour as a Gentleman, a Christian, or a President of the United States, after the treaty he has signed, to entertain such sentiments. I have a moral assurance that the representation of the Regicide Directory is absolutely false and groundless. If it be, it is a stronger mark of their audacity and insolence, and still a stronger proof of the support they mean to give to the mischievous faction they are known to nourish there to the ruin of those States, and to the end, that no British affections should ever arise in that important part of the world, which would naturally lead to a cordial, hearty British Alliance upon the bottom of mutual interest and ancient affection. It shews, in what part it is, and with what a weapon, they mean a deadly blow at the heart of Great Britain. One really would have expected, when this new Constitution of theirs, which had been announced as a great reform, and which was to be, more than any of their former experimental schemes, alliable with other Nations, that they would, in their very first publick Act and their declaration to the collected representation of Europe and America, have affected some degree of moderation, or, at least, have observed a guarded silence with regard to their temper and their views. No such thing; they were in haste to declare the principles which are spun into the primitive staple of their frame. They were afraid that a moment's doubt should exist about them. In their very infancy they were in haste to put their hand on their infernal altar, and to swear the same immortal hatred to England which was sworn in the succession of all the short-lived constitutions that preceded it. With them every thing else perishes, [303] almost as soon as it is formed; this hatred alone is immortal. This is their impure Vestal fire that never is extinguished; and never will it be extinguished whilst the system of Regicide exists in France. What! are we not to believe them? Men are too apt to be deceitful enough in their professions of friendship, and this makes a wise man walk with some caution through life. Such professions, in some cases, may be even a ground of further distrust. But when a man declares himself your unalterable enemy! No man ever declared to another a rancour towards him, which he did not feel. *Falsos in amore odia non fingere,* said an Author, who points his observations so as to make them remembered.

Observe, my Lord, that from their invasion of Flanders and Holland to this hour, they have never made the smallest signification of a desire of Peace with this Kingdom, with Austria, or indeed, with any other power, that I know of. As superiours, they expect others to begin. We have complied, as you may see. The hostile insolence, with which they gave such a rebuff to our first overture in the speech from the Throne, did not hinder us from making, from the same Throne, a second advance. The two Houses, a second time, coincided in the same sentiments with a degree of apparent unanimity, (for there was no dissentient voice but yours) with which, when they reflect on it, they will be as much ashamed, as I am. To this our new humiliating overture (such, at whatever hazard, I must call it) what did the regicide Directory answer? Not one publick word of a readiness to treat. No, they feel their proud situation too well. They never declared, whether they would grant peace to you or not. They only signified to you their pleasure, as to the Terms, on which alone they would, in any case, admit you to it. You shewed your general disposition to peace, and, to forward it, you left every thing open to negotiations. [304] As to any terms you can possibly obtain, they shut out all negotiation at the very commencement. They declared, that they never would make a peace, by which any thing, that ever belonged to France, should be ceded. We would not treat with the Monarchy, weakened as it must obviously be in any circumstance of restoration, without a reservation of something for indemnity and security, and that too in words of the largest comprehension. You treat with the Regicides without any reservation at all. On their part, they assure you formally and publickly, that they will give you nothing in the name of indemnity or security, or for any other purpose.

It is impossible not to pause here for a moment, and to consider the manner in which such declarations would have been taken by your Ancestors from a Monarch distinguished for his arrogance; an arrogance, which, even more than his ambition, incensed and combined all Europe against him. Whatever his inward intentions may have been, did Lewis the 14th ever make a declaration, that the true bounds of France were the Ocean, the Mediterranean and the Rhine? In any overtures for peace, did he ever declare, that he would make no sacrifices to promote it? His declarations were always directly to the contrary; and at the Peace of Ryswick his actions were to the contrary. At the close of the War, almost in every instance victorious, all Europe was astonished, even those who received them were astonished, at his concessions. Let those, who have a mind to see, how little, in comparison, the most powerful and ambitious of all Monarchs is to be dreaded, consult the very judicious, critical observations on the Politicks of that Reign, inserted in the Military Treatise of the Marquis de Montalembert. Let those, who wish to know what is to be dreaded from an ambitious republick, consult no author no military critick, no historical critick. Let them open [305] their own eyes, which degeneracy and pusillanimity have shut from the light that pains them, and let them not vainly seek their security in a voluntary ignorance of their danger.

To dispose us towards this peace—an attempt, in which our Author has, I do not know whether to call it, the good or ill fortune to agree with whatever is most seditious, factious and treasonable in this country, we are told by many dealers in speculation, but not so distinctly by the Author himself, (too great distinctness of affirmation not being his fault)—but we are told, that the French have lately obtained a very pretty sort of constitution, and that it resembles the British constitution as if they had been twinned together in the womb. *Mire sagaces fallere hospites discrimen obscurum.* It may be so; but I confess I am not yet made to it; nor is the Noble Author. He finds the "elements" excellent; but the disposition very inartificial indeed. Contrary to what we might expect at Paris, the meat is good, the cookery abominable. I agree with him fully in the last; and if I were forced to allow the first, I should still think with our old coarse bye-word, that the same power, which furnished all their former *restaurateurs,* sent also their present cooks. I have a great opinion of Thomas Paine, and of all his productions. I remember

his having been one of the Committee for forming one of
their annual Constitutions, I mean the admirable Constitution of 1793—after having been a Chamber Counsel to the
no less admirable Constitution of 1791. This pious patriot
has his eyes still directed to his dear native country, notwithstanding her ingratitude to so kind a benefactor. This outlaw
of England, and lawgiver to France, is now, in secret probably, trying his hand again; and inviting us to him by making
his Constitution such, as may give his disciples in England
some plausible pretext for going into the house that he has
opened. We have discovered, it [306] seems, that all, which
the boasted wisdom of our ancestors has laboured to bring to
perfection for six or seven centuries, is nearly or altogether
matched in six or seven days, at the leisure hours and sober
intervals of Citizen Thomas Paine.

But though the treacherous tapster Thomas
Hangs a new Angel two doors from us,
As fine as daubers' hands can make it,
In hopes that strangers may mistake it;
We think it both a shame and sin
To quit the good old Angel Inn.

Indeed in this good old House, where every thing, at
least, is well aired, I shall be content to put up my fatigued
horses, and here take a bed for the long night that begins to
darken upon me. Had I, however, the honour (I must now call
it so) of being a Member of any of the Constitutional Clubs,
I should think I had carried my point most completely. It is
clear, by the applauses bestowed on what the Author calls
this new Constitution, a mixed Oligarchy, that the difference
between the Clubbists and the old adherents to the Monarchy of this country is hardly worth a scuffle. Let it depart in
peace, and light lie the earth on the British Constitution! By
this easy manner of treating the most difficult of all subjects,
the Constitution for a great Kingdom, and by letting loose

an opinion, that they may be made by any adventurers in speculation in a small given time and for any Country, all the ties, which, whether of reason or prejudice, attach mankind to their old, habitual, domestic Governments, are not a little loosened: all communion, which the similarity of the basis has produced between all the Governments that compose what we call the Christian World and the Republic of Europe, would be dissolved. By these hazarded speculations France is more approximated to us in Constitution than in situation, and in proportion as we recede from the ancient system of Europe, we approach to [307] that connection which alone can remain to us, a close alliance with the new discovered moral and political world in France.

These theories would be of little importance, if we did not, not only know, but, sorely feel, that there is a strong Jacobin faction in this Country, which has long employed itself in speculating upon Constitutions, and to whom the circumstance of their Government being home bred and prescriptive, seems no sort of recommendation. What seemed to us to be the best system of liberty that a nation ever enjoyed, to them seems the yoke of an intolerable slavery. This speculative faction had long been at work. The French Revolution did not cause it: it only discovered it, increased it, and gave fresh vigour to its operations. I have reason to be persuaded, that it was in this Country, and from English Writers and English Caballers, that France herself was instituted in this revolutionary fury. The communion of these two factions upon any pretended basis of similarity is a matter of very serious consideration. They are always considering the formal distributions of power in a constitution: the moral basis they consider as nothing. Very different is my opinion: I consider the moral basis as every thing; the formal arrangements, further than as they promote the moral principles of Government, and the keeping desperately wicked persons as the subjects of laws and not the makers of them, to be of little importance.

What signifies the cutting and shuffling of Cards, while the Pack still remains the same? As a basis for such a connection, as has subsisted between the powers of Europe, we had nothing to fear, but from the lapses and frailties of men, and that was enough; but this new pretended Republic has given us more to apprehend from what they call their virtues, than we had to dread from the vices of other men. Avowedly and systematically they have given the upper hand to all the [308] vicious and degenerate part of human nature. It is from their lapses and deviations from their principle, that alone we have any thing to hope.

I hear another inducement to fraternity with the present Rulers. They have murdered one Robespierre. This Robespierre they tell us was a cruel Tyrant, and now that he is put out of the way, all will go well in France. Astraea will again return to that earth from which she has been an Emigrant, and all nations will resort to her golden scales. It is very extraordinary, that the very instant the mode of Paris is known here, it becomes all the fashion in London. This is their jargon. It is the old *bon ton* of robbers, who cast their common crimes on the wickedness of their departed associates. I care little about the memory of this same Robespierre. I am sure he was an execrable villain. I rejoiced at his punishment neither more nor less than I should at the execution of the present Directory or any of its Members. But who gave Robespierre the power of being a Tyrant? and who were the instruments of his tyranny? The present virtuous Constitution-mongers. He was a Tyrant, they were his satellites and his hangmen. Their sole merit is in the murder of their colleague. They have expiated their other murders by a new murder. It has always been the case among this banditti. They have always had the knife at each others' throats, after they had almost blunted it at the throats of every honest man. These people thought, that, in the commerce of murder, he was like to have the better of the bargain, if any time was lost: they therefore took one of their short revolutionary methods, and massacred him in a manner so perfidious and cruel, as would shock all humanity, if the stroke was not struck by the present Rulers on one of their own Associates. But this last act of infidelity and murder is to expiate all the rest, and to qualify them for the amity of an humane and virtuous [309] Sovereign and civilized People. I have heard that a Tartar believes, when he has killed a Man, that all his estimable qualities pass with his cloaths and arms to the murderer. But I have never heard, that it was the opinion of any savage Scythian, that if he kills a brother villain, he is *ipso facto* absolved of all his own offences. The Tartarian doctrine is the most tenable opinion. The murderers of Robespierre, besides what they are entitled to by being engaged in the same tontine of Infamy, are his Representatives; have inherited all his murderous qualities, in addition to their own private stock. But it seems, we are always to be of a party with the last and victorious Assassins. I confess, I am of a different mind; and am, rather inclined, of the two, to think and speak less hardly of a dead ruffian, than to associate with the living. I could better bear the stench of the gibbeted murderer, than the society of the bloody felons who yet annoy the world. Whilst they wait the recompense due to their ancient crimes, they merit new punishment by the new offences they commit. There is a period to the offences of Robespierre. They survive in his Assassins. Better a living dog, says the old proverb, than a dead lion; not so here. Murderers and hogs never look well till they are hanged. From villainy no good can arise, but in the example of its fate. So I leave them their dead Robespierre, either to gibbet his memory, or to deify him in their pantheon with their Marat and their Mirabeau.

It is asserted, that this government promises stability. God of his Mercy forbid! If it should, nothing upon earth besides itself can be stable. We declare this stability to be the ground of our making peace with them. Assuming it therefore, that the Men and the System are what I have described, and that they have a determined hostility against this country, an hostility not only of policy but of predilection—then I think that every rational being would go [310] along with me in considering its permanence as the greatest of all possible evils. If, therefore, we are to look for peace with such a thing in any of its monstrous shapes, which I deprecate, it must be in that state of disorder, confusion, discord, anarchy and insurrection, such as might oblige the momentary Rulers to forbear their attempts on neighbouring States, or to render these attempts less operative, if they should kindle new wars. When was it heard before, that the internal repose of a determined and wicked enemy, and the strength of his government, became the wish of his neighbour, and a security against either his malice or his ambition? The direct contrary has always been inferred from that state of things; accordingly, it has ever been the policy of those, who would preserve themselves against the enterprizes of such a malignant and mischievous power, to cut out so much work for him in his own States, as might keep his dangerous activity employed at home.

It is said in vindication of this system, which demands the stability of the regicide power as a ground for peace with them, that when they have obtained, as now it is said, (though not by this noble Author) they have, a permanent Government, they will be *able* to preserve amity with this Kingdom, and with others who have the misfortune to be in their neighbourhood. Granted. They will be *able* to do so, without question; but are they willing to do so? Produce the act, produce the declaration. Have they made any single step towards it? Have they ever once proposed to treat?

The assurance of a stable peace, grounded on the stability of their system, proceeds on this hypothesis, that their hostility to other Nations has proceeded from their Anarchy at home, and to the prevalence of a Populace which their government had not strength enough to master. This [311] I utterly deny. I insist upon it as a fact, that in the daring com-

mencement of all their hostilities, and their astonishing perseverance in them, so as never once in any fortune, high or
low, to propose a treaty of peace to any power in Europe, they
have never been actuated by the People. On the contrary,
the People, I will not say have been moved, but impelled by
them, and have generally acted under a compulsion, of which
most of Us are, as yet, thank God, unable to form an adequate idea. The War against Austria was formally declared by
the unhappy Louis 16th; but who has ever considered Louis
16th, since the Revolution, to have been the Government?
The second regicide Assembly, then the only Government,
was the Author of that War, and neither the nominal King nor
the nominal People had any thing to do with it further than
in a reluctant obedience. It is to delude ourselves to consider
the state of France, since their Revolution, as a state of Anarchy. It is something far worse. Anarchy it is, undoubtedly,
if compared with Government pursuing the peace, order,
morals, and prosperity of the People. But regarding only the
power that has really guided, from the day of the Revolution
to this time, it has been of all Governments the most absolute, despotic, and effective, that has hitherto appeared on
earth. Never were the views and politics of any Government
pursued with half the regularity, system and method, that a
diligent observer must have contemplated with amazement
and terror in theirs. Their state is not an Anarchy, but a series
of short-lived Tyrannies. We do not call a Republic with annual Magistrates an Anarchy. Theirs is that kind of Republic;
but the succession is not effected by the expiration of the
term of the Magistrate's service, but by his murder. Every
new Magistracy succeeding by homicide, is auspicated by ac-
cusing its predecessors [312] in the office of Tyranny, and it
continues by the exercise of what they charged upon others.

This strong hand is the law, and the sole law, in their
State. I defy any person to show any other law, or if any such
should be found on paper, that it is in the smallest degree, or

in any one instance, regarded or practised. In all their successions, not one Magistrate, or one form of Magistracy, has
expired by a mere occasional popular tumult. Every thing
has been the effect of the studied machinations of the one
revolutionary cabal, operating within itself upon itself. That
cabal is all in all. France has no Public; it is the only nation I
ever heard of where the people are absolutely slaves, in the
fullest sense, in all affairs public and private, great and small,
even down to the minutest and most recondite parts of their
household concerns. The Helots of Laconia, the Regardants
to the Manor in Russia and in Poland, even the Negroes in
the West Indies know nothing of so searching, so penetrating, so heart-breaking a slavery. Much would these servile
wretches call for our pity under that unheard-of yoke, if for
their perfidious and unnatural Rebellion, and for the murder
of the mildest of all Monarchs, they did not richly deserve a
punishment not greater than their crime.

On the whole, therefore, I take it to be a great mistake,
to think that the want of power in the government furnished
a natural cause of war: whereas, the greatness of its power,
joined to its use of that power, the nature of its system, and
the persons who acted in it, did naturally call for a strong military resistance to oppose them, and rendered it not only just,
but necessary. But, at present, I say no more on the genius
and character of the power set up in France. I may probably trouble you with it more at large hereafter. This subject
calls for a very full exposure; [313] at present, it is enough
for me, if I point it out as a matter well worthy of consideration, whether the true ground of hostility was not rightly
conceived very early in this war, and whether any thing has
happened to change that system, except our ill success in a
war, which, in no principal instance, had its true destination
as the object of its operations. That the war has succeeded ill
in many cases, is undoubted; but then let us speak the truth
and say, we are defeated, exhausted, dispirited, and must sub-

mit. This would be intelligible. The world would be inclined to pardon the abject conduct of an undone Nation. But let us not conceal from *ourselves* our real situation, whilst, by every species of humiliation, we are but too strongly displaying our sense of it to the Enemy.

The Writer of the Remarks in the last week of October appears to think that the present Government in France contains many of the elements, which, when properly arranged, are known to form the best practical governments; and that the system, whatever may become its particular form, is no longer likely to be an obstacle to negotiation. If its form now be no obstacle to such negotiation, I do not know why it was ever so. Suppose that this government promised greater permanency than any of the former, (a point, on which I can form no judgment) still a link is wanting to couple the permanence of the government with the permanence of the peace. On this not one word is said: nor can there be, in my opinion. This deficiency is made up by strengthening the first ringlet of the chain that ought to be, but that is not, stretched to connect the two propositions. All seems to be done, if we can make out, that the last French edition of Regicide is like to prove stable.

As a prognostic of this stability, it is said to be accepted by the people. Here again I join issue with the [314] Fraternizers, and positively deny the fact. Some submission or other has been obtained, by some means or other, to every government that hitherto has been set up. And the same submission would, by the same means, be obtained for any other project that the wit or folly of man could possibly devise. The Constitution of 1790 was universally received. The Constitution, which followed it, under the name of a Convention, was universally submitted to. The Constitution of 1793 was universally accepted. Unluckily, this year's Constitution, which was formed and its *genethliacon* sung by the noble Author while it was yet in embryo, or was but just come bloody from the womb, is the only one which in its very formation has been generally resisted by a very great and powerful party in many parts of the kingdom, and particularly in the Capital. It never had a popular choice even in show. Those who arbitrarily erected the new building out of the old materials of their own Convention, were obliged to send for an Army to support their work. Like brave Gladiators, they fought it out in the streets of Paris, and even massacred each other in their House of Assembly in the most edifying manner, and for the entertainment and instruction of their Excellencies the Foreign Ambassadors, who had a box in this constitutional Amphitheatre of a free People.

At length, after a terrible struggle, the Troops prevailed over the Citizens. The Citizen Soldiers, the ever famed National Guards, who had deposed and murdered their Sovereign, were disarmed by the inferior trumpeters of that Rebellion. Twenty thousand regular Troops garrison Paris. Thus a complete Military Government is formed. It has the strength, and it may count on the stability of that kind of power. This power is to last as long as the Parisians think proper. Every other ground of stability, but from military force and terrour, is clean out of the [315] question. To secure them further, they have a strong corps of irregulars, ready armed. Thousands of those Hell-hounds called Terrorists, whom they had shut up in Prison on their last Revolution, as the Satellites of Tyranny, are let loose on the people. The whole of their Government, in its origination, in its continuance, in all its actions, and in all its resources, is force; and nothing but force. A forced constitution, a forced election, a forced subsistence, a forced requisition of soldiers, a forced loan of money.

They differ nothing from all the preceding usurpations, but that to the same odium a good deal more of contempt is added. In this situation, notwithstanding all their military force, strengthened with the undisciplined power of the Terrorists, and the nearly general disarming of Paris, there would almost certainly have been before this an insurrection against them, but for one cause. The people of France languished for Peace. They all despaired of obtaining it from the coalesced powers, whilst they had a gang of professed Regicides at their head; and several of the least desperate Republicans would have joined with better men to shake them wholly off, and to produce something more ostensible, if they had not been reiteratedly told that their sole hope of peace was the very contrary to what they naturally imagined. That they must leave off their cabals and insurrections, which could serve no purpose, but to bring in that Royalty, which was wholly rejected by the coalesced Kings. That, to satisfy them, they must tranquilly, if they could not cordially, submit themselves to the tyranny and the tyrants they despised and abhorred. Peace was held out, by the allied Monarchies, to the people of France, as a bounty for supporting the Republick of Regicides. In fact, a coalition, begun for the avowed purpose of destroying that den of [316] Robbers, now exists only for their support. If evil happens to the Princes of Europe, from the success and stability of this infernal business, it is their own absolute crime.

We are to understand, however, (for sometimes so the Author hints) that something stable in the Constitution of Regicide was required for our amity with it; but the noble Remarker is no more solicitous about this point, than he is for the permanence of the whole body of his October Speculations. "If," says he, speaking of the Regicide, "they can obtain a practicable Constitution, even for a limited period of time, they will be in a condition to re-establish the accustomed relations of peace and amity." Pray let us leave this bushfighting. What is meant by *a limited period of time?* Does it mean the direct contrary to the terms, "an *unlimited* period?" If it is a limited period, what limitation does he fix as a ground for his opinion? Otherwise, his limitation is unlimited. If he only requires a Constitution that will last while the treaty goes on, ten days existence will satisfy his demands. He knows that France never did want a practicable Constitution nor a Government, which endured for a limited period of time. Her Constitutions were but too practicable; and short as was their duration, it was but too long. They endured time enough for treaties which benefited themselves and have done infinite mischief to our cause. But, granting him his strange thesis, that, hitherto, the mere form or the mere term of their Constitutions, and, not their indisposition, but their instability, has been the cause of their not preserving the relations of Amity—how could a Constitution, which might not last half an hour after the noble Lord's signature of the treaty, in the company, in which he must sign it, endure its observance? If you trouble yourself at all with their Constitutions, you are [317] certainly more concerned with them after the treaty, than before it, as the observance of conventions is of infinitely more consequence, than the making them. Can any thing be more palpably absurd and senseless, than to object to a treaty of peace, for want of durability in Constitutions, which had an actual duration, and to trust a Constitution, that at the time of the writing had not so much as a practical existence? There is no way of accounting for such discourse in the mouths of men of sense, but by supposing, that they secretly entertain a hope, that the very act of having made a peace with the Regicides will give a stability to the Regicide system. This will not clear the discourse from the absurdity, but it will account for the conduct, which such reasoning so ill defends. What a round-about way is this to peace! To make war for the destruction of Regicides, and then to give them peace in order to insure a stability, that will enable them to observe it! I say nothing of the honour displayed in such a system. It is plain it militates with itself almost in all the parts of it. In one part it supposes stability in their Constitution, as a ground of a stable peace. In another part, we are to hope for peace in a different way; that is, by splitting this brilliant orb into little stars, and this would make the face of heaven so fine. No! there is no system upon which the peace, which in humility we are to supplicate, can possibly stand.

I believe, before this time, that the mere form of a Constitution, in any country, never was fixed as the sole ground of objecting to a treaty with it. With other circumstances it may be of great moment. What is incumbent on the assertors of the 4th week of October system to prove, is not whether their then expected Constitution was likely to be stable or transitory, but whether it promised to this country and its allies, and to the peace and settlement of all Europe, more good will, or more good faith, than any of [318] the experiments which have gone before it. On these points I would willingly join issue.

Observe first the manner, in which the Remarker describes (very truly, as I conceive) the people of France, under that auspicious Government, and then observe the conduct of that Government to other Nations. "The people without any established Constitution; distracted by popular convulsions; in a state of inevitable bankruptcy; without any commerce; with their principal Ports blockaded, and without a Fleet that could venture to face one of our detached Squadrons." Admitting, as fully as he had stated it, this condition of France, I would fain know how he reconciles this condition with his ideas of *any kind of a practicable Constitution,* or *duration for a limited period,* which are his *sine qua non* of Peace. But, passing by contradictions as no fair objections to reasoning, this state of things would naturally, at other times, and in other Governments, have produced a disposition to peace, almost on any terms. But, in that state of their Country, did the Regicide Government solicit peace or amity with other Nations, or even lay any specious grounds for it in propositions of affected moderation, or in the most loose and general conciliatory language? The direct contrary. It was but a very few days before the noble writer had commenced his

Remarks, as if it were to refute him by anticipation, that his France thought fit to lay out a new territorial map of dominion, and to declare to us and to all Europe what Territories she was willing to allot to her own Empire, and what she is content (during her good pleasure) to leave to others.

This their Law of Empire was promulgated without any requisition on that subject, and proclaimed in a style, and upon principles, which never had been heard of in the annals of arrogance and ambition. She prescribed the limits to her Empire, not upon principles of treaty, convention, [319] possession, usage, habitude, the distinction of tribes, nations, or languages, but by physical aptitudes. Having fixed herself as the Arbiter of physical dominion, she construed the limits of Nature by her convenience. That was nature, which most extended and best secured the Empire of France.

I need say no more on the insult offered, not only to all equity and justice, but to the common sense of mankind, in deciding legal property by physical principles, and establishing the convenience of a Party as a rule of public Law. The noble Advocate for Peace has indeed perfectly well exploded this daring and outrageous system of pride and tyranny. I am most happy in commending him, when he writes like himself. But hear, still further, and in the same good strain, the great patron and advocate of amity with this accommodating, mild and unassuming power, when he reports to you the Law they give, and its immediate effects. "They amount," says he, "to the sacrifice of Powers, that have been the most nearly connected with us: the direct, or indirect annexation to France of all the ports of the Continent, from Dunkirk to Hamburgh; an immense accession of Territory; and, in one word, THE ABANDONMENT OF THE INDEPENDENCE OF EUROPE!" This is the Law (the Author and I use no different terms) which this new Government, almost as soon as it could cry in the cradle, and as one of the very first acts, by which it auspicated its entrance into function as the Pledge it gives of the firmness of its Policy—such is the Law, that this proud Power prescribes to abject Nations. What is the comment upon this Law, by the great Jurist, who recommends us to the Tribunal which issued the Decree? "An obedience to it, would be (says he) dishonourable to us, and exhibit us to the present age and to posterity, as submitting to the Law prescribed to us by our Enemy."

[320] Here I recognize the voice of a British Plenipotentiary: I begin to feel proud of my Country. But, alas, the short date of human elevation! The accents of dignity died upon his tongue. This Author will not assure us of his sentiments for the whole of a Pamphlet; but in the sole energetick part of it, he does not continue the same through an whole sentence, if it happens to be of any sweep or compass. In the very womb of this last sentence, pregnant, as it should seem, with a Hercules, there is formed a little Bantling of the mortal race, a degenerate puny parenthesis, that totally frustrates our most sanguine views and expectations, and disgraces the whole gestation. Here is this destructive parenthesis, "unless some adequate compensation be secured *to us*"—To US! The Christian world may shift for itself—Europe may groan in Slavery—we may be dishonoured by receiving Law from an Enemy—but all is well, provided the compensation *to us* be adequate! To what are we reserved? An *adequate* compensation "for the Sacrifice of Powers the most nearly connected with us"; an *adequate* compensation "for the direct or indirect annexation to France of all the Ports of the Continent, from Dunkirk to Hamburgh"; an *adequate* compensation "for the abandonment of the independence of Europe!" Would that when all our manly sentiments are thus changed, our manly language were changed along with them; and that the English tongue were not employed to utter what our Ancestors never dreamed could enter into an English heart!

But let us consider this matter of adequate compensation. Who is to furnish it? From what funds is it to be drawn? Is it by another Treaty of Commerce? I have no objections to Treaties of Commerce, upon principles of commerce. Traffick for traffick; all is fair. But—commerce, in exchange for empire, for safety, for glory! We set out in our dealing with a miserable cheat upon ourselves. I know [321] it may be said that we may prevail on this proud, philosophical, military Republick, which looks down with contempt on Trade, to declare it unfit for the Sovereign of Nations to be *eundem Negotiatorem et Dominum;* that, in virtue of this maxim of her State, the English in France may be permitted, as the Jews are in Poland and in Turkey, to execute all the little inglorious occupations; to be the sellers of new and the buyers of old Cloaths; to be their Brokers and Factors, and to be employed in casting up their debits and credits, whilst the master Republick cultivates the arts of Empire, prescribes the forms of peace to nations, and dictates laws to a subjected world. But are we quite sure that when we have surrendered half Europe to them in hope of this compensation, the Republick will confer upon us those privileges of dishonour? Are we quite certain, that she will permit us to farm the Guillotine; to contract for the provision of her twenty thousand Bastiles; to furnish transports for the myriads of her Exiles to Guiana; to become Commissioners for her naval Stores, or to engage for the cloathing of those Armies which are to subdue the poor Reliques of Christian Europe? No! She is bespoke by the Jew Subjects of her own Amsterdam for all these services.

But if these, or matters similar, are not the compensations the Remarker demands, and that, on consideration, he finds them neither adequate nor certain, who else is to be the Chapman, and to furnish the purchase money at this market of all the grand principles of Empire, of Law, of Civilization, of Morals, and of Religion, where British faith and honour are to be sold by inch of candle? Who is to be the *dedecorum pretiosus emptor?* Is it the *Navis Hispanae Magister?* Is it to be furnished by the Prince of Peace? Unquestionably. Spain as yet possesses mines of gold and silver; and may give us in *pesos duros* an adequate [322] compensation for our honour and our virtue. When these things are at all to be sold, they are the vilest commodities at market.

It is full as singular as any of the other singularities in this work, that the Remarker, talking so much as he does of cessions and compensations, passes by Spain in his general settlement, as if there were no such Country on the Globe: as if there were no Spain in Europe, no Spain in America. But this great matter of political deliberation cannot be put out of our thoughts by his silence. She *has* furnished compensations—not to you, but to France. The Regicide Republick, and the still nominally subsisting Monarchy of Spain, are united, and are united upon a principle of jealousy, if not of bitter enmity to Great Britain. The noble Writer has here another matter for meditation. It is not from Dunkirk to Hamburgh that the ports are in the hands of France: they are in the hands of France from Hamburgh to Gibraltar. How long the new Dominion will last, I cannot tell; but France the Republick has conquered Spain, and the ruling Party in that Court acts by her orders and exists by her power.

The noble Writer, in his views into futurity, has forgotten to look back to the past. If he chooses it, he may recollect, that on the prospect of the death of Philip the Fourth, and still more on the event, all Europe was moved to its foundations. In the Treaties of Partition, that first were entered into, and in the war that afterwards blazed out to prevent those Crowns from being actually or virtually united in the House of Bourbon, the predominance of France in Spain, and, above all, in the Spanish Indies, was the great object of all these movements in the Cabinet and in the Field. The grand alliance was formed upon that apprehension. On that apprehension the mighty war was continued during such a number of years, as the degenerate and pusillanimous [323] impatience of our dwindled race can hardly bear to have reckoned—a war, equal within a few years in duration, and not perhaps inferiour in bloodshed, to any of those great contests for Empire, which in History make the most awful matter of recorded Memory.

Ad confligendum venientibus undique Poenis,
Omnia cum belli trepido concussa tumultu
Horrida contremuere sub altis aetheris auris,
In dubioque fuit sub utrorum regna cadendum
Omnibus humanis esset terrâque marique—

When this war was ended (I cannot stay now to examine how) the object of the war was the object of the Treaty. When it was found impracticable, or less desirable than before, wholly to exclude a branch of the Bourbon race from that immense succession, the point of Utrecht was to prevent the mischiefs to arise from the influence of the greater upon the lesser branch. His Lordship is a great Member of the Diplomatick Body; he has of course all the fundamental Treaties, which make the Public Statute Law of Europe, by heart; and indeed no active Member of Parliament ought to be ignorant of their general tenor and leading provisions. In the Treaty, which closed that war, and of which it is a fundamental part, because relating to the whole Policy of the Compact, it was agreed, that Spain should not give any thing from her territory in the West Indies to France. This Article, apparently onerous to Spain, was in truth highly beneficial. But, oh, the blindness of the greatest Statesman to the infinite and unlooked-for combinations of things which lie hid in the dark prolifick womb of Futurity! The great Trunk of Bourbon is cut down; the withered branch is worked up into the construction of a French Regicide Republick. Here we have, formed, a new, unlooked-for, monstrous, heterogeneous alliance; a double-natured Monster; Republick above and Monarchy below. There is no Centaur of fiction, no poetic [324] Satyr of the Woods; nothing short of the Hieroglyphick Monsters of Aegypt, Dog in Head and Man in Body, that can give an idea of it. None of these things can subsist in nature; so at least it is thought. But the moral world admits Monsters which the physical rejects.

In this Metamorphosis, the first thing done by Spain, in the honey-moon of her new servitude, was, with all the hardihood of pusillanimity, utterly to defy the most solemn Treaties with Great Britain and the Guarantee of Europe. She has yielded the largest and fairest part of one of the largest and fairest Islands in the West Indies, perhaps on the Globe, to the usurped Powers of France. She compleats the title of those Powers to the whole of that important central Island of Hispaniola. She has solemnly surrendered to the Regicides and butchers of the Bourbon family, what that Court never ventured, perhaps never wished, to bestow on the Patriarchal stock of her own august House.

The noble Negotiator takes no notice of this portentous junction, and this audacious surrender. The effect is no less than the total subversion of the Balance of Power in the West Indies, and indeed every where else. This arrangement, considered in itself, but much more as it indicates a compleat Union of France with Spain, is truly alarming. Does he feel nothing of the change this makes in that part of his description of the state of France, where he supposes her not able to face one of our detached Squadrons? Does he feel nothing for the condition of Portugal under this new Coalition? Is it for this state of things he recommends our junction in that common alliance as a remedy? It is surely already monstrous enough. We see every standing principle of Policy, every old governing opinion of Nations, compleatly gone; and with it the foundation of all their establishments. Can Spain keep herself internally where [325] she is, with this connexion? Does he dream, that Spain, unchristian, or even uncatholic, can exist as a Monarchy? This Author indulges himself in speculations of the division of the French Republick. I only say, that with much greater reason he might speculate on the Republicanism and the subdivision of Spain.

It is not peace with France, which secures that feeble Government; it is that peace, which, if it shall continue, decisively ruins Spain. Such a peace is not the peace, which the remnant of Christianity celebrates at this holy season. In it there is no glory to God on high, and not the least tincture of good will to Man. What things we have lived to see! The King of Spain in a group of Moors, Jews, and Renegadoes, and the Clergy taxed to pay for his conversion! The Catholick King in the strict embraces of the most unchristian Republick! I hope we shall never see his Apostolick Majesty, his Faithful Majesty, and the King, defender of the faith, added to that unhallowed and impious Fraternity.

The Noble Author has glimpses of the consequences of Peace as well as I. He feels for the Colonies of Great Britain, one of the principal resources of our Commerce and our Naval Power, if Piratical France shall be established, as he knows she must be, in the West Indies, if we sue for peace on such terms as they may condescend to grant us. He feels that their very Colonial System for the Interiour is not compatible with the existence of our Colonies. I tell him, and doubt not I shall be able to demonstrate, that, being what she is, if she possesses a rock there we cannot be safe. Has this Author had in his view, the transactions between the Regicide Republick and the yet nominally subsisting Monarchy of Spain?

I bring this matter under your Lordship's consideration, that you may have a more compleat view, than this Author [326] chooses to give of the *true France* you have to deal with, as to its nature, and to its force and its disposition. Mark it, my Lord, France in giving her Law to Spain, stipulated for none of her indemnities in Europe, no enlargement whatever of her Frontier. Whilst we are looking for indemnities from France, betraying our own safety in a sacrifice of the independence of Europe, France secures hers by the most important acquisition of Territory ever made in the West Indies, since their first settlement. She appears (it is only in appearance) to give up the Frontier of Spain, and she is compensated, not in appearance, but in reality, by a Territory, that makes a dreadful Frontier to the Colonies of Great Britain.

It is sufficiently alarming, that she is to have the possession of this great Island. But all the Spanish Colonies virtually are hers. Is there so puny a whipster in the *petty form* of the School of Politicks, who can be at a loss for the fate of the British Colonies, when he combines the French and Spanish consolidation with the known critical and dubious dispositions of the United States of America, as they are at present, but which, when a Peace is made, when the basis of a Regicide ascendancy in Spain is laid, will no longer be so good as dubious and critical? But I go a great deal further, and on much consideration of the condition and circumstances of the West Indies, and of the genius of this new Republick, as it has operated, and is likely to operate on them, I say, that if a single Rock in the West Indies is in the hands of this *transatlantic Morocco*, we have not an hour's safety there.

The Remarker, though he slips aside from the main consideration, seems aware that this arrangement, standing as it does, in the West Indies, leaves us at the mercy of the new Coalition, or rather at the mercy of the sole guiding part of it. He does not indeed adopt a supposition, such as I make, [327] who am confident that any thing which can give them a single good port and opportune piratical station there, would lead to our ruin; the Author proceeds upon an idea, that the Regicides may be an existing and considerable territorial power in the West Indies, and, of course, her piratical system more dangerous and as real. However, for that desperate case, he has an easy remedy; but surely, in his whole shop, there is nothing so extraordinary. It is, that we three, France, Spain, and England, (there are no other of any moment) should adopt some "*analogy*" in the interiour systems of Government in the several Islands, which we may respectively retain after the closing of the War." This plainly can be done only by a Convention between the Parties, and I believe it would be the first war ever made to terminate in an analogy of the interiour Government of any country, or any parts of such countries. Such a partnership in domestick Government is, I think, carrying Fraternity as far as it will go.

It will be an affront to your sagacity, to pursue this matter into all its details; suffice it to say, that if this Convention for analogous domestick Government is made, it immediately gives a right for the residence of a Consul (in all likelihood some Negro or Man of Colour) in every one of your Islands; a Regicide Ambassador in London will be at all your meetings of West India Merchants and Planters, and, in effect, in all our Colonial Councils. Not one Order of Council can hereafter be made, or any one Act of Parliament relative to the West India Colonies even be agitated, which will not always afford reasons for protests and perpetual interference. The Regicide Republic will become an integrant part of the Colonial Legislature; and, so far as the Colonies are concerned, of the British too. But it will be still worse; as all our domestick affairs are interlaced, more or less intimately, with our external, this intermeddling must every [328] where insinuate itself into all other interiour transactions, and produce a co-partnership in our domestick concerns of every description.

Such are the plain inevitable consequences of this arrangement of a system of analogous interiour Government. On the other hand, without it, the Author assures us, and in this I heartily agree with him, "that the correspondence and communications between the neighbouring Colonies will be great; that the disagreements will be incessant, and that causes even of National Quarrels will arise *from day to day.*" Most true. But, for the reasons I have given, the case, if possible, will be worse by the proposed remedy, by the triple fraternal interiour analogy; an analogy itself most fruitful, and more foodful, than the old Ephesian Statue with the three tier of breasts. Your Lordship must also observe how infinitely this business must be complicated by our interference in the slow-paced Saturnian movements of Spain, and the rapid parabolick flights of France. But such is the Disease, such is the Cure, such is and must be the Effect of Regicide Vicinity.

But what astonishes me is, that the Negotiator, who has certainly an exercised understanding, did not see, that every person, habituated to such meditations, must necessarily pursue the train of thought further than he has carried it; and must ask himself, whether what he states so truly of the necessity of our arranging an analogous interiour Government, in consequence of the Vicinity of our Possessions in the West Indies, does as extensively apply, and much more forcibly, to the circumstance of our much nearer Vicinity with the Parent and Author of this mischief. I defy even his acuteness and ingenuity to shew me any one point in which the cases differ, except that it is plainly more necessary in Europe than in America. Indeed, the further we trace the details of the proposed peace, the more your Lordship will [329] be satisfied, that I have not been guilty of any abuse of terms, when I use indiscriminately (as I always do in speaking of arrangements with Regicide) the words Peace and Fraternity. An analogy between our interiour Governments must be the consequence. The noble Negotiator sees it as well as I do. I deprecate this Jacobin interiour analogy. But, hereafter, perhaps, I may say a good deal more upon this part of the subject.

The noble Lord insists on very little more, than on the excellence of their Constitution, the hope of their dwindling into little Republicks, and this close copartnership in Government. I hear of others indeed that offer, by other arguments, to reconcile us to this peace and Fraternity; the Regicides, they say, have renounced the Creed of the Rights of Man, and declared Equality a Chimera. This is still more strange than all the rest. They have apostatised from their Apostacy. They are renegadoes from that impious faith, for which they subverted the ancient Government, murdered their King, and imprisoned, butchered, confiscated, and banished their fellow Subjects; and to which they forced every man to swear at the peril of his Life. And now, to reconcile themselves to the world, they declare this Creed, bought by so much blood, to be an imposture and a Chimera. I have no doubt that they always thought it to be so, when they were destroying every thing at home and abroad for its establishment. It is no strange thing to those who look into the nature of corrupted man, to find a violent persecutor a perfect unbeliever of his own Creed. But this is the very first time that any man or set of men were hardy enough to attempt to lay the ground of confidence in them, by an acknowledgement of their own falsehood, fraud, hypocrisy, treachery, heterodox doctrine, persecution, and cruelty. Every thing we hear from them is new, and to use a phrase of their own, *revolutionary.* Every thing supposes a total [330] revolution in all the principles of reason, prudence, and moral feeling.

If possible, this their recantation of the chief parts in the Canon of the Rights of Man, is more infamous, and causes greater horror than their originally promulgating, and forcing down the throats of mankind that symbol of all evil. It is raking too much into the dirt and ordure of human nature to say more of it.

I hear it said too, that they have lately declared in favour of property. This is exactly of the same sort with the former. What need had they to make this declaration, if they did not know, that by their doctrines and practices they had totally subverted all property? What Government of Europe, either in its origin or its continuance, has thought it necessary to declare itself in favour of property? The more recent ones were formed for its protection against former violations. The old consider the inviolability of property and their own existence as one and the same thing; and that a proclamation for its safety would be sounding an alarm on its danger. But the Regicide Banditti knew that this was not the first time they have been obliged to give such assurances, and had as often falsified them. They knew that after butchering hundreds of men, women and children, for no other cause, than to lay hold on their property, such a declaration might have a chance of encouraging other nations to run the risque of establishing a commercial House amongst them. It is notorious that these very Jacobins, upon an alarm of the Shopkeepers of Paris, made this declaration in favour of Property. These brave Fellows received the apprehensions expressed on that head with indignation; and said, that property could be in no danger, because all the world knew it was under the protection of the *Sansculottes.* At what period did they not give this assurance? Did they not give it, when they fabricated [331] their first constitution? Did they not then solemnly declare it one of the rights of a Citizen (a right, of course, only declared and not then fabricated) to depart from his Country, and choose another *Domicilium,* without detriment to his property? Did they not declare, that no property should be confiscated from the children, for the crime of the parent? Can they now declare more fully their respect for property, than they did at that time? And yet was there ever known such horrid violences and confiscations, as instantly followed under the very persons now in power, many of them leading Members of that Assembly, and all of them violators of that engagement, which was the very basis of their Republick—confiscations in which hundreds of men, women and children, not guilty of one act of duty in resisting their usurpation, were involved? This keeping of their old is, then, to give us a confidence in their new engagements. But examine the matter and you will see, that the prevaricating sons of violence give no relief at all, where at all it can be wanted. They renew their old fraudulent declaration against confiscations,

Regicide Peace IV

and then they expressly exclude all adherents to their ancient lawful Government from any benefit of it: that is to say, they promise, that they will secure all their brother plunderers in their share of the common plunder. The fear of being robbed by every new succession of robbers, who do not keep even the faith of that kind of society, absolutely required, that they should give security to the dividends of Spoil; else they could not exist a moment. But it was necessary, in giving security to robbers, that honest men should be deprived of all hope of restitution; and thus their interests were made utterly and eternally incompatible. So that it appears, that this boasted security of property is nothing more than a seal put upon its destruction: this ceasing of confiscation is to secure the confiscators against the innocent proprietors. That very [332] thing, which is held out to you as your cure, is that which makes your malady, and renders it, if once it happens, utterly incurable. You, my Lord, who possess a considerable, though not an invidious, Estate, may be well assured, that if by being engaged, as you assuredly would be, in the defence of your Religion, your King, your Order, your Laws, and Liberties, that Estate should be put under confiscation, the property would be secured, but in the same manner, at your expence.

But, after all, for what purpose are we told of this reformation in their principles, and what is the policy of all this softening in ours, which is to be produced by their example? It is not to soften us to suffering innocence and virtue, but to mollify us to the crimes and to the society of robbers and ruffians! But I trust that our Countrymen will not be softened to that kind of crimes and criminals; for if we should, our hearts will be hardened to every thing which has a claim on our benevolence. A kind Providence has placed in our breasts a hatred of the unjust and cruel, in order that we may preserve ourselves from cruelty and injustice. They who bear cruelty, are accomplices in it. The pretended gentleness which excludes that charitable rancour, produces an indifference which is half an approbation. They never will love where they ought to love, who do not hate where they ought to hate.

There is another piece of policy, not more laudable than this, in reading these moral lectures, which lessens our hatred to Criminals, and our pity to sufferers, by insinuating that it has been owing to their fault or folly, that the latter have become the prey of the former. By flattering us, that we are not subject to the same vices and follies, it induces a confidence, that we shall not suffer the same evils by a contact with the infamous gang of robbers who have thus robbed and butchered our neighbours before our faces. We must [333] not be flattered to our ruin. Our vices are the same as theirs, neither more nor less. If any faults we had, which wanted this French example to call us to a "*softening* of character, and a review of our social relations and duties," there is yet no sign that we have commenced our reformation. We seem, by the best accounts I have from the world, to go on just as formerly, "some to undo, and some to be undone." There is no change at all: and if we are not bettered by the sufferings of war, this peace, which, for reasons to himself best known, the Author fixes as the period of our reformation, must have something very extraordinary in it; because hitherto ease, opulence, and their concomitant pleasure, have never greatly disposed mankind to that serious reflexion and review which the Author supposes to be the result of the approaching peace with vice and crime. I believe he forms a right estimate of the nature of this peace; and that it will want many of those circumstances which formerly characterized that state of things.

If I am right in my ideas of this new Republick, the different states of peace and war will make no difference in her pursuits. It is not an enemy of accident, that we have to deal with. Enmity to us and to all civilized nations is wrought into the very stamina of its constitution. It was made to pursue the purposes of that fundamental enmity. The design will go on regularly in every position and in every relation. Their

hostility is to break us to their dominion: their amity is to debauch us to their principles. In the former we are to contend
with their force; in the latter with their intrigues. But we stand
in a very different posture of defence in the two situations. In
war, so long as Government is supported, we fight with the
whole united force of the kingdom. When under the name of
peace the war of intrigue begins, we do not contend against
our enemies with the whole force of the kingdom. No—[334]
we shall have to fight (if it should be a fight at all, and not an
ignominious surrender of every thing which has made our
country venerable in our eyes and dear to our hearts) we shall
have to fight with but a portion of our strength against the
whole of theirs. Gentlemen who not long since thought with
us, but who now recommend a Jacobin peace, were at that
time sufficiently aware of the existence of a dangerous Jacobin faction within this kingdom. A while ago, they seemed to
be tremblingly alive to the number of those, who composed
it; to their dark subtlety; to their fierce audacity; to their
admiration of every thing that passes in France; to their eager
desire of a close communication with the mother faction
there. At this moment, when the question is upon the opening of that communication, not a word of our English Jacobins. That faction is put out of sight and out of thought. "It
vanished at the crowing of the cock." Scarcely had the Gallick
harbinger of peace and light began to utter his lively notes,
than all the cackling of us poor Tory geese to alarm the garrison of the Capitol was forgot.[1] There was enough of indemnity before. Now a complete act of oblivion is passed about
the Jacobins of England, though one would naturally imagine
it would make a principal object in all fair deliberation upon
the merits of a project of amity with the Jacobins of France.
But however others may chuse to forget the faction, the fac-

1. Hic auratis volitans argenteus anser
   Porticibus, GALLOS in limine adesse canebat.

tion does not chuse to forget itself, nor, however gentlemen may chuse to flatter themselves, it does not forget them.

Never in any civil contest has a part been taken with more of the warmth, or carried on with more of the arts of a party. The Jacobins are worse than lost to their country. Their hearts are abroad. Their sympathy with the Regicides of France is complete. Just as in a civil contest, they exult in [335] all their victories; they are dejected and mortified in all their defeats. Nothing that the Regicides can do, (and they have laboured hard for the purpose) can alienate them from their cause. You and I, my dear Lord, have often observed on the spirit of their conduct. When the Jacobins of France, by their studied, deliberated, catalogued files of murder, with the poignard, the sabre and the tribunal, have shocked whatever remained of human sensibility in our breasts, then it was they distinguished the resources of party policy. They did not venture directly to confront the public sentiment; for a very short time they seemed to partake of it. They began with a reluctant and sorrowful confession: they deplored the stains which tarnished the lustre of a good cause. After keeping a decent time of retirement, in a few days crept out an apology for the excesses of men cruelly irritated by the attacks of unjust power. Grown bolder, as the first feeling of mankind decayed and the colour of these horrors began to fade upon the imagination, they proceeded from apology to defence. They urged, but still deplored, the absolute necessity of such a proceeding. Then they made a bolder stride, and marched from defence to recrimination. They attempted to assassinate the memory of those, whose bodies their friends had massacred; and to consider their murder as a less formal act of justice. They endeavoured even to debauch our pity, and to suborn it in favour of cruelty. They wept over the lot of those who were driven by the crimes of Aristocrats to republican vengeance. Every pause of their cruelty they considered as a return of their natural sentiments of benignity and justice. Then they had recourse to history; and found out all the recorded cruelties that deform the annals of the world, in order that the massacres of the regicides might pass for a common event; and even that the most merciful of Princes, who suffered by their hands, should bear the iniquity of all the tyrants who have at any time infested the earth. In [336] order to reconcile us the better to this republican tyranny, they confounded the bloodshed of war with the murders of peace; and they computed how much greater prodigality of blood was exhibited in battles and in the storm of cities, than in the frugal well-ordered massacres of the revolutionary tribunals of France.

As to foreign powers, so long as they were conjoined with Great Britain in this contest, so long they were treated as the most abandoned tyrants and, indeed, the basest of the human race. The moment any of them quits the cause of this Government, and of all Governments, he is re-habilitated; his honour is restored; all attainders are purged. The friends of Jacobins are no longer despots; the betrayers of the common cause are no longer traitors.

That you may not doubt that they look on this war as a civil war, and the Jacobins of France as of their party, and that they look upon us, though locally their countrymen, in reality as enemies, they have never failed to run a parallel between our late civil war and this war with the Jacobins of France. They justify their partiality to those Jacobins by the partiality which was shewn by several here to the Colonies; and they sanction their cry for peace with the Regicides of France by some of our propositions for peace with the English in America.

This I do not mention, as entering into the controversy how far they are right or wrong in this parallel, but to shew that they do make it, and that they do consider themselves as of a party with the Jacobins of France. You cannot forget their constant correspondence with the Jacobins whilst it was in their power to carry it on. When the communication is again opened, the interrupted correspondence will commence. We cannot be blind to the advantage which such a party affords to Regicide France in all her views; and, on the other hand, what an advantage Regicide France [337] holds out to the views of the republican party in England. Slightly as they have considered their subject, I think this can hardly have escaped the writers of political ephemerides for any month or year. They have told us much of the amendment of the Regicides of France, and of their returning honour and generosity. Have they told any thing of the reformation, and of the returning loyalty of the Jacobins of England? Have they told us of *their* gradual softening towards royalty; have they told us what measures *they* are taking for "putting the crown in commission," and what approximations of any kind *they* are making towards the old constitution of their country? Nothing of this. The silence of these writers is dreadfully expressive. They dare not touch the subject: but it is not annihilated by their silence, nor by our indifference. It is but too plain, that our constitution cannot exist with such a communication. Our humanity, our manners, our morals, our religion, cannot stand with such a communication: the constitution is made by those things, and for those things: without them it cannot exist; and without them it is no matter whether it exists or not.

It was an ingenious parliamentary Christmas play, by which, in both Houses, you anticipated the holidays—it was a relaxation from your graver employment—it was a pleasant discussion you had, which part of the family of the constitution was the elder branch? Whether one part did not exist prior to the others; and whether it might exist and flourish if "the others were cast into the fire?"[1] In order to make this saturnalian amusement general in the family, you sent it

1. See Debates in Parliament upon Motions, made in both Houses, for prosecuting Mr. Reeves for a Libel upon the Constitution, Dec. 1795.

down stairs, that judges and juries might partake of the entertainment. The unfortunate antiquary and augur, who is the
butt of all this sport, may suffer in the roystering horseplay
[338] and practical jokes of the servants' hall. But whatever
may become of him, the discussion itself and the timing it
put me in mind of what I read, (where I do not recollect)
that the subtle nation of the Greeks were busily employed,
in the church of Santa Sophia, in a dispute of mixed natural philosophy, metaphysics and theology, whether the light
on mount Tabor was created or uncreated, and were ready
to massacre the holders of the unfashionable opinion, at
the very moment when the ferocious enemy of all philosophy and religion, Mahomet the Second, entered through a
breach into the capital of the Christian World. I may possibly suffer much more than Mr. Reeves, (I shall certainly
give much more general offence) for breaking in upon this
constitutional amusement concerning the created or uncreated nature of the two Houses of Parliament, and by calling
their attention to a problem, which may entertain them less,
but which concerns them a great deal more, that is, whether
with this Gallick Jacobin fraternity, which they are desired
by some writers to court, all the parts of the Government,
about whose combustible or incombustible qualities they are
contending, may "not be cast into the fire" together. He is
a strange visionary, (but he is nothing worse) who fancies,
that any one part of our constitution, whatever right of pri-
mogeniture it may claim, or whatever astrologers may divine
from its horoscope, can possibly survive the others. As they
have lived, so they will die together. I must do justice to the
impartiality of the Jacobins. I have not observed amongst
them the least predilection for any of those parts. If there has
been any difference in their malice, I think they have shewn
a worse disposition to the House of Commons than to the
Crown. As to the House of Lords, they do not speculate at
all about it; and for reasons that are too obvious to detail.

The question will be concerning the effect of this French [339] fraternity on the whole mass. Have we any thing to apprehend from Jacobin communication, or have we not? If we have not, is it by our experience, before the war, that we are to presume, that, after the war, no dangerous communion can exist between those, who are well affected to the new constitution of France, and ill affected to the old constitution here?

In conversation I have not yet found nor heard of any persons except those who undertake to instruct the publick, so unconscious of the actual state of things, or so little prescient of the future, who do not shudder all over, and feel a secret horror at the approach of this communication. I do not except from this observation those who are willing, more than I find myself disposed, to submit to this fraternity. Never has it been mentioned in my hearing, or from what I can learn in my inquiry, without the suggestion of an Alien Bill, or some other measures of the same nature, as a defence against its manifest mischief. Who does not see the utter insufficiency of such a remedy, if such a remedy could be at all adopted? We expel suspected foreigners from hence; and we suffer every Englishman to pass over into France, to be initiated in all the infernal discipline of the place—to cabal, and to be corrupted, by every means of cabal and of corruption, and then to return to England, charged with their worst dispositions and designs. In France he is out of the reach of your police; and when he returns to England, one such English emissary is worse than a legion of French, who are either tongue-tied, or whose speech betrays them. But the worst Aliens are the ambassador and his train. These you cannot expel without a proof (always difficult) of direct practice against the State. A French ambassador, at the head of a French party, is an evil which we have never experienced. The mischief is by far more visible than the remedy. But, after all, every such [340] measure as an Alien Bill, is a measure of hostility, a preparation for it, or a cause of dispute that shall bring it on. In effect, it is fundamentally contrary to a relation of amity, whose essence is a perfectly free communication. Every thing done to prevent it will provoke a foreign war. Every thing, when we let it proceed, will produce domestick distraction. We shall be in a perpetual dilemma; but it is easy to see which side of the dilemma will be taken. The same temper, which brings us to solicit a Jacobin peace, will induce us to temporise with all the evils of it. By degrees our minds will be made to our circumstances. The novelty of such things, which produces half the horror and all the disgust, will be worn off. Our ruin will be disguised in profit, and the sale of a few wretched baubles will bribe a degenerate people to barter away the most precious jewel of their souls. Our constitution is not made for this kind of warfare. It provides greatly for our happiness, it furnishes few means for our defence. It is formed, in a great measure, upon the principle of jealousy of the crown; and as things stood, when it took that turn, with very great reason. I go farther. It must keep alive some part of that fire of jealousy eternally and chastely burning, or it cannot be the British constitution. At various periods we have had tyranny in this country, more than enough. We have had rebellions with more or less justification. Some of our Kings have made adulterous connections abroad, and trucked away, for foreign gold, the interests and glory of their crown. But, before this time, our liberty has never been corrupted. I mean to say, that it has never been debauched from its domestick relations. To this time it has been English Liberty, and English Liberty only. Our love of Liberty, and our love of our Country, were not distinct things. Liberty is now, it seems, put upon a larger and more liberal bottom. We are men, and as men, undoubtedly, nothing [341] human is foreign to us. We cannot be too liberal in our general wishes for the happiness of our kind. But in all questions on the mode of procuring it for any particular community, we ought to be fearful of admitting those, who have no interest in it, or who have, perhaps, an interest against it, into the consultation. Above all, we cannot be too cautious in our communication with those, who seek their happiness by other roads than those of humanity, morals and religion, and whose liberty consists, and consists alone, in being free from those restraints, which are imposed by the virtues upon the passions.

When we invite danger from a confidence in defensive measures, we ought, first of all, to be sure, that it is a species of danger against which any defensive measures, that can be adopted, will be sufficient. Next, we ought to know that the spirit of our Laws, or that our own dispositions, which are stronger than Laws, are susceptible of all those defensive measures which the occasion may require. A third consideration is whether these measures will not bring more odium than strength to Government; and the last, whether the authority that makes them, in a general corruption of manners and principles, can ensure their execution? Let no one argue from the state of things, as he sees them at present, concerning what will be the means and capacities of Government when the time arrives, which shall call for remedies commensurate to enormous evils.

It is an obvious truth, that no constitution can defend itself. It must be defended by the wisdom and fortitude of men. These are what no constitution can give. They are the gifts of God; and he alone knows, whether we shall possess such gifts at the time we stand in need of them. Constitutions furnish the civil means of getting at the natural; it is all that in this case they can do. But our Constitution has more impediments, than helps. Its excellencies, [342] when they come to be put to this sort of proof, may be found among its defects.

Nothing looks more awful and imposing than an ancient fortification. Its lofty embattled walls, its bold, projecting, rounded towers that pierce the sky, strike the imagination and promise inexpugnable strength. But they are the very things that make its weakness. You may as well think of opposing one of these old fortresses to the mass of artillery brought by a French irruption into the field, as to think of resisting by your old laws and your old forms the new destruction which the corps of Jacobin engineers of to-day prepare for all such forms and all such laws. Besides the debility and false principle of their construction to resist the present modes of attack, the Fortress itself is in ruinous repair, and there is a practicable breach in every part of it.

Such is the work. But miserable works have been defended by the constancy of the garrison. Weather-beaten ships have been brought safe to port by the spirit and alertness of the crew. But it is here that we shall eminently fail. The day that by their consent the seat of Regicide has its place among the thrones of Europe, there is no longer a motive for zeal in their favour; it will at best be cold, unimpassioned, dejected, melancholy duty. The glory will seem all on the other side. The friends of the Crown will appear not as champions, but as victims; discountenanced, mortified, lowered, defeated, they will fall into listlessness and indifference. They will leave things to take their course; enjoy the present hour, and submit to the common fate.

Is it only an oppressive night-mare, with which we have been loaded? Is it then all a frightful dream, and are there no Regicides in the world? Have we not heard of that prodigy of a ruffian, who would not suffer his benignant [343] Sovereign, with his hands tied behind him and stripped for execution, to say one parting word to his deluded people—of Santerre, who commanded the drums and trumpets to strike up to stifle his voice, and dragged him backward to the machine of murder? This nefarious villain (for a few days I may call him so) stands high in France, as in a republick of robbers and murderers he ought. What hinders this monster from being sent as ambassador to convey to his Majesty the first compliments of his brethren, the Regicide Directory? They have none that can represent them more properly. I anticipate the day of his arrival. He will make his public entry into London on one of the pale horses of his brewery. As he knows that we are pleased with the Paris taste for the orders of Knighthood,[1] he will fling a bloody sash across his shoulders with the order of the Holy Guillotine, surmounting the Crown, appendant to the ribband. Thus adorned, he will proceed from Whitechapel to the further end of Pall-Mall, all the musick of London playing the Marseillois Hymn before him, and escorted by a chosen detachment of the *Legion de l'Echaffaud.* It were only to be wished that no ill-fated loyalist for the imprudence of his zeal may stand in the pillory at Charing-Cross, under the statue of King Charles the First, at the time of this grand procession, lest some of the rotten eggs, which the Constitutional Society shall let fly at his indiscreet head, may hit the virtuous murderer of his King. They might soil the state dress, which the Ministers of so many crowned heads have admired, and in which Sir Clement Cotterel is to introduce him at St. James's.

If Santerre cannot be spared from the constitutional [344] butcheries at home, Tallien may supply his place, and in point of figure with advantage. He has been habituated to commissions; and he is as well qualified, as Santerre, for this. Nero wished the Roman people had but one neck. The wish of the more exalted Tallien, when he sat in judgment, was, that his Sovereign had eighty-three heads, that he might send one to every one of the departments. Tallien will make an excellent figure at Guildhall, at the next Sheriff's feast. He may open the ball with my Lady Mayoress. But this will be after he has retired from the public table, and gone into the private room for the enjoyment of more social and unreserved conversation with the Ministers of State and the

---

1. "*In the Costume assumed by the members of the legislative body, we almost behold the revival of the extinguished insignia of Knighthood,*" &c. &c. See A View of the relative State of Great-Britain and France at the commencement of the year 1796.

Judges of the Bench. There these Ministers and Magistrates will hear him entertain the worthy Aldermen with an instructing and pleasing narrative of the manner, in which he made the rich citizens of Bordeaux squeak, and gently led them by the publick credit of the guillotine to disgorge their anti-revolutionary pelf.

All this will be the display, and the town-talk, when our Regicide is on a visit of ceremony. At home nothing will equal the pomp and splendour of the *Hôtel de la République*. There another scene of gaudy grandeur will be opened. When his citizen Excellency keeps the festival, which every citizen is ordered to observe, for the glorious execution of Louis the Sixteenth, and renews his oath of detestation of Kings, a grand ball, of course, will be given on the occasion. Then what a hurly burly; what a crowding; what a glare of a thousand flambeaus in the square; what a clamour of footmen contending at the door; what a rattling of a thousand coaches of Duchesses, Countesses and Lady Marys, choaking the way and overturning each other in a struggle, who should be first to pay her court to the *Citoyenne*, the spouse of the twenty-first husband, he the husband of the thirty-first wife, and to hail her in the rank of honourable [345] matrons before the four days duration of marriage is expired! Morals, as they were: decorum, the great outguard of the sex, and the proud sentiment of honour, which makes virtue more respectable, where it is, and conceals human frailty, where virtue may not be, will be banished from this land of propriety, modesty, and reserve.

We had before an Ambassador from the most Christian King. We shall have then one, perhaps two, as lately, from the most antichristian Republick. His chapel will be great and splendid; formed on the model of the Temple of Reason at Paris, while the famous ode of the infamous *Chênier* will be sung, and a prostitute of the street adored as a Goddess. We shall then have a French Ambassador without a suspicion of

Popery. One good it will have: it will go some way in quieting the minds of that Synod of zealous protestant Lay Elders who govern Ireland on the pacific principles of polemick theology, and who now, from dread of the Pope, cannot take a cool bottle of claret, or enjoy an innocent parliamentary job with any tolerable quiet.

So far, as to the French communication here. What will be the effect of our communication there? We know, that our new brethren, whilst they every where shut up the churches, increased, in Paris at one time, at least four fold the opera-houses, the play-houses, the publick shows of all kinds, and, even in their state of indigence and distress, no expence was spared for their equipment and decoration. They were made an affair of state. There is no invention of seduction, never wholly wanting in that place, that has not been increased; brothels, gaming-houses, every thing. And there is no doubt, but when they are settled in a triumphant peace, they will carry all these arts to their utmost perfection, and cover them with every species of imposing magnificence. They have all along avowed them as a part of their policy; [346] and whilst they corrupt young minds through pleasure, they form them to crimes. Every idea of corporal gratification is carried to the highest excess, and wooed with all the elegance that belongs to the senses. All elegance of mind and manners is banished. A theatrical, bombastick, windy phraseology of heroic virtue, blended and mingled up with a worse dissoluteness, and joined to a murderous and savage ferocity, forms the tone and idiom of their language and their manners. Any one who attends to all their own descriptions, narratives and dissertations, will find in that whole place more of the air of a body of assassins, banditti, house-breakers, and outlawed smugglers, joined to that of a gang of strolling players, expelled from and exploded in orderly theatres, with their prostitutes in a brothel, at their debauches and bacchanals, than any thing of the refined and perfected virtues, or the polished, mitigated vices, of a great capital.

Is it for this benefit we open "the usual relations of peace and amity?" Is it for this our youth of both sexes are to form themselves by travel? Is it for this that with expence and pains we form their lisping infant accents to the language of France? I shall be told that this abominable medley is made rather to revolt young and ingenuous minds. So it is in the description. So perhaps it may in reality to a chosen few. So it may be when the Magistrate, the Law and the Church, frown on such manners, and the wretches to whom they belong; when they are chased from the eye of day, and the society of civil life, into night-cellars, and caves and woods. But when these men themselves are the magistrates; when all the consequence, weight and authority of a great nation adopt them; when we see them conjoined with victory, glory, power and dominion, and homage paid to them by every Government, it is not possible that the downhill should not be slid into, recommended by every [347] thing which has opposed it. Let it be remembered that no young man can go to any part of Europe without taking this place of pestilential contagion in his way: and whilst the less active part of the community will be debauched by this travel, whilst children are poisoned at these schools, our trade will put the finishing hand to our ruin. No factory will be settled in France, that will not become a club of complete French Jacobins. The minds of young men of that description will receive a taint in their religion, their morals, and their politicks, which they will in a short time communicate to the whole kingdom.

Whilst every thing prepares the body to debauch, and the mind to crime, a regular church of avowed Atheism, established by law, with a direct and sanguinary persecution of Christianity, is formed to prevent all amendment and remorse. Conscience is formally deposed from its dominion over the mind. What fills the measure of horror is, that schools of Atheism are set up at the publick charge in every part of the country. That some English parents will be wicked enough to send their children to such schools there is no doubt. Better this Island should be sunk to the bottom of the sea, than that (so far as human infirmity admits) it should not be a country of Religion and Morals.

With all these causes of corruption, we may well judge what the general fashion of mind will be through both sexes and all conditions. Such spectacles and such examples will overbear all the laws that ever blackened the cumbrous volumes of our statutes. When Royalty shall have disavowed itself; when it shall have relaxed all the principles of its own support; when it has rendered the systems of Regicide fashionable, and received it as triumphant in the very persons who have consolidated that system by the perpetration of every crime, who have not only massacred the prince, but the very laws and magistrates which were the [348] support of royalty, and slaughtered with an indiscriminate proscription, without regard to either sex or age, every person that was suspected of an inclination to King, Law or Magistracy— I say, will any one dare to be loyal? Will any one presume, against both authority and opinion, to hold up this unfashionable, antiquated, exploded constitution?

The Jacobin faction in England must grow in strength and audacity; it will be supported by other intrigues, and supplied by other resources, than yet we have seen in action. Confounded at its growth, the Government may fly to Parliament for its support. But who will answer for the temper of a House of Commons elected under these circumstances? Who will answer for the courage of a House of Commons to arm the Crown with the extraordinary powers that it may demand? But the ministers will not venture to ask half of what they know they want. They will lose half of that half in the contest: and when they have obtained their nothing, they will be driven by the cries of faction either to demolish the feeble works they have thrown up in a hurry, or, in effect, to abandon them. As to the House of Lords, it is not worth mentioning. The Peers ought naturally to be the pillars of the Crown: but when their titles are rendered contemptible, and their property invidious and a part of their weakness and not of their strength, they will be found so many degraded and trembling individuals, who will seek by evasion to put off the evil day of their ruin. Both Houses will be in perpetual oscillation between abortive attempts at energy, and still more unsuccessful attempts at compromise. You will be impatient of your disease, and abhorrent of your remedy. A spirit of subterfuge and a tone of apology will enter into all your proceedings, whether of law or legislation. Your Judges, who now sustain so masculine an authority, will appear more on their [349] trial, than the culprits they have before them. The awful frown of criminal justice will be smoothed into the silly smile of seduction. Judges will think to insinuate and sooth the accused into conviction and condemnation, and to wheedle to the gallows the most artful of all delinquents. But they will not be so wheedled. They will not submit even to the appearance of persons on their trial. Their claim to this exemption will be admitted. The place, in which some of the greatest names which ever distinguished the history of this country have stood, will appear beneath their dignity. The criminal will climb from the dock to the side-bar, and take his place and his tea with the counsel. From the bar of the counsel, by a natural progress, he will ascend to the bench, which long before had been virtually abandoned. They, who escape from justice, will not suffer a question upon reputation. They will take the crown of the causeway: they will be revered as martyrs; they will triumph as conquerors. Nobody will dare to censure that popular part of the tribunal, whose only restraint on misjudgment is the censure of the publick. They, who find fault with the decision, will be represented as enemies to the institution. Juries, that convict for the crown, will be loaded with obloquy. The Juries, who acquit, will be held up as models of justice. If Parliament orders a prosecution and fails, (as fail it will), it will be treated to its face as guilty of a conspiracy maliciously to prosecute. Its care in discovering a conspiracy against the state will be treated as a forged plot to destroy the liberty of the subject; every such discovery, instead of strengthening Government, will weaken its reputation.

In this state, things will be suffered to proceed, lest measures of vigour should precipitate a crisis. The timid will act thus from character; the wise from necessity. Our laws had done all that the old condition of things dictated [350] to render our Judges erect and independent; but they will naturally fail on the side, upon which they had taken no precautions. The judicial magistrates will find themselves safe as against the Crown, whose will is not their tenure; the power of executing their office will be held at the pleasure of those, who deal out fame or abuse as they think fit. They will begin rather to consult their own repose and their own popularity, than the critical and perilous trust that is in their hands. They will speculate on consequences, when they see at Court an ambassador, whose robes are lined with a scarlet dyed in the blood of Judges. It is no wonder, nor are they to blame, when they are to consider how they shall answer for their conduct to the criminal of to-day turned into the magistrate of to-morrow.

The Press—

The Army—

When thus the helm of justice is abandoned, an universal abandonment of all other posts will succeed. Government will be for a while the sport of contending factions, who whilst they fight with one another will all strike at her. She will be buffeted and beat forward and backward by the conflict of those billows; until at length, tumbling from the Gallick coast, the victorious tenth wave shall ride, like the bore, over all the rest, and poop the shattered, weather-beaten, leaky, water-logged vessel, and sink her to the bottom of the abyss.

Among other miserable remedies that have been found

in the *materia medica* of the old college, a change of Ministry will be proposed; and probably will take place. They who go out can never long with zeal and good will support Government in the hands of those they hate. In a situation of fatal dependence on popularity, and without one aid from the little remaining power of the Crown, it is not to be expected that they will take on them that odium which more [351] or less attaches upon every exertion of strong power. The Ministers of popularity will lose all their credit at a stroke, if they pursue any of those means necessary to give life, vigour, and consistence to Government. They will be considered as venal wretches, apostates, recreant to all their own principles, acts, and declarations. They cannot preserve their credit but by betraying that authority of which they have been the usurpers.

To be sure no prognosticating symptoms of these things have as yet appeared. Nothing even resembling their beginnings. May they never appear! May these prognostications of the author be justly laughed at and speedily forgotten! If nothing as yet to cause them has discovered itself, let us consider in the author's excuse, that we have not yet seen a Jacobin legation in England. The natural, declared, sworn ally of sedition, has not yet fixed its headquarters in London.

There never was a political contest, upon better or worse grounds, that by the heat of party spirit may not ripen into civil confusion. If ever a party adverse to the Crown should be in a condition here publickly to declare itself, and to divide, however unequally, the natural force of the kingdom, they are sure of an aid of fifty thousand men, at ten days warning, from the opposite coast of France. But against this infusion of a foreign force, the Crown has its guarantees, old and new. But I should be glad to hear something said of the assistance, which loyal subjects in France have received from other powers in support of that lawful government, which secured their lawful property. I should be glad to know, if they are so disposed to a neighbourly, provident and sympathetick attention to their publick engagements, by what means they are to come at us. Is it from the powerful States of Holland we are to reclaim our guarantee? Is it from the King of Prussia and his steady good affections and his powerful navy, [352] that we are to look for the guarantee of our security? Is it from the Netherlands, which the French may cover with the swarms of their citizen soldiers in twenty-four hours, that we are to look for this assistance? This is to suppose too that all these powers have no views offensive or necessities defensive of their own. They will cut out work for one another, and France will cut out work for them all.

That the Christian Religion cannot exist in this country with such a fraternity, will not, I think, be disputed with me. On that religion, according to our mode, all our laws and institutions stand as upon their base. That scheme is supposed in every transaction of life; and if that were done away, every thing else, as in France, must be changed along with it. Thus religion perishing, and with it this constitution, it is a matter of endless meditation what order of things would follow it. But what disorder would fill the space between the present and that which is to come, in the gross, is no matter of doubtful conjecture. It is a great evil, that of a civil war. But in that state of things, a civil war which would give to good men and a good cause some means of struggle, is a blessing of comparison that England will not enjoy. The moment the struggle begins, it ends. They talk of Mr. Hume's Euthanasia of the British Constitution, gently expiring without a groan in the paternal arms of a mere Monarchy. In a Monarchy! Fine trifling indeed! There is no such Euthanasia for the British Constitution—

*   *   *

Notes

The references to "vol. i." and "vol. ii." are to the "Select Works" of Burke. For many of the notes which follow, as in the case of those two volumes, the editor has to tender his best thanks to John Frederick Boyes, Esq.

Letter I

Page 62, line 2. *Our last conversation.* Burke assumes for his correspondent the same point of view as his own. Cp. post, p. 77, l. 8. The letters are therefore not controversial in *form.* The Monthly Review, April, 1815, describes them as "addressed to those advocates of the peace who had originally been partizans of the war: and it was only with persons of this description that Mr. B. deigned to enter into controversy." This is true of the ultimate public whom he hoped to influence, but not of the ostensible correspondent.

L. 4. *unpleasant appearances.* The continued manifestations of a desire for peace with France.

L. 8. *disastrous events.* The military disasters of the allies on the Continent, beginning with the battle of Fleurus in 1794, and followed by the separate treaties of peace successively made with the Republic by Tuscany, Prussia, Sweden, Holland, and Spain, leaving only Great Britain and Austria at war with it.

L. 23. *in its aphelion,* i.e. in its deviation from its normal path. Burke would have hailed the returning popularity of the war in 1798 as a return to this normal path.

L. 33. *same periods of infancy,* &c. The allusion is to an ever-popular but false theory of history, which may be traced as early as Polybius. In Burke's time this theory was put forth in many forms. Churchill, Gotham, Book iii:

Let me not only the distempers know
Which in all states from common causes flow:
But likewise, those, which, by the will of fate,

On each peculiar mode of Empire wait:
Which in its very constitution lurk,
Too sure at last to do their destin'd work.

[354] So Young, Second Letter on Pleasure: "It has often been observed that it is with states as with men. They have their birth, growth, health, distemper, decay, and death. Men sometimes drop suddenly by an apoplexy, states by conquest; in full vigour both . . . . On the soft beds of luxury most kingdoms have expired. Casti, Animali Parlanti, Canto iv:

E tutti li politici systemi
In se di destruzion racchiudon' semi."

As to England, Mr. Hallam remarks that it differs from all free governments of powerful nations which history has recorded by manifesting, after the lapse of several centuries, not merely no symptoms of decay, but a more expansive energy. Middle Ages, vol. ii. chap. viii.

P. 63, L. 3. *similitudes—analogies.* The hint has been developed by Mill, in his account of Fallacies of Generalization, Logic, Book 5. "Bodies politic," says Mr. Mill, "die; but it is of disease, or violent death. They have no old age."

L. 10. *moral essences.* Cp. post, p. 139, l. 28.

L. 14. *There is not,* &c. Specific attempts to create a "philosophy of history" have at length ceased with the extinction of the German schools of speculative philosophy. Burke's criticism thoroughly agrees with the general spirit of the best historians.

L. 29. *It is often impossible, in these political enquiries,* &c. Burke derived his observations from a favourite author: "La conservation des estats est chose qui vraysemblablement surpasse nostre intelligence: c'est comme dict Platon, chose puissante et de difficile dissolution, qu'une police civile; elle dure souvent contre les maladies mortelles et intestines, contre les injures des loix injustes, contre la tyrannie, contre le desbordement et ignorance des magistrats, license et sedition des peuples." Montaigne, Liv. iii., chap. 9. In an earlier chapter of Montaigne, and in Bolingbroke, we have the duration of states compared with that of individuals.

P. 64, L. 1. *remained nearly as they have begun.* e.g. China.

L. 3. *spent their vigour,* &c. e.g. the Mahomedan Caliphate, the monarchy of Charlemagne, &c.

L. 4. *blazed out,* &c. The allusion is clearly to the Mogul Empire

LETTER I

in the time of Aurungzebe. "Most nations," says Young, in the letter above quoted, "have been gayest when nearest to their end, and like a taper in the socket have blazed as they expired."

L. 5. *meridian of some.* Ancient Rome, Venice, Holland, are instances.

L. 9. *plunged in unfathomable abysses,* &c. Burke has in mind the phrase "Mersus profundo pulchrior evenit."

L. 16. *death of a man.* Among many instances that will occur to the reader, Pericles is perhaps the best.

IBID. *his disgust.* Coriolanus is an instance.

IBID. *his retreat.* Burke probably alludes to Pitt, and his disastrous withdrawal from public affairs in 1768–1770. See vol. i. p. 206, where the revolt of [355] America from England is traced to this cause. The resignation of Charles V. is another instance, in its effects on the Netherlands.

L. 17. *his disgrace.* The allusion is probably to the Constable Charles de Bourbon, whose disgrace at the French court led to the misfortunes sustained by France under Francis I.

L. 18. *A common soldier.* The allusion is to Arnold of Winkelried, whose self-devotion on the field of Sempach secured the freedom of Switzerland.

IBID. *a child.* The allusion is to Hannibal, and the oath administered to him at twelve years old, by his father Hamilcar. Cp. p. 348, l. 14.

IBID. *a girl at the door,* &c. The allusion is to Joan of Arc, who according to one version of her story (probably the true one) acted as ostler at a small inn.

P. 65, L. 9. *humbled—weakened—endangered.* By the independence of America, established by the aid of France.

L. 13. *high and palmy state.* Hamlet, Act i. sc. 1.

L. 29. *a vast, tremendous, unformed spectre.* Burke is thinking of Virgil's "Monstrum horrendum, informe, ingens." Burke seems to have been the first Englishman who discerned accurately the portentous shape which France was assuming. This powerful description was fully justified during the following years.

P. 66, L. 7. *poison of other States,* &c. A new application of the proverb that "one man's meat is another's poison."

NOTES

L. 17. *finest parts of Europe.* The Austrian Netherlands, the Rhine, Savoy and Nice, Lombardy.

L. 28. *At first,* &c. Burke himself was among those who believed France to be crushed as a nation by the Revolution: but he soon undeceived himself.

P. 67, L. 15. *publick—never regarded,* &c. Burke has in mind the famous Roman maxim, "non de republica desperare."

L. 18. *Dr. Brown.* The work was his "Estimate of the Manners and Principles of the Times." See vol. i. p. 88, and the Editor's note.

L. 27. *Pythagoras.* Burke probably means Archimedes, and alludes to the well-known story of his great discovery in solid geometry.

L. 32. *as in the Alps,* goitre *kept* goitre, &c. The phrase is Juvenal's:

Quis tumidum guttur miratur in Alpibus?

Sat. xiii. l. 162.

P. 68, L. 5. *never did the masculine spirit,* &c. This great stir in the public mind occurred when Burke was a young man lately arrived in London, and just turning his attention to public affairs. It profoundly affected him, and influenced his whole life.

L. 33. *eye of the mind is dazzled and vanquished.* Burke copies the phrase, "In bello oculi primi vincuntur."

P. 69, L. 6. *palpable night.* "Palpable darkness," Par. Lost, xii. 188.

[356] **L. 29.** *at no time has the wealth,* &c. See the Third Letter, pp. 254–306, where this is proved in detail.

L. 31. *vast interest to preserve—great means of preserving it.* "You must not consider the money you spend in your defence, but the fortune you would lose if you were not defended; and further, you must recollect you will pay less to an immediate war, than to a peace with a war establishment and a war to follow it . . . . Your empire cannot be saved by a calculation." Grattan, Speech on Downfall of Buonaparte. Reference to the use of the argument by Bacon and Swift will be given in a note to the Third Letter.

P. 70, L. 7. *If our wealth commands us,* &c. So B. Jonson, "The Fox," Act vi. sc. 12:

These possess wealth as sick men possess fevers,
Which trulier may be said to possess them.

The conceit is derived from a classical source: "Ea invasit homines habendi cupido ut possideri magis quam possidere videamur": Pliny,

LETTER I

Letters, B. ix. Lett. 30. So Archbishop Leighton, Commentary on 1 St. Peter, iv. 8: "Hearts glued to the poor riches they possess or rather are possessed by." Leighton repeats it in his "Commentary on the Ten Commandments."

L. 8. *poor indeed.* Shakspeare, Othello, Act iii. sc. 3:

He that filches from me my good name,
Robs me of that which not enriches him,
And makes me poor indeed.

L. 21. *He is the Gaul,* &c. Alluding to the story of Brennus, Livy, Lib. v. cap. 48.

L. 27. *that state which is resolved,* &c. i.e. Republican France.

P. 71, L. 9. *petty peculium.* Burke alludes to the additions by conquest to the colonial empire, which went on until both the French and the Dutch were left without any colonies at all.

L. 10. *ambiguous in their nature.* He alludes to the conquest of Martinique with its population of revolutionary people of colour.

L. 12. *any one of those points,* &c. i.e. in his conquests on the border of France, especially Austrian Flanders.

L. 19. *When Louis the Fourteenth,* &c. Burke describes the most critical period in the War of the Grand Alliance.

L. 36. *puppet shew of a naval power.* See p. 164, where Burke maintains that England ought to have made a campaign with 100,000 men on the Continent.

P. 72, L. 5. *nothing in human affairs,* &c. The common phrase "Nihil humani alienum."

L. 12. *our account,* &c. See note to p. 270, l. 6.

L. 25. *pale cast,* &c. Hamlet, Act iii. sc. 2, transposed:

"And thus the native hue of resolution
Is sicklied o'er with the pale cast of thought," &c.

L. 32. *prolific error,* i.e. prolific of other errors. Cp. vol. i. p. 137, l. 31.

[357] **P. 73, L. 5.** *early victories.* The capture of Valenciennes, Condé, Quesnoy, Landrécy, and Toulon. See the Introduction.

L. 13. *desertion.* Prussia deserted the campaign as soon as it began to fail.

L. 15. *mutual accusations.* Between England and Austria.

NOTES

P. 74, L. 7. *cry is raised against it.* Burke alludes to the public indignation which followed on the passing of the "Gagging Act" of 1794.

L. 9. *most efficient member,* &c. Burke alludes to the failure of the prosecutions of Hardy and Horne Tooke at the Old Bailey in 1794.

L. 11. *highest tribunal of all.* Parliament.

L. 34. *Mussabat tacito,* &c. Lucretius, Lib. vi. 1178.

P. 75, L. 17. *poisonous jaws,* &c. The allusion is to the fascination said to be exercised by serpents over birds.

L. 24. *It is in the nature,* &c. The modern historian will hardly sympathise with Burke's lament over the failure of the State prosecutions, nor could Burke himself have seriously wished to recall the days of Scroggs and Jefferies. Besides, his wishes had been amply satisfied in the State Trials in Scotland, where, owing to the difference in procedure, all the prisoners had been convicted.

L. 34. *what the bulk of us must ever be.* A powerful statement of the weaknesses inherent in democracies.

P. 76, L. 16. Burke now powerfully enforces that view of the nature of the war of which he was the author, and for a long time the sole expositor. It was perfectly true, and in a year or two its truth was obvious to every one.

L. 20. *a system — an armed doctrine.* Grattan, Speech on Downfall of Buonaparte: "Sirs, the French Government is war; it is a Stratocracy elective, aggressive, and predatory. . . . . Their constitution is essentially war, and the object of that war is the downfall of Europe . . . . Not an army, but a military government in march!" Again: "If the government of any other country contains an insurrectionary principle, as France did when she offered to aid the insurrections of her neighbours, your interference is warranted: if the government of another country contains the principle of universal empire, as France did and promulgated, your interference is justifiable." It was no easy task to prove to the English government and people how the France of the Directory differed from the France of Louis XIV. Macaulay, in a passage founded on the present one, has admirably described Mr. Pitt's own blindness to what was so distinctly seen by Burke: "He went to war: but he would not understand the peculiar nature of that war. He was obstinately blind to the plain fact that he was contending against a state which was also a sect, and that the new quarrel between England and France was of quite a different kind from the old quarrels

LETTER I

about colonies in America and fortresses in the Netherlands. He had to combat frantic enthusiasm, restless activity, the wildest and most audacious spirit of innovation: and he acted as if he had [358] had to deal with the harlots and fops of the old court of Versailles, with Madame de Pompadour and the Abbé Bernis." "Biographies," Pitt.

L. 25. *in every country.* See the Second Letter, p. 155.

IBID. *a Colossus.* &c. Burke alludes to the famous Colossus which bestrode the harbour of Rhodes. Jacobin sympathies in England were rapidly extinguished after Burke's death, when the struggle with France became a struggle for national existence.

P. 77, L. 6. *To their power* = "as far as in them lies."

P. 78, L. 28. *Regicides—first to declare war.* This statement, pertinaciously repeated in the early Parliamentary debates on the Peace question, is not strictly true. England was the first to break off all diplomatic communication with France. The King recalled Lord Gower from Paris, and commanded that ordinary relations should cease with Chauvelin after the 10th of August, 1792, when the French monarchy was abolished. Chauvelin, whom the Convention still continued in London, was only communicated with as representing the monarchy, and on the execution of the King in January, 1793, he received from the English government notice to quit England. It is true that the French government had already instructed him to the same effect, but these instructions were unknown to the English government.

P. 79, L. 16. *some unhappy persons.* The Duke of Choiseul, and other "emigrants" in British service, were shipwrecked and taken prisoners near Calais in 1795. Choiseul was condemned by the Directory, but saved by the Revolution of Brumaire. He lived to take part in the Revolution of 1830, and became aide-de-camp to Louis Philippe.

P. 80, L. 11. *afflicted family of Asgill.* Charles Asgill, a young captain in the British army in America, chosen by lot to be surrendered to the enemy's mercy in reprisal for the execution of Huddy, April 12, 1782. Asgill's mother appealed to the King and Queen of France to intercede in her son's behalf. The intercession was successful: and Asgill visited Paris to acknowledge in person the exertions of Marie Antoinette.

P. 81, L. 22. *a war of Government,* &c. Such it unquestionably was in 1793. Whether it continued to be so when the French government avowedly carried it on for the purpose of destroying the European balance of power, and annihilating England, is another question.

NOTES

P. 82, L. 1. *Speech from the Throne.* Intended to stop the mouths of the opposition and prepare the way for negotiations with France. See Introduction. It had neither effect.

L. 15. *gipsey jargon.* The phrase is borrowed from the account given in the Annual Register of the nomenclature adopted by the Convention.

P. 83, L. 15. *"Citizen Regicides,"* &c. In Burke's most effective Parliamentary style, and scarcely a caricature of the attitude assumed by the ministry. The passage reminds us of Thomson, Britannia:

Whence this unwonted patience, this weak doubt,
[359] This tame beseeching of rejected peace,
This weak forbearance?

L. 24. *patient suitors,* &c. The picture which follows is in that vein of profound and scornful irony of which Burke was almost as great a master as his countryman Swift.

L. 25. *sanguinary tyrant Carnot.* Burke has no word of toleration, much less of praise, for a single statesman of the Revolution. Cp. the allusion to Hoche, p. 221. Carnot's vote for the death of the King outweighed everything else in the eyes of his critic.

L. 27. *down of usurped pomp.* Carnot was one of the Directors, who lived in the palace of the Luxembourg.

P. 84, L. 15. *Trophonian Cave.* The rites of the deity Trophonius were celebrated in a cave near Lebadea, in Boeotia. Pausanias denies the tradition to which Burke here alludes, that none ever laughed after once visiting the cave.

L. 33. *speeches and messages in former times.* Burke's usual line of argument. Cp. vol. i. p. 267. Burke in the next page qualifies this reference to the past, to avoid the charge of "pedantry."

P. 86, L. 29. *squander away the fund of our submissions.* Burke gloomily anticipates the time when this humiliating attitude on the part of England may really become necessary. Cp. vol. ii. p. 128, l. 26.

L. 33. *Barthélemy.* This able diplomatist, who negotiated the Treaties with Spain and Prussia, afterwards became a Director. Allied with Carnot, his upright and statesmanlike opposition produced the Revolution of Fructidor. Carnot escaped: but Barthélemy was dragged through the streets of Paris, and before the windows of the Luxembourg, in an iron cage, on his way to the convict settlement of Cayenne.

Letter I

P. 89, L. 34. *ten immense and wealthy provinces.* Burke proceeds to characterize the pretensions of France to the "Rhine, Alps, and Mediterranean" boundary.

P. 90, L. 25. *a law,* &c. The decree of the Convention incorporating Belgium with France, like Savoy and Nice.

L. 34. *sacred Rights of Man.* See vol. ii. p. 149. The allusion is, of course, ironical.

P. 91, L. 7. *cooped and cabined in.* "Cribbed, cabined, and confined." Macbeth, Act iii. sc. 4.

P. 92, L. 22. *over-running of Lombardy.* This had taken place early in the year (1796).

L. 23. *Piedmont—its impregnable fortresses.* Alessandria, Tortona, Coni, Ceva, and others. See Hamley's Operations of War, p. 142.

L. 25. *instances for ever renewed—Genoa.* The Ligurian republic was constituted in the next year, and the French policy thus completed.

L. 27. *half the Empire.* Swabia and Bavaria, overrun by Moreau in this year.

[360] **P. 94, L. 17.** *"in the lowest deep, a lower deep."* Par. Lost, Book iv. l. 76.

P. 95, L. 2. *"None but itself,"* &c. The line "None but himself can be his parallel," is quoted from Theobald, in Martinus Scriblerus, as a specimen of fustian.

P. 96, L. 4. *Light lie the earth,* &c. The phrase, repeated from Letter IV (p. 351) is from the well-known elegy of Prior on Col. Villiers:

Light lie the earth, and flourish green the bough.

The conception is borrowed, through the Latins, from the Greek elegiac authors. Meleager in Anthol.;

Παμμῆτορ γῆ χαῖρε, σὺ τὸν πάρος οὐ βαρὺν εἴς σε
Αἰσιγένην καὐτὴ νῦν ἐπέχοις ἀβαρής.

See Martial, Ep. Lib. v. 34. Juv. Sat. vii. 207, &c.

P. 99, L. 6. *"If it be thus,"* &c. St. Luke, xxiii. 31.

L. 12. *wax into our ears,* &c. Burke alludes to the story of Ulysses and the Sirens, Odyssey, Book xii.

L. 14. *Reubel, Carnot, Tallien.* The two former were Directors: but Tallien had by this time ceased to be a leading politician. He had sunk into obscurity as a member of the Council of Five Hundred. He afterwards went to Egypt, and in 1801 appeared in London as a prisoner, on which occasion he was feted by the Opposition.

L. 15. *Domiciliary Visitors.* Under the law of August 1792, 3000 persons were at once dragged away to prison in one night.

L. 17. *Revolutionary Tribunals.* The famous Revolutionary Tribunal, which took cognizance of treason against the Republic, was instituted by Danton, who was himself condemned by it. It had ceased to exist in December 1794, after employing its vigour during the last six months against the party of Robespierre. It sent to the guillotine 2,774 persons, including the Queen and the Princess Elizabeth.

L. 18. *Septembrizers.* Alluding to the massacres at Paris in September 1792, in which 1500 persons perished. The "Septembriseur" *par excellence* was Tallien.

L. 26. *little national window.* One of the pleasantries which enlivened the despatches from Carrier to the Convention, describing his cruelties in La Vendée.

L. 28. *declaration of the Government.* The Whitehall Declaration, which filled Burke with unbounded admiration, to which he more than once recurs (see pp. 156, 318), was from the pen of Lord Grenville.

P. 101, L. 2. *Plutarch.* The allusion is not in Plutarch. Burke is thinking of Cicero, De Oratore, Lib. III, cap. 34, where the critic recalls the satire poured on Pericles by the comedians, who nevertheless ascribed to him such force and power of engaging attention "ut in eorum mentibus qui audissent quasi aculeos quosdam relinqueret."

[361] **L. 18.** *With their spear,* &c. The allusion is to the story of C. Popilius Laenas.

P. 102, L. 34. *Ut lethargicus,* &c. Horace, Sat. Lib. ii. 3. 30.

P. 104, L. 8. *competence to act.* Cp. vol. i. p. 254. Burke's observations on the necessity of popular support to a great war, though apparently quite modern in spirit, were based on history, as he presently shows.

P. 104, L. 25. *country of old called* ferax monstrorum. Burke quotes as usual from memory, "Asia, terra ferax miraculorum," Plin. Epist. 173.

L. 34. *muster of our strength.* The remarkable estimate which follows excludes, as usual with Burke, the mass of the people, who are regarded (P. 105, l. 15) as merely the "objects of protection," and the "means of force." It is curious that one who had laid down the rational doctrine of the causes of hostility between people and government contained in vol. i. p. 75 (Present Discontents), should now see no anomaly in the existence of an incurable Jacobin faction numbering one-fifth of the effective forces of the country.

P. 106, L. 10. *By passing from place to place,* &c. Cp. vol. ii. p. 180.

L. 18. *naturally disposed to peace.* The observation is true: and it illustrates Pitt's difficulty. The mass of his supporters in the country were interested in peace.

L. 19. *languid and improvident.* Dryden, the Medal:

The wise and wealthy love the surest way,
And are content to thrive and to obey:
But wisdom is to sloth too great a slave.

P. 107, L. 11. *But strong passions awaken the faculties,* &c. Burke clearly has in mind the lines of Akenside, "Pleasures of the Imagination," Bk. ii.

"Passion's fierce illapse
Rouses the mind's whole fabric, with supplies
Of daily impulse, keeps the elastic powers
Intensely poised," &c.

P. 108, L. 14. *Pope—dying notes.* See the last fifty lines of the two dialogues called "Epilogue to the Satires."

L. 15. *Johnson.* See the first sixty lines of "London" (1738).

L. 17. *Glover.* See his poem, London, or the Progress of Commerce, and the pathetic ballad, Admiral Hosier's Ghost.

L. 35. *driven by a popular clamour,* &c. See Lord Stanhope's History of England.

P. 110, L. 25. *Guarda-Costas.* The coast-guards of Spanish America, whose insolence to English ships was a main cause of the war.

IBID. *Madrid Convention.* Made in 1713, for thirty years. It secured to England the "Assiento," or contract for supplying Spanish America with African slaves.

L. 26. *Captain* Jenkins's *ears.* Exhibited in the House of Commons as having being cut off by a Spanish captain.

L. 34. *dilatory pleas, exceptions of form.* Proceedings under the old [362] legal system, which deferred the consideration of the question without touching its merits. Moving and carrying the *previous question* has the same effect in parliamentary debate.

P. 113, L. 7. *contending to be admitted at a moderate premium.* Burke states the circumstances of the loan voted in December, 1795, with the partiality to be expected. For the facts, see the notes, post, to pp. 254–60.

L. 26. *When I came to England.* In 1750.

L. 29. *Aire and Calder.* The improvement of the navigation of these rivers, which connected the West Riding with the port of Hull, may be said to be the first step in the construction of those two great networks of canals and railways, which have played so important a part in developing English trade and manufactures. Burke returns to the subject in the Third Letter, p. 290.

P. 118, L. 26. *three great immoveable pillars.* Cp. vol. i. p. 295, note to p. 73, l. 17.

P. 121, L. 14. *"Of large discourse,"* &c. Hamlet, Act iv. sc. 4.

P. 122, L. 8. *If the war,* &c. In these three brief paragraphs Burke puts his argument for the war into a compendious and striking form. Compare with the whole argument Bacon's very similar plea for a Holy War. As will be seen, Burke evidently had Bacon in mind in some other passages: "Such people as have utterly degenerated from the laws of Nature, as have in their very body and frame of estate a monstrosity, and may be truly accounted, according to the examples we have formerly recited, common enemies and grievances of mankind and disgraces and reproaches to human nature—such people all nations are interested or ought to be interested to reform." "When the constitution of a State and the fundamental laws and customs of the same, if laws they may be called, are against the laws of Nature and of Nations, then I say a war upon them is lawful."

P. 123, L. 31. *abolition of the law.* Cp. vol. ii. p. 191.

P. 125, L. 9. *Jacobinism is the revolt,* &c. So Southey, Essay on Popular Disaffection: "Of mere men of letters, wherever they exist as a separate class, a large proportion are always enlisted in hostility, open or secret, against the established order of things."

L. 27. *regular decree.* The allusion is to the frantic efforts made under the Convention to get rid of Christianity and even faith in a God and the soul. They came to an end with the acknowledgment of Deism as the national faith, and the establishment of the Festival of the Supreme Being by Robespierre in 1794.

LETTER I

P. 126, L. 2. *profane apotheosis.* The allusion is to the funeral honours paid to the remains of Marat in the Pantheon.

L. 8. *rites in honour of Reason.* Burke alludes to the scene of Nov. 10, 1793, when the Commune of Paris enthroned a superannuated prostitute in Nôtre Dame as the goddess of Reason. Similar scenes were repeated throughout the country.

L. 11. *schools founded at the publick expence.* By the Convention. They [363] were mere primary schools, in which were to be taught reading, writing, arithmetic, and the republican catechism.

L. 23. *Manners are what,* &c. Burke draws his arguments from the old, French school itself. Massillon (Vices et Vertus des Grands): "Moeurs cultivées, bienséances voisines de la vertu." Again, "Les bienséances qui sont inseparables du rang, et qui sont comme la première école de la vertu."

P. 127, L. 8. *five or six hundred drunken women.* It may be objected that Burke has no business to charge upon the Directory all the excesses of the Assembly and Convention. The presumption in the eyes of any candid observer was now in favour of reaction. Burke had denied the reality of the reaction in his then unpublished Fourth Letter.

L. 17. *paradoxes.* Cp. vol. ii. p. 277, l. 13.

L. 20. *at which morality is perplexed,* &c. The same idea is admirably expressed by Molière: "Ne fatiguez point mon devoir par les propositions d'une facheuse extrémité dont peut être nous n'aurons pas besoin." Mons. Pourceaugnac, Act i, Scene 4.

L. 24. *improving instincts into morals.* On this doctrine, so often insisted on by Burke, see Introduction to vol. ii. p. 40, &c.

P. 128, L. 12. *common civil contract.* Here again Burke goes back to the early legislation of the Revolution. Subsequent legislation, in European countries least to be suspected of revolutionism, has justified the advocates of the measure.

P. 130, L. 21. *cannibalism.* Burke follows Bacon, in the Tract on a Holy War, in arguing from the cannibalism, among other traits, of the American Indians that their territory was forfeited by the Law of Nations, and that the Spaniards, or any one else, might lawfully invade it.

P. 132, L. 21. *papers and seals.* Cp. vol. i. p. 288, &c.

L. 24. *Nothing is so strong,* &c. Burke's sketch of the European system may remind the reader of the relations of the Greek communities as reflected in Herodotus and Thucydides.

L. 33. *As to war—sole means of justice.* Burke uses a saying of Bacon, "Wars are the highest trials of right," Observations on a Libel.

P. 133, L. 28. *several orders.* i.e. church, nobles, and commons.

P. 134, L. 2. *continued in greater perfection,* &c. As in Venice, Holland, and Switzerland. This was natural enough. The power of a Crown counterbalanced the authority of the upper orders.

L. 25. *formed resolution,* &c. Peace had however been made by France with all Europe except England and Austria.

P. 135, L. 11. *never in a state,* &c. Cp. Introduction to vol. ii. pp. 44–45.

L. 32. *praetorian law.* The "Equity" of Roman law.

IBID. *Law of Neighbourhood.* So M. de Puisaye, quoted by Southey, "Public Opinion and the Political Reformers": "It is with the independence of nations as with the liberty of individuals, they have a right to do everything which involves no wrong to others. So long as my neighbour demeans [364] himself conformably to the laws his conduct is no concern of mine: but if he converts his house into a brothel or commence a manufactory there which should poison my family with its unwholesome stench, I prosecute him for a nuisance."

P. 137, L. 9. *ground of action—ground of war.* So Bacon, On a War with Spain. "Wars (I speak not of ambitious, predatory wars) are suits of appeal to the Tribunal of God's justice."

P. 138, L. 1. *trifling points of honour,* &c. Imitated by Casti, Anim. Parl. Canto iii.:

Due passi più o men lunghi, più o men corti,
Un inchino talor più o men profondo,
Capace è di mandar sossopra il mondo.

L. 5. *wild-cat skins.* In the American settlements.

P. 139, L. 23. *bailliages.* Districts of judicature.

P. 140, L. 4. *France is out of her bounds.* Burke means that the emigrants were the real France. Sheridan often refers to this striking expression of Burke on the subject: "Look at the map of Europe: there, where a great man (who however was always wrong on this subject) said he looked for France, and found nothing but a chasm." Speech,

Letter I

Dec. 8, 1802. Again, Aug. 13, 1807: "France,"—as Mr. Burke described it—"a blank in the map of Europe."

P. 142, L. 9. *negro slaves.* Burke alludes to the blacks of Hayti.

L. 15. *Oppression makes,* &c. Ecclesiastes vii. 7.

L. 19. *bitterness of soul.* Burke evidently had in mind the lines of Addison (The Campaign) describing the cry of Europe for deliverance from Louis XIV:

States that their new captivity bemoan'd,
Armies of martyrs that in exile groan'd,
Sighs from the depth of gloomy dungeons heard,
And prayers in bitterness of soul preferr'd.

This poem was sometimes quoted in the debates on peace in Parliament.

P. 143, L. 30. *Algiers.* The argument had been advanced by Fox, on the occasion of the famous debate, Dec. 15, 1792, when Burke first took his seat on the Treasury bench. Mr. Fox moved the house to send a minister to Paris to treat with the provisional government. "If we objected to the existing form of government in France, we had as strong objections to the form of government at Algiers; yet at Algiers we had a consul." The argument from Mahomedan communities is derived from the controversial theologians of a preceding age. See Hooker, Eccl. Pol. iv. 7, &c.

P. 146, L. 22. *"Thus painters write,"* &c. Prior, "Protogenes and Apelles." Apelles of Co (Cos) visits his brother artist at Rhodes, and not finding him at home, draws a perfect circle on a panel:

And will you please, sweet-heart, said he,
To show your master this from me?
[365] By it he presently will know
How painters write their names at Co.

Burke alludes to Grenville's master-hand similarly displayed in the Declaration.

P. 149, L. 30. *whom my dim eyes,* &c. Burke has in mind a pathetic triplet from Pope's Homer:

Two, while I speak, my eyes in vain explore,
Two from one mother sprung—my Polydore,
And lov'd Lycaon; now perhaps no more!

Iliad, xxii. 63.

NOTES

LETTER II

P. 155, L. 23. *wherever the race,* &c. i.e. in America as well as in Europe. Incidents in Hayti and in Spanish America suggested the observation. Cp. post, p. 231.

P. 156, L. 29. *our friends.* The Duke of Portland and his followers.

P. 157, L. 15. *Conquest of France.* Cp. vol. ii. p. 291, l. 4.

P. 158, L. 24. *linked by a contignation,* i.e. by a structural tie. The image is Shaksperian:

> It is a massy wheel,
> To whose huge spokes ten thousand lesser things
> Are mortis'd and adjoin'd.
>
> Hamlet, Act iii. sc. 3.

P. 159, L. 16. *Centrifugal war.* The expression aptly characterizes the war policy of the Allies. Cp. 163, l. 12, where it is explained as a "scheme of war that repels as from a centre," i.e. France itself.

P. 160, L. 22. *nothing to hold an alliance together.* Burke proceeds to show why the coalition failed. His thorough and exact analysis of the situation may be relied on.

P. 161, L. 11. *worse than a negative interest.* Because all the West Indian possessions of European powers other than Spain were originally encroachments on Spain. Spain has been losing the West Indies piecemeal ever since she gained them.

L. 20. *No continental power,* &c. The dilemma was complete.

P. 163, L. 5. *contemptible factories.* Pondicherry, Karikal, &c.

L. 8. *Cape of Good Hope.* The Cape was in those times only valuable in connexion with India and the East. British policy and enterprise has made it the nucleus of a great group of colonial states.

L. 25. *declines still more.* The decline of Holland as a colonial power was measured by the failing prosperity of the Dutch East Indian Company.

P. 164, L. 23, foll. The passage which follows, expanding the criticisms on the general plan of the war, and alluding to the unfortunate campaign in [366] the West Indies, was inserted by Burke in a subsequent edition. It ends p. 167, l. 28. It belongs to the period of the Third Letter.

LETTER II

L. 35. *fierce barbarians.* The negroes of Hayti and Guadaloupe.

P. 165, L. 7. *ally in the heart of the country.* Burke was always for stirring the strong anti-revolutionary elements which existed unused in France. The subsequent history of French factions has amply shown how much might have been done in this way.

P. 166, L. 15. *made for the seat,* &c. Burke has in mind the early settlement of the Spaniards in the West Indies, when Hayti was the centre of government, and the transfer of West Indian supremacy to the French with the possession of the west of the island.

IBID. *not improved as the French division had been.* The extraordinary prosperity of French Hayti is a striking feature in colonial history. See the Editor's History of European Colonies.

L. 21. *reclamation* = protest.

P. 167, L. 1. *ties of blood.* Burke derives the hint from Bacon, speaking of the Social War: "You speak of a naturalisation in blood; there was a naturalisation indeed in blood." "Of General Naturalisation."

L. 34. *I see, indeed, a fund,* &c. Burke alludes to the ecclesiastical electorates of Cologne, Trèves, and Mainz, and to the large sovereign bishoprics of Liège, Paderborn, Munster, &c. These it was proposed to secularize and cede some parts to Austria and Prussia in compensation for the Austrian Netherlands and the Rhenish possessions of Prussia.

P. 169, L. 4. *Substitutions,* i.e. family settlements. Cp. vol. ii. p. 207, l. 17.

P. 170, L. 19. *there is no doctrine whatever,* &c. Burke repeats the observation from Bolingbroke (On the true use of Retirement, &c.), who borrows it from Montaigne, Essais, Liv. i. ch. 40: "Toute opinion est assez forte pour se faire espouser au prix de la vie."

L. 30. *with all their heart,* &c. The phrase is borrowed from the Church of England Catechism.

L. 33. *strike the sun out of heaven.* Burke has in mind Gray, The Bard:

Fond impious man! think'st thou the sanguine cloud
Rais'd by thy breath can quench the orb of day?

P. 171, L. 7. *"carried along with the general motion,"* &c.:

For as in Nature's swiftness, with the throng
Of flying orbs whilst ours is borne along,
All seems at rest to the deluded eye,

Moved by the soul of the same harmony;
So carried on by your unwearied care
We rest in peace, and yet in motion share.
Dryden, Lines to the Lord Chancellor.

L. 17. *evil for its good.* Milton, Par. Lost, Book iv. 110.

L. 18. *nothing, indeed,* &c. Borrowed from Aristotle, Ἀρχὴ ἀνδρὰ δείξει.

[367] **P. 176, L. 9.** *Montalembert.* This veteran soldier and politician had cast in his lot with the Revolution.

L. 13. *The diplomatic politicians,* &c. This ingenious account of the growth of an aggressive policy on the part of France, though based on notorious historical facts, is difficult to justify specifically.

L. 23. *Russia and Prussia.* The rise of the former dated from Peter the Great, of the latter from Frederick.

L. 26. *by the very collision,* &c. The Seven Years' War.

P. 177, L. 4. *French party.* See p. 175, l. 16.

L. 19. *Out the word came.* The allusion is to the arguments in the Encyclopédie and elsewhere. The politicians, of course, never employed the word except in theoretical discussions, before the Revolution.

P. 178, L. 10. *Austrian match.* Between the Dauphin and Marie Antoinette.

P. 179, L. 4. *commercial treaty.* Made by Mr. Pitt in 1784.

L. 10. *facilitated—but did not produce it.* Burke can hardly escape the charge of bending his facts to his theory. Political ambition alone would never have produced the treaty.

L. 17. *unhappy American quarrel.* Here again the alliance of France with the revolted Colonies may be accounted for without assuming an unnatural ambition on the part of France.

L. 26. *produced by their republican principles.* But cp. p. 182, post, where the policy of the old monarchy is shown not to have been repugnant to republics.

L. 30. *in a great extent of country.* The example of the United States destroyed at once the old illusion that a non-monarchical government could only suit with small states. Cp. vol. ii. p. 224, l. 35.

LETTER II

P. 180, L. 31. *found in monarchies stiled absolute.* Burke repeats a well-known conclusion of Gibbon.

P. 181, L. 8. *entire circle of human desires.* Burke alludes to an idea put forth by Montesquieu and developed in Goldsmith's Traveller. It is fully explained in the note to vol. i. p. 237, l. 31. Burke's account of the growth of English civilization has been well amplified by Guizot: "The general character of European civilization has especially distinguished the civilization of England. It was exhibited in that country with more sequence and greater clearness than in any other. In England the civil and religious orders, aristocracy, democracy, monarchy, local and central institutions, moral and political development, have increased and advanced together . . . . Not one of the ancient elements of society ever completely perished; no special principle was ever able to obtain an exclusive dominion. There has always been a simultaneous development of all the different powers, and a sort of compromise between the claims and the interests of all of them. . . . . It cannot, for instance, be denied that the simultaneous development of the different social elements caused England to advance more rapidly than any of the continental states towards the true aim and object of all society—the [368] establishment of a free and regular government. . . . . Besides, the essence of Liberty is the simultaneous manifestation of all interests, of all rights, of all forces, and of all social elements. England had therefore made a nearer approach to liberty than the greater number of other states."—Lectures on Civilization, Lect. ix, Beckwith's translation.

L. 16. *direct object.* Burke alludes to the specific provisions in its favour, from Magna Charta to the Habeas Corpus Act.

L. 21. *as great to spend,* &c. Cp. vol. i. p. 285, l. 34. Since 1832 the people have been less disposed to expenditure.

L. 29. *above my power of praise.* Burke's general estimate of Pitt has been fully confirmed by modern opinion. Supreme in influence over Parliament, and the first of the great school of English financial statesmen, he failed signally as a war-minister.

P. 182, L. 27. *We go about asking when assignats will expire,* &c. "The French, beginning with bankruptcy at home, had proceeded abroad on the maxim of Machiavelli, that men and arms will find money and provide for themselves." Southey, Essay on State of Public Opinion and the Political Reformers.

P. 183, L. 6. *Jinghiz Khan.* A famous Asiatic conqueror of the twelfth century.

L. 28. *Harrington—never could imagine,* &c. Harrington uniformly derives all government from property. A man, he argues, with no estate, either in land, goods, or money, can have nothing to govern, and therefore no share in government. A state of things in which the people, not owning at least two thirds of the land, are supreme, he denominates "an Anarchy." See his System of Politics in Aphorisms.

L. 33. *"The mine exhaustless."* Burke is followed here by an opponent: "Nothing in point of resources is beyond the reach of a revolutionary government: whereas regular governments have their limitations in this point."—Marquis of Lansdowne's Speech on the Address, 1801.

P. 184, L. 4. *copying music.* Burke is perhaps thinking of Rousseau.

IBID. *plaidoyers.* Law proceedings.

L. 10. must *be destroyed.* Burke copies the "Delenda est Carthago" of Scipio.

P. 185, L. 32. *diligent reader of history.* "A century after the expulsion of James, Louis XVI was anxious to draw wisdom from the fate of the Stuarts. He was continually reading over the lives of Charles I and James II, and even, it is said, added comments with his own hand on the margin. Determined to avoid their erring policy, he, as we have already seen, temporised and yielded on every possible occasion."— Lord Mahon's Essay on the French Revolution.

P. 186, L. 35. *but one republic.* i.e. America.

P. 187, L. 13. *paid to his enemies.* i.e. to the new French government.

L. 20. *husbandmen or fishermen.* As in New England.

P. 188, L. 6. *you may call this France,* &c. We have elsewhere the idea [369] of a country or city being itself in exile when the worthy have departed and the worthless remain. Coriolanus, when banished by the citizens, retaliates as he departs:

"I banish you,
And here remain with your uncertainties," &c.

Act iii. Scene 3.

And Carew to Master William Montague:

LETTER III

Thus divided from your noble parts
The kingdom lives in exile.

"Non te civitas, non regia domus in exilium miserunt, sed tu utrasque."
Cicero, quoted in letters of Swift to Gay.

P. 189, L. 1. *a circumstance which,* &c. The allusion is to the months
of July and August, 1796, during which Burke was at Bath, prostrate
under the malady which in the next year carried him off.

LETTER III

P. 193, L. 24. *"Vast species."* Cowley's lines on Pindar:

The phoenix Pindar is a vast species alone.

P. 198, L. 22. *bundle of State-Papers.* The correspondence between
Lord Malmesbury and Delacroix, beginning Dec. 17 and ending Dec.
20, 1796, together with the long Royal Declaration of Dec. 27. The
correspondence was presented to the House of Commons Dec. 28.

L. 31. *"paths of pleasantness,"* &c. Proverbs iii. 17.

P. 200, L. 31. *rehearsal at Basle.* See ante, p. 86, &c.

P. 201, L. 9. *"garrit aniles,"* &c. Hor. Sat. ii. 6. 77.

L. 18. *"malignant and a turban'd Turk."* See end of Othello.

L. 33. *In the disasters of their friends,* &c. "Nous avons tous assez de
force pour supporter les maux d'autrui." Rochefoucauld, Max. xix.
Popularized in England through the "Thoughts on Various Subjects"
by Pope and Swift. Very humourously expressed by Villemain in his
"Souvenirs" when speaking of Talleyrand: "Il paraissait quelquefois
d'une *résignation* trop grande sur le malheur de ses amis."

P. 203, L. 1. *boulimia.* Raging hunger.

L. 8. *"shreds and patches."* Hamlet, Act iii. sc. 3.

L. 9. *mumping cant* = Beggars' set phrases. To "mump" is to go
begging. Cp. vol. i. p. 175, l. 6.

L. 11. *"Where the gaunt mastiff,"* &c. Pope, Moral Essays, Ep. iii.
l. 195.

L. 22. *neighbouring vice.* The allusion is to the Aristotelian theory
of Virtues, which places each in a mean state between two vices.

L. 28. *speech of the Minister.* Mr. Pitt's speech of Dec. 30, 1796.

NOTES

P. 204, L. 18. *Virgil proposed,* &c. Georgics, Book iii. l. 25.

L. 19. *hides his head,* &c. Bonaparte had forced the passage of the [370] Mincio, April 30, 1796, cutting off the Austrian general Beaulieu from Mantua, and forcing him to retreat upon the passes of the Tyrol.

P. 210, L. 7. *in this mother country of freedom,* &c.:

Onde provò con riflessioni egregie
La libertà delle prigioni regie.

Casti, Animali Parlanti, Canto xvi.

Casti's work was published in the beginning of the present century. The coincidences with Burke are too many to be accidental.

L. 32. *patriarchal rebels.* Lafayette, Latour-Maubeuge, and Bureau de Pusy. Burke goes on to speak particularly of Lafayette, who had been taken prisoner in the territory of Liège in August, 1792. General Fitzpatrick as early as March, 1794, had moved the Commons for an address to the Crown with the object of procuring his release. This motion was opposed by Burke, and lost by a large majority. The motion was repeated Dec. 16, 1796, warmly supported by Fox, and again lost. The Peace of Campo Formio, made shortly after the publication of this letter, set Lafayette at liberty.

P. 211, L. 10. *that family.* The Austrian.

L. 33. *not only of no real talents.* Burke's estimate of Lafayette is just.

P. 212, L. 3. *fifth of October.* An account of this deportation from Versailles to Paris is given in Burke's "Reflections." See Select Works, vol. ii. pp. 164–65.

L. 16. *This officer,* &c. Smith was taken prisoner in an attempt to cut out some vessels from the Havre. The French government had him sent to Paris, and imprisoned in the Temple as a spy. He managed to escape, together with the royalist Phelippeaux, an officer of engineers, by means of a forged order for transporting them to another place of confinement. Phelippeaux accompanied Smith to the East, and aided him in the famous defence of Acre in 1799, which stopped the advance of Bonaparte in Syria.

P. 215, LL. 20 foll. *Muse of fire—ascended the highest heaven of invention—swelling scene—Potentates for fellow-actors—port of Mars—dogs of war—famine, fever,* &c. Burke has freely used the opening lines of Shakespeare's Henry V:

O for a muse of fire, that would ascend
The brightest heaven of invention!

LETTER III

A kingdom for a stage, princes to act,
And monarchs to behold the swelling scene!
Then should the warlike Harry, like himself,
Assume the port of Mars; and at his heels,
Leash'd in like hounds, should famine, sword, and fire,
Crouch for employment.

Burke evidently assumed that the passage was well-known to his readers.

[371] **P. 216, L. 28.** *"Which has so often stormed Heaven, and with a pious violence forced down blessings,"* &c. St. Matthew xi. 14.

Regnum coelorum violenza pate
Da caldo amore è di viva speranza
Che vence la divina volontade.
Dante, Paradiso, Canto xx. l. 94.

By tears, and groans, and never ceasing care
And all the pious violence of prayer.
Young's Last Day, Book ii.

We by devotion borrow from his throne,
And almost make omnipotence our own:
We force the gates of Heaven by fervent prayer,
And call forth triumph out of man's despair.
Young's Force of Religion.

P. 217, L. 9. *Freinshemius.* The continuator of the Roman historian Livy.

L. 29. *Never, no never,* &c. "Nunquam aliud natura, aliud Sapientia dixit." Juvenal.

L. 32. *of Belvedere.* The Belvedere palace at Rome.

IBID. *universal robber.* Bonaparte, who during the past year had stripped the states of North Italy in succession of their choicest art-treasures as part of the price of peace.

P. 218, L. 3. *Vehement passion does not,* &c. Addison, Spectator, No. 408: "We may generally observe a pretty nice proportion between the strength of reason and passion . . . . The weaker understandings have generally the weaker passions."

L. 8. *If ever there was a time that calls on us for no vulgar conception of things, and for exertions in no vulgar strain.* "This sincere and solid compliment I would pay them (the French people and commanders), of saying and showing, that we must omit no human preparations

NOTES

which the heart and head of man can contrive and execute." Sheridan, Speech on Traitorous Correspondence, &c., April 28, 1798.

L. 18. *De la Croix.* The minister who conducted the negotiations with Lord Malmesbury.

L. 31. *His Majesty has only to lament. A poor possession to be left to a great monarch:*

> invenietque
> Nil sibi legatum praeter plorare, suisque.
>
> Hor. Sat. II. v. 9.

P. 220, L. 17. *former declaration.* The *Whitehall Declaration.* See ante, pp. 99–100.

P. 221, L. 16. *Regicide fleet.* A fleet of seventeen vessels sailed from Brest in December, 1796, for a descent upon Ireland, relying on the support of the inhabitants. It retreated to France without landing any troops. [372] Seven ships were lost by a storm. Hoche lost his way, and got back to Brest several days after the rest of his fleet, after being hotly pursued by Lord Bridport.

L. 33. *practised assassin Hoche.* The allusion is to the execution of the invaders at Quiberon. Driven by the national army to an isolated rock, and unable to escape to the British ships, all surrendered and were shot. Many of the wretched *émigrés* who thus perished were personally known to Burke.

P. 224, L. 5. *mask of a Davus or a Geta.* Characters of slaves in the Roman comedy.

P. 225, L. 15. *hypothecated in trust.* By the Treaty of Peace with Prussia, concluded at Basle April 5, 1795, the left bank of the Rhine was to be occupied by the French pending a general pacification. The French evacuated the Prussian territories on the right bank.

L. 26. *Lucchesini.* An Italian adventurer who had ingratiated himself with Frederick the Great, and had ever since been a diplomatist of high repute. Burke's contemptuous mention of him here is interesting, for it was he who negotiated for Prussia after the battle of Jena.

L. 33. *Prince of Peace.* Properly, "Prince of the Peace," a title conferred on Godoy in honour of the disgraceful peace negotiated by him between France and Spain, July 22, 1796. By this peace, the Spanish part of St. Domingo, and the Spanish possessions in North America were ceded to France.

LETTER III

P. 226, L. 3. *Tetrarch.* So called by Burke, contemptuously, from his holding his crown on the sufferance of the Republic. Cp. post, p. 339, l. 32. The Sardinian king saved his crown by suing for mercy at the first irruption of Bonaparte in 1796. He ceded to the French Savoy and Nice, together with the right of occupying Coni, Ceva, Tortona, Alessandria, and six less important fortresses, and the right of passing and repassing through his dominions at any time.

L. 21. *admission of French garrisons.* The fate of Genoa had been clear since the first occupation of its soil in 1794. The French easily democratized the old commonwealth, and in May of this year (1797) it was abolished and replaced by a "Ligurian Republic," which had a Directory and Councils like France.

L. 25. *early sincerity.* The Grand-Duke of Tuscany, weak in mind and insignificant in position, created general amusement by being the first member of the alliance to detach himself from it. This he did early in 1795.

L. 32. *placed Leghorn,* &c. Leghorn was seized by the French in June, 1796, notwithstanding the peace made by the Grand-Duke. They expected to seize abundance of English property, and, disappointed in this, pillaged their own allies.

P. 227, L. 16. *"murdering piece."* The technical name for this species of pictures; like "landscape."

[373] **L. 27.** *sunk deep into the vale,* &c. Pius VI was over eighty years of age.

P. 228, L. 8. *regenerated law.* Burke alludes to the revival of the study of Civil Law at Bologna.

L. 9. *hideously metamorphosed.* In 1798 the same process was extended to Rome itself.

L. 14. *work which defied the power,* &c. The drainage of the Pontine marshes had been attempted at intervals by several Popes: but no progress was made until the time of Pius VI, who restored the canal of Augustus and constructed the modern road on the line of the Appian way. It is not correct to say that the same task defied the engineers of ancient Rome. Their works had fallen into decay.

P. 229, L. 16. *at all times—powerful squadron.* The Mediterranean had been evacuated by the British squadron employed on that station in consequence of the demands of the war in the West Indies.

NOTES

L. 21. *despotic mistress of that sea.* "The Mediterranean a French lake."

P. 230, L. 9. *himself the victim,* &c. The allusion is to the assassination of Gustavus (III) by Ankarström, March 16, 1792.

L. 16. *late Empress — new Emperor.* Catherine II had died Nov. 17, 1796, leaving Paul I her successor. Burke's expectations from Paul were justified. The unprincipled aggressions of France after the peace of Campo Formio drew him into the alliance: and the tide of events on the continent was first changed by the Italian campaign in 1799, in which Suwarrow bore so important a part.

P. 231, L. 19. *As long as Europe,* &c. Though the possessory interest of Europe in America has practically ceased, time has confirmed Burke's diplomatic dictum that "America is to be considered as part of the European system."

L. 24. *attempts to plant Jacobinism instead of liberty.* The allusion is to the arrogant bearing and intrigues of the French envoy in the United States, where the French confidently hoped to Jacobinize the government as in Holland and Genoa. The Directory instructed their representative to take no notice of Washington, and to appeal to the people.

P. 232, L. 25. *if any memory,* &c. The qualification was necessary. This antiquated distinction of parties, fading early in Burke's career (cp. vol. i. p. 72, l. 11), was now mere matter of history.

L. 33. *by their union have once saved it.* An ingenious account of the desertion of the Portland Whigs, with Burke at their head, in 1792.

P. 233, L. 16. *other party.* The followers of Fox.

P. 234, L. 25. *distinguished person.* Lord Auckland, a shrewd man bred to the law, had risen to some eminence as a diplomatic agent of Mr. Pitt's.

P. 238, L. 14. *when the fortune of the war began to turn.* In 1793.

L. 32. *noble person himself.* Lord Auckland. In the debates of the early part of 1795 he had opposed the peace proposals.

[374] **P. 239, L. 7.** *no foundation for attributing,* &c. Lord Auckland sent to Burke a copy of the pamphlet on the day of its publication (Oct. 28, 1795), with a note confessing the authorship, but stating that as regards the public he neither sought to avow the publication nor wished to disavow it. Burke's remarks on the authorship were therefore justifiable.

LETTER III

L. 14. *riggs of old Michaelmas.* Stormy weather about that time. (Rigs = capricious tempests.)

L. 19. *Speech from the throne.* The speech on the opening of the Session in 1795.

P. 242, L. 4. *As to our Ambassador, this total want of reparation for the injury was passed by under pretence of despising it.*

It is the cowish terror of his spirit
That dares not undertake: he'll not feel wrongs
That tie him to an answer.

Lear, Act iv. sc. 2.

P. 243, L. 15. *non omnibus dormio.* The allusion is to a story contained in Plutarch's Eroticus, of one Galba, and Maecenas: Ὥσπερ καὶ ὁ Ῥωμαῖος ἐκεῖνος Κάββας εἱστία Μαικήναν, εἶτα ὁρῶν διαπληκτιζόμενον ἀπὸ νευμάτων πρὸς τὸ γύναιον, ἀπέκλινεν ἡσυχῇ τὴν κεφαλὴν, ὡς δὴ καθεύδων, ἐν τούτῳ δὴ τῶν οἰκετῶν τινος προσρυέντος ἔξωθεν τῇ τραπέζῃ, καὶ τὸν οἶνον ὑφαιρουμένου, διαβλέψας, "Κακόδειμον," εἶπεν, "οὐκ οἶσθα, ὅτι μόνῳ Μαικήνᾳ καθεύδω;"

L. 32. *two confidential communications.* Both delivered to Delacroix by Lord Malmesbury on Saturday morning, Dec. 17, 1796. The first contained the proposed terms of peace so far as they related to France, the second so far as they related to Spain and Holland. The Confidential Memorials were not signed by Lord Malmesbury, though his signature was affixed to the note to which they were appended: and the Directory returned the memorials to him on Sunday stating that they could recognize no unsigned documents, and demanding an *ultimatum* properly signed, within twenty-four hours. On Monday, Lord Malmesbury returned the memorials properly signed, with a statement that they contained not an ultimatum, but a project subject to discussion. Later in the same day he received the peremptory notice to quit Paris in forty-eight hours.

P. 246, L. 21. *German War.* So called at first: afterwards best known as the Seven Years' War.

P. 247, L. 29. *the Empire and the Papacy.* Neither of the two Cardinal powers of mediaeval Europe, now in their political decay, were so formidable to progress as is now often supposed. The continual attacks directed against them proceeded mainly from the politicians, and date back long before 1789.

P. 248, L. 13. *body of republics.* Alluding especially to the Ligurian and Cispadane Republics in Italy. The establishment of the Partheno-paean Republic confirmed Burke's augury.

[375] **L. 19.** *universal empire—universal revolution.* In a very short time the justice of the charge was confessed by the best friends of France. No sooner was the peace of Campo Formio signed than the attacks on Rome, Switzerland, and Naples, made it clear that faith would be kept by the Directory on no other terms than a submission to republican principles.

P. 249, L. 2. *Scrap of equivalents.* His contemptible list of proposed cessions to France in exchange for the Austrian Netherlands.

P. 250, L. 7. *very dubious struggle.* The result of the war in the rest of the West Indies was still doubtful.

P. 252, L. 10. *family of thieves.* The allusion is to the division of power between the two assemblies—the Council of Ancients and the Council of Five Hundred.

L. 29. *The identical men,* &c.

Da riguardo servil, da melensaggine
Vinte per uso,—un anima non hanno
Capace d'una bella scelleraggine.

Casti, Animali Parlanti, Cant. xi.

L. 30. *original place—dirtiest of chicaners.* The allusion is to the two lawyers Rewbel and Lepaux.

P. 254, L. 23. *"The slothful man,"* &c. Proverbs xxii. 13.

P. 255, L. 4. *open subscription*—of eighteen millions, proposed by Mr. Pitt, December 7, 1795. For every £100 in cash the subscriber became entitled to £120 3 per cents., and £25 4 per cents., with further addition in the Long Annuities. The loan was notoriously not an open competition. It was placed in the hands of the mercantile house of Boyd. The circumstances attending the loan were brought to light by Mr. W. Smith in a motion for a Committee of Enquiry. An ample account may be seen in the Parliamentary History.

L. 8. *whiff and wind of it,* &c.

With the whiff and wind of his fell sword
The unnerved father falls.

Hamlet, Act ii. Scene 2.

L. 25. *Ne te quaesiveris extra.* Persius, Sat. i. 7.

P. 256, L. 18. *ritually,* i.e. formally, properly.

LETTER III

P. 257, L. 2. *very lucrative bargain.* The premium on the loan amounted to no less a sum than £2,160,000!

P. 258, L. 14. *The love of lucre,* &c. i.e. as productive of capital. Burke may have had the following passage in his ear when he wrote the above clause: "The inclination is natural in them all, pardonable in those who have not yet made their fortunes: and as lawful in the rest as love of power or love of money can make it. But as natural, as pardonable, and as lawful as this inclination is, where it is not under check of the civil power, or when a corrupt ministry," &c. Swift, *Examiner,* No. xxiv.

L. 23. *"with all its imperfections,"* &c. This well-known phrase from Hamlet is a favourite quotation with Burke. See vol. i. p. 243, l. 28.

[376] **P. 260, L. 27.** *"wherever a man's treasure,"* &c. Luke xii. 34.

P. 267, L. 18. *"Modo sol nimius,"* &c. Ovid, Met. Lib. v. 483.

P. 269, L. 1. *How war,* &c. Milton, Sonnet xvii. l. 7.

L. 19. *Proving its title,* &c. Among many embodiments of this commonplace, Shakespeare's is perhaps the best:

"Therefore, brave conquerors! for so you are,
That war against your own affections,
And the huge army of the world's desires," &c.
                    Love's Labour's Lost, Act i. Scene 1.

P. 270, L. 5. *"palmy state."* Cp. note, p. 65, l. 13, ante.

L. 6. *brighter lustre than in the present,* &c. Burke alludes to the English campaign in the Low Countries under the Duke of York. The British contingent took the field at the investment of Valenciennes, which surrendered to the Duke of York, July 28, 1793. A month after, the Duke was besieging Dunkirk: but was forced to raise the siege suddenly by the arrival of overwhelming reinforcements to the enemy. He took the lead in the succeeding year, capturing all the posts between Courtray and Lille; and the English contingent was distinguished in the repulse of the French at Tournay, May 10, 1794. The English ranks were greatly thinned by the terrible fighting at Turcoing, on the 18th and 22nd, while the severe losses they inflicted on the enemy drew from the Convention a decree denying all quarter to the British and Hanoverian troops. Moreau and several other French generals, to their honour, refused to execute this savage decree. A month afterwards, the decisive battle of Fleurus gave Flanders to the French. At the head of an overwhelming number of troops, Pichegru drove the Duke into

Holland. The states of Holland having submitted to the French early in 1795: and the English army, pursued by Macdonald and Moreau, had to retreat through a practically hostile country into German territory. They embarked at Bremerhaven for England, 1795.

L. 21. *distant possessions.* West Indies.

L. 23. *neighbouring colonies.* The British West Indies.

IBID. *one sweeping law,* &c. That of August, 1793, which decreed a levy of the people *en masse* until the enemy should be driven from the soil of the Republic.

P. 271, L. 6. *invasion.* The alarm of invasion naturally began to be felt as England was gradually deserted by the Allies, as a consequence of the great development of France, and her bitterness against England. After the Peace of Campo Formio England was left absolutely alone, and the probability of invasion was redoubled.

L. 13. *forty years ago.* In the time of the elder Pitt and his vigorous war-policy.

P. 272, L. 27. *much more to dread.* See Burke's famous Letter to a Noble Lord.

P. 273, L. 1. *The excesses of delicacy,* &c. The argument is amplified in a note [377] of Southey's: "It is the lowest class which supplies the constant consumption of society. It is they who are cut off by contagious diseases, who are poisoned in manufactories, who supply our fleets and armies. The other class of society are exempt from most of these chances of destruction, yet they produce little or no surplus of population, and the families of all such as have been truly illustrious soon become extinct. The most thoughtful people taken as a body are the least prolific. An increase of animal life depends on something more than animal passion, or the abundance of the means of subsistence."

L. 9. *whose name,* &c. These touching words allude to the recent death of the author's only son in 1794.

L. 13. *the ancients.* Burke alludes to his favourite philosopher, Aristotle.

P. 282, L. 24. The allusion is to the statutory registration of deeds in that county.

P. 286, L. 26. *"migravit ab aure voluptas."* Hor. Ep. ii. 1. 187.

P. 287, L. 23. *all the three theatres.* The famed old ones of Drury

LETTER IV

Lane and Covent Garden, and the "Little Theatre" in the Haymarket, made popular by Foote and Colman.

P. 288, L. 10. *my first political tract.* The "Observations on the State of the Nation." See ante, p. 245. The publication of the quarto edition of his works evidently attracted Burke's attention anew to this early production.

P. 299, L. 18. *The different Bills.* The first bill, originated by a private company, was introduced in the previous session (1795–6), supported by the leading merchants, and by the East India Company. It was defeated by the interest of the corporation of London. The second bill, containing the rival scheme of the corporation, was introduced early in 1797.

P. 303, L. 1. *bore*—an exceptionally high tide.

P. 304, L. 34. *Famish their virtues,* &c. The image belongs to Young: "Eusebius, though liberal to the demands of nature, rank, and duty, starves vice, caprice, and folly." Letter on Pleasure, iii.

P. 305, L. 7. *mines of Newfoundland.* The fisheries. The expulsion of the French from St. Pierre and Miquelon (see Introduction) had thrown them exclusively into English hands.

LETTER IV

P. 309, L. 27. *eternal duration.* See for examples the conclusion of Horace's Odes and Ovid's Metamorphoses.

P. 310, L. 4. *Parisian September.* The allusion is to the memorable September of 1792.

L. 7. *pleasant author.* Voltaire.

L. 32. *Rider's Almanack.* Then and long afterwards the best popular almanack.

P. 312, L. 2. *Second edition.* Burke waited to watch the effect of Lord [378] Auckland's work on the public. It had been out about two months when the criticism was begun.

L. 12. *Qualis in aethereo.* Tibullus, Lib. iv. Carm. 2.

L. 16. *simple country folk.* Burke was no longer in Parliament: he lived in retirement at Beaconsfield.

P. 314. The style here, as in many other parts, is that of a speech in debate.

NOTES

P. 317, L. 5. *Esto perpetua.* Father Paul Sarpi's dying prayer for his country (Venice). See Dr. Johnson's Life of him.

P. 318, L. 7. *restored the two countries,* &c. Thomson alludes to the idea, "Liberty," Part iv.:

Since first the rushing flood
Urged by almighty power, this favoured isle
Turned flashing from the Continent aside,
Indented shore to shore responsive still.

P. 319, L. 21. *"That strain I heard,"* &c. Milton, Lycidas.

L. 23. *a style which,* &c. Burke somewhat unfairly contrasts the flimsy style of Auckland's pamphlet with that of Grenville's Declaration. The compositions were in different kinds.

P. 321, L. 16. *first republic in the world.* Holland.

L. 27. *Pomoerium.* The limit of the precincts of ancient Rome.

P. 322, L. 2. *boulimia.* See ante, p. 203, l. 1.

L. 19. *Doctor in Molière.* See "Le Malade Imaginaire."

P. 323, L. 18. *opinion of some.* See the opening of the first chapter. That empires fall by their own weight is not only an ill-formed analogy, but formed on false premises. A tree, or a building, never falls by its own weight until some other cause has done its work.

P. 324, L. 11. *"once to doubt,"* &c. Othello, Act iii. sc. 3.

L. 25. *excellent Berkeley.* Bishop Berkeley's Queries, mainly directed to the condition of Ireland, make an important epoch in the history of Political Economy.

P. 326, L. 12. *dare not be wise.* "Sapere aude." Horace, Epistles, i. 2. 40.

L. 15. *"To-morrow and to-morrow,"* &c. See Macbeth, Act v. sc. 5.

P. 327, L. 27. *the famous Jurieu.* Pierre Jurieu (1637–1713) a Protestant theologian of some eminence, had satisfied himself by study of the Prophets and Apocalypse that the year 1689 would witness the final triumph of Protestantism over Rome. As the time approached, so jubilant were the partisans of his views that a medal was struck in his honour with the legend "Jurius Propheta." The year 1689 however, passed without seeing his predictions fulfilled. Jurieu reapplied himself to his studies, and discovered that he had made an error of twenty-six years, and that 1715 was the real date of the second advent of the

Messiah and the fall of Antichrist. Before this date the prophet died. Among his numerous writings is a curious one [379] entitled "Les Soupirs de la France esclave qui respire après la liberté." It denounced the tyranny of Louis XIV, and asserted the sovereignty of the people.

L. 29. *Mr. Brothers.* Richard Brothers was a harmless fanatic who prophesied and published various pamphlets containing his prophecies. In 1792 "he was commanded by the Lord God to go down to the House of Parliament and acquaint the members for their own personal safety and the general benefit of the country that the time of the world was come to fulfil the 7th chapter of Daniel." But on his publishing his prophetic mission to George III to "deliver up his crown, that all his power and authority might cease," he was taken up on a warrant, on suspicion of treasonable practices. One member of Parliament, a Mr. Halhed, believed in him, and repeatedly strove to bring his wrongs before the house.

P. 328, L. 35. *gemitus Columbae.* Cooings. Isaiah lix. 11 (Vulg.).

P. 330, L. 3. *untimely wisdom,* &c. "Eventus ille stultorum magister," Livy.

P. 332, L. 17. *Jourdan Coupe-tête.* Matthew Jourdan, the illiterate ruffian who devastated the Comtat Venaissin, and executed the horrible "Massacre de la Glacière" at Avignon. The Revolutionary Tribunal rid the world of him in 1794.

L. 18. *whose Predecessor,* &c. Joseph the Second.

P. 333, L. 14. *Juignie—Cardinal de Rochefoucault.* Juigné, Bishop of Chalons, had taken part in the famous sitting of the 4th of August, 1789, and proposed a *Te Deum* in celebration of it. He was now in exile at Constance. As to the Cardinal de Rochefoucault, see note to vol. ii. p. 213, l. 31.

L. 16. *their very beings.* Perhaps borrowed from what Grattan had said of the famous preacher Dr. Kirwan: "In feeding the lamp of charity he had almost exhausted the lamp of life." Speech on the Address, Jan. 19, 1792.

P. 334, L. 15. *D'Espremenil.* D'Espremenil had been a minister before the Revolution. On the establishment of the Convention he had retired to the country, and ceased to take any part in politics. From his country seat he was suddenly called before the Revolutionary tribunal, condemned, and executed, in 1794.

NOTES

L. 17. *Malesherbes.* The famous ally of Turgot, in his plans for saving France by timely fiscal and constitutional reforms. He had been the king's advocate at his trial. After the king's execution, he also retired to the country: whence he was brought before the Revolutionary tribunal, condemned, and executed with D'Espremenil. Sainte-Beuve calls him "ce Franklin de vieille race."

P. 335, L. 13. *"last that wore the imperial purple."* The prophecy was to meet with a striking fulfilment.

P. 336, L. 13. *humility and submission—silent adoration—trembling wings.* [380] As in the fine passage page 163, Burke is using classical materials. Pope, Essay on Man, i. 91:

> Hope humbly then; with trembling pinions soar:
> Wait the great teacher Death, and God adore.

P. 337, L. 4. *old Trivulzio.* The famous old general was then (1515) in his seventy-fourth year. The battle of Marignano was fought by him at the head of a French army. It gained Francis I, for a short time, possession of the whole Duchy of Milan.

IBID. *battle of Marignan.* Burke quotes from memory the famous description of this battle in Mezeray, Book iii: "Il se trouva sur le champ quatorze mille Suisses morts et pres de quatre mille François: ceux-là pour la plus grande part brisez de coups de canons ou percez de traits d'arbaleste, et ceux-cy fendus et hachez par d'horribles et larges playes. Aussi Trivulce, qui s'estoit trouvé à dix-huit batailles, disoit que celle-cy estoit une bataille de géants, et que toutes les autres n'estoient en comparison que des jeux d'enfans."

L. 14. *Origenist,* &c. So Young, Satire vi:

> Dear Tillotson! be sure, the best of men!
> Nor thought be more than thought great Origen—
> "Though once upon a time he misbehav'd,
> Poor Satan! doubtless he'll at length be saved."

P. 338, L. 13. *usurper, murderer, regicide.* Claudius. See Hamlet, Act iii. sc. 3.

L. 33. *massacre at Quiberon.* The captured French emigrants, not being recognised as belligerents, were all shot. Burke alludes to this in the Third Letter, p. 170, where he speaks of the "practised assassin Hoche."

P. 339, L. 16. *Taedet harum,* &c. Terence, Eun. ii. 3. 6.

Letter IV

L. 24. *Muscadin.* Perfumed with musk.

L. 32. *Tetrarchs.* Cp. p. 226, l. 3.

P. 340, L. 31. *"pride, pomp, and circumstance."* Othello, Act iii. sc. 3.

P. 342, L. 2. *Anacharsis Cloots.* Jean Baptiste Clootz, or, properly, Klotz, a wealthy German settled in Paris, and greatly inflamed with revolutionary ideas. He assumed the name Anacharsis in honour of the philosophic Scythian, when travelling in Europe before the Revolution. His early exploit is abundantly described by Burke. He afterwards added to his assumed title of "Ambassador of the Human Race" that of "Personal Enemy of God." By a decree of the 26th of August, 1792, the title of citizen was conferred upon him: on which occasion he thanked the French people at the bar of the Convention, and pronounced a panegyric on the regicide Ankarström. Cp. note to p. 230, l. 9, ante. He perished a victim to the Terror, March 23, 1794.

P. 343, L. 1. *their Cotterel.* Sir Clement Cotterell was a high official of the Court of George III.

[381] **L. 5.** *gaudy day.* An annual festival.

P. 344, L. 3. *grown philosophick.* This keen sarcasm refers not only to the late Emperor, Joseph the Second, and to Louis XVI, but to such living sovereigns as the Grand Duke of Tuscany. See p. 226, where he is spoken of as a "pacific Solomon."

L. 6. *Cappadocia.* Burke of course means that Prussia had become to France what Cappadocia was to Rome; a humble province of the regicide empire.

L. 8. *Judean representation.* Burke likens Austria to Judea, as he has just likened Prussia to Cappadocia.

L. 14. *daughter.* Marie Antoinette.

L. 26. *Moriamur, &c.* The story of the unanimous enthusiasm of the Hungarian Diet is apocryphal. The words were used by Charles, Maria Theresa's husband, and a certain number of the nobles repeated it after him: but the majority murmured, and demanded a readjustment of taxation.

P. 346, L. 15. *Lord Auckland—Duke of Bedford.* The latter was one of the leaders of the opposition in the Lords.

P. 347, L. 23. *I do not believe, &c.* Burke is right. Washington bore no hatred to Great Britain.

P. 348, L. 15. *infernal altar.* The allusion is to the story of Hannibal, as stated by Livy. Cp. note to p. 64, l. 18.

L. 28. *an Author who points,* &c. Tacitus.

P. 350, L. 10. *Marquis de Montalembert.* This veteran soldier was still living, and actively employed in the service of the Republic. He wrote more than one "Military Treatise."

L. 26. *Mire sagaces,* &c. Horace, Odes, Lib. ii. 5. 22.

L. 32. *old coarse bye-word.* "God sends meat, and the devil sends cooks."

L. 35. *Thomas Paine.* The author of the Rights of Man had been installed as a member of the Convention.

P. 351, L. 10. *house that he has opened.* Burke goes on in his happiest vein of humour, to apply to Paine the amusing lines of Swift on the old and the new Angel Inns.

L. 32. *light lie the earth,* &c. Cp. ante, p. 96, l. 4.

P. 352, L. 7. *Republic of Europe.* The argument is amplified in the First Letter.

L. 24. *I have reason to be persuaded,* &c. Cp. the earlier pages of the Reflections (Select Works, vol. ii.). Thiers, in his History, says that the French political clubs were modelled on those of England.

L. 29. *formal distributions—moral basis.* See the arguments in vol. ii. p. 278, and following.

P. 353, L. 15. *Astraea.* The goddess of Justice, said to have quitted the earth when the Golden Age ceased.

P. 354, L. 6. *I have heard that a Tartar believes,* &c. Butler, Hudibras (Part i. c. 2):

[382] So a wild Tartar, when he spies
A man that's handsome, valiant, wise,
If he can kill him thinks t' inherit
His wit, his beauty, and his spirit.

So Shaftesbury, Essay on the Freedom of Wit and Humour: "For, in good earnest, to destroy a philosophy in hatred to a man implies as errant a Tartar-notion as to destroy or murder a man, in order to plunder him of his wit, and get the inheritance of his understanding."

L. 14. *tontine of Infamy.* A happy stroke. A Tontine (so named from

LETTER IV

its inventor) is a lottery in which the longest livers divide the produce of the stock, with its accumulations. Cp. vol. ii. p. 361, l. 7.

L. 26. *Murderers and hogs*, &c. This grim humour is borrowed from Bacon's "Spurious" Apophthegms, No. 16.

L. 30. *Pantheon.* Cp. ante, note to p. 126, l. 2.

P. 357, L. 10. *regardants.* A "villain regardant" is the old legal term for an ordinary serf.

L. 11. *even the Negroes*, &c. Burke goes too far. At this time the condition of the negroes in the British West Indies, which Burke had been the first to characterise adequately, in a juvenile production forty years before, was being widely discussed.

L. 26. *more at large hereafter.* See the Second Letter.

P. 358, L. 34. *genethliacon.* A birth-song. Burke's observation is correct. It was the strength of the opposition in the Assembly, and the goodness of their cause, that led to the Revolution of Fructidor, and the triumph of the war-party, in 1797.

P. 361, L. 35. *"splitting this brilliant orb,"* &c.:

Give me my Romeo, and when he shall die,
Take him and cut him out in little stars,
And he shall make the face of heaven so fine,
That all the world shall fall in love with night.
Romeo and Juliet, Act iii. sc. 2.

P. 365, L. 8. *eundem Negotiatorem*, &c. The Roman *negotiator* or factor was usually a slave.

L. 14. *master Republick cultivates the arts*, &c. The allusion is to Virgil's well-known lines:

Tu regere imperio populos, Romane, memento;
Hae tibi erunt artes.

L. 33. *by inch of candle.* By auction; the time for bidding limited by an inch of candle.

IBID. *dedecorum pretiosus*, &c. Horace, Odes, Lib. iii. 6. 32.

L. 35. *Prince of Peace.* See ante, p. 225, and the note.

P. 366, L. 2. *pesos duros.* Dollars.

L. 24. *death of Philip the Fourth.* Burke works out this hint in the First Letter, p. 111.

NOTES

[383] **P. 369, L. 6.** *this holy season.* Cp. p. 312. From the two passages it may be concluded that the work was begun late in December 1795.

P. 370, L. 19. *transatlantic Morocco.* Burke alludes to the political rights which according to French principles were granted to the free blacks and men of colour in the French West Indies, and to the stimulus which this would give to communities originally founded on piracy, and always addicted to it.

P. 372, L. 28. Here ends that part of the critique upon Auckland's Letter which Burke corrected for the press. The following pages, down to p. 376, l. 28, were made up by Bishop King from loose uncorrected papers.

P. 373, L. 7. *bought by so much blood.* Burke has in mind his favourite lines from Addison's Cato:

Remember, O my friends, the laws, the rights,
The generous plan of power deliver'd down
From age to age, by your renown'd forefathers —
So dearly bought, the price of so much blood —
O let it never perish in your hands,
But piously transmit it to your children.

P. 376, L. 1. *They never will love,* &c. Dr. Johnson "loved a good hater."

For in base mind nor friendship dwells, nor enmity.
　　　　　　Spenser, Faery Queen, Book iv, canto iv, st. 11.

L. 16. *best accounts I have,* &c. Burke alludes to the strict retirement in which he was living, since the death of his son.

L. 18. *"some to undo,"* &c. The line is from Denham's "Cooper's Hill."

L. 28. Here the original terminates. The remaining portion of this letter does not belong to Burke's confutation of Lord Auckland. It was added by Bishop King from a separate copy, already put into type, but never finished or published. The Bishop says that it formed part of the Third Letter of Burke's original scheme (see p. 148), and was laid aside in consequence of the rupture of the negotiations.

P. 377, L. 17. *tremblingly alive.* The expression is Pope's. Essay on Man, i. 197.

L. 24. *"vanished at the crowing,"* &c. Shakespeare, Hamlet.

LETTER IV

L. 26. *us poor Tory geese.* The allusion is to the story of the Capitol of Rome saved from the Gauls by the cackling of geese, Livy, Lib. v. c. 47.

L. 33. *Hic auratis,* &c. Virgil, Aen. viii. 655.

P. 378. This bitter tirade, which applies to most of Burke's former political associates, cannot be read without pain. It must be remembered that he did not publish it.

P. 383, L. 13. *jewel of their souls,* &c. Othello, Act iii. sc. 5.

P. 384, L. 31. *awful and imposing.* The allusion is clearly to Windsor Castle, as seen on the approach from the uplands of Buckinghamshire, where Burke was living in retirement.

P. 385, L. 30. *for a few days,* &c. This indicates that the fragment was [384] written while Malmesbury's negotiations were yet going on, and a favourable conclusion was anticipated.

P. 387, L. 17. *coaches of Duchesses, Countesses, and Lady Marys:*

Monsieur much complains at Paris
Of wrongs from Dutchesses, and Lady Marys.
Pope, Dunciad, Book ii.

P. 389, L. 2. *Is it for this that our youth of both sexes are to form themselves by travel?* Wordsworth illustrates the warning:

Not in my single self alone I found,
But in the minds of all ingenuous youth,
Change and subversion from that hour. No shock
Given to my moral nature had I known
Down to that very moment.
The Prelude, Book x.

Much of this book may be read to show the working of the French Revolution on the minds of many of the young men of England.

P. 392, L. 32. *Tenth wave.* Silius Italicus, xiv. 121.

Non aliter Boreas Rhodopes a vertice praeceps
Cum sese immisit *decimoque volumine* pontum
Expulit in terras.

So Taylor, "Mercy of the Divine Judgments": "If Pharaoh will not be cured by one plague he shall have ten, and if ten will not do it, the great and tenth wave which is far bigger than all the rest." Young, The Brothers, Act iv.:

This, Fate, is thy tenth wave, and quite o'erwhelms me.

NOTES

P. 394, L. 26. *Mr. Hume's Euthanasia,* &c. In his early Essay "On the British Government," Hume argues from a fallacy already confuted by Burke (see p. 62) that the "English constitution" must end either in a republic or an absolute monarchy. The latter he thought the easiest and most natural.